Primary Documents to accompany
Liberty, Equality, Power
A History of the American People
Volume I: To 1877

John M. Murrin
Paul E. Johnson
James M. McPherson
Gary Gerstle
Emily S. Rosenberg
Norman L. Rosenberg

Prepared by
Marvin E. Schultz
Ouachita Technical College

HARCOURT
BRACE

Harcourt Brace College Publishers
Fort Worth   Philadelphia   San Diego   New York   Orlando   Austin   San Antonio
Toronto   Montreal   London   Sydney   Tokyo

Publisher	Ted Buchholz
Acquisitions Editor	Drake Bush
Developmental Editor	Sue Lister
Marketing Manager	Steven Drummond
Production Manager	Tad Gaither
Production Services	Seaside Publishing Services
Text Design and Composition	Seaside Publishing Services
Text Type	11/12 Bembo

Material on pages 4–5 from THE LAWS OF BURGOS, 1512–1513: ROYAL ORDINANCES FOR THE GOOD GOVERNMENT AND TREATMENT OF THE INDIANS, trans. Lesley Baird Simpson. Reprinted by permission of John Howell Books. Material on pages 6–8 from THE BROKEN SPEARS by Miguel Leon Portilla. Copyright © 1962, 1990 by Beacon Press. Reprinted by permission of Beacon Press.

Requests for permission to make copies of any part of the work should be mailed to: Permissions Department, Harcourt Brace & Company, 6277 Sea Harbor Drive, Orlando, FL 32887-6277.

Address for Editorial Correspondence:
Harcourt Brace College Publishers, 301 Commerce Street, Suite 3700, Fort Worth, TX 76102

Address for Orders:
Harcourt Brace College Publishers, 6277 Sea Harbor Drive, Orlando, FL 32887-6277
1-800-782-4479 or 1-800-433-0001 (in Florida)

ISBN: 0-15-502200-8

Printed in the United States of America
  6 7 8 9 0 1 2 3 4   023   9 8 7 6 5 4 3 2
Harcourt Brace College Publishers

Preface

Voices from the past articulate history most eloquently. Primary sources, such as those presented here, are crucial to comprehending the development of the United States because they provide firsthand descriptions of, or reflections upon, occurrences that profoundly shaped the nation. For that reason, scholars rely heavily on such material for their knowledge of the past. Unfortunately, college students usually do not have access to eyewitness accounts, and they often conclude that history is nothing more than a rather dull compilation of obscure events and even-more-obscure dates. This documents package has been prepared so that students may hear some of the distant voices for themselves and come to realize that individuals, not "facts," are the critical element in history. By studying the selections presented in these two volumes, students will understand more fully the social, cultural, and political topics developed in *Liberty, Equality, and Power: A History of the American People.* They will find as well that they have gained a deeper awareness of and appreciation for the history of the American people.

The relationships among liberty, equality, and power provide one of the major themes in the nation's history, and the documents included in this book highlight that relationship. American perceptions of liberty, equality, and power have changed markedly over time, however, and the selections will help students understand the evolution of those ideals. Consequently, the earliest items emphasize the conflicts that occurred when European powers laid claim to the "New World." As the British gained dominance over much of North America, the English belief that power often threatened liberty became pervasive in the American colonies. The documents from the Revolutionary War era make clear that fear. Following independence, a developing market economy significantly affected attitudes toward liberty and power, while at the same time the emergence of democracy seemed to place more and more importance on the individual. During the nineteenth century, then, many Americans enjoyed the benefits of liberty and freedom. Numerous others, on the other hand, did not. The material reveals that for those people, the struggle to achieve equality lasted until well into the twentieth century. In addition to a growing egalitarianism during the 1900s, the expansive role of the United States in international affairs had significant implications. A number of the more recent documents therefore stress the importance of military and diplomatic efforts as the nation sought to ensure its fundamental ideals of liberty and equality while rising to a position of unprecedented world power.

Studying history can be a challenging, sometimes intimidating, task, and this ancillary is designed to help students as much as possible as they explore the national heritage. Each chapter begins with an introduction that places the selections in a broad historical context and that reiterates the themes developed in the corresponding textbook chapter. Moreover, the documents have individual introductions that survey the material and describe its importance to the history of the United States. A series of questions at the conclusion of each chapter encourages students to discuss the material they have just read. The questions focus on issues of liberty, equality, and power, but they also serve as a springboard to a broader understanding of American history. Indeed, one of the greatest advantages of using primary sources is that they allow the reader to become the historian and discover intellectual concepts or historical themes that they find of particular interest. Students may work individually with the questions, but they will gain much more from their efforts if they work with a study partner, a small group, or the entire class. Such an approach will bring the broadest range of understanding and experience to the discussion, which will in turn help make the material more vibrant, history more alive, learning more dynamic.

Many people have helped with the preparation of these two volumes, and I deeply appreciate their assistance. Several deserve special recognition. Professor Donald S. Frazier of McMurry University provided crucial help in the initial stage of the project. The staff of the Mary Counts Burnett Library at Texas Christian University offered invaluable support, especially Brenda Barnes and Cheryl Sussman of the Government Documents department. Finally, I am grateful to Shelia Kaye Jenkins of Ouachita Technical College for her help in the final preparation of the book.

Marvin E. Schultz
Ouachita Technical College

Contents

Chapter 1
When Old Worlds Collide:
Contact, Conquest, Catastrophe

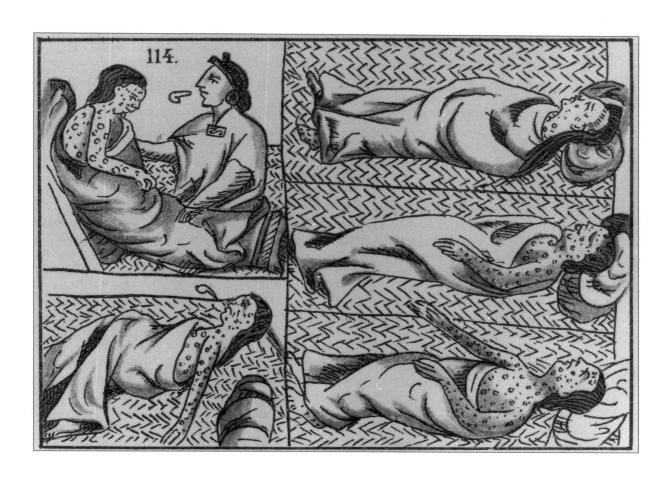

*Native Americans had no acquired immunity to many of the viruses and bacteria
European explorers carried, and, as a result, the native population died
by the millions. Smallpox germs were the real victors in the struggle
between the Aztecs and the Spanish invaders.*

*L*iberty, equality, and power provide three currents that have profoundly shaped the history of the American people; the relationship among those forces serves as a critical theme in the national heritage. As the large-scale migration of Europeans and Africans to the Americas began, however, issues of power clearly prevailed. In particular, the Spanish claimed all of the western hemisphere, an assertion ultimately legitimized by papal authority. Spain used that blessing to create an unprecedented global empire that linked Africa, America, and Europe. On the other hand, perhaps as early as 14,000 years ago, Asiatic tribes crossed Beringia, populating the vast land stretching from the Arctic to the Antarctic and creating complex societies that antedated much of Western culture. Many of these native inhabitants fiercely resisted European incursion, forcing the Spaniards to rely on legal devices and military strength to establish their power in the Americas. Consequently, contact between Europeans and Indians developed into conflicts that often had catastrophic consequences.

Papal Bull *Inter Caetera*
May 4, 1493*

Concern that Columbus's discoveries might have infringed on Portuguese claims led Pope Alexander VI to define the region that Spain could explore and develop. This Bull, which established a demarcation line west of the Canary Islands, served as the foundation for Spanish movement into the western hemisphere and set the stage for the long-term development of an Hispanic Latin America. The document reveals several important elements that characterized early efforts to gain control over America, including the struggle between European states to claim newly found territories, the influence of the church as a secular power, and the role of Christian zeal in the European occupation of the Americas.

To the illustrious sovereigns, our very dear son in Christ, Ferdinand, king, and our very dear daughter in Christ, Isabella, queen of Castile, Leon, Aragon, Sicily, and Granada, health and apostolic benediction. Among other works well pleasing to the Divine Majesty and cherished of our heart, this assuredly ranks highest, that in our times especially the Catholic faith and the Christian religion be exalted and be everywhere increased and spread, that the health of souls be cared for and that barbarous nations be overthrown and brought to the faith itself. . . . [R]ecognizing that as true Catholic kings and princes, such as we have always known you to be, and as your illustrious deeds already known to the whole world declare, you not only eagerly desire, but with every effort, zeal, and diligence, without regard to hardships, expenses, dangers, with the shedding even of your blood, are laboring to that end; recognizing also that you have long since dedicated to this purpose your whole soul and all your endeavors—as witnessed in these times with so much glory to the Divine Name in your recovery of the kingdom of Granada from the yoke of the Saracens—we therefore are rightly led, and hold it as our duty, to grant you . . . those things whereby . . . you may be enabled for the honor of God himself and the spread of the Christian rule to carry forward your holy and praiseworthy purpose so pleasing to immortal God. We have indeed learned that you, who for a long time had intend-

---

*From *European Treaties Bearing of the History of the United States and Its Dependencies to 1648*, ed. Frances G. Davenport (Washington, D.C.: Carnegie Institution, 1917), I:71–78.

ed to seek out and discover certain islands and mainlands remote and unknown and not hitherto discovered by others, to the end that you might bring to the worship of our Redeemer and the profession of the Catholic faith their residents and inhabitants, having been up to the present time greatly engaged in the siege and recovery of the kingdom itself of Granada were unable to accomplish this holy and praiseworthy purpose; but the said kingdom having at length been regained, as was pleasing to the Lord, you, with the wish to fulfill your desire, chose our beloved son, Christopher Columbus, . . . to make diligent quest for these remote and unknown mainlands and islands through the sea, where hitherto no one had sailed; and they at length, with divine aid and with the utmost diligence sailing in the ocean sea, discovered certain very remote islands and even mainlands that had not been discovered by others; wherein dwell very many people living in peace, and, as reported, going unclothed and not eating flesh. Moreover, as your aforesaid envoys are of opinion, these very peoples living in the said islands and countries, believe in one God, the Creator in heaven, and seem sufficiently disposed to embrace the Catholic faith and be trained in good morals. And it is hoped that, were they instructed, the name of the Savior, our Lord Jesus Christ, would easily be introduced into the said countries and islands. Also, on one of the chief of these aforesaid islands the said Christopher has already caused to be put together and built a fortress fairly equipped, wherein he has stationed as garrison certain Christians, companions of his, who are to make search for other remote and unknown islands and mainlands. In the islands and countries already discovered are found gold, spices, and very many other precious things of divers kinds and qualities. Wherefore, as becomes Catholic kings and princes, after earnest consideration of all matters, especially of the rise and spread of the Catholic faith, . . . you have purposed with the favor of divine clemency to bring under your sway the said mainlands and islands with their residents and inhabitants and to bring them to the Catholic faith. Hence, heartily commending in the Lord this your holy and praiseworthy purpose, and desirous that . . . the name of our Savior be carried into those regions, we exhort you very earnestly in the Lord and by your reception of holy baptism, whereby you are bound to our apostolic commands, . . . to lead the peoples dwelling in those islands and countries to embrace the Christian religion. . . . And, in order that you may enter upon so great an undertaking with greater readiness and heartiness endowed with the benefit of apostolic favor, we, . . . by the authority of Almighty God conferred upon us in blessed Peter and of the vicarship of Jesus Christ, which we hold on earth, do by tenor of these presents, should any of the said islands have been found by your envoys and captains, give, grant, and assign to you and your heirs and successors, kings of Castile and Leon, forever, together with all their dominions, cities, camps, places, and villages, and all rights, jurisdictions, and appurtenances, all islands and mainlands found and to be found, discovered and to be discovered towards the west and south, by drawing and establishing a line from the Arctic pole . . . to the Antarctic pole, . . . no matter whether the said mainlands and islands are found and to be found in the direction of India or towards any other quarter, the said line to be distant one hundred leagues toward the west and south from any of the islands commonly known as the Azores and Cape Verde. With this proviso, however, that none of the islands and mainlands, . . . beyond the said line towards the west and south, be in the actual possession of any Christian king or prince up to the birthday of the Lord Jesus Christ just past from that which the present year one thousand four hundred and thirty-three begins. And we make, appoint, and depute you and your said heirs and successors lords of them all with full and free power, authority, and jurisdiction of every kind; with this proviso however, that by this our gift, grant, and assignment no right acquired by any Christian prince, who may be in actual possession of said islands and mainlands prior to the said birthday of our Lord Jesus Christ, is hereby to be understood to be withdrawn or taken away. Moreover we command you in virtue of holy obedience that, employing all due diligence . . . you should appoint to the aforesaid mainlands and islands worthy, God-fearing, learned, skilled, and experienced men, in order to instruct the aforesaid inhabitants in the Catholic faith and train them in good morals. Furthermore, under penalty of excommunication . . . , we strictly forbid all persons . . . to dare, without your special permit or that of your aforesaid heirs and successors, to go for the purpose of trade or any other reason to the islands or mainlands . . . towards the west and south [of the said line]. We trust in Him from whom empires and governments and all good things proceed, that, should you, with the Lord's guidance, pursue this holy and praiseworthy undertaking, in a short while your hardships and endeavors will attain the most felicitous result, to the happiness and glory of all Christendom. . . . Let no one, therefore, infringe, or with rash boldness contravene, this our recommendation, exhortation, requisition, gift, grant, assignment, constitution, deputation, decree, mandate, prohibition, and will. . . .

The Laws of Burgos, 1512*

Promulgated by Queen Juana, daughter of Isabella, these statutes institutionalized the *encomienda* in the New World, sought to ensure the religious salvation of the natives, and defined the social and economic status of the Indians. Perhaps more importantly, the use of carefully articulated laws offered the Spanish a means to establish, and to justify, their power over the natives. By passing these statutes to ensure the salvation of the Indians, the Spanish ensured the destruction of native culture. As with all legal codes, the Laws of Burgos reveal much about the attitudes and presumptions of those in power, while also providing some insight into the lives of those the laws are meant to control.

WHEREAS, the King, my Lord and Father, and the Queen, my Mistress and Mother, . . . always desired that the chiefs and Indians of the Island of Española [Hispaniola] be brought to a knowledge of our Holy Catholic Faith, and, . . .

WHEREAS, it has become evident through long experience that nothing has sufficed to bring the said chiefs and Indians to a knowledge of our Faith (necessary for their salvation), since by nature they are inclined to idleness and vice, and have no manner of virtue or doctrine (by which our Lord is discovered), and that the principal obstacle in the way of correcting their vices and having them profit by and impressing them with the doctrine is that their dwellings are remote from the settlements of the Spaniards who . . . reside in the said Island, because, although at the time the Indians go to serve them they are indoctrinated in and taught the things of our Faith, after serving they return to their dwellings where, because of the distance and their own evil inclinations, they immediately forget what they have been taught and go back to their customary idleness and vice, and when they come to serve again they are as new in the doctrine as they were at the beginning, because, although the Spaniard who accompanies them to their village . . . reminds them of it and reprehends them, they, having no fear of him, do not profit by it and tell him to leave them in idleness, since that is their reason for returning to their said village, and that their only purpose and desire is to do with themselves what they will, without regard for any virtue, and, . . .

WHEREAS, it is our duty to seek a remedy for it in every way possible, it was considered by the King . . . and by several members of my council and by persons of good life, letters, and conscience, and they . . . gave it as their opinion that the most beneficial thing that could be done at present would be to remove the said chiefs and Indians to the vicinity of the villages and communities of the Spaniards—this for many considerations—and thus, by continual asso-

---

*From *The Laws of Burgos of 1512–1513: Royal Ordinances for the Good Government and Treatment of the Indians*, trans. Lesley Baird Simpson (San Francisco: John Howell Books, 1960), 11–14, 16–18, 21, 23–24, 26–28, 32, 42–45. Used by permission.

ciation with them, as well as by attendance at church on feast days to hear Mass and the divine offices, and by observing the conduct of the Spaniards, as well as the preparation and care that the Spaniards will display in demonstrating and teaching them, while they are together, the things of our Holy Catholic Faith, it is clear that they will the sooner learn them and, having learned them, will not forget them as they do now. . . .

THEREFORE, . . . it was agreed that for the improvement and remedy of all the aforesaid, the said chiefs and Indians should forthwith be brought to dwell near the villages and communities of the Spaniards who inhabit that Island, so that they may be treated and taught and looked after as is right and as we have always desired; and so I command that henceforth that which is contained below be obeyed and observed as follows: . . .

II

We order and command that all chiefs and Indians dwelling on the Island of Española, now or in the future, shall be brought from their present dwelling places to the villages and communities of the Spaniards who reside . . . on the said Island; and in order that they be brought of their own volition and suffer no harm from the removal, we hereby command Don Diego Columbus, our Admiral, Viceroy, and Governor of the said Island . . . to have them brought in the manner that seems best, with the least possible harm to the said chiefs and Indians. . . .

III

. . . [T]he citizens to whom the said Indians are given in encomienda shall . . . be obliged to erect a structure to be used as a church; . . . and in this said church he shall place an image of Our Lady and a bell with which to call the Indians to prayer; and the person who has them in encomienda shall be obliged to have them called by the bell at nightfall and go with them to the said church, and have them cross themselves and bless themselves, and together recite the *Ave Maria,* the *Pater Noster,* the *Credo,* and the *Salve Regina,* in such wise that all of them shall hear the said person, and the said person hear them, so that he may know who is performing well and who ill, and correct the one who is wrong. . . .

IV

Also, in order to discover how each one is progressing in things of the Faith, we command that every two weeks the said person who has them in charge shall examine them to see what each one knows particularly and to teach them what they do not know; and he shall also teach them the Ten Commandments and the Seven Deadly Sins and the Articles of the Faith, that is, to those he thinks have the capacity and ability to learn them; but all this shall be done with great love and gentleness. . . .

IX

. . . [W]hoever has fifty Indians or more in encomienda shall be obliged to have a boy (the one he considers most able) taught to read and write, and the things of our Faith, so that he may later teach the said Indians, because the Indians will more readily accept what he says than what the Spaniards and settlers tell them. . . .

X

. . . [E]ach and every time an Indian falls sick in a place where there is a priest, the priest shall be obliged to go to him and recite the Credo and other profitable things of our Holy Catholic Faith, and, if the Indian shall know how to confess, he shall confess him, without charging him any fee for it; . . . and also that they shall go with a Cross to the Indians who die and shall bury them without charging any fee for it or for the confession. . . .

XII

. . . [A]ll the Spanish inhabitants and settlers who have Indians in encomienda shall be obliged to have all infants baptized within a week of their birth, or before, if it is necessary; and if there is no priest to do so, the person in charge of the said estate shall be obliged to baptize them, according to the custom in such emergencies. . . .

Harcourt Brace & Company

XIII

. . . [A]fter the Indians have been brought to the estates, all the founding [of gold] . . . shall be done in the manner prescribed below: that is, the said persons who have Indians in encomienda shall extract gold with them for five months in the year, and at the end of these five months, the said Indians shall rest forty days; . . . and in all the said forty days no one shall employ any Indians in extracting gold. . . . And we command that . . . the persons who have the said Indians in encomienda shall be obliged, during these forty days of rest, to indoctrinate them in . . . our Faith more than on other days, because they will have the opportunity and means to do so. . . .

XVI

. . . [A]mong the other things of our Faith that shall be taught to the Indians, they shall be made to understand that they may not have more than one wife at a time, nor may they abandon her. . . .

XVIII

. . . [N]o pregnant woman, after the fourth month, shall be sent to the mines, . . . but shall be kept on the estates and utilized in housekeeping tasks, such as making bread, cooking, and weeding; and after she bears her child she shall nurse it until it is three years old, and in all this time she shall not be sent to the mines . . . or used in anything else that will harm the child. . . .

XIX

. . . [T]hat all those . . . who have Indians in encomienda . . . shall be obliged to give each of them a hammock in which to sleep continually; and they shall not allow them to sleep on the ground, as hitherto they have been doing. . . .

XXIV

. . . [N]o person or persons shall dare to beat any Indian with sticks, or whip him, or call him dog, or address him by any other name than his proper name alone; and if an Indian should deserve to be punished for something he has done, the said person having him in charge shall bring him to the visitor for punishment. . . .

Aztec Accounts of the Spanish Arrival in Mexico*

The conquest of Mexico proved to be one of the most dramatic contacts between Spaniards and Native Americans. Defeating the Aztecs cleared the way for the Spanish to claim Mexico and, ultimately, large portions of North America. Moreover, the Aztecs' incredible wealth dazzled the imaginations of Europeans, making the search for gold a major force in the exploration and exploitation of the entire western hemisphere. Consequently, the capture of the Aztec capital of Tenochtitlán marked a crucial step in Spain's rise to world power. The three documents that follow offer various versions of that monumental occurrence. The first account, taken from several Aztec sources, provides an Indian view of the events that took place in 1520 and 1521.

Motecuhzoma now arrayed himself in his finery, preparing to go out to meet them. The other great princes also adorned their persons, as did the nobles and their chieftains and knights. They all went out together to meet the strangers.

---

*From *The Broken Spears: The Aztec Account of the Conquest of Mexico,* ed. Miguel Leon-Portilla (Boston: Beacon Press, 1962, 1990), 63–69, 105–109. Originally published in Spanish under the title *Visíon de las Vencidas* (Mexico City: Universidad Nacional Autonoma de Mexico, 1959). Reprinted by permission of Beacon Press.

Harcourt Brace & Company

They brought trays heaped with the finest flowers—the flower that resembles a shield; the flower shaped like a heart; in the center, the flower with the sweetest aroma; and the fragrant yellow flower, the most precious of all. They also brought garlands of flowers, and ornaments for the breast, and necklaces of gold, necklaces hung with rich stones, necklaces fashioned in the petatillo style.

Thus Motecuhzoma went out to meet them. . . . He presented many gifts to the Captain and his commanders, those who had come to make war. Then he hung the gold necklaces around their necks and gave them presents of every sort as gifts of welcome.

When Motecuhzoma had given necklaces to each one, Cortés asked him: "Are you Motecuhzoma? Are you the king? Is it true that you are the king Motecuhzoma?"

And the king said: "Yes, I am Motecuhzoma." Then he stood up to welcome Cortés; he came forward, bowed his head low and addressed him in these words: "Our lord, you are weary. The journey has tired you, but now you have arrived on the earth. You have come to your city, Mexico. You have come here to sit on your throne, to sit under its canopy.

"The kings who have gone before, your representatives, guarded it and preserved it for your coming. The kings . . . ruled for you in the City of Mexico. The people were protected by their swords and sheltered by their shields.

"Do the kings know the destiny of those they left behind, their prosperity? If only they are watching! If only they see what I see!

"No, it is not a dream. I am not walking in my sleep. I am not seeing you in my dreams. . . . I have seen you at last! I have met you face to face! I was in agony for five days, for ten days, with my eyes fixed on the Region of the Mystery. And now you have come out of the clouds and mists to sit on your throne again.

"This was foretold by the kings who governed your city, and now it has taken place. You have come back to us; you have come down from the sky. Rest now, and take possession of your royal houses. Welcome to your land, my lords!"

When Motecuhzoma had finished, La Malinche translated his address into Spanish so that the Captain could understand it. Cortés replied in a strange and savage tongue, speaking first to La Malinche: "Tell Motecuhzoma that we are his friends. There is nothing to fear. We have wanted to see him for a long time, and now we have seen his face and heard his words. Tell him that we love him well and that our hearts are contented."

When the Spaniards entered the Royal House, they placed Motecuhzoma under guard and kept him under their vigilance. They also placed a guard over Itzcuauhtzin, but the other lords were permitted to depart. . . .

In the morning the Spaniards told Motecuhzoma what they needed in the way of supplies: tortillas, fried chickens, hens' eggs, pure water, firewood, and charcoal. Also: large clean cooking pots, water jars, pitchers, dishes, and other pottery. Motecuhzoma ordered that it be sent to them. The chiefs who received this order were angry with the king and no longer revered or respected him. But they furnished the Spaniards with all the provisions they needed—food, beverages, and water, and fodder for the horses.

When the Spaniards were installed in the palace, they asked Motecuhzoma about the city's resources and reserves and about the warriors' ensigns and shields. They questioned him closely and then demanded gold.

Motecuhzoma guided them to it. They surrounded him and crowded close with their weapons. He walked in the center while they formed a circle around him.

When they arrived at the treasure house called Teucalen, the riches of gold and feathers were brought out to them: ornaments made of quetzal feathers, richly worked shields, disks of gold, the necklaces of the idols, gold nose plugs, gold greaves, and bracelets and crowns.

Harcourt Brace & Company

The Spaniards immediately stripped the feathers from the gold shields and ensigns. They gathered all the gold into a great mound and set fire to everything else, regardless of its value. Then they melted the gold down into ingots. As for the precious green stones, they took only the best of them; the rest were snatched up by the Tlaxcaltecas. The Spaniards searched throughout the whole treasure house, questioning and quarreling, and seized every object they thought was beautiful.

Next they went to Motecuhzoma's storehouse in the place called Totocalo, where his personal treasures were kept. The Spaniards grinned like little beasts and patted each other with delight.

When they entered the hall of treasures, it was as if they had arrived in Paradise. They searched everywhere and coveted everything; they were slaves to their own greed. All of Motecuhzoma's possessions were brought out: fine bracelets, necklaces with large stones, ankle rings with little gold bells, the royal crowns and all the royal finery—everything that belonged to the king and was reserved to him only. They seized these treasures as if they were their own, as if this plunder were merely a stroke of good luck. . . .

[The Spaniards] advanced cautiously, with their standard-bearer in the lead. . . . The Tlaxcaltecas and the other allies followed close behind. The Tlaxcaltecas held their heads high and pounded their breasts with their hands, hoping to frighten us with their arrogance and courage. They sang songs as they marched, but the Aztecs were also singing. It was as if both sides were challenging each other with their songs. They sang whatever they happened to remember and the music strengthened their hearts. . . .

Then all the Aztecs sprang up and charged into battle. The Spaniards were so astonished that they blundered here and there like drunkards; they ran through the streets with the warriors in pursuit. This was when the taking of captives began. A great many allies from Tlaxcala, Acolhuacan, Chalco, and Xochimilcho were overpowered by the Aztecs, and there was a great harvesting of prisoners, a great reaping of victims to be sacrificed. . . .

The Aztecs took their prisoners to Yacacolco, hurrying them along the road under the strictest guard. Some of the captives were weeping, some were keening, and others were beating their palms against their mouths.

When they arrived in Yacacolco, they were lined up in long rows. One by one they were forced to climb to the temple platform, where they were sacrificed by the priests. The Spaniards went first, then their allies, and all were put to death.

As soon as the sacrifices were finished, the Aztecs arranged the Spaniards' heads in rows on pikes. They also lined up their horses' heads. They placed the horses' heads at the bottom and the heads of the Spanish above, and arranged them all so that the faces were toward the sun. However, they did not display any of the allies' heads. All told, fifty-three Spaniards and four horses were sacrificed there in Yacacolco. . . .

The Spanish blockade caused great anguish in the city. The people were tormented by hunger, and many starved to death. There was no fresh water to drink, only stagnant water and the brine of the lake, and many people died of dysentery.

The only food was lizards, swallows, corn cobs and the salt grasses of the lake. The people also ate water lilies and the seeds of the colorin, and chewed on deer hides and pieces of leather. They roasted and seared and scorched whatever they could find and then ate it. They ate the bitterest weeds and even dirt.

Nothing can compare with the horrors of that siege and the agonies of the starving. We were so weakened by hunger that, little by little, the enemy forced us to retreat. Little by little they forced us to the wall.

Harcourt Brace & Company

Report of Hernando Cortés*
October 30, 1520

Hernando Cortés, commander of the Spanish conquistadors who defeated the Aztecs, provided Emperor Charles V with the following description of some of the initial events in Tenochtitlán. Cortés offered one explanation for his phenomenal success by describing the Aztec legend that prophesied a conqueror who would arrive from the East. In addition, he offered the first account of the remarkable riches that helped encourage and finance the European drive for power in the Americas.

When we had passed the bridge, the Señor Muteczuma came out to receive us, attended by about two hundred nobles, . . . in two processions in close proximity to the houses on each side of the street, which is very wide and beautiful, and so straight that you can see from one end of it to the other, although it is two thirds of a league in length, having on both sides large and elegant houses and temples. Muteczuma came through the center of the street, attended by two lords. . . . He was supported on the arms of both, and as we approached, I alighted and advanced close to salute him; but the two attendant lords stopped me to prevent my touching him, and he and they both performed the ceremony of kissing the ground; after which he directed his brother who accompanied him to remain with me; the latter accordingly took me by the arm, while Muteczuma, with his other attendant, walked a short distance in front of me, and after he had spoken to me, all the other nobles also came up to address me, and then went away in two processions with great regularity, one after the other, and in this manner returned to the city . . . [where we] reached a very large and splendid palace, in which we were to be quartered, which had been fully prepared for our reception. He there took me by the hand and led me into a spacious saloon, in front of which was a court, through which we entered. Having caused me to sit down on a piece of rich carpeting, . . . he told me to wait his return there, and then went away. After a short space of time, when my people were all bestowed in their quarters, he returned with many and various jewels of gold and silver, feather-work, and five or six thousands pieces of cotton cloth, very rich and of varied texture and finish. After having presented these to me, . . . he discoursed as follows:—

"It is now a long time since, by means of written records, we learned from our ancestors that neither myself nor any of those who inhabit this region were descended from its original inhabitants, but from strangers who emigrated hither from a very distant land; and we have also learned that a prince, whose vassals they all were, conducted our people into these parts, and then returned to his native land. He afterward came again to this country, after the lapse of much time, and found that his people had intermarried with the native inhabitants, by whom they had many children, and had built towns in which they resided; and when he desired them to return with him, they were unwilling to go, nor were they disposed to acknowledge him as their sovereign; so he departed from the country, and we have always heard that his descendants would come to conquer this land, and reduce us to subjection as his vassals; and according to the direction from which you say you have come, namely, the quarter where the sun rises, and from what you say of the great lord or king who sent you hither, we believe and are assured that he is our natural sovereign, especially as you say that it is a long time since you first had knowledge of us. Therefore be assured that we will obey you, and acknowledge you for our sovereign in place of the great lord whom you mention, and that there shall be no default or decep-

---

*From *The Despatches of Hernando Cortés, the Conqueror of Mexico, Addressed to the Emperor Charles V. Written During the Conquest, and Containing a Narrative of its Events,* trans. George Folsom (New York: Wiley and Putnam, 1843), 85–89, 107–109.

tion on our part. And you have the power in all this land, I mean wherever my power extends, to command what is your pleasure, and it shall be done in obedience thereto, and all that we have is at your disposal. And since you are in your own proper land and your own house, rest and refresh yourselves after the toils of your journey, and the conflicts in which you have been engaged, which have been brought upon you, as I well know, by all the people from Puntunchan to this place; and I am aware that the Cempoallans and Tlascalans have told you much evil of me, but believe no more than you see with your own eyes, especially from those who are my enemies, some of whom were once my subjects, and having rebelled upon your arrival, make these statements to ingratiate themselves in your favor. . . ." I answered him in respect to all that he said, expressing my acknowledgments, and adding whatever the occasion seemed to demand, especially endeavoring to confirm him in the belief that your Majesty was the sovereign that he had looked for; and after this he took his leave, and having gone, we were liberally supplied with fowls, bread, fruits, and other things required for the use of our quarters.

I one day spoke to Muteczuma and said that your Highness needed gold for certain works that he had ordered to be completed, and I wished him to send some of his people, and I would send some of mine, to the lands and abodes of those lords who had submitted themselves on that occasion, to ask them to supply your Majesty with some part of what they possessed; since besides the necessity your Majesty had for the gold, it would serve as a beginning of their fealty, and your Highness would form a better opinion of their disposition to render him service by such demonstrations; and I also requested that he himself would give me the gold he had, as well as other things, in order that I might transmit them to your Majesty. He immediately requested that I would designate the Spaniards whom I wish to send on this business, and he distributed them two by two, and five by five, among many provinces and cities; . . . and with them he sent some of his own people and directed them to go to the governors of provinces and cities, and say that I commanded each one of them to give a certain proportion of gold, which he prescribed. Accordingly all those caciques to whom he sent contributed freely what he demanded of them, as well as jewels as plates and leaves of gold and silver, and whatever else they possessed; and melting down all that admitted it, we found that the fifth part belonging to your Majesty amounted to 32,400 pesos of gold and upwards, without reckoning the jewels of gold and silver, the feather-work, and precious stones, together with many other valuable articles that I set apart for your Majesty, worth more than 100,000 ducats.

The Conquest of Mexico*

Bernal Díaz del Castillo, who served in the army that captured Tenochtitlán, wrote a history of that campaign in 1568. The following passages describe first the Aztec attack that drove the Spaniards from Tenochtitlán, and then the fighting that marked the final stages of the conquest, including the carnage that accompanied the Spanish victory over the Aztecs.

[During the fighting for the city] many companies of Mexicans came to the causeway and . . . we could not fend them off, on the contrary they kept on following us thinking that this very night they would carry us off to be sacrificed.

When we had retreated near to our quarters and had already crossed a great opening where there was much water, the arrows, javelins, and stones could no longer reach us. [Then] there was sounded the dismal drum of Huichilobos and many other shells and horns and things like trumpets and the sound of them all was terrifying, and we all looked towards the lofty Cue

---

*From Bernal Díaz del Castillo, *The True History of the Conquest of New Spain*, ed. and pub. Genaro García in Mexico, trans. Alfred P. Maudslay (London: The Hakluyt Society, 1912), 148–151, 185–187.

where they were being sounded, and saw that our comrades whom they had captured . . . were being carried by force up the steps, and they were taking them to be sacrificed. When they got them up to a small square . . . where their accursed idols are kept, we saw them place plumes on the heads of many of them and with things like fans they forced them to dance before Huichilobos, and after they had danced they immediately placed them on their backs on some rather narrow stones which had been prepared as [a place of] sacrifice, and with the stone knives they sawed open their chests and drew out their palpitating hearts and offered them to the idols that were there, and they kicked the bodies down the steps, and Indian butchers who were waiting below cut off the arms and feet and flayed the faces, and prepared it afterwards like glove leather with the beards on, and kept those for the festivals when they celebrated drunken orgies, and the flesh they ate in *chilmole*. In the same way they sacrificed all the others and ate the legs and arms and offered the hearts and blood to their idols, as I have said, and the bodies, that is their entrails and feet, they threw to the tigers and lions which they kept in the house of carnivores. . . .

. . . [L]et us speak of the dead bodies and heads that were in the houses where Guatemoc had taken refuge. I say on my oath, Amen, that all the houses and the palisades in the lake were full of heads and corpses and I do not know how to describe it for in the streets and the courts of Tlatelolco there was no difference, and we could not walk except among corpses and heads of dead Indians. I have read about the destruction of Jerusalem, but I know not for certain if there was greater mortality than this, for of the great number of the warriors from all the provinces and towns subject to Mexico who had crowded in [to the city] most of them died, . . . thus the land and the lake and the palisades were full of dead bodies, and stank so much that no one could endure it, and for this reason, as soon as Guatemoc was captured, each one of the Captains went to his own camp, . . . and even Cortés was ill from the stench which assailed his nostrils, and from headache, during the days we were in Tlatelolco. . . .

[A]s there was so great a stench in the city, Guatemoc asked permission of Cortés for all the Mexican forces left in the city to go out to the neighboring pueblos, and they were promptly told to do so. I assert that during three days and nights they never ceased streaming out and all three causeways were crowded with men, women and children, so thin, yellow, dirty and stinking, that it was pitiful to see them. When the city was free of them, Cortés went to examine it and we found the houses full of corpses and there were some poor Mexicans, who could not move out, still among them, and what they excreted from their bodies was a filth such as thin swine pass which have been fed nothing but grass, and all the city was as though it had been ploughed up and the roots of the herbs dug out and they had eaten them and even cooked the bark of some of the trees, and there was no fresh water to be found, only salt water. I also wish to state that they did not eat the flesh of their own Mexicans, only that of our people and our Tlaxcalan allies whom they had captured, and there had been no births for a long time, as they had suffered so much from hunger and thirst and continual fighting.

The Travels of Cabeza de Vaca*
1528–1536

Álvar Núñez, Cabeza de Vaca, accompanied the tragic Pánfilo de Narváez expedition of 1528. The explorers traveled through Florida, but they failed to reestablish contact with their supporting flotilla and found themselves abandoned. After eight years of traveling westward, a group of

---

[6]From Álvar Núñez, Cabeza de Vaca, *The Journey of Álvar Núñez, Cabeza de Vaca, and His Companions from Florida to the Pacific, 1528–1536*, ed. A. F. Bandalier, trans. Fanny Bandalier (New York: A. S. Barnes & Company, 1905), 26–28, 31–32, 117–118, 121–123.

survivors reached northern Mexico. Cabeza de Vaca published his observations of the journey in 1542, providing the earliest description of the southernmost region of what would become the United States. His account sparked additional explorations into the area, which provided Spain with a claim to much of North America. In their efforts to solidify that claim, the Spanish often faced powerful opposition from the Indian tribes that Cabeza de Vaca had visited.

The country between our landing place and the village and country of Apalachen [probably near the Apalachicola River in the Florida panhandle] is mostly level; the soil is sand and earth. All throughout it there are very large trees and open forests containing nut trees, laurels, and others of the kind called resinous, cedar, juniper, water oak, pines, oak and low palmetto, like those of Castilla. Everywhere there are many lagunes, large and small, some very difficult to cross, partly because they are so deep, partly because they are covered with fallen trees. Their bottom is sandy, and in the province of Apalachen the lagunes are much larger than those we found previously. . . . The animals we saw there were three kinds of deer, rabbits and hares, bears and lions and other wild beasts, among them one that carries its young in a pouch on its belly as long as the young are small, until they are able to look for their sustenance, and even then, when they are out after food and people come, the mother does not move until her little ones are in the pouch again. The country . . . has good pasture for cattle; there are birds of many kinds in large numbers; geese, ducks, wild ducks, muscovy ducks, Ibis, small white herons (egrets), herons and partridges. We saw many falcons, marsh-hawks, sparrow-hawks, pigeon-hawks and many other birds. . . .

There were men . . . who swore they had seen two oak trees, each as thick as the calf of a leg, shot through and through by arrows, which is not surprising if we consider the force and dexterity with which they shoot. I myself saw an arrow that penetrated the base of a poplar tree for half a foot in length. All the many Indians from Florida we saw were archers, and, being very tall and naked, at a distance they appear giants.

Those people are wonderfully built, very gaunt and of great strength and agility. Their bows are as thick as an arm, from eleven to twelve spans long, shooting an arrow at 200 paces with unerring aim. . . .

From the island of Ill-Fate [a coastal barrier island, perhaps Galveston] on, all the Indians whom we met as far as to here have the custom of not cohabiting with their wives when they are pregnant, and until the child is two years old.

Children are nursed to the age of twelve years, when they are old enough to gather their own food. We asked them why they brought their children up in that way and they replied, it was owing to the great scarcity of food all over that country, since it was common (as we saw) to be without it two or three days, and even four, and for that reason they nursed the little ones so long to preserve them from perishing through hunger. And even if they should survive, they would be very delicate and weak. When one falls sick he is left to die in the field unless he be somebody's child. Other invalids, if unable to travel, are abandoned; but a son or brother is taken along.

There is also a custom for husbands to leave their wives if they do not agree, and remarry whom they please; this applies to the young men, but after they have had children they stay with their women and do not leave them.

When, in any village, they quarrel among themselves, they strike and beat each other until worn out, and only then do they separate. Sometimes their women step in and separate them, but men never interfere in these brawls. Nor do they ever use bow and arrow, and after they have fought and settled the question, they take their lodges and women and go out in the fields to live apart from the others until their anger is over, and when they are no longer angry and their resentment has passed away they return to the village and are as friendly again as if nothing happened. There is no need of mediation. When the quarrel is between unmarried people they go to some of their neighbors, who, even if they be enemies, will receive them well, with great festivities and gifts of what they have, so that, when pacified, they return to their village wealthy. . . .

Those Indians are the readiest people with their weapons of all I have seen in the world, for when they suspect the approach of an enemy they lay awake all night with their bows within reach and a dozen of arrows, and before one goes to sleep he tries his bow, and should the string not be to his liking he arranges it until it suits him. Often they crawl out of their dwellings so as not to be seen and look and spy in every direction after danger, and if they detect anything, in less than no time are they all out in the field with their bows and arrows. Thus they remain until daybreak, running hither and thither whenever they see danger or suspect their enemies might approach. When day comes they unstring their bows until they go hunting.

The strings of their bows are made of deer sinews. They fight in a crouching position, and while shooting at each other talk and dart from one side to the other to dodge the arrows of the foe. In this way they receive little damage from our crossbows and muskets. On the contrary, the Indians laugh at those weapons, because they are not dangerous to them on the plains over which they roam. They are only good in narrows and in swamps.

Horses are what the Indians dread most, and by the means of which they will be overcome.

Whoever has to fight Indians must take great care not to let them think he is disheartened or that he covets what they own; in war they must be treated very harshly, for should they notice either fear or greed, they are the people who know how to abide their time for revenge and to take courage from the hearts of their enemy. After spending all their arrows, they part, going each their own way, and without attempting pursuit, although one side might have more men than the other; such is their custom.

Many times they are shot through and through with arrows, but do not die from the wounds as long as the bowels or heart are not touched; on the contrary, they recover quickly. Their eyesight, hearing and senses in general are better, I believe, than those of any other men upon earth. They can stand, and have to stand, much hunger, thirst and cold, being more accustomed and used to it than others. This I wished to state here, since, besides that all men are curious to know the habits and devices of others, such as might come in contact with those people should be informed of their customs and deeds, which will be of no small profit to them.

Discussion

1. How do the documents reveal, and what do they imply about, the various sources and manifestations of Spanish power in the western hemisphere?

2. What do the documents suggest about cultural differences between Spaniards and Native Americans, and how do those differences relate to the development of Spanish power?

3. How do the assertions of Spanish power implicit in the Laws of Burgos and the conquest of Mexico conform to the Papal Bull of 1493?

4. Unlike the Aztecs, some Indians resisted the Spanish for centuries. What does the account by Cabeza de Vaca reveal about the Indians' power to defend their culture?

5. What do the Laws of Burgos, the Aztec description of the conquest, and Cabeza de Vaca's account show about Indian attitudes toward power? What do the documents disclose about Native-American attitudes regarding equality?

6. Columbus assumed that Indians would be easy to convert to Christianity. The Laws of Burgos recognize that conversion will be a difficult process. What explains this change of attitude?

Chapter 2

The Challenge to Spain and the Spectrum of European Settlement

NOVA BRITANNIA.

OFFERING MOST

Excellent fruites by Planting in
VIRGINIA.

Exciting all such as be well affected
to further the same.

The London Company sold stock, held lotteries, and published brochures such as this to promote their Virginia colony. While these promotional efforts hinted at instant wealth, they masked the desperate need for additional settlers and laborers.

*M*ore than ten million people moved to the Americas in the three hundred years after the voyages of Columbus. In addition to those from Spain, the emigrants came from a variety of cultures, including French, Dutch, African, and English. As a result, other European states threatened Spanish hegemony in the western hemisphere, initiating power struggles in the region that lasted well into the eighteenth century. Each of these groups, furthermore, carried with them different political and economic ideals, providing a broad spectrum of settlement that significantly shaped the development of American society. For many individuals, commerce provided the primary impetus to the development of the so-called New World. Others, particularly the English, were more concerned with establishing permanent settlements. Englishmen shared a deep faith in specific civil rights that had evolved over centuries but were generally dated from the Magna Carta of 1215. As English settlers came to dominate the Atlantic coast of North America, they established a tradition of liberty that had a vital influence on the development of the United States.

The Conversion of the Savages in New France, 1610*

The following letter, written by the Huguenot poet, lawyer, and historian Marc Lescarbot to Maria de Medici, the Catholic queen of France, touches on French attitudes toward European colonization of the Americas while providing a brief description of Acadia (modern Nova Scotia). From the early 1600s to the 1760s, North America became the prize in a monumental conflict between European powers; Lescarbot's critical comments regarding other nations portend that bitter international confrontation. This document also describes briefly the egalitarianism of tribal democracy that characterized many Indian societies.

It remains . . . to deplore the wretched condition of these people who occupy a country so large that the old world bears no comparison with it. . . . Dense ignorance prevails in all these countries, where there is no evidence that they have ever felt the breath of the Gospel, except in the last century when the Spaniard carried thither some light of the Christian religion, together with his cruelty and avarice. But this was so little that it should not receive much consideration, since by the very confession of those who have written their histories, they have killed almost all the natives of the country, who, only seventy years ago . . . numbered more than twenty millions. For more than twenty-five years, the English have retained a foothold in the country, called in honor of the deceased Queen of England, Virginia. . . . But that country carries on its affairs with so much secrecy, that very few persons know anything definite about it. . . . As to our French people, I have complained enough . . . of our lack of zeal either in reclaiming these poor erring ones, or in making known, exalted, and glorified, the name of God in the lands beyond the seas, where it never has been proclaimed. . . . But why is it that the Church, which has so much wealth; why is it that the Nobility, who expend so much needlessly, do not establish some fund for the execution of so holy a work? Two courageous Gentlemen, Sieurs de

---

*From *The Jesuit Relations and Allied Documents: Travels and Explorations of the Jesuit Missionaries in New France, 1610–1791,* 73 vols., ed. Reuben Gold Thwaites (Cleveland: Burrows Brothers Company, 1896–1901), I:61–77.

Monts and de Poutrincourt, have . . . shown such great zeal in this work, that they have weakened their resources by their outlays, and have done more than their strength justified them in doing. . . .

This Port Royal, the home of sieur de Poutrincourt is the most beautiful earthly habitation that God has ever made. It . . . can securely harbor twenty thousand ships. . . . Furthermore, there can be caught . . . great quantities of herring, smelt, sardines, barbels, codfish, seals and other fish; and as to shell-fish, there is an abundance of lobsters, crabs, palourdes, cockles, mussels, snails, and porpoises. But whoever is disposed to go beyond the tides of the sea will find in the rivers quantities of sturgeon and salmon, and will have plenty of sport in landing them. . . .

The people who are at Port Royal . . . are called Souriquois and . . . are governed by Captains called Sagamores. . . . At Port Royal, the name of the . . . Sagamore . . . is Membertou. He is at least a hundred years old, and may in the course of nature live more than fifty years longer. He has a number of families whom he rules, not with so much authority as does our King . . . , but with sufficient power to harangue, advise, and lead them to war, to render justice to one who has a grievance, and like matters. He does not impose any taxes upon the people, but if there are any profits from the chase he has a share of them, without being obliged to take part in it. It is true that they sometimes make him presents of Beaver skins and other things, when he is occupied in curing the sick. . . . Now this Membertou to-day, by the grace of God, is a Christian, together with all his family, having been baptized, and twenty others with him, on last Saint John's day, the 24th of June. . . .

Charter of the Dutch West India Company, 1621*

During the colonial period, Americans developed a powerful faith in free enterprise and popular government. The importance of trade in the development of the Americas is evident in the following charter, granted by the States General of the United Netherlands in June 1621 in an effort to gain access to the lucrative products of the western hemisphere. The selection makes clear the Dutch emphasis on commerce rather than on conquest and settlement. In its description of corporate organization and procedure, the charter also reflects the egalitarianism that marked the republican government of the Netherlands. Although American republicanism grew more directly out of English constitutionalism, the Dutch faith in liberty, property, and toleration became a significant element of American culture.

Be it known, that we knowing the prosperity of these countries, and the welfare of their inhabitants depends principally on navigation and trade, . . . and desiring that the aforesaid inhabitants should not only be preserved in their former navigation, traffic, and trade, but also that their trade may be encreased as much as possible . . . : And we find by experience, that without the common help, assistance, and interposition of a General Company, the people . . . cannot be profitably protected and maintained in their great risk from pirates, extortion and otherwise, which will happen in so very long a voyage. We have, therefore, . . . found it good, that the navigation, trade, and commerce, in parts of the West-Indies, and Africa, and other places hereafter described, should not henceforth be carried on any otherwise than by the common united strength of the merchants and inhabitants of these countries; and that for that end there shall be erected one General Company, which we . . . will maintain and strengthen with our Help,

---

*From *The Federal and State Constitutions, Colonial Charters, and Other Organic Laws of the States Territories, and Colonies Now or Heretofore Forming the United States of America,* 7 vols., ed. Francis N. Thorpe (Washington, D.C.: U.S. Government Printing Office, 1909), I:59–67.

Favour and assistance . . . and moreover furnish them with a proper Charter, and with the following Privileges and Exemptions, to wit, That for the Term of four and twenty Years, none of the Natives or Inhabitants of these countries shall be permitted to sail to or from the said lands, or to traffic on the coast and countries of *Africa* from the *Tropic of Cancer* to the *Cape of Good Hope,* nor in any countries of *America,* or the *West-Indies,* beginning at the fourth end of *Terra Nova,* by the straights of *Magellan, La Maire,* or any other straights and passages situated thereabouts to the straights of *Anian,* as well on the north sea as the south sea, nor on any islands situated on the one side or the other, or between both; nor in the western or southern countries reaching, lying, and between both meridians, from the *Cape of Good Hope,* in the East, to the east end of *New Guinea,* in the West, inclusive, but in the name of the United Company of these United Netherlands. . . .

II. That, moreover, the aforesaid Company may, . . . make contracts, engagements and alliances with the limits herein before prescribed, make contracts, engagements and alliances with the princes and natives of the countries comprehended therein, and also build any forts and fortifications there, to appoint and discharge Governors, people for war, and officers of justice, and other public officers, for the preservation of the places, keeping good order, police and justice, and in like manner for the promoting of trade; . . . Moreover, they advance the peopling of those fruitful and unsettled parts, and do all that the service of those countries, and the profit and increase of trade shall require. . . .

V. And should it be necessary for the establishment, security, and defence of this trade, to take any troops with them, we will . . . furnish the said Company with such troops, provided they be paid and supported by the Company. . . .

VIII. That we will not take any ships, ordnance, or ammunition belonging to the company, for the use of this country, without the consent of the said company.

IX. We have moreover incorporated this company, and favoured them with privileges, . . . that they may pass freely with all their ships and goods without paying any toll to the United Provinces. . . .

XI. And that this company may be strengthened by a good government, to the greatest profit and satisfaction of all concerned, we have ordained, that the said government shall be vested in five chambers of managers; one at Amsterdam, . . . one chamber in Zealand, . . . one chamber at the Maeze, . . . one chamber in North Holland, . . . and the fifth chamber in Friesland. . . .

XIV. That the first managers shall serve for the term of six years, and then one-third part of the number of managers shall be changed by lot; and two years after a like third part, and the two next following years, the last third part; and so on successively the oldest in the service shall be dismissed; and in the place of those who go off, . . . three others shall be nominated by the managers, . . . together with the principal adventurers . . . , from which the aforesaid Provinces, the deputies, or the magistrates, shall make a new election of a manager. . . .

XV. That the accounts of the furniture and outfit of the vessels, with their dependencies, shall be made up three months after the departure of the vessels, and one month after, copies shall be sent to us, and to the respective chambers. . . .

XVI. That every six years they shall make a general account of all outfits and returns, together with all the gains and losses of the company; . . . which accounts shall be made public . . . , to the end that every one who is interested may, upon hearing of it, attend; and if by the expiration of the seventh year, the accounts are not made out in manner aforesaid, the managers shall forfeit their commissions, which shall be appropriated to the use of the poor. . . . And notwithstanding there shall be a dividend made of the profits of the business, so long as we find that *ten per cent* shall have been gained.

Harcourt Brace & Company

XVIII. That so often as it shall be necessary to have a general meeting of the aforesaid chambers, . . . [at least nineteen persons] shall be deputed by us for the purpose of helping to direct the aforesaid meeting of the company.

XIX. By which general meeting . . . all the business of this Company . . . shall be managed and finally settled, provided, that in the case of resolving upon a war, our approbation shall be asked.

XXXI. The manager shall not deliver or sell to the Company, in whole or in part, any of their own ships, merchandise or goods; nor buy or cause to be bought, of the said Company, directly or indirectly, any goods or merchandise, nor have any portion or part therein, on forfeiture of one year's commissions for the use of the poor, and the loss of Office.

XXXII. The managers shall give notice by advertisement, as often as they have a fresh importation of goods and merchandise, to the end that every one may have a seasonable knowledge of it, before they proceed to a final sale. . . .

XXXV. That all the goods of this Company which shall be sold by weight shall be sold by one weight, to wit, that of Amsterdam; and that all such goods shall be put on board ship, or in store without paying any excise, import, or weigh-money. . . .

XXXVI. That the . . . managers shall not be arrested, attached or encumbered, in order to obtain from them an account of the administration of the Company, nor for the payment of the wages of those who are in the service of the Company, but those who shall pretend to take the same upon them, shall . . . refer the matter to their ordinary judges. . . .

XXXIX. We have moreover promised . . . that we will defend this Company against every person in free navigation and traffic, and assist them with a million of guilders. . . .

XL. And if by a violent and continued interruption of the aforesaid navigation and traffic, the business within the limits of their Company shall be brought to an open war, we will . . . give them for their assistance sixteen ships of war, . . . with four good well sailing yachts, . . . which shall be properly mounted and provided in all respects, . . . upon condition that they shall be manned, victualled, and supported at the expense of the Company, and that the Company shall be obliged to add thereto sixteen like ships of war and four yachts . . . ; Provided that all the ships of war and merchant-men . . . shall be under an admiral appointed by us according to the previous advise of the aforesaid General Company, and shall obey our commands, together with the resolutions of the Company. . . .

XLIV. The managers of this Company shall solemnly promise and swear, that they will act well and faithfully in their administration, and make good and just accounts of their trade: That they in all things will consult the greatest profit of the Company: . . . That they will not give the principal members any greater advantage in the payments or distribution of money than the least. . . .

XLV. All which privileges . . . together with the assistance herein before mentioned . . . we have . . . given . . . to the aforesaid Company; . . . promising moreover that they shall enjoy them peaceably and freely; ordaining that the same shall be observed and kept by all the magistrates, officers and subjects of the United Netherlands. . . . And that none may pretend ignorance hereof, we command that the contents of this charter shall be notified by publication, or an advertisement, where, and in such manner, as is proper; for we have found it necessary for the service of this country. . . .

Harcourt Brace & Company

John Hawkins's First Voyage, 1562–1563[*]
Recorded by Richard Hakluyt

Sir John Hawkins stirred English interest in the Americas with his successful voyage in the 1560s. The following account of that venture played an important role in suggesting the wealth to be made in the Atlantic trade, especially in what became a centuries-long commerce in slaves. The importation of African slaves had crucial implications for the United States. Slavery shaped attitudes toward liberty for more than two hundred years, and the search for racial equality has lasted well through the twentieth century. In addition, the slavery question helped generate an intense conflict over the nature of political power in the United States that culminated in civil war during the 1860s.

Master John Hawkins having made divers voyages to the isles of the *Canaries,* and there by his good and upright dealing being grown in love and favour with the people, informed himself amongst them, by diligent inquisition, of the state of the West *India,* whereof he had received some knowledge of the instructions of his father, but increased the same by the advertisements and reports of that people. And being amongst other particulars that *Negroes* were very good merchandise in *Hispaniola,* and that store of *Negroes* might easily be had upon the coast of *Guinea,* resolved himself to make trial thereof, and communicated that device with his worshipful friends in *London.* . . . All which persons liked so well of his intention, that they became liberal contributors and adventurers in the action. For which purpose there were three good ships immediately provided: . . . in which small fleet *Master Hawkins* took with him not above 100 men, for fear of sickness and other inconveniences, whereunto men in long voyages are commonly subject.

With this company he put off and departed from the coast of *England* in the month of October, 1562, and in his course touched first at *Tenriffe,* where he received friendly entertainment. From thence he passed to *Sierra Leona,* upon the coast of *Guinea,* which place by the people is called *Tagarin,* where he stayed some good time, and got into his possession, partly by the sword and partly by other means, to the number of 300 *Negroes* at the least, besides other merchandises which that country yieldeth. With this prey he sailed over the ocean sea unto the island of *Hispaniola,* and arrived at the port of *Isabella*: and there he had reasonable utterance of his English commodities, as also of some part of his *Negroes,* trusting the Spaniards no further, than that by his own strength he was able to master them. From the port *Isabella* he went to *Puerta de Plata,* where he made like sales, standing always upon his guard: from thence also he sailed to *Monte Christi,* another port on the north side of *Hispaniola,* and the last place of his touching, where he had peaceable traffic, and made vent of the whole number of his *Negroes:* for which he received in those three places, by way of exchange, such a quantity of merchandise that he did not only lade his own three ships with hides, ginger, sugars, and some quantity of pearls, but he freighted also two other hulks with hides and other like commodities, which he sent into *Spain.* And thus, leaving the island, he returned . . . , passing out by the islands of the *Caicos,* without further entering into the Bay of *Mexico,* in this his first voyage to the *West India.* And so, with prosperous success and much gain to himself and the aforesaid adventurers, he came home, and arrived in the month of September, 1563.

---

[*]From *Voyages of the Elizabethan Seamen: Select Narratives from the "Principal Navigations" of Hakluyt,* ed. Edward John Payne (London: Oxford University Press, 1907), 6–8.

Harcourt Brace & Company

The First Charter of Virginia, 1606*

Under the provisions of the following charter, granted by King James I, the London Company established the first permanent English settlement in North America. While the document addresses matters of trade, it differs markedly from the West India Company charter in its attention to settlement and development. In 1624, the king overturned the charter, making Virginia a royal colony. Thus, very early on the seeds of discord between colonial sovereignty and English power were planted in the New World. An important factor in that struggle was the colonials' insistence that they enjoyed the "Liberties, Franchises, and Immunities" of Englishmen—a declaration made explicitly in the Virginia Company charter.

WHEREAS . . . Sir *Thomas Gates,* and Sir *George Somers,* Knights, *Richard Hackluit,* Clerk, Prebendary of *Westminister,* and *Edward-Maria Wingfield, Thomas Hanham,* and *Ralegh Gilbert,* Esqrs., *William Parker, and George Popham,* Gentlemen, and divers others of our loving Subjects, have been humble Suitors unto us, that We would vouchsafe unto them our License, to make Habitation, Plantation, and to deduce a colony of sundry of our People into that part of *America* commonly called VIRGINIA, and other parts and Territories in *America,* either appertaining unto us or which are not now actually possessed by any *Christian* Prince or People, . . . lying, and being all along the Sea Coasts, between four and thirty Degrees of *Northerly* Latitude . . . and five and forty Degrees of the same Latitude . . . ;

And to that End, and for the more speedy Accomplishment of their said intended Plantation and Habitation there, are desirous to divide themselves into two several Colonies and Companies; the one consisting of certain . . . Adventurers, of our City of *London* . . . , which do desire to begin their Plantation and Habitation in some fit and convenient Place, between four and thirty and one and forty Degrees of the said Latitude, alongst the Coasts of *Virginia,* and the Coasts of *America* aforesaid: And the other consisting of sundry . . . Adventurers, of our Cities of *Bristol* and *Exeter,* and of our Town of *Plimouth,* . . . which do desire to begin their Plantation and Habitation in some fit and convenient Place, between eight and thirty Degrees and five and forty Degrees of the said Latitude, all alongst the said Coasts of *Virginia* and *America,* as that coast lyeth:

We, greatly commending . . . their Desires for the Furtherance of so noble a Work, which may, by the Providence of Almighty God, hereafter tend to the Glory of his Divine Majesty, in propagating the *Christian* Religion to such People, as yet live in Darkness and miserable Ignorance of the true Knowledge and Worship of God, and may in time bring the Infidels and Savages, living in those parts, to human Civility, and to a settled and quiet Government: DO by these our Letters Patents, graciously accept of, and agree to, their humble and well-intended Desires;

And do therefore . . . GRANT and agree, that the said . . . Adventurers of and for our City of *London,* . . . shall be called the *first Colony;* And they shall and may begin their said first Plantation and Habitation, at any Place upon the said Coast of *Virginia* or *America,* . . . between the said four and thirty and one and forty Degrees of the said Latitude; And that they shall have all the Lands, Woods, Soil, Grounds, Havens, Ports, Rivers, Mines, Minerals, Marshes, Waters, Fishings, Commodities, and Hereditaments, whatsoever, from the said first Seat of their

---

*From *The Federal and State Constitutions , Colonial Charters, and Other Organic Laws of the State Territories, and Colonies Now or Heretofore Forming the United States of America,* ed. Francis N. Thorpe (Washington, D.C.: U.S. Government Printing Office, 1909) VII: 3783–3789.

Harcourt Brace & Company

Plantation and Habitation for the space of fifty like *English* miles, all along the said Coasts of *Virginia* and *America*, towards the *West* and *Southwest*, as the Coast lyeth, with all the Islands within one hundred Miles over and against the Sea Coast; And also . . . from the said Place of their first Plantation and Habitation for the space of fifty like *English* Miles, all alongst the said Coasts of *Virginia* and *America*, towards the *East* and *Northeast*, or towards the *North*, as the Coast lyeth, together with all the Islands within one hundred Miles, directly over against the said Sea Coast; And also . . . from the same fifty Miles every way on the Sea Coast, directly into the main Land, by the Space of one hundred like *English* Miles; And shall and may inhabit and remain there; and shall and may also build and fortify within any the same, for their better Safeguard and defence. . . .

And we do likewise . . . GRANT and agree, that the said [associates] of the Town of *Plimouth*, . . . shall be called the *second Colony*; And that they shall and may begin their said Plantation . . . at any Place upon the said Coast of *Virginia* and *America*, . . . between eight and thirty Degrees of the said Latitude, and five and forty Degrees of the same Latitude; And that they shall have all Lands, Soils, Grounds, Havens, Ports, Rivers, Mines, Minerals, Woods, Marshes, Waters, Fishings, Commodities, and Hereditaments, whatsoever, from the first Seat of their Plantation and Habitation by the Space of fifty like *English* Miles, as is aforesaid, all alongst the said Coasts of *Virginia* and *America*, towards the *West* and *Southwest*, or towards the *South*, as the Coast lyeth, and all the Islands within one hundred Miles, directly over against the said Sea Coast; And also . . . from the said Place of their first Plantation and Habitation for the Space of fifty like Miles, all alongst the said Coasts of *Virginia* and *America*, towards the *East* and *Northeast*, or towards the *North*, as the Coast lyeth, and all the Islands also within one hundred Miles, directly over against the same said Sea Coast; And also . . . from the same fifty Miles every way on the Sea Coast, directly into the main Land, by the Space of one hundred like *English* Miles; And shall and may inhabit and remain there; and shall and may also build and fortify within any the same for their better Safeguard. . . .

Provided always, . . . that the Plantation and Habitation of such of the said Colonies, as shall last plant themselves, as aforesaid, shall not be made within one hundred like *English* miles of the other of them, that first began to make their Plantation. . . .

And we do also ordain . . . that each of the said Colonies shall have a Council, which shall govern and order all Matters and Causes, which shall arise, grow, or happen, to or within the several Colonies, according to such Laws, Ordinances, and Instructions, as shall be, in that behalf, given and signed with Our Hand. . . .

And that also there shall be a Council, established here in *England*, which shall, in like manner, consist of thirteen Persons, to be, for that Purpose, appointed by Us, . . . which shall be called our *Council of Virginia*; And shall . . . have the superior Managing and Direction, only of and for all Matters that shall or may concern the Government . . . of the said several Colonies. . . .

And moreover, we do GRANT and agree . . . that the said several Councils . . . lawfully may . . . give and take Order, to dig, mine, and search for all manner of Mines of Gold, Silver, and Copper . . . within any Part of their said several Colonies . . . ; And to Have and enjoy the Gold, Silver, and Copper . . . to the Use and Behoof of the same Colonies . . . ; Yielding therefore to Us . . . the fifth Part only of all the same Gold and Silver, and the fifteenth Part of all the same Copper. . . .

And that they shall, or lawfully may, establish and cause to be made a Coin, to pass current there between the people of those several Colonies, for the more Ease of Traffick and Bargaining between and amongst them and the Natives there. . . .

And we do likewise . . . give full Power and Authority . . . to the said several Companies . . . that they . . . may . . . travel thitherward, and to abide and inhabit there . . . such and so many

Harcourt Brace & Company

of our Subjects, as shall willingly accompany them . . . ; With sufficient Shipping, and . . . Armour, Weapons, Ordinance, Powder, Victual, and all other things, necessary for the said Plantations, and for their Use and Defence there. . . .

Moreover, we do . . . GIVE AND GRANT Licence unto the said [associates] . . . of the said Colonies, that they . . . may, . . . for their several Defences, encounter, expulse, repel, and resist, as well by Sea as by Land, by all Ways and Means whatsoever, all . . . Persons, as without special Licence of the said several Colonies and Plantations, shall attempt to inhabit within the said several Precincts and Limits of the said several Colonies and Plantations, . . . or that shall enterprise or attempt . . . the Hurt, Detriment, or Annoyance, of the said several Colonies or Plantations:

Giving and granting, by these Presents, unto the . . . Associates of the said [colonies] . . . Power and Authority to take and surprise, by all Ways and Means whatsoever, all and every Person or Persons, with their Ships, Vessels, Goods, and other Furniture, which shall be found trafficking, into any Harbour or Harbours, Creek or Creeks, or Place, within the limits or Precincts of the said several Colonies and Plantations, not being of the same Colony, until such time, as they, being of any Realms, or Dominions under our Obedience, shall pay, or agree to pay, to the . . . Treasurer of that Colony . . . two and a half upon every Hundred, of anything so by them trafficked, bought, or sold; And being Strangers, and not Subjects under our Obeysance, until they shall pay five upon every Hundred, of such Wares and Merchandises, as they shall traffick, buy or sell, as aforesaid; WHICH Sums of Money, or Benefit, as aforesaid, for and during the Space of one and twenty Years . . . shall wholly be emploied to the Use, Benefit, and Behoof of the said several Plantations where such Traffick shall be made; And after the said one and twenty Years ended, the same shall be taken to the use of Us, our Heirs, and Successors. . . .

And we do further . . . GIVE AND GRANT unto the . . . Associates of the said first Colony and Plantation, and to the . . . Associates of the said second Colony and Plantation, that they . . . may transport the Goods, Chattels, Armour, Munition, and Furniture, needful to be used by them, for their said Apparel, Food, Defence, or otherwise in Respect of the said Plantations . . . during the Time of seven Years, . . . for the better Relief of the said several Colonies and Plantations, without any Customs, Subsidy, or other Duty. . . .

Also we do . . . DECLARE . . . that all and every the Persons being our Subjects, which shall dwell and inhabit within every or any of the said Colonies and Plantations, and every of their children, which shall happen to be born within any of the Limits and Precincts of the said several Colonies and Plantations, shall HAVE and enjoy all Liberties, Franchises, and Immunities . . . as if they had been abiding and born, within this our Realm of *England*. . . .

Moreover, . . . we . . . declare and set forth, that if any Person or Persons . . . shall, at any time or times hereafter, transport any wares Merchandises, or Commodities, out of any of our Dominions, with a Pretence to land, sell, or otherwise dispose of them, within . . . of the said Colonies and Plantations, and yet nevertheless, being at Sea, or after he hath landed . . . , shall carry the same into any other Foreign Country, with a Purpose there to sell or dispose of the same, without the Licence of Us . . . ; That then, all the Goods and Chattels of such Person or Persons, . . . together with the said Ship or Vessel, wherein such Transportation was made, shall be forfeited to Us. . . .

And finally, we . . . GRANT and agree to and with the said [associates of both colonies], that We, . . . upon Petition in that Behalf to be made, shall . . . GIVE and GRANT, unto such Persons, their Heirs, and Assigns, as the Council of that Colony . . . shall for that Purpose, nominate and assign all lands, Tenements, and Hereditaments, which shall be within the Precincts limited for that Colony. . . .

The Laws of Virginia, 1619*

The following code constitutes the first statutes enacted by a general assembly in North America; they therefore mark an important step in the evolution of popular government. Like all laws, they mirror the society that created them, and they help the modern reader gain some understanding of life in early Virginia. At the same time, by disclosing what authorities considered to be criminal activities, the statutes shed light on perceptions of power and liberty at the beginning of English settlement in the New World.

By this present General Assembly be it enacted that no injury or oppression be wrought by the *English* against the Indians whereby the present peace might be disturbed, & ancient quarrels might be revived. . . .

Against Idleness, gaming, drunkenness, & excess in apparel, the Assembly hath enacted as followeth: . . .

Be it enacted, that if any man be found, to live as an Idler or renegade though a freed man, it shall be lawful for that Incorporation or Plantation to which he belongeth to appoint him a master to serve for wages till he show apparent signs of amendment.

Against gaming at Dice & Cards be it ordained . . . that the winner or winners shall lose all his or their winnings & both winners and losers shall forfeit ten shillings a man, one ten shillings whereof to go to the discoverer, & the rest to charitable & pious uses in the Incorporation where the faults are committed.

Against drunkenness be it also decreed, that if any private person be found culpable thereof, for the first time he is to be reproved privately by the Minister, the second time, publicly, the Third time to lie in bolts 12 hours in the House of the Provost Marshall & to pay his fees, and if he still continue in that vice, to undergo such severe punishment as the Governor & Council of Estate shall think fit to be inflicted upon him. But if any Officer offend in this crime, the first time he shall receive a reproof from the Governor, the second time he shall openly be reproved in the Church by the minister, & the third time he shall first be committed & then degraded. . . .

Against excess of apparel, that every man be assessed in the Church for all the public contributions, if he be unmarried according to his own apparel, if he be married, according to his own & his wife's, or either by their apparel.

As touching the Instruction of drawing some of the better disposed of the Indians to converse with our people & to live & labor among them, the Assembly . . . think it fit to enjoin . . . those of the Colony neither utterly to reject them, nor yet to draw them to come in. But in case they will of themselves come voluntarily . . . to do service, in killing of Deer, Fishing, beating Corn, & other works that then five or six may be admitted to every such place, and no more, & that with the consent of the Governor, provided that good guard in the night be kept upon them, for generally . . . they are a most treacherous people, & quickly gone when they have done a villainy. . . .

Be it enacted . . . that for . . . the conversion of the Indians to Christian Religion, each town, city, Borough, & particular plantation do obtain unto themselves by just means a certain number of the natives' children to be educated by them in the true Religion & civic course of life, of which children the most towardly boys . . . to be brought up by them . . . so as to be fitted for the College intended for them, that from thence they may be sent to that of conversion.

---

*From *Journals of the House of Burgesses of Virginia, 1619–1658/59,* ed. H. R. McIlwaine (Richmond: Virginia State Library, 1915), 9–11, 13–14.

Harcourt Brace & Company

As touching the business of planting corn, the present Assembly doth ordain, that year by year, all & every householder and householders, have in store for every servant he or they shall keep, & also for his or their own persons, . . . one spare barrel of corn to be delivered out yearly either upon sale or exchange, as need shall require. . . .

About the Plantation of Mulberry trees be it enacted that every man . . . do for seven years together every year plant and maintain in growth six Mulberry trees at the least. . . .

Be it farther enacted, as concerning silk flax that those men that are . . . settled . . . do this next year plant & Dress 100 plants. . . .

For hemp also both *English* & Indian, & for *English* Flax and Anise seeds, we do require . . . all householders of this Colony, that have any those seeds, to make trial thereof the next season.

Moreover be it enacted . . . that every householder do yearly plant & maintain ten vines, until they have attained to the art & experience of dressing a vineyard, either by their own industry, or by the instructions of some [other person]. . . .

Be it further ordained . . . that all contracts made in *England* between the owners of land & their Tenants and the servants which they shall sent hither, may be caused to be duly performed. . . .

Be it established also . . . that no crafty or advantageous means . . . put in practice for the enticing away the Tenants & Servants of any particular plantation from the place where they are Seated. . . .

That no man do sell or give any Indians any piece, shot, or powder, or any other arms offensive or defensive, upon pain of being held a Traitor to the Colony, & of being hanged, as soon as the fact is proved, without all redemption.

That no man do sell or give any of the greater hounds to the Indians, or any *English* dog of quality, as a Mastiff, Greyhound, Blood hound, land or water Spaniel, or any other dog or bitches whatever, of the *English* race, upon pain of forfeiting 5 pounds *sterling* to the public uses of the Incorporation where he dwelleth.

That no man may go above twenty miles from his dwelling place, nor upon any voyage whatsoever shall be absent from thence for the space of seven days together, without first having made the Governor, or commander of the same place acquainted therewith. . . .

That no man shall purposely go to any Indian towns, habitations or places of resort, without leave from the Governor or commander of that place where he liveth upon pain of paying 40 shillings to public uses. . . .

That no man living in this Colony, but shall between this and the first of *January* next ensuing come or send to the Secretary of State, to enter . . . all his servants' names, & for what term, or upon what conditions they are to serve. . . . Also whatsoever, Masters or people do come over to this plantation, that within one month of their arrival . . . , they shall likewise resort to the Secretary of State & shall Certify him upon what terms or conditions they be come hither. . . .

All Ministers in this Colony shall once a year . . . bring to the Secretary of Estate a true account of all Christenings, burials, & marriages. . . . Likewise where there be no ministers, that the commanders of the place do supply the same duty.

No man without leave from the Governor shall kill any Neat cattle whatsoever, young or old, especially kine, Heifers, or Cowcalves, & shall be careful to preserve their Steers & Oxen, & to bring them to the plow & such profitable uses, & without having obtained leave as aforesaid shall not kill them upon penalty of forfeiting the value of the Beast so killed.

Whosoever shall take any of his neighbors' boats, oars, or canoes without leave from the owner shall be held and esteemed as a felon and so proceeded against; also he that shall take away by violence or stealth any canoes or other things from the Indians shall make valuable restitution to the said Indians, and shall forfeit, if he be freeholder, five pounds; if a servant 40 shillings, or endure a whipping. . . .

All ministers shall duly read divine service, and exercise their ministerial function according to the Ecclesiastical Laws and orders of the church of *England,* and every *Sunday* in the afternoon shall Catechize such as are not yet ripe to come to the Communion. . . .

The Ministers and Churchwardens shall seek to prevent all ungodly disorders; the committers whereof if, upon good admonitions and mild reproof they will not forbear the said scandalous offenses, as suspicions of whoredom, dishonest company keeping with women and such like, they are to be presented and punished accordingly.

If any person after two warnings, do not amend his or her life in point of evident suspicion of Incontinency or of the commission of any other enormous sins, that then he or she be presented by the Churchwardens and suspended for a time from the church by the minister. In which Interim if the same person do not amend and humbly submit him or herself to the church, he is then fully to be excommunicate and soon after a writ or warrant to be sent from the Governor for the apprehending of his person & seizing all his goods. . . .

For reformation of swearing, every freeman and Master of a family after thrice admonition shall give 5 shillings or the value upon present demands, to the use of the church where he dwelleth; and every servant after the like admonition, except his Master discharge the fine, shall be subject to whipping. Provided, that . . . the said servant shall acknowledge his fault publicly in the Church. . . .

No man shall trade into the Bay either in Shallop, pinnace, or ship without the Governor's License, and without putting in security, that neither himself, nor his Company shall force or wrong the Indians. . . .

All persons whatsoever upon Sabbath days shall frequent divine service & sermons both forenoon and afternoon; & all such as bear arms, shall bring their pieces, Swords, powder, & shot. And Every one that shall transgress this Law, shall forfeit three shillings a time to the use of the Church. . . .

No maid or woman servant . . . shall contract herself in marriage without either the consent of her parents or her Master or Mistress, or of the magistrate & Minister of the place both together. . . .

Be it enacted by the present assembly, that whatsoever servant hath heretofore, or shall hereafter contract himself in *England* . . . to serve any Master here in *Virginia,* and shall afterward, against his said former contract, depart from his Master without leave, or being once embarked, shall abandon the ship he is appointed to come in, & so being left behind, shall put himself into the service of any other man that will bring him hither; that then at the same servant's arrival here, he shall first serve out his time, with that Master that brought him hither and afterward also shall serve out his time with his former Master according to his covenant.

The Mayflower Compact, 1620*

Unsure of the legal authority for their colony, and concerned by the number of "strangers" in their midst, Pilgrim immigrants from the Netherlands and England promulgated this agreement before establishing their settlement at Plymouth, Massachusetts. Although the document is remarkably brief, the ideas expressed in the compact have exerted tremendous influence on the American people. By creating a "body politick," the emigrants put into place government by the

---

*From William Bradford, *Bradford's History of Plymouth Plantation, 1606–1646,* ed. William T. Davis (New York: Charles Scribner's Sons, 1908), 107.

majority with the consent of the minority. The Mayflower Compact, therefore, stands as an early American effort to provide some balance between the power of government and the liberties of individuals.

> In the name of God, Amen. We whose names are under-written, the loyal subjects of our dread sovereign Lord, King James, by the grace of God, of Great Britain, France, and Ireland King, defender of the faith, etc., having undertaken, for the glory of God, and advancement of the Christian faith, and honor of our king and country, a voyage to plant the first colony in the Northern parts of Virginia, do by these presents solemnly and mutually in the presence of God, and of one another, covenant and combine ourselves together into a civil body politick, for our bettering ordering and preservation and furtherance of the ends aforesaid; and by virtue hereof to enact, constitute, and frame such just and equal laws, ordinances, acts, constitutions, and offices, from time to time, as shall be thought most meet and convenient for the general good of the Colony, unto which we promise all due submission and obedience. In witness whereof we have hereunder subscribed our names at Cape Cod the 11th of November, in the year of the reign of our sovereign lord, King James, of England, France, and Ireland, the eighteenth, and of Scotland the fifty-fourth. Anno Domino 1620.

A Model of Christian Charity, 1630*

This sermon, famous because of John Winthrop's plea that the Puritans establish a model community in New England, also shows the importance of the covenant in Calvinist thinking. The ideal of the covenant helped to shape the development of constitutional republicanism in the United States by insisting that those in power recognize the liberties of the people over whom they govern. In addition, the conviction that the Puritans were chosen by God for a unique destiny later manifested itself in the growth of a powerful United States that conquered much of North America before assuming a role as a leading international power.

> Thus stands the case between God and us. We are entered into a Covenant with Him for this work. We have taken out a commission. The Lord hath given us leave to draw our own articles. We have professed to enterprise these and those ends, upon these and those accounts. We have hereupon besought of Him favor and blessing. Now if the Lord shall please to hear us, and bring us in peace to the place we desire, then hath he ratified this Covenant and sealed our Commission, and will expect a strict performance of the articles contained in it; but if we shall neglect the observation of these articles which are the ends we have propounded, and, dissembling with our God, shall fall to embrace this present world and prosecute our carnal intentions, seeking great things for ourselves and our posterity, the Lord will surely break out in wrath against us; be revenged of such a (sinful) people, and make us know the price of the breach of such a Covenant.
>
> Now the only way to avoid this shipwreck, and to provide for our posterity, is to follow the council of Micah, *to do justly, to love mercy, to walk humbly with our God*. For this end, we must be knit together, in this work, as one man. We must entertain each other in brotherly affection. We must be willing to abridge ourselves of our superfluities, for the supply of other's necessities. We must uphold a familiar commerce together in all meekness, gentleness, patience, and liberality. We must delight in each other; make other's condition our own; rejoice together, mourn

---

*From Robert C. Winthrop, *Life and Letters of John Winthrop, Governor of the Massachusetts-Bay Company at the Time of Their Emigration to New England*, 2d ed. (Boston: Little, Brown, and Company, 1869), II:18–20.

together, labor and suffer together, always having before our eyes our commission and community in the work, as members of the same body. So shall we *keep the unity of the spirit in the bond of peace.* The Lord will be our God, and delight to dwell among us, as his own people, and will command a blessing upon us in all our ways. So that we shall see much more of his wisdom, power, goodness, and truth, than formerly we have been acquainted with. We shall find that the God of Israel is among us, when ten of us shall be able to resist a thousand of our enemies; when he shall make us a praise and a glory, that men shall say of succeeding plantations, "The Lord make it like that of *New England.*" For we must consider that we shall be as a City upon a hill. The eyes of all people are upon us. Soe that if we shall deal falsely with our God in this work we have undertaken, and so cause him to withdraw his present help from us, we shall be made a story and a by-word throughout the world. We shall open the mouths of enemies to speak evil of the ways of God, and all professors for God's sake. We shall shame the faces of many of God's worthy servants, and cause their prayers to be turned into curses upon us till we be consumed out of the good land whither we are a-going. . . .

Therefore let us choose life that we, and our seed may live, by obeying His voice and cleaving to Him, for He is our life and our prosperity.

Discussion

1. Based on the documents, what expressions of egalitarianism existed at the time that large-scale emigration of Europeans and Africans to the Americas began? What examples of inequality do the documents reveal?

2. Several of the selections show that efforts to capitalize on the wealth of the western hemisphere played a key role in the development of the Americas. What assertions of power and expressions of liberty exist in those documents? What does that suggest about concepts of power and liberty in early colonial America?

3. How do the documents hint that future power struggles will ensue in the Americas?

4. The Virginia Charter claims the "liberties of Englishmen" for its settlers. Based on the various English documents, what might those liberties have been?

5. What do the documents suggest about different understandings of power and liberty that might have existed between the people who settled Virginia and the colonists who landed in Massachusetts?

Harcourt Brace & Company

Chapter 3
England Discovers Its Colonies:
Upheaval, War, Trade, and Empire

Public notices of slave auctions were common by the eighteenth century. Like advertisements today, they focused on what buyers of the day wanted to know: that the slaves are healthy and thus a good investment and that they orginated on the "Rice Coast" of Africa and are knowledgeable in growing rice.

*B*y the middle of the seventenenth century, England had established a firm hold on much of the Atlantic seaboard, and the American colonies became an integral part of an increasingly powerful English state. Colonial policies, therefore, became much more sophisticated during the seventeenth century as royal authorities sought to protect imperial interests by establishing a mercantilistic economy, by creating new colonies, and by organizing the Dominion of New England. Colonial Americans throughout the period continued to claim their rights as Englishmen, and England enjoyed great success in strengthening the empire while recognizing the liberties of its subjects. Nevertheless, turmoil characterized the era, particularly the disputes between Parliament and the king that led to the Civil War and to the Glorious Revolution. Intense conflicts also occurred in the colonies, generally between settlers and royal governors. Consequently, some Americans expressed concern that assertions of English power, if unchecked, might ultimately threaten liberty.

The Navigation Act of 1651*

International rivalries led England to place a growing emphasis on mercantilistic commercial policies beginning in the 1650s. The following document, designed to eliminate the competition that Dutch merchants presented, was the first in a series of Navigation Acts regulating trade in the English empire. Although mercantilism often proved advantageous to Americans, many of the colonials at first feared the Navigation Acts as dangerous expressions of royal power. Restricting trade, they believed, limited their ability to gain property, which posed a dire threat to the most fundamental of their liberties. Moreover, the mercantilistic assumption that colonies existed to benefit the mother country implied that the English viewed colonists as inferiors, not as equals.

> For the Increase of the Shipping and the Encouragement of the Navigation of this Nation, which under the good Providence and Protection of God, is so great a means of the Welfare and Safety of this Commonwealth; be it Enacted by this present Parliament and the Authority thereof, That from [December 1] . . . forwards, no Goods or Commodities whatsoever of the Growth, Production, or Manufacture of Asia, Africa or America; or of any part thereof; or of any Islands belonging to them . . . shall be Imported or brought into this Commonwealth of England, or into Ireland, or any other lands, . . . in any other Ship or Ships, Vessel or Vessels whatsoever, but onely in such as do truly and without fraud belong onely to the People of this Commonwealth, or the Plantations thereof, as the Proprietors or right Owners thereof; and whereof the Master and Mariners are also for the most part of them of the People of this Commonwealth, under the penalty of the forfeiture and loss of all those Goods that shall be imported contrary to this Act. . . .
>
> And it is further Enacted by the Authority aforesaid, that no Goods or Commodities of the Growth, Production, or Manufactures of Europe, or of any part thereof, shall . . . be imported or brought into this Commonwealth of England, or into Ireland, or any other Lands, . . . to this Commonwealth belonging, or in their possession, in any Ship or Ships, Vessel or Vessels

---

*From C. H. Firth and R. S. Rait, *Acts and Ordinances of the Interregnum: 1642–1660,* 3 vols. (London: Wyman and Sons, 1911), II:559–61.

whatsoever, but in such as do truly and without fraud belong onely to the people of this Commonwealth, as the True Owners and Proprietors thereof, and in no other, except onely such Forin Ships and Vessels as do truly and properly belong to the people of that countrey or Place, of which the said Goods are the Growth, Production, or Manufacture; or to such Ports where the said Goods can onely be, or most usually are first shipped for Transportation; And that under the same penalty of forfeiture and loss expressed in the former branch of this act. . . .

And it is further Enacted . . . , That no sort of Cod-fish, Ling, Herring, Pilchard, or any other kinde of salted Fish, usually fished for and caught by the people of this Nation; nor any Oyl made, or that shall be made of any kinde of Fish whatsoever; nor any Whale-fins, or Whale-bones, shall from henceforth be Imported . . . but onely such as shall be caught in Vessels that do or shall truly and properly belong to the people of this Nation. . . : And the said Fish to be cured and the Oyl aforesaid made by the people of this Commonwealth. . . .

And it is further Enacted . . . That no sort of . . . salted Fish whatsoever, which shall be caught and cured for the people of this Commonwealth, shall be . . . exported from any place or places belonging to this Commonwealth, in any other Ship or Ships, Vessel or Vessels save onely in such as do truly and properly appertain to the people of this Commonwealth, as Right Owners. . . .

Religious Toleration in Carolina, 1696*

The Fundamental Constitutions of Carolina established a detailed, often impractical, political system for the new colony. At the same time, the constitution guaranteed a degree of religious tolerance by moving away from many of the more doctrinaire attitudes that earlier settlers had held. The following selection suggests the complexity of the overall document. The passage also provides a broad definition of faith that ensured a liberty of conscience, which served as an important precedent in the creation of religious freedom in the United States.

[Article] Ninety-five. No man shall be permitted to be a freeman of Carolina, or to have any estate or habitation within it, that doth not acknowledge a God; and that God is to be publickly and solemnly worshipped. . . .

Ninety-seven. But since the natives of that place, who will be concerned in our plantation, are utterly strangers to Christianity, whose idolatry, ignorance, or mistake gives us no right to expel or use them ill; and those who remove from other parts to plant there will unavoidably be of different opinions concerning matters of religion, the liberty thereof they will expect to have allowed them, and it will not be reasonable for us, on this account, to keep them out, that civil peace may be maintained amidst diversity of opinions, and our agreement and compact with all men may be duly and faithfully observed; the violation whereof, upon what pretence soever, cannot be without great offence to Almighty God, and great scandal to the true religion which we profess; and also that Jews, heathens, and other dissenters from the purity of Christian religion may not be scared and kept at a distance from it, but, by having an opportunity of acquainting themselves with the truth and reasonableness of its doctrines, and the peaceableness and inoffensiveness of its professors, and, by good usage and persuasion, and all those convincing methods of gentleness and meekness, suitable to the rules and designs of the gospel, be won over to embrace and unfeignedly receive the truth; therefore, any seven or more persons agree-

*From *The Federal and State Constitutions, Colonial Charters, and Other Organic Laws of the States, Territories, and Colonies Now or Heretofore Forming the United States of America,* 7 vols., ed. Francis N. Thorpe (Washington, D.C.: U.S. Government Printing Office, 1909), V:2783–2785.

ing in any religion, shall constitute a church or profession, to which they shall give some name, to distinguish it from others.

Ninety-eight. The terms of admittance and communion with any church or profession shall be written in a book, and therein may be subscribed by all members of the said church or profession; which book shall be kept by the public register of the precinct wherein they reside.

Ninety-nine. The time of every one's subscription and admittance shall be dated in the said book or religious record.

One hundred. In the terms of communion of every church or profession, these following shall be three; without which no agreement or assembly of men, upon pretence of religion, shall be accounted a church or profession within these rules:

1st. "That there is a God."

II. "That God is publickly to be worshipped."

III. "That it is lawful and the duty of every man, being thereunto called by those that govern, to bear witness to truth; and that every church or profession shall, in their terms of communion, set down the external way whereby they witness a truth as in the presence of God, whether it be by laying hands on or kissing the bible, as in the Church of England, or by holding up the hand, or by any other sensible way."

One hundred and one. No person above seventeen years of age shall have any benefit or protection of the law, or be capable of any place of profit or honor, who is not a member of some church or profession, having his name recorded in some one, and but one religious record at once.

One hundred and two. No person of any other church or profession shall disturb or molest any religious assembly.

One hundred and three. No person whatsoever shall speak anything in their religious assembly irreverently or seditiously of the government or governors, or of state matters.

One hundred and four. Any person subscribing the terms of communion, in the record of the said church or profession, before the precinct register, and any five members of the said church or profession, shall be thereby made a member of the said church or profession.

One hundred and five. Any person striking out his own name out of any religious record, or his name being struck out by any officer thereunto authorized by each church or profession respectively, shall cease to be a member of that church or profession.

One hundred and six. No man shall use any reproachful, reviling, or abusive language against any religion of any church or profession; that being the certain way of disturbing the peace, and of hindering the conversion of any to the true faith, by engaging them in quarrels and animosities, to the hatred of the professors of that profession which otherwise they might be brought to assent to.

One hundred and seven. Since charity obliges us to wish well to the souls of all men, and religion ought to alter nothing in any man's civil estate or right, it shall be lawful for slaves, as well as others, to enter themselves, and be of what church or profession any of them shall think best, and therefore, be as fully members as any freeman. But yet no slave shall hereby be exempted from that civil dominion his master hath over him, but be in all things in the same state and condition as he was in before.

One hundred and eight. Assemblies, on what pretence soever of religion, not observing and performing the above said rules, shall not be esteemed as churches, but unlawful meetings, and be punished as other riots.

One hundred and nine. No person whatever shall disturb, molest, or persecute another for his speculative opinions in religion, or his way of religion.

Harcourt Brace & Company

Bacon's Rebellion, 1676*

One of the most dramatic events in seventeenth-century America occurred with Bacon's Rebellion. This violent upheaval reflected many of the power struggles that characterized the colonies—pitting easterner against westerner, established elite against the disadvantaged, English authority against local interests. In the end, the reaction to the insurrection helped strengthen royal control over Virginia. Perhaps not coincidentally, a century later Virginians would play critical roles in another rebellion, one that ended the king's power in America. The following account of Bacon's Rebellion was written by Robert Beverley several years after the event, but he had a first-hand interest in the affair since his father had helped Governor Sir William Berkeley quell the insurrection.

This Addition of Mischief to Minds already full of Discontent, made People ready to vent all their Resentment against the poor *Indians*. There was nothing to be got by Tobacco; neither could they turn any other Manufacture to Advantage; so that most of the poorer Sort were willing to quit their unprofitable Employments, and go Voluntiers against the *Indians*.

At first they flock'd together tumultuously, running in Troops from one Plantation to another without a Head; till at last the seditious Humour of Colonel *Nath. Bacon*, led him to be of the Party. This *Gentlemen* had been brought up at one of the Inns of Court in *England,* and had a moderate Fortune. He was young, bold, active, of an inviting Aspect, and powerful Elocution. In a Word, he was every way qualified to head a giddy and unthinking Multitude. Before he had been Three Years in the Country, he was, for his extraordinary Qualifications, made one of the Council, and in great Honour and Esteem among the people. For this Reason he no sooner gave Countenance to this riotous Mob, but they all presently fix'd their Eyes upon him for their General, and accordingly made their Addresses to him. As soon as he found this, he harangued them publickly. He aggravated the *Indian* Mischiefs, complaining, that they were occasion'd for want of a due Regulation of their Trade. He recounted particularly the other Grievances and Pressures they lay under; and pretended, that he accepted of their Command with no other Intention, but to do them and the Country Service, in which he was willing to encounter the greatest Difficulties and Dangers. He farther assured them, he would never lay down his Arms, till he had revenged their Sufferings upon the *Indians*, and redress'd all their other Grievances.

By these Insinuations, he wrought his Men into so perfectly a Unanimity, that they were once and all at his Devotion. He took care to exasperate them to the utmost, by representing all their Misfortunes. After he had begun to muster them, he dispatch'd a Messenger to the Governour, by whom he aggravated the Mischief done by the *Indians*, and desired a Commission of General to go out against them. This Gentleman was in so great Esteem at that Time with the Council, that the Governour did not think fit to give him a flat Refusal: But sent him Word, he would consult the Council, and return him a further Answer.

In the mean time, *Bacon* was expeditious in his Preparations, and having all Things in Readiness, began his March, depending on the Authority the People had given him. He would not lose so much Time, as to stay for his Commission; but dispatched several Messengers to the Governour to hasten it. On the other Hand, the Governour, instead of a Commission, sent positive Orders to him to disperse his Men, and come down in Person to him, upon Pain of being declared a Rebel.

This unexpected Order, was a great Surprize to *Bacon*, and not a little Trouble to his Men. However, he was resolved to prosecute his first Intentions, depending upon his Strength, and Interest with the People. Nevertheless, he intended to wait upon the Governour, but not alto-

---

*From Robert Beverley, *The History and Present State of Virginia* (London: R. Parker, 1705), Book I, 69–77.

gether defenceless. Pursuant to this Resolution, he took about Forty of his Men down with him in a Sloop to *James-Town*, where the Governour was with his Council.

Matters did not succeed there to Mr. *Bacon's* Satisfaction; wherefore he express'd himself a little too freely. For which being suspended from the Council, he went away again in a Huff with his Sloop and Followers. The Governour fill'd a Long-Boat with Men, and pursued the Sloop so close, that Colonel *Bacon* removed into his Boat to make more Haste. But the Governour had sent up by Land to the Ships at *Sandy-Point*, where he was stopp'd, and sent down again. Upon his Return he was kindly received by the Governour, who, knowing he had gone a Step beyond his Instructions in having suspended him, was glad to admit him again of the Council; after which he hoped all Things might be pacified.

Notwithstanding this, Col. *Bacon* still insisted upon a Commission to be General of the Voluntiers, and to go out against the *Indians;* from which the Governour endeavour'd to disswade him, but to no Purpose, because he had some secret Project in View. He had the Luck to be countenanced in his Importunities, by the News of fresh Murder and Robberies committed by the *Indians.* However, not being able to accomplish his Ends by fair Means, he stole privately out of Town; and having put himself at the Head of Six Hundred Voluntiers, marched directly to *James-Town*, where the Assembly was then sitting. He presented himself before the Assembly, and drew up his men in Battalia before the House wherein they sat. He urged to them his Preparations; and alleged, that if the Commission had not been delay'd so long, the War against the *Indians* might have been finish'd.

The Governour resented this insolent Usage worst of all, and now obstinately refused to grant him any thing, offering his naked Breast against the presented Arms of his Followers. But the Assembly, fearing the fatal Consequence of provoking a discontented Multitude ready arm'd, who had the Governour, Council and Assembly entirely in their Power, address'd the Governour to grant *Bacon* his Request. They prepar'd themselves the Commission, constituting him General of the Forces of *Virginia*, and brought it to the Governour to be signed.

With much Reluctancy his Excellency sign'd it, and thereby put the Power of War and Peace into *Bacon's* Hands. Upon this he march'd away immediately, having gain'd his End, which was in effect a Power to secure a Monopoly of the Indian Trade to himself and his Friends.

As soon as General *Bacon* had march'd to such a convenient Distance from *James-Town*, that the Assembly thought they might deliberate with Safety, the Governour, by their Advice, issued a Proclamation of Rebellion against him, commanding his Followers to surrender him, and forthwith disperse themselves. Not contented with this, he likewise gave Orders at the same time, for raising the Militia of the Country against him.

The People being much exasperated, and General *Bacon* by his Address and Eloquence having gain'd an absolute Dominion over their Hearts, they unanimously resolved, that not a Hair of his Head shou'd fall to the Ground, much less that they shou'd surrender him as a Rebel. Therefore, they kept to their Arms, and instead of proceeding against the Indians, they march'd back to *James-Town*; directing their Fury against such of their Friends and Country-men, as should dare to oppose them.

The Governour seeing this, fled over the Bay to *Accomack*, whither he hoped the Infection of *Bacon's* Conspiracy had not reach'd. But there, instead of People's receiving him with open Arms, in Remembrance of the former Services he had done them; they began to make Terms with him for Redress of their Grievances, and for the Ease and Liberty of Trade. Thus Sir *William*, who had been almost the Idol of the People, was, by reason of the loyal Part he acted, abandon'd by all; except some few, who went over to him from the Western Shore in Sloops and Boats. So that it was some time before he could make head against *Bacon*: But he left him to range through the Country at Discretion.

Harcourt Brace & Company

General *Bacon* at first held a Convention of such of the Chief Gentlemen of the Country, as would come to him, especially of those about *Middle-Plantation,* who were near at Hand. At this Convention they made a Declaration to justifie his unlawful Proceedings; and obliged People to take an Oath of Obedience to him as their General. Then, by their Advice, on Pretence of the Governour's Abdication, he call'd an Assembly, by Writs sign'd by himself, and Four others of the Council. . . .

By this Time the Governour had got together a small Party to side with him. These he furnished with Sloops, Arms and Ammunition, in order to cross the Bay, and oppose the Malcontents. By this Means there happen'd some skirmishes, in which several were kill'd, and others taken Prisoners. Thus, they were going on by a Civil War to destroy one another, and lay waste their Infant Country; when it pleased God, after some Months confusion, to put an end to their Misfortunes, as well as to *Bacon's* Designs, by his natural Death.

He died at Dr. *Green's*, in *Gloucester* County: But where he was bury'd was never yet discover'd; tho' afterward there was great Enquiry made, with Design to expose his Bones to publick Infamy.

In the mean while, those Disorders occasion'd a general Neglect of Husbandry, and a great Destruction of the Stocks; so that People had a dreadful Prospect of Want and Famine. But the Malcontents being thus disunited by the Loss of their General, in whom they all confided, they began to squabble among themselves; and every Man's Business was how to make the best Terms he could for himself.

Lieutenant-General *Ingram* (whose true Name was *Johnson*) and Major-General *Walklate* surrender'd on Condition of Pardon for themselves and their Followers; tho' they were both forced to submit to an Incapacity of bearing Office in that Country for the future.

Peace being thus restored, Sir *William Berkeley* return'd to his former Seat of Government, and every Man to his several Habitation.

The Glorious Revolution in America, 1689*

In 1688, Parliament's fear of a Catholic dynasty under the House of Stuart led to the Glorious Revolution and the joint sovereignty of William and Mary. Americans took advantage of events in England to remove Edmond Andros, governor of the Dominion of New England. James II had established the Dominion to consolidate his power in the northern colonies, which many colonials viewed as a dangerous threat to their political rights and their personal liberty. Nathaniel Byfield, a New England merchant, sent an account of the overthrow of Governor Andros to friends in London in June 1689. In his letter, he included the declaration of grievances that had sparked the uprising.

. . . II. To get us within the reach of the Desolation [King James II] desired for us, it was no improper thing that we should first have our Charter vacated . . . before it was possible for us to appear at Westminster in the legal Defence of it; and without fair leave to answer for ourselves the Crimes falsly laid to our Charge, we were put under a President and a Council, without any liberty for an Assembly, which the other American plantations have. . . .

III. The Commission was as Illegal for the Form of it, as the Way of obtaining it was Malicious and Unreasonable; yet we made no Resistance thereunto as we could easily have done; but chose to give all mankind a Demonstration of our being a People sufficiently dutiful and loyal to our King: and . . . we took Pains to make our selves believe . . . That his Magesty's

---

* "Declaration of the Gentlemen, Merchants and Inhabitants of Boston, and the Country Adjacent," April 18, 1689, in *Narratives of the Insurrections, 1675–1690,* ed. Charles M. Andrews (New York: Charles Scribner's Sons, 1915), 175–82.

Desire was no other than the happy Encrease and Advance of these Provinces by their more immediate dependence on the Crown of England. And we were convinced of it by the Courses immediately taken to damp and spoyl our Trade; whereof Decayes and Complaints presently filled all the Country; while in the mean time neither the Honour nor the Treasury of the King was at all advanced by this new Model of our Affairs, but a considerable Charge added unto the Crown.

IV. In little more than a half a Year we saw this Commission superseded by another yet more absolute and Arbitrary, with which Sir Edmond Andross arrived as our Governour: who besides his Power, with the Advice and Consent of his Council, to make Laws and raise Taxes as he pleased, had also the Authority by himself to Muster and Imploy all Persons residing in the Territory as occasion shall serve; and to transfer such Forces to any English Plantation in America, as occasion shall require. And several Companies of Souldiers were now brought from Europe, to support what was to be imposed on us . . . .

V. The Government was no sooner in these hands, but Care was taken to load Preferments principally upon such Men as were Strangers to and Haters of the People. . . . But of all Oppressors we were chiefly squeez'd by a Crew of Abject Persons fetched from New York, to be the tools of the Adversary . . . ; by these were extraordinary and intollerable Fees extorted from every one upon all Occasions, without any Rules but those of their own Avarice and Beggary; . . . nor could a small Volume contain the other Illegalities done by these Horse-leeches in the two or three Years that they have been sucking us. . . .

VI. It was now plainly affirmed, both . . . in open Council [and] . . . in private Converse, that the People of New-England were all slaves, and the only difference between them and Slaves is their not being bought and sold; and it was a Maxim delivered in open Court unto us by one of the Council, that we must not think the Priviledges of English men would follow us to the End of the World: Accordingly we have been treated with multiplied Contradictions to Magna Carta, the Rights of which we laid claim unto. . . . Packt and pickt Juries have been very common things among us. . . . Without a Verdict, yea, without a Jury sometimes People have been fined most unrighteously; and some . . . have been kept in long and close Imprisonment without any the least Information appearing against them, or an Habeas Corpus allowed unto them. . . .

VII. . . . [T]here was one very comprehensive Abuse given to us; Multitudes of pious and sober Men . . . scrupled the Mode of Swearing on the Book, desiring that they might Swear with an uplifted hand, agreeable to the ancient Custom of the Colony; and though we think we can prove that the Common Law amongst us . . . not only indulges, but even commands and enjoins the Rite of lifting the Hand in Swearing; yet they that had this Doubt, were still put by from serving upon any Juries; and many of them were most unaccountably Fined and Imprisoned. . . .

Because these Things could not make us miserable fast enough, there was a notable Discovery made of we know not what flaw in all our Titles to our Lands; and tho, besides our purchase of them from the Natives, and besides our actual peaceable unquestioned possession of them for near threescores Years, and besides the promise of K. Charles II . . . , That no man here shall receive any Prejudice in his Free-hold or Estate, . . . Yet we were every day told, That no Man was owner of a Foot of Land in all the Colony. . . .

IX. All the Council were not ingaged in all these ill Actions, but those of them which were true Lovers of their Country were seldom admitted to, and seldomer consulted at the Debates which produced these unrightous Things: Care was taken to keep them under Disadvantage; and the Governour, with five or six more, did what they would. We bore all these, and many more such Things, without making any attempt for any relief; only Mr. [Increase] Mather, purely out of respect unto the Good of his Afflicted Country, undertook a Voyage unto England;

Harcourt Brace & Company

which when these Men suspected him to be preparing for, they used all manner of Craft and Rage, not only to interrupt his Voyage, but to ruin his Person too...

X. And yet that our Calamity might not be terminated here, we are again Briar'd in the Perplexities of another Indian War; how, or why, is a mystery too deep for us to unfold. And tho' 'tis judged that our Indian Enemies are not above 100 in Number, yet an Army of One thousand English hath been raised for the Conquering of them; which Army of our poor Friends and Brethren now under Popish Commanders (for in the Army as well as in the Council, the Papists are in Commission) has been under such a Conduct, ... and the whole War hath been so managed, that we cannot but suspect in it a Branch of the Plot to bring us low. ...

XI. We did nothing against these Proceedings, but only cry to our God. ... We have been quiet hitherto, and so still we should have been, had not the Great God at this time laid us under double engagement to do something for our Security. ... For first, we are informed that the rest of English America is alarmed with just and great Fears, that they may be attaqu'd by the French, who have lately (it is said) already treated many of the English with worse than Turkish Cruelties. ... Moreover, we have understood, (though the Governour has taken all imaginable care to keep us all ignorant thereof) that the Almighty God hath been pleased to prosper the noble Undertaking of the Prince of Orange, to preserve the three Kingdoms from the horrible brinks of Popery and Slavery, and to bring to a condign Punishment those worst of Men, by whom English liberties had been destroy'd. ...

XII. We do therefore seize upon the Persons of those few ill Men which have been (next to our Sins) the grand Authors of our Miseries; resolving to secure them, for what Justice, Orders from his Highness with the English parliament shall direct, lest, ere we are aware, we find ... ourselves to be by them given away to a Forreign Power, before such Orders can reach unto us; for which Orders we now humbly wait.

Edmond Andros's Report, 1690*

Governor Edmond Andros submitted the following account of events in New England to the Lords of Trade. In the report, he emphasized his loyalty to royal policy while describing the treasonous nature of the rebels. His superiors accepted his interpretation of the uprising, and they exonerated him. More ominous to Americans, the Glorious Revolution did little to limit the king's power over the settlers. Indeed, only a few years later William III created the Board of Trade in order to centralize and strengthen his authority. As the seventeenth century ended, substantive differences concerning power and liberty existed between the crown and the colonies.

That in the yeare 1686 Sir Edmond Andros was by comision under the Greate Seale of England appoynted to succeed the President Dudley and Council in the government of the Massachusetts Colony, the Provinces of Hampshire and Maine and the Narragansett Country, to w'ch was annexed the Colonys of Rhode Island New Plymouth and the County of Cornwall.

In the yeare 1687 the Collony of Connecticott was also annexed and in the yeare 1688 he received a new Commission for all New England including the Province of New Yorke and East and West Jersey. ...

---

* "Declaration of the Gentlemen, Merchants and Inhabitants of Boston, and the Country Adjacent," April 18, 1689, in *Narratives of the Insurrections, 1675–1690*, ed. Charles M. Andrews (New York: Charles Scribner's Sons, 1915), 229–36.

Harcourt Brace & Company

Sir Edmond Andros upon receipt of his Commission went to New Yorke and Albany of which the Indians having notice, altho' they were then mett in Councill about goeing to Canada came thither, and were setled, and confirmed under his government. . . .

The severall Provinces and Coloneys in New England being soe united, the revenue continued and setled in those parts, for the support of the government, amounted to about twelve thousand pounds *per annum* and all places were well and quietly setled and in good posture. . . .

He was always ready to give grants of vacant lands and confirme defective titles as authorized (the late Corporation not having passed or conveyed any persuant to the directions in their Charter) but not above twenty have passed the seal in the time of his government.

Courts of Judicature were setled in the severall parts, soe as might be convenient for the ease and benefitt of the subject, and Judges appoynted to hold the Terms and goe the Circuite throughout the Dominion, to administer justice in the best manner and forme, and according to the lawes Customes and statutes of the realm of England, and some peculiar locall prudentiall laws of the Country, not repugnant therto; and fees regulated for all officers.

That particuler care was taken for the due observance of the severall Acts made for the encouragement of navigation and regulateing the plantation trade, whereby the lawfull trade and His Majestys revenue of Customs was considerably increased.

The Indians throughout the govern't continued in good order and subjection untill, towards the letter end of the yeare 1688, by some unadvised proceedings of the Inhabitants in the Eastern parts of New England, the late rupture with the Indians there comenced, severall being taken and some killed, when Sir Edmond Andros was at New Yorke more than three hundred miles distant from that place; and upon his speedy returne to Boston (having viewed and setled all parts to the Westward) great part of the garrison soldiers with stores and other necessary were imediately sent Eastward to reinforce those parts, and vessells to secure the coast and fishery, and further forces raysed and appoynted to be under the command of Majr Gen'll Winthrop, who falling sick and declineing the service, by advice of the Councill he went with them in person and by settlement of several garrisons, frequent partyes, marches and pursuits after the enemy, sometimes above one hundred miles into the desart further than any Christian settlement, in w'ch the officers and souldiers of the standing forces always imployed, takeing and destroying their forts and settlem'ts, corne, provision, ammunicion and canooes, dispersed and reduced them to the uttermost wants and necessitys, and soe secured the Countrey, . . . not the least loss, damage of spoyle hapned to the inhabitants or fishery, and the Indians were ready to submitt at mercy.

About the latter end of March 1688 Sir Edmond Andros returned for Boston, leaveing the garrisons and souldiers in the Easterne parts in good condition , sufficiently furnished with provisions and all stores and implyments of warr and vessells for defence of the coast and fishery.

On the 18th of April 1689 severall of His Maj'ties Councill in New England haveing combined and conspired togeather with those who were magistrates and officers in the late Charter Government annually chosen by the people, and severall other persons, to subvert and overthrow the government, and in stead thereof to introduce their former Commonwealth; and haveing by their false reports and aspersions gott to their assistance the greatest part of the people, whereof appeared in arms at Boston under the command of those who were Officers in the sayd former popular government, to the number of about two thousand horse and foote; which strange and sudden appearance being wholly a surprize to Sir Edmond Andros, as knowing noe cause or occasion for the same, but understanding that severall of the Councill were at the Councill Chamber where . . . they were to meet, . . . he and those with him went hither. And tho' (as he passed) the streets were full of armed men, yett none offered him or those that were with him the least rudeness or incivillity, but on the contrary usuall respect; but when he came to the Councill Chamber he found severall of the sayd former popular Majestrates and other chiefe persons then present, with those of the Councill, who had noe suitable regard to him, or the peace and quiet of the Countrey, but instead of giving any assistance to support the Government, made him a prisoner and also imprisoned some members of the Councill and other officers, who in pursuance of their respective dutyes and stations attended on him, and kept him for the space of ten months under severe and close confinement untill by His Ma'ties comand they were sent for England to answer what might be objected them, Where, after summons given to the pretended Agents of New England and their twice appearance at the Councill Board, nothing could be objected by them or others, they were discharged. In the time of his confinement being denyed the liberty of discourse or conversation with any person, his own servants to attend him, or any communication or correspondence with any by letters, he hath noe particular knowledge of their further proceedings, but hath heard and understands:—

That soone after the confinem't of his person, the Confederates [took the] fort and Castle from the Officers that had the comand of them, whom they also imprisoned and dispersed the few souldiers belonging to the two standing Companeys then there, as they did the rest, when they recalled the forces imployed against . . . the Indians Eastward . . . in w'ch service halfe a company of the standing forces at New York being also imployed, the officers were surprised and brought prisoners to Boston, and the souldiers dispersed, as the remaining part of them at New Yorke were afterwards upon the revolucion there. The other company was, and remained, at Fort Albany. . . . And the Confederates at Boston possessed themselves of all His Ma'ties stores, armes ammunicion and other implements of warr, and disabled His Ma'ties man of war the *Rose* frigatt by securing the Comander and bringing her sayles on shoare; and at the same time haveing imprisoned the secretary and some other officers, they broke open the Sec'rys Office and seized and conveyed away all records papers and wrightings.

Those Members of His Ma'ties Councill that were in confederacy with the before mencioned popular Majestrates and other chiefe actors in this revolucion, tooke upon them the government, by the name of a Councill, who not content with the inconveniency they had brought on themselves in the Massachusetts Colony, but to the ruine of the poore neighbours, on the twentieth of April gave orders for the drawing off the forces from Pemyquid and other garrisons and places in the Easterne parts, far without the lymitts of their Collony and where the seate of warr with the Indians was, and to seize severall of the officers, and for calling home the vessells appoynted to gard the sea coast and fishery; w'ch was done accordingly, and the forces disbanded, when most of the souldiers belonging to the standing Companys there were dispersed; of which, . . . the Indians [taking] notice, (and being supplyed with Ammunicion and provision out of a vessell sent from Boston by some of the chiefe conspirators before the insurrection to trade with them) they were encouraged and enabled to renew and pursue the warr; and by the assistance of some French who have been seen amongst them and engageing of severall other Indians before unconcerned, increased their numbers, that in a very short tyme severall hundreds of Their Ma'ties subjects were killed and carryed away captive; The Fort at Pemyquid taken; the whole Cuntry of Cornwall, the greatest part of the Province of Maine, and part of the Province of New Hampshire destroyed and deserted; and the principall trade of that country, w'ch consisted in a considerable fishery, the getting of masts, yards, etc. for the supply of His Ma'tyes navy Royall, and boards and other lumber for the supply of the other West India plantacions, is almost wholy ruined.

By the encouragem't and perswasion of those of . . . Massachusetts[,] the severall other provinces and collonys in New England as far as New Yorke have disunited themselves, and set up their former separate Charter, or popular governments without Charter, and by that meanes the whole revenue of the Crowne continued and setled in the severall parts for the support of the Government is lost and destroyed.

Harcourt Brace & Company

The usuall time for election of new Majestrates at Boston comeing on in the beginning of May 1689, great controversie arose about the setling of Civill Government; some being for a new election, and others that the Majestrates chosen and sworne in 1686 before the alteracion should reassume; the latter of w'ch was concluded on by them and the pretended representatives of the severall townes of the Massachusetts, and assumed by the sd Majestrates accordingly, and thereupon the old Charter Government, tho' vacated in Westminster Hall, was reassumed without any regard to the Crowne of England, and they revived and confirmed their former laws contrary and repugnant to the laws and statutes of England, setled their Courts of Judicature, and appoynted new officers, and have presumed to try and judge all cases civill and criminall, and to pass sentence of death on severall of Their Ma'ties subjects, some of whom they have caused to be executed.

Altho in the revenue continued on the Crowne for suport of the government dureing his time, the country pay'd but the old establisht rate of a penny in the pound *per Annum* as given and practised for about fifty yeares past, the present Administrators have of their own authority, for not above six months, raysed and exacted from the people of the Massachusetts Collony seven rates and a half.

Since the insurrection and alteracion in New England they doe tollerate an unlimited irregular trade, contrary to the severall acts of the Plantations, Trade and Navigacion, now so little regarded as in the time of their former Charter Government; they esteeming noe laws to be binding on them but what are made by themselves, nor admitt English laws to be pleaded there, or appeales to His Ma'tie. And many shipps and vessells have since arrived from Scotland, Holland, Newfoundland, and other places prohibitted, they having imprisoned His Ma'ties Collector, Surveyor and searcher, and displaced other Customhouse officers.

That they sent to Albany to treat with the Indians in those parts, particularly with the Five Nations, Masquaes etc. and invited them to Boston; which is of ill and dangerous consequence, by makeing the sayd Indians particularly acquainted with the disunion and separate governments, and shewing them the countrey and disorders thereof, as far as Boston, giveing thereby the greatest advantage to the French of gaining or subdueing the sayd Indians and attempting Fort Albany (the most advanced frontier into the country and great mart of the beaver and peltry trade) and of infesting other parts.

The forces raysed and set out by them the last summer, notwithstanding the great encouragem't they promised of eight pounds per head for every Indian should be killed, besides their pay, proved neither effectuall to suppresse the enemy or secure the country from further damage and murthers; and upon the winters approaching the forces were recalled and the country left exposed to the enemy, who have already over runn and destroyed soe great a part thereof. And now by the assistance of the French of Canada may probably proceed further into the heart of the country, being soe devided and out of order unless it shall please His Ma'tie by his owne authority to redress the same, and put a stop to the French and Indians, and thereby prevent the ruine or loss of that whole dominion of New England and consequently of Their Maj'ties other American Plantacions, endangered not only by the want of provisions, but by the many ships, vessells, seamen and and other necessarys in New England, capable to supply and transport any force, may annoy or attempt those plantations; but may be by His Ma'ties authority and comands effectually setled and preserved, and of service against the French or any other Their Ma'ties enemys in those parts, with no greater land force then is necessary to be continued there, and a sufficient revenue raysed to defray the charge thereof, by dutyes and rates, as heretofore hath been practiced amongst them and is usual in other Their Ma'ties plantacions.

Harcourt Brace & Company

Creation of the Board of Trade, 1696*

The following declaration reorganized the Board for Foreign Plantations, created in 1660, by centralizing control of the colonies in the hands of the king rather than in Parliament. The document stresses the role that board members played in promoting and regulating trade, but it also charged them with reviewing the acts of colonial assemblies. William III, it appeared to Americans, was as intent as his Stuart predecessors had been on asserting his power at the expense of Americans' economic and political liberties.

His Majesties Commission for promoting the Trade of this Kingdom and for inspecting and improving His Plantations in America and elsewhere.

WILLIAM the Third by the Grace of God King of England, Scotland, France and Ireland, Defender of the Faith &a. To our Keeper of oure Great Seale of England or Chancellor of England . . . , Our President of Our Privy Council . . . , Our first Commissioner of Our Treasury And our Treasurer of England . . . , Our first Commissioner of our Admiralty and Our Admirall of England . . . , And our principall Secretarys of State . . . , And the Chancellor of Our Exchequer . . . , To Our Right Trusty and Right Well beloved Cousin and Councillor John Earl of Bridgewater, and Ford Earl of Tankerville, To our Trusty and Well beloved Sir Philip Meadows, Knt, William Blaithwaite, John Pollexfen, John Locke, Abraham Hill, and John Methwen, Esquires, Greeting. . . .

KNOW YEE therefor that We reposing espetiall Trust and Confidence in your Discretions, Abilityes and Integrities . . . authorize and appoint . . . you, to be Our Commissioners during our Royal Pleasure, for promoting the Trade of our Kingdome, and for Inspecting and Improving our Plantations in America and elsewhere. . . .

And We do hereby further Impower and require you Our said Commissioners to take into your care all Records, Grants and Papers remaining in the Plantation Office or thereunto belonging.

And likewise to inform your selves of the present condition of Our respective Plantations, as well as with regards to the administration of the Government and Justice in those places, as in relations to the Commerce thereof; And also to inquire into the Limits of Soyle and Product of Our severall Plantations and how the same may be improved, and of the best means for easing and securing Our Colonies there, and how the same may be rendered most usefull and beneficiall to our said Kingdom of England.

And We do hereby further impower and require you Our said Commissioners, more particularly and in a principal manner to inform your selves what Navall Stores may be furnished from Our Plantations, and in what Quantities, and by what methods Our Royall purpose of having our Kingdom supplied with Navall Stores from thence may be made practicable and promoted; And also to inquire into and inform your selves of the best and most proper methods of settling and improving in Our Plantations, such other Staples and other Ma[n]ufactures as Our subjects of England are now obliged to fetch and supply themselves withall from other Princes and States; And also what Staples and Manufactures may be best encouraged there, and what Trades are taken up and excercised there, which are or may prove prejudiciall to England, by furnishing themselves or other Our Colonies with what has been usually supplied from England; And to finde out proper means of diverting them from such Trades, and whatsoever else may turne to the hurt of Our Kingdom of England.

---

*From *American History Told by Contemporaries*, 5 vols., ed. Albert Bushnell Hart (New York: The Macmillan Company, 1914), II:129–31.

And to examin and look into the usuall Instructions given to the Governors of Our Plantations, and to see if any thing may be added, omitted or changed therein to advantage; To take and Account yearly by way of Journall of the Administration of Our Governors there, and to draw-out what is proper to be observed and represented unto Us; and as often as occasion shall require to consider of proper persons to be Governors or Deputy Governors, or to be of Our Councill or of Our Councill at Law, or Secretarys, in Our respective Plantations, in order to present their Names to Us in Councill.

And We do hereby further Authorize and impower you Our said Commissioners, to examin into and weigh such Acts of the Assemblies of the Plantations respectively as shall from time to time be sent or transmitted hither for Our Approbation; And to set down and represent as aforesaid the Usefulness or Mischief thereof to Our Crown, and to Our said Kingdom of England, or to the Plantations themselves, in case the same should be established for Laws there; And also to consider what matters may be recommended as fitt to be passed in the Assemblies there, To heare complaints of Oppression and maladministrations, in Our Plantations, in order to represent as aforesaid what you in your Discretions shall thinke proper; And also to require an Account of all Monies given for Publick uses by the Assemblies in Our Plantations, and how the same are and have been expended or laid out.

Discussion

1. English authorities believed that their policies preserved liberty and at the same time protected the interests of the empire. Based on the documents, why might Americans have viewed those policies as dangerous assertions of power?

2. How do the guarantee of religious toleration in the Fundamental Constitutions and the declaration of grievances in 1689 express concepts of liberty? To what degree, if any, are they also expressions of equality?

3. How does the statement of religious toleration compare to the "Model of Christian Charity" sermon presented in the previous chapter? How might any similarities or differences in the ideals they express be explained?

4. The American colonies experienced several insurrections during the seventeenth century. According to the descriptions of Bacon's Rebellion and the overthrow of Governor Edmond Androse, what were the critical issues of power and liberty that shaped those rebellions?

Chapter 4
Expansion, Diversity, and Anglicization in Provincial America

As early as 1647, Massachusetts towns were required to tax residents in support of elementary schools. The New England Primer *was used to promote both literacy and the spirtual welfare of New England children.*

The European population of North America rose markedly in the eighteenth century, creating a period of turmoil as direct confrontations between the various states that claimed the region revealed a continuing power struggle to assert control over the New World. In the English settlements, rapid growth led to several crises, including the need for an expanding currency. Such a population explosion also accelerated the development of regional differentiation between the Lower South, the Upper South, the Mid-Atlantic colonies, the backcountry, and New England. On the other hand, even as society grew more sophisticated and complex, Americans continued to share a common faith in their English heritage and its emphasis on individual liberties. Americans embraced the ideals of the Enlightenment as well, which greatly influenced their understanding of those liberties. In addition, the colonies witnessed a powerful wave of revivalism, beginning early in the century but peaking around 1740, yet another common experience and one that helped strengthen religious toleration. Over time, then, Colonials developed institutions that reflected English traditions. At the same time, many settlers were becoming aware that their household economy was making them different from Englishmen at home.

In Defense of Paper Money, 1724★

By the early eighteenth century, numerous Americans believed that a disparity of wealth was depriving them of any prospects for the economic security critical to preserving their rights as Englishmen. The problem, they insisted, stemmed from the scarcity of money in the colonies. Most major transactions had to be conducted in specie, which, because of mercantilistic policies, tended to flow to England rather than circulate within the colonies. Issuing paper money seemed to offer a solution to the dilemma, but many officials disproved of currency as inflationary. Thus, a struggle ensued between those people in positions of economic and political power and those who feared that conservative monetary policies threatened their liberty. William Burnet, who served as governor of New York and New Jersey, wrote this letter to gain support from his superiors for paper money in the colonies. His essay reveals common attitudes toward, and the complexities of, the issue.

I am very sensible of the disadvantage I lye under in writing upon this argument, and the misfortune it is to any cause to have already appeared in an odious light, as I am but too well convinced in the case of paper money Acts in the Plantations, by your Lordships last words in your letter of the 17th of june—*That Bills for encreasing of Paper money will meet with no encouragement*—I hope your Lordships will not think it presumption in me even after this declaration to endeavor to give you a more favorable opinion of such Acts and if I go too far in this, it is owing to the encouragement your Lordships have given me by receiving what I have offered on all occasions in so kind a manner and admitting the best constructions that my weak Reasonings will bear[.]

★From *American History Told by Contemporaries*, 5 vols., ed. Albert Bushnell Hart (New York: The Macmillan Company, 1914), II:251–53.

I have already in my letter of the 12th of May last used several Arguments to justify the Paper Act in New Jersey, and therein I observed how well the Bills of New York keep up their credit and the reasons why they have not fall'n in value as those of Carolina and New England and that under a good regulation these Acts are both of Service to the Trade of the Plantations and of great Britain, for which that I may not repeat I beg leave to refer to my said letter of the 12th of May last and desire your Lordships would again take into your consideration when you are to determine your opinion on this present Act.—

But there are many things there only hinted at which I shall now lay before your Lordships and in which I shall cheifly [sic] argue from what is to be gathered from experience of Great Britain itself from observing the nature of credit and the events it has under gone, and in this I hope I may be the more patiently heard because what experience I have was purchased at no very cheap rate[.]

Credit ought to be supported if it is possible, both by *reason* and *common opinion*. Reason tho ever so strong will not always do alone in the Beginning if common opinion is against it but it will carry all before it at the long run: Common opinion or humor will generally do for a time without reason nay, against it. But then it is often attended with vast mischeif and danger—Of this we have a fatal Instance in the famous south Sea Scheme, which being left to common opinion without restraint has produced the most terrible effects possible. If there had been a possitive Law, making all Bargains for South Sea Stock above some fixed Price as 150. void and making it a legal tender at 100 all these mischeifs would have been avoided but this would have been called *compulsive Paper Credit,* yet because in Reason it is worth so much as long as the Nation stands and because the Parliament has always kept their engagements all clamors against this would soon have blown over and no enemies would have been found to it but Brokers[.]

To make this appear it is enough to prove, that at the bottom all the present voluntary credit stands upon this very foundation at last & no other[.]

It is very certain that there is no proportion between the Specie & the great quantity of Bank Bills and Bankers Notes, commonly current who lend their notes on the several Branches of Government Securitys and seldom at a Rate under *par* very often above *par* When the Government is safe this would do when there is any danger, Common opinion pulls down her own work & Bankers break in abundance, and the Bank itself is put to Extremitys. An Instance of this I remember at the time of the Preston affair—The Bank would have broke in a few days, if the victory there had not happened as soon as it did[.]

And the Reason was plainly this because when they had paid away all their Specie they had nothing left but Exchequer Notes, and such other Securitys to exchange for their remaining Bank Notes, and these would have been at such a discount that they must have been broke, and compounded for such Payment at the Best[.]

Thus it is plain that the foundation in Reason of the credit of the Bank it self not to speak of the Private Goldsmiths in the Government Security remaining at *Par* and yet the Parliament is so good as to provide an interest on these Exchequer Bills, and to pay the Bank so much more per cent for circulation whereas in fact when foul weather comes the Bank is a Staff of Reed and must lean on the Government to prop itself up and so increase the load instead of easing it[.]

And this humour keeps up the imaginary value, when there is no real occasion for it; all Government Securities being at the same time commonly above par[.] But upon any ill News the like Humour beats down all voluntary credit, in the same manner as it does Exchequer Bills &c and really carries the General Discredit as much further than it ought as it had advanced credit beyond its reasonable bounds before and if once the Bank had broke, then all this would have appeared to a demonstration[.] . . .

Harcourt Brace & Company

From all which I beg to conclude, that it is not the names things get for the present but the real nature of them, that will be found to hold against all events & that in the instance of Paper money where it is regulated by just Laws and where the Publick have not acted contrary to them their credit is in reason better established than the credit of any private Persons or Society and that the method used to catch the common opinion of mankind by offering them money when they please is nothing but a fashionable Bubble which People are every day sufferers by when a Banker breaks & even the best founded Societys can not maintain their Credit when there is the Greatest need of them. But that all Credit finally centers in the Security of ye Governmt[.]

I take the liberty further to observe to your Lordships on how many occasions the Government of Great Britain has found it impracticable to raise all the money wanted within the year from whence all the present debts of the nation have arisen: The same necessity lyes often upon the Plantations where frequently a sum of ready money is wanted, which it would be an intollerable Tax to raise at once, and therefore they are forced to imitate the Parliament at home, in anticipating upon remote funds. And as there is no Bank nor East India company nor even private subscribers capable of lending the Province the money they want at least without demanding the extravagant Interest of 8 Pr Cent which is the common Interest here, but would ruin the publick to pay since this is a Case there is no possible way left to make distant funds provide ready money, when it is necessarily wanted, but making paper Bills to be sunk by such funds. Without this Carolina would have been ruined by their Indian War[.] Boston could not have supported theirs nor could any of the Provinces have furnished such considerable sums to the Expeditions against Canada[.] Nor could at present any of the necessary repairs of this Fort be provided for, nor the arrears of the Revenue be discharged, which is done by this Act in a Tax to be levyed in 4 years nor indeed any publick Service readily and sufficiently effected[.]

And I may add one thing more that this manner of compulsive credit does in fact keep up its value here and that it occasions much more Trade and business than would be without it and that more Species is exported to England by reason of these Paper Bills than could be if there was no circulation but of Specie for which reason all the merchants here seem well satisfied with it.

Paper Money Outlawed, 1740*

This proclamation by the Lords Commissioners for Trade and Plantations (the Board of Trade) made it difficult for a colony to issue paper money. The need for currency, however, remained a problem throughout the colonial era. Debtors and poor Americans, furthermore, continued to resent the policy that they viewed as an assertion of power and a danger to liberty.

WHEREAS, for preventing the many & great Inconveniences that had arisen in some of his Majesty's Colonies & Plantations in America, by passing Laws for Striking Bills of Credit, & issuing out the same, in lieu of money, the respective Governors & Commanders in chief of his Majesty's Colonies & Plantations for the time being, have been particularly instructed not to give their Assent to or pass any such laws for the future, without a Clause inserted in such Act, declaring that the same shall not take Effect, until the said Act shall have been approved and

*From *American History Told by Contemporaries,* 5 vols., ed. Albert Bushnell Hart (New York: The Macmillan Company, 1914–), II:254.

confirm'd by his Majesty his Heirs or Successors: and whereas notwithstanding such his Majesty's Commanders to the said Governors in that behalf, Paper Bills of Credit have been created & issued in his Majesty's said Colonies & Plantations by Virtue of Acts of Assembly there, making it obligatory on all persons to take such Bills of Credits, in payment for Debts, Dues & Demands . . . and a great Discouragement has been brot on the Com'erce of this Kingdom by occasioning a Confusion in Dealings and a lessening of Credit in those parts; And whereas an humble Address was presented, the last Session by the House of Commons, to his Majesty, That he would be graciously pleased to require & command the respective Governors of his Colonies & Plantation in America, punctually & effectually to observe his Majtys Royal Instructions not to give Assent to or to pass any Act, whereby Bills of Credit may be issued in lieu of money, without a Clause to be inserted in such Act, declaring that the same shall be approved by his Majesty:

It is therefore his Majesty's Will & Pleasure, & you are hereby also further required & commanded under pain of his Majesty's highest displeasure and of being removed, from your Governmt punctually & effectually to observe his Majesty's Royal Instruction not to give Assent to or pass any Act, whereby Bills of Credit may be issued in lieu of money without a Clause be inserted in such Act, declaring that the same shall not take Effect, until the said Act shall be approved by his Majesty, his Heirs or Successors.

Considerations on the Nature of Laws, 1721*

This essay from *Cato's Letters* provides an example of the political writing that attracted great attention in the colonies early in the eighteenth century. The document reveals many of the Enlightenment ideals regarding liberty, equality, and power that shaped American thinking during the period. According to Cato, natural law established two fundamental rights: equity, or justice, and the right to defend that equity. The premise had profound implications for colonial attitudes toward those in power, because the essay concludes that a community may resist unjust laws. In 1776, Thomas Jefferson institutionalized such concepts in the Declaration of Independence.

The Mischiefs that are daily done, and the Evils that are daily suffered in the World, are sad proofs how much human Malice exceeds human wisdom. Law only provides against the Evils which it knows or foresees; but when Laws fail, we must have Recourse to Reason and Nature, which are the only Guides in the making of Laws. *Stirpem Juris a Natura repertam,* says Cicero; there never would have been any Law against any Crime, if Crimes might have been safely committed, against which there was no Law; For every Law supposes some Evil, and can only punish or restrain the Evils which already exist.

But as positive Laws, let them be ever so full and perspicuous, can never entirely prevent the Arts of crafty Men to evade them, or the Power of great ones to violate them; hence new Laws are daily making, and new Occasions for more are daily arising: So that the utmost that Wisdom, Virtue, and Law can do, is to lessen or qualify, but never totally abolish Vice and Enormity. Law is therefore a Sign of the Corruption of Man; and many Laws are Signs of the Corruption of a State.

Positive Laws deriving their Force from the Law of Nature, by which we are directed to make occasional Rules, which we call Laws, according to the Exigences of Times, Places, and

---

*From *Cato's Letters; or, Essays on Liberty, Civil and Religious, and Other Important Subjects,* 3d corrected ed., 4 vols. (New York: Russell and Russell, 1733), II:64–70.

Harcourt Brace & Company

Persons, grow obsolete, or cease to be, as soon as they cease to be necessary: And it is as much against the law of Nature to execute Laws, when the first Cause of them ceases, as it is to make Laws, for which there is no Cause, or a bad Cause. This would be to subject Reason to Force, and to apply a Penalty where there is no Crime. Law is right Reason, commanding Things that are good, and forbidding Things that are bad; it is a Distinction and Declaration of Things just and unjust, and of the Penalties or Advantages annexed to them.

The Violation therefore of Law does not constitute a Crime where the Law is bad; but the Violation of what ought to be Law, is a Crime even when there is no Law. The Essence of Right and Wrong, does not depend on Words and Clauses inserted in a Code or a Statute-Book, much less upon the Conclusions and Explications of Lawyers; but upon Reason and the Nature of Things, antecedent to all Laws. In all Countries, Reason is or ought to be consulted, before Laws are enacted; and they are always worse than none, where it is not consulted. Reason is in some Degree given to all Men, and *Cicero* says, that whoever has Reason, has right Reason; that Virtue is but perfect Reason, and that all nations having Reason for their Guide, all Nations are capable of arriving at Virtue.

From this Reasoning of his, it would follow, that every People are capable of making Laws; and that Laws, where they are bad, are gained by Corruption, Faction, Fear, or Surprize; and are rather their Misfortune, than the Effects of their Folly. The Acts of *Caesar* were confirmed by the Senate and the People; but the Senate was awed, and the Tribunes and People were bribed: Arms and Money procured him a Law to declare him lawless. But, as the most pompous Power can never unsettle the everlasting Land-marks between Good and Evil, no more than those between Pleasure and Pain; *Caesar* remained still a Rebel to his Country, and his Acts remained wicked and tyrannical.

Let this stand for an Instance, that Laws are not always the Measure of Right and Wrong. And as positive Laws often speak when the Law of Nature is silent, the Law of Nature sometimes speaks, when positive Laws say nothing. . . .

It is impossible to devise Laws sufficient to regulate and manage every Occurrence and Circumstance of Life, because they are often produced and diversified by Causes that do not appear; and in every Condition of Life, Men must have, and will have, great Allowances made to their own natural Liberty and Discretion: But every Man who consents to this Proposition, that *every Man should do all the Good, and prevent all the Evil that he can.* This is the voice of the Law of Nature; and all Men would be happy by it, if all Men would practise it. This Law leads us to see, that the Establishment of Falshood and Tyranny (by which I mean the Privilege of One or a Few to mislead and oppress All) cannot be justly called Law, which is the impartial Rule of Good and Evil, and can never be the Sanction of Evil alone.

It has been often said, that Virtue is its own Reward; and it is very true, not only from the Pleasure that attends the Consciousness of doing well, and the Fame that follows it, but in a more extensive Sense, from the Felicity which would accrue to every Man, if all Men would pursue Virtue: But as this Truth may appear too general to allure and engage particular Men, who will have always their own single selves most at Heart, abstracted from all the rest; therefore in the making of Laws, the Pleasures and Fears of particular Men, being the great Engines by which they are to be governed, must be consulted; Vice must be rendered detestable and dangerous; Virtue amiable and advantageous. Their Shame and Emulation must be raised, their private Profit and Glory, Peril and Infamy, laid before them. . . .

Rewards and Punishments therefore constitute the whole Strength of Laws; and the Promulgation of Laws, without which they are none, is an Appeal to the Sense and Interest of Men, which of the two they will chuse.

The two great Laws of human Society, from whence all the rest derive their Course and Obligation, are those of Equity and Self-preservation: By the First, all Men are bound alike not to hurt one another; by the Second, all Men have a Right alike to defend themselves: . . . All the Laws of Society are entirely reciprocal, and no Man ought to be exempt from their Force; and whoever violates this primary Law of Nature, ought by the Law of Nature to be destroyed. He who observes no Law, forfeits all Title to the Protection of Law. It is a Wickedness not to destroy a Destroyer; and all the ill Consequences of Self-defence are chargeable upon him who occasioned them.

Many Mischiefs are prevented, by destroying One who shews a certain Disposition to commit many. To allow a Licence to any Man to do Evil with Impunity, is to make Vice triumph over Virtue, and Innocence Prey to the Guilty. If Men be obliged to bear great and publick Evils, when they can upon better Terms oppose and remove them; they are obliged by the same Logick, to bear the total Destruction of Mankind. If any Man may destroy whom he pleases without Resistance, he may extinguish the human Race without Resistance. For, if you settle the Bounds of Resistance, you allow it; and if you do not fix its Bounds, you leave Property at the Mercy of Rapine, and Life in the Hands of Cruelty.

It is said, that the Doctrine of Resistance would destroy the Peace of the World: But it may be more truly said, that the contrary Doctrine would destroy the World itself, as it has already some of the best Countries in it. I must indeed own, that if one Man may destroy all, there would be a great and lasting Peace when Nobody was left to break it.

The Law of Nature does not only allow us, but obliges us, to defend ourselves. It is our Duty, not only to ourselves, but to the Society. . . .

So that the Conduct of Men, who when they are ill treated, use Words rather than Arms, and practise Submission rather than Resistance, is owing to a prudential Cause, because there is Hazard in Quarrels and War, and their Case may be made worse by an Endeavour to mend it; and not to any Consession of Right in those that do them wrong. When Men begin to be wicked, we cannot tell where that Wickedness will end; we have Reason to fear the worst, and provide against it.

Such is the Provision made by Laws: They are Checks upon the unruly and partial Appetites of Men, and intended for Terror and Protection. But as there are already Laws sufficient every where, to preserve Peace between private Particulars, the great Difficulty has hitherto been to find proper checks for those who were to check and administer the Laws. To settle therefore a thorough Impartiality in the Laws, both as to their End and Execution, is a Task worthy of human Wisdom, as it would be the Cause and Standard of Civil Felicity. In the Theory, nothing is more easy than this Task: Yet who is able to perform it, if they who can will not?

No Man in Society ought to have any Privilege above the rest, without giving the Society some Equivalent for such his Privilege. Thus Legislators, who compile good Laws, and good Magistrates who execute them, do, by their honest Attendance upon the Publick, deserve the Privileges and Pay which the Publick allows them; and Place and power are the Wages paid by the People to their own Deputies and Agents. Hence it has been well said, that a chief Magistrate is . . . "above the private members of the Community, but the Community itself is above him."

Wherever, therefore, the Laws are honestly intended and equally executed, so as to comprehend in their Penalties and Operation the Great as well and as much as the Small, and hold in awe the Magistrates as much as the Subject, that Government is good, that People are happy.

On Self-Denial, 1734*

As the preceding selection shows, political philosophers embraced virtue as crucial to society. In the following essay, which first appeared in *The Pennsylvania Gazette*, Benjamin Franklin offers his reflections on virtue. To his contemporaries, Franklin epitomized the enlightened individual of the eighteenth century. A successful and wealthy publisher, he devoted much of his life to philosophical rumination and scientific research. Franklin, as shown in the following document, occasionally revealed an iconoclasm that in many ways reflected the independent mindedness of some colonists and a new confidence in the possibilities of human benevolence.

It is commonly asserted, that *without self-denial there is no virtue,* and that the greater the self-denial is, the greater is the virtue.

If it were said, that he who cannot deny himself any thing he inclines to, though he knows it will be to his hurt, has not the virtue of resolution or fortitude, it would be intelligible enough; but as it stands, the proposition seems obscure or erroneous.

Let us consider some of the virtues singly.

If a man has no inclination to wrong people in his dealings; if he feels no temptation to it, and therefore never does it, can it be said, that he is not a just man? If he is a just man, has he not the virtue of justice?

If to a certain man, idle diversions have nothing in them that is tempting, and therefore he never relaxes his application to business for their sake, is he not an industrious man; or has he not the virtue of industry?

I might in like manner instance in all the rest of the virtues; but to make the thing short, as it is certain, that the more we strive against the temptation to any vice, and practise the contrary virtue, the weaker will that temptation be, and the stronger will be that habit; till at length the temptation hath no force, or entirely vanishes: does it follow from thence, that in our endeavours to overcome vice, we grow continually less and less virtuous, till at length we have no virtue at all!

If self-denial be the essence of virtue, then it follows, that the man who is naturally temperate, just, &c., is not virtuous, but that in order to be virtuous, he must, in spite of his natural inclinations, wrong his neighbors, and eat and drink, &c., to excess.

But, perhaps it may be said, that by the word *virtue,* in the above assertion, is meant *merit,* and so it should stand; thus without self-denial there is no merit; and the greater the self-denial the greater the merit.

The self-denial here meant must be, when our inclinations are toward vice, or else it would still be nonsense.

By merit is understood desert; and when we say a man merits, we mean that he deserves praise and reward.

We do not pretend to merit any thing of God, for he is above our services, and the benefits he confers on us are the efforts of his goodness and bounty.

All merit then is with regard to one another, and from one another.

Taking then the proposition as it stands—

If a man does me a service, from a natural benevolent inclination, does he deserve less of me than another, who does me the like kindness against his inclination?

*From Benjamin Franklin, "On Self Denial," *The Pennsylvania Gazette,* February 18, 1734, in *Memoirs of Benjamin Franklin. Written by Himself, and Continued by His Grandson and Others,* 2 vols. (Philadelphia: McCarty & Davis, 1837), II:470–71.

If I have two journeymen, one naturally industrious, the other idle, but both perform a day's work equally good, ought I to give the latter the most wages?

Indeed lazy workmen are commonly observed to be more extravagant in their demands than the industrious; for if they have not more for their work, they cannot live as well as the industrious. But though it be true to a proverb, that *lazy folks take the most pains,* does it follow that they deserve the *most money?* If you were to employ servants in affairs of trust, would you pay more wages to one you know were naturally honest, than for one naturally roguish, but who had lately acted honestly: for currents whose natural channels are dammed up, til a new course is by time worn sufficiently deep, and become natural, are apt to break their banks. If one servant is more valuable than another, has he not more merit than the other, and yet this is not on account of superior self-denial. Is a patriot praiseworthy, if public support is natural to him?

Is a pacing horse less valuable for being a natural pacer?

Nor in my opinion has any man less merit for having in general naturally virtuous inclinations.

The truth is, that temperance, justice, charity, &c., are virtues whether practised with or against our inclinations; and the man who practises them, merits our love and esteem: and self-denial is neither good nor bad, but as it is applied. He that denies a vicious inclination, is virtuous in proportion to his resolution; but the most perfect virtue is above all temptation; such as the virtue of the saints in heaven: and he who does any foolish, indecent, or wicked thing, merely because it is contrary to his inclination, like some mad enthusiasts I have read of, who ran almost in public naked, under the notion of taking up the cross, is not practising the reasonable science of virtue, but is a lunatic.

Electrical Kite, 1752*

Benjamin Franklin, who became an outspoken proponent of colonial unity and, eventually, independence, often represented American interests before the intellectual and political leaders of Europe. In that capacity he certainly provided an invaluable service as a powerful defender of American liberty. One reason for his accomplishments as a diplomat was the immense fame he had gained through his experiments with electricity. He described his most famous experiment in the following letter to an English colleague.

As frequent mention is made in public papers from Europe of the success of the Philadelphia experiment for drawing the electric fire from the clouds by means of pointed rods of iron erected on high buildings &c. it may be agreeable to the curious to be informed that the same experiment has succeeded in Philadelphia, though made in a different and more easy manner, which is as follows:

Make a small cross of two light strips of cedar, the arms so long as to reach to the four corners of a large thin silk handkerchief when extended; tie the corners of the handkerchief to the extremities of the cross, so you have the body of a kite; which being properly accommodated with a tail, loop, and string, will rise in the air, like those made of paper; but this being of silk is fitter to bear the wet and wind of a thunder gust without tearing. To the top of the upright stick of the cross is to be fixed a very sharp pointed wire, rising a foot or more above the wood.

---

*Franklin to Peter Collionson, October 16, 1752, in *Memoirs of Benjamin Franklin. Written by Himself, and Continued by His Grandson and Others,* 2 vols. (Philadelphia: McCarty & Davis, 1837), II:284.

To the end of the twine, next the hand, is to be tied a silk ribbon, and where the silk and twine join, a key may be fastened. This kite is to be raised when a thunder-gust appears to be coming on, and the person who holds the string must stand within a door or window, or under some cover, so that the silk ribbon may not be wet; and care must be taken that the twine does not touch the frame of the door or window. As soon as any of the thunder clouds come over the kite, the pointed wire will draw the electric fire from them, and the kite, with all the twine, will be electrified, and the loose filaments of the twine will stand out every way, and be attracted by an approaching finger. And when the rain has wetted the kite and twine, so that it can conduct the electric fire freely, you will find it stream out plentifully from the key on the approach of your knuckle. At this key the phial may be charged; and from electric fire thus obtained, spirits may be kindled, and all other electric experiments be performed, which are usually done by the help of a rubbed glass globe or tube, and thereby the sameness of the electric matter with that of lightening completely demonstrated.

Reasons for Establishing the Colony of Georgia, 1733*

In the 1730s a number of influential Englishmen founded Georgia. Proprietors believed that the new settlements would protect South Carolina from the Spanish and thereby ensure British power in the region. They hoped, too, that Georgia would serve as a haven for England's "deserving" poor by providing economic opportunity—and consequently some degree of liberty—for disadvantaged Britons. Written by Benjamin Martin of London, the following essay underscores the philanthropic and practical concerns that led to the creation of the colony. The piece also expresses the benevolence that characterized many Enlightenment reformers.

If half of these [estimated four thousand persons imprisoned each year for debt, about one third of whom never recover], or only five hundred of them, were to be sent to Georgia every year to be incorporated with those foreign Protestants who are expelled their own country for religion, what great improvements might not be expected in our trade, when those, as well as foreigners, would be so many new subjects gained by England? For, while they are in prison, they are absolutely lost,—the public loses their labor, and their knowledge. If they take the benefit of the Act of Parliament that allows them liberty on their delivery of their all to their creditors, they come destitute into the world again. As they have no money and little credit, they find it almost impossible to get into business, especially when our trades are overstocked. They, therefore, by contracting new debts, must return again into prison, or, how honest soever their dispositions may be, by idleness and necessity will be forced into bad courses, such as begging, cheating, or robbing. These, then, likewise, are useless to the state; not only so, but dangerous. But these (it will be said) may be serviceable by their labor in the country. To force them to it, I am afraid, is impracticable; to suppose they will voluntarily do it, I am sure is unlikely. The Colony of Georgia will be proper asylum for these. This will make the act of parliament of more effect. Here they will have the best motive for industry; a possession of their own, and no possibility of subsisting without it.

I have heard it said that our prisons are the properest places for those that are thrown into them, by keeping them from being hurtful to others. Surely this way of thinking is something too severe. Are these people, with their liberty to lose our compassion? Are they to be shut up from our eyes, and excluded also from our hearts? Many of very honest dispositions fall into

---

*From Thaddeus M. Harris, *Biographical Memorials of James Oglethorpe, Founder of the Colony of Georgia in North America* (Boston: Freeman and Bolles, 1841), 343–45.

decay, nay, perhaps, because they are so, because they cannot allow themselves that latitude which others take to be successful. The ways that lead to a man's ruin are various. Some are undone by overtrading, others by want of trade; many by being responsible for others. Do all these deserve such hardship? If a man sees a friend, a brother, a father going to a prison, where felons are to be his society, want and sickness his sure attendants, and death, in all likelihood his only, but *quick* relief; if he stretches out his hand to save him from immediate slavery and ruin, he runs the risk of his own liberty, and at last loses it; is there any one who will say, this man is not an object of compassion? Not so, but of esteem, and worth preserving for his virtue? But supposing that idleness and intemperance are the usual cause of his ruin. Are these crimes adequate to such a punishment as confinement for life? But even yet granting that these unhappy people deserve no indulgence, it is certainly imprudent in any state to lose the benefit of the labor of so many thousands.

But the public loss, by throwing men into prison, is not confined to them only. They have many of them wives and children. These are, also, involved in their ruin. Being destitute of a support, they must perish, or else become a burden on their parishes by an inability to work, or a nuisance by their thefts. These, too, are useless to society.

In short, all those who can work yet are supported in idleness by any mistaken charity, or are sustained by their parishes, which are at this time, through all England overburdened by indolent and lazy poor;—all those who add nothing by their labor to the welfare of the state, are useless, burdensome, or dangerous to it. What is to be done with these necessitous? Nobody, I suppose, thinks that they should continue useless. It will be then an act of charity to these, and of merit to the public, for any one to propose, forward, and perfect a better expedient for making them useful. If he cannot, he is surely just to acquiesce, till a better be found, in the present design of settling them in Georgia.

Sinners in the Hands of an Angry God*

Early in the eighteenth century, an emotional reaction against the rationality of the Enlightenment led to a powerful revivalism known as the Great Awakening that swept Britain and its American colonies. The revival had a monumental influence on the development of American religion, education, and society, while the evangelical rejection of established authority eventually strengthened the movement for independence. New England minister Jonathan Edwards played a dominant role in the Awakening, and his passionate message is clearly evident in the following sermon.

. . . So that thus it is, that natural men are held in the hand of God over the pit of Hell; they have deserved the fiery pit, and are already sentenced to it; and God is dreadfully provoked, his anger is as great towards them as to those that are actually suffering the executions of the fierceness of his wrath in hell, and they have done nothing in the least to appease or abate that anger, neither is God in the least bound by any promise to hold 'em up one moment; the devil is waiting for them, hell is gaping for them, the flames gather and flash about them, and would fain lay hold on them and swallow them up; the fire pent up in their own hearts is struggling to break out; and they have no interest in any Mediator, there are no means within reach that can be any security to them. In short they have no refuge, nothing to take hold of; all that preserves them every moment is the mere arbitrary will, and uncovenanted, unobliged forbearance of an incensed God. . . .

---

*From *Selected Sermons of Jonathan Edwards,* ed. H. Norman Gardiner (New York: The Macmillan Company, 1904), 78–97.

This that you have heard is the case of every one of you that are out of Christ. The world of misery, that lake of burning brimstone, is extended abroad under you. *There* is the dreadful pit of the glowing flames of the wrath of God; there is hell's wide gaping mouth open; and you have nothing to stand upon, nor anything to take hold of. There is nothing between you and hell but the air; 'tis only the power and mere pleasure of God that holds you up.

Your wickedness makes you as it were heavy as lead, and to tend downwards with great weight and pressure towards hell; and if God should let you go, you should immediately sink and swiftly descend and plunge into the bottomless gulf, and your healthy constitution, and your own care and prudence, and best contrivance, and all your righteousness, would have no more influence to uphold you and keep you out of hell than a spider's web would have to stop a falling rock. Were it not that so is the sovereign pleasure of God, the earth would not bear you one moment; for you are a burden to it; the creation groans with you; the creature is made subject to the bondage of your corruption, not willingly; the sun don't willingly shine upon you to give you light to serve sin and Satan; the earth don't willingly yield her increase to satisfy your lusts; nor is it willingly a stage for your wickedness to be acted upon; the air don't willingly serve you for breath to maintain the flame of life in your vitals, while you spend your life in the service of God's enemies. God's creatures are good, and were made for men to serve God with, and don't willingly subserve to any other purpose, and groan when they are abused to purposes directly contrary to their nature and end. And the world would spew you out, were it not for the sovereign hand of him who hath subjected it in hope. There are the black clouds of God's wrath now hanging directly over your heads, full of the dreadful storms, and big with thunder; and were it not for the restraining hand of God, it would immediately burst forth upon you. The sovereign pleasure of God, for the present, stays his rough wind; otherwise it would come with fury, and your destruction would come like a whirlwind, and you would be like the chaff of the summer threshing floor. . . .

The God that holds you over the pit of hell, much as one holds a spider or some loathsome insect over the fire, abhors you, and is dreadfully provoked; his wrath towards you burns like fire; he looks upon you as worthy of nothing else, but to be cast into fire; he is of purer eyes than to bear to have you in his sight; you are ten thousand times so abominable in his eyes, as the most hateful and venomous serpent is in ours. You have offended him infinitely more than ever a stubborn rebel did his prince: and yet it is nothing but his hand that holds you from falling into the fire every moment. 'Tis ascribed to nothing else, that you did go to hell the last night; that you was suffered to awake again in this world after you closed your eyes to sleep; and there is no other reason to be given why you have not dropped into hell since you arose in the morning, but that God's hand has held you up. There is no other reason to be given why you haven't gone to hell since you have sat here in the house of God, provoking his pure eyes by your sinful wicked manner of attending his solemn worship. Yea, there is nothing else that is to be given as a reason why you don't this very moment drop down into hell.

O sinner! consider the fearful danger you are in. 'Tis a great furnace of wrath, a wide and bottomless pit, full of the fire of wrath, that you are held over in the hand of that God whose wrath is provoked and incensed as much against you as against many of the damned in hell. You hang by a slender thread, with the flames of divine wrath flashing about it, and ready every moment to singe it and burn it asunder; and you have no interest in any Mediator, and nothing to lay hold of to save yourself, nothing to keep off the flames of wrath, nothing of your own, nothing that you ever have done, nothing that you can do, to induce God to spare you one moment. . . .

How dreadful is the state of those that are daily and hourly in danger of this great wrath and infinite misery! But this is the dismal case of every soul in this congregation that has not been born again, however moral and strict, sober and religious, they may otherwise be. Oh, that you would consider it, whether you be young or old! There is reason to think that there are many in this congregation now hearing this discourse, that will actually be subjects of this very misery to all eternity. We know not who they are, or in what seats they sit, or what thoughts they now have. It may be they are now at ease, and hear all these things without much disturbance, and are now flattering themselves that they are not the persons, promising themselves that they shall escape. If we knew that there was one person, and but one, in the whole congregation, that was to be the subject of this misery, what an awful thing it would be to think of! If we knew who it was, what an awful sight it would be to see such a person! How might all the rest of the congregation lift up a lamentable and bitter cry over him! But alas! instead of one, how many is it likely will remember this discourse in hell! And it would be a wonder, if some that are now present should not be in hell in a very short time, before this year is out. And it would be no wonder if some persons that now sit here in some seats of this meeting-house in health, and quiet and secure, should be there before to-morrow morning. Those of you that finally continue in a natural condition, that shall keep out of hell the longest, will be there in a little time! 'Tis doubtless the case that of some that heretofore you have seen and known, that never deserved hell more than you and that heretofore appeared as likely to have been now alive as you. Their case is past all hope; they are crying in extreme misery and perfect despair. But here you are in the land of the living and in the house of God, and have an opportunity to obtain salvation. What would not those poor, damned, hopeless souls give for one day's such opportunity as you now enjoy!

And now you have an extraordinary opportunity, a day wherein Christ has flung the door of mercy wide open, and stands in the door calling and crying with a loud voice to poor sinners; a day wherein many are flocking to him and pressing into the Kingdom of God. Many are daily coming from the east, west, north and south; many that were very likely in the same miserable condition that you are in are in now a happy state, with their hearts filled with love to him that has loved them and washed them from their sins in his own blood, and rejoicing in the hope of the glory of God. How awful it is to be left behind at such a day! . . .

Are there not many here that have lived long in the world that are not to this day born again, and so are aliens from the commonwealth of Israel and done nothing ever since they have lived but treasure up wrath against the day of wrath? Oh, sirs, your case in an especial manner is extremely dangerous; your guilt and hardness of heart is extremely great. . . . You had need to consider yourselves and wake thoroughly out of sleep; you cannot bear the fierceness and the wrath of the infinite God.

And you that are young men and young women, will you neglect this precious season that you now enjoy, when so many others of your age are renouncing all youthful vanities and flocking to Christ? You especially have now an extraordinary opportunity; but if you neglect it, it will soon be with you as it is with those persons that spent away all the precious days of youth in sin and are now come to such a dreadful pass in blindness and hardness.

And you children that are unconverted, don't you know that you are going down to hell to bear the dreadful wrath of that God that is now angry with you every day and every night? Will you be content to be children of the devil, when so many other children in the land are converted and are become the holy and happy children of the King of kings?

And let every one that is yet out of Christ and hanging over the pit of hell, whether they be old men and women or middle-aged or young people or little children, now hearken to the loud calls of God's word and providence. . . . God seems now to be hastily gathering in the elect in all parts of the land; and probably the bigger part of adult persons that ever shall be saved will be brought in now in a little time, and . . . the election will obtain and the rest will be blinded. If this should be the case with you, you will eternally curse this day, and will curse the day that ever you was born to see such a season of the pouring out of God's Spirit, and will wish that

Harcourt Brace & Company

you had died and gone to hell before you had seen it. Now . . . the axe is in an extraordinary manner laid at the root of the trees, that every tree that bringeth not forth good fruit may be hewn down and cast into the fire.

Therefore let every one that is out of Christ now awake and fly from the wrath to come. The wrath of Almighty God is now undoubtedly hanging over great part of this congregation. Let every one fly out of Sodom. *"Haste and escape for your lives, look not behind you, escape to the mountain, lest ye be consumed."*

Discussion

1. Economic policies often involve matters of power as well as concerns for liberty or equality. How do the documents regarding paper money reveal such issues? What does the selection on Georgia suggest about the relationship between economic concerns and power and liberty?

2. What does Cato's discourse on the nature of laws imply about the legitimate power of government? What role does virtue play in society? How might the essay have influenced American attitudes toward liberty?

3. In his sermon, Jonathan Edwards described the awesome power of God, yet the Great Awakening encouraged individualism and religious toleration. Is there anything in the document that suggests how the individual might have gained importance during the revival? Does Edwards appear to advocate toleration in his message?

4. How do the documents reveal the Anglicization of American society during the eighteenth century? Do any of the documents show the emergence of distinctive American ideals; if so, how?

Chapter 5
War, Victory, and Imperial Reform

Causes often use religious symbolism when they want to suggest the righteousness of their cause and the evil of their opponents. This often meant having the devil appear next to your opponent, suggesting a common link between their ideas.

*C*olonial wars plagued the mid-eighteenth century as European powers fought among themselves and against Native Americans to gain control over the territory east of the Mississippi River. English colonists viewed New Spain and New France as the epitome of tyranny, so in their eyes the struggle for the continent was also a battle to preserve liberty. That battle seemed to have been fought successfully when Great Britain defeated France in 1763 and gained extensive new colonial holdings. Faced with defiant Indians, a huge empire, and burdensome debt, however, royal authorities determined to enact a series of comprehensive imperial reforms. To many Americans, those reforms seemed to pose as serious a threat to their rights as had ever been presented by the French and Spanish. Ironically, then, at the height of British power in North America, the colonies would begin to resist Parliament's authority.

The Albany Plan, 1754*

*B*enjamin Franklin proposed a unified colonial government as a means to meet the French and Indian threat. The Albany Congress modified the proposal and presented it to the various general assemblies, which roundly rejected the Albany Plan. According to Franklin, the colonies feared that the president-general could assert undue power, and in 1754 colonists certainly did not trust each other enough to turn authority over to a central council. Royal authorities also ultimately ruled against the plan because they doubted that the colonists could cooperate and because they feared the precedent of such a union. Nevertheless, Franklin remained dedicated to unity, and, despite the failure of his first effort to bring the thirteen colonies together, his commitment would bear fruit in the years after 1763.

That the said general government be administered by a President-General, to be appointed and supported by the crown; and a Grand Council, to be chosen by the representatives of the people of the several colonies met in their respective Assemblies—who shall meet for the first time at the city of Philadelphia, being called by the President-General as soon as conveniently may be after his appointment.

That there shall be a new election of the members of the Grand Council every three years; and, on the death or resignation of any member, his place should be supplied by a new choice at the next sitting of the Assembly of the colony he represented.

That after the first three years, when the proportion of money arising out of each colony to the general treasury can be known, the number of members to be chosen shall from time to time, in all ensuing elections, be regulated by that proportion, yet so as that the number to be chosen by any one province be not more than seven, nor less than two.

That the Grand Council shall meet once in every year, and oftener if occasion require, at such time and place as they shall adjourn to at the last preceding meeting, or as they shall be called to meet at by the President-General on any emergency; he having first obtained in writing the consent of seven of the members to such call, and sent due and timely notice to the whole.

---

*"Plan of Union," in *The Works of Benjamin Franklin,* 10 vols., ed. Jared Sparks (Chicago: Townsend MacCoun, 1882), III:36–55.

That the Grand Council have power to choose their speaker; and shall neither be dissolved, prorogued, nor continued sitting longer than six weeks at one time, without their own consent or the special command of the crown.

That the members of the Grand Council shall be allowed for their service ten shillings sterling per diem, during their session and journey to and from the place of meeting; twenty miles to be reckoned a day's journey.

That the assent of the President-General be requisite to all acts of the Grand Council, and that it be his office and duty to cause them to be carried into execution.

That the President-General, with the advice of the Grand Council, hold or direct all Indian treaties, in which the general interest of the colonies may be concerned; and make peace or declare war with Indian nations.

That they make such laws as they judge necessary for regulating all Indian trade.

That they make all purchases, from the Indians for the crown, of lands not now within the bounds of particular colonies, or that shall be within their bounds when some of them are reduced to more convenient dimensions.

That they make new settlements on such purchases, by granting lands in the King's name, reserving a quit-rent to the crown for the use of the general treasury.

That they make laws for regulating and governing such new settlements, till the crown shall think fit to form them into particular governments.

That they raise and pay soldiers and build forts for the defence of any of the colonies, and equip vessels of force to guard the coasts and protect the trade on the ocean, lakes, or great rivers; but they shall not impress men in any colony, without the consent of the legislature.

That for these purposes, they have power to make laws, and lay and levy such general duties, imposts, or taxes, as to them shall appear most equal and just (considering the ability and other circumstances of the inhabitants in the several colonies), and such as may be collected with the least inconvenience to the people; rather discouraging luxury, than loading industry with unnecessary burthens.

That they may appoint a General Treasurer and Particular Treasurer in each government, when necessary; and from time to time may order the sums in the treasury of each government into the general treasury; or draw on them for special payments, as they find most convenient.

Yet no money to issue, but by joint orders of the President-General and Grand Council; except where sums have been appropriated to particular purposes, and the President-General is previously empowered by an act to draw such sums.

That the general accounts shall be yearly settled and reported to the several Assemblies.

That a quorum of the Grand Council, empowered to act with the President-General, do consist of twenty-five members; among whom there shall be one or more from a majority of the colonies.

That the laws made by them for the purposes aforesaid shall not be repugnant, but, as near as may be, agreeable to the laws of England, and shall be transmitted to the King in Council for approbation, as soon as may be after their passing; and if not disapproved within three years after presentation, to remain in force.

That, in case of the death of the President-General, the Speaker of the Grand Council for the time being shall succeed, and be vested with the same powers and authorities, to continue till the King's pleasure be known.

That all military commission officers, whether for land or sea service, to act under this general constitution, shall be nominated by the President-General; but the approbation of the Grand Council is to be obtained, before they receive their commissions. And all civil officers are to be nominated by the Grand Council, and to receive the President-General's approbation before they officiate.

Harcourt Brace & Company

But, in case of vacancy by death or removal of any officer civil or military under this constitution, the Governor of the province in which such vacancy happens may appoint, till the pleasure of the President-General and Grand Council can be known.

That the particular military as well as civil establishments in each colony remain in their present state, the general constitution notwithstanding; and that on sudden emergencies any colony may defend itself, and lay the accounts thence arising before the President-General and Grand Council, who may allow and order payment of the same, as far as they judge such accounts just and reasonable.

Questions of Arbitrary Power and Liberty*

In 1763, the radical journalist John Wilkes became a notorious spokesman for liberty with the following virulent attack, in the *North Briton* No. 45, on King George III and the Bute and Grenville administrations. Questioning the motives for, and the provisions of, the peace settlement with France, he condemned the Treaty of Paris and the king's speech that defended it at the close of Parliament in April. More importantly, he implored his readers to ignore the government's call for acceptance of the treaty and warned them of the threat to liberty that despotic monarchs presented. In the second document that follows, parliament assured the king that they would prosecute Wilkes, an effort that helped make him a martyr in the eyes of his followers. His willingness to take so bold a stand, and the penalty he paid for it, won Wilkes the admiration of many Americans by the end of the 1760s.

. . . Every friend of his country must lament that a prince of so many great and amiable qualities, whom England truly reveres, can be brought to give the sanction of his sacred name to the most odious measures, and to the most unjustifiable public declarations, from a throne ever renowned for truth, honour, and unsullied virtue. . .

The *Preliminary Articles of Peace* were such as have drawn the contempt of mankind on our wretched negotiators. All our most valuable conquests are agreed to be restored, and the *East-India company* would have been infallibly ruined by a single article of this fallacious and baneful negotiation. No hireling of the minister has been hardy enough to dispute this; yet the minister himself has made our sovereign declare, *the satisfaction which he felt at the re-establishment of peace upon conditions so honouroble to his crown, and so beneficial to his people.* As to the *entire approbation* of parliament, which is so vainly boasted of, the world knows how that was obtained. The large debt on the *Civil List,* already above half a year in arrear, shews pretty clear the transactions of the winter. It is, however, remarkable, that the minister's speech dwells on the *entire approbation* given by parliament to the *Preliminary Articles,* which I will venture to say, he must by this time be ashamed of; for he has been brought to confess the total want of that knowledge, accuracy and precision, by which such immense advantages, both of trade and territory, were sacrificed to our inveterate enemies. Those gross blunders, are, indeed, in some measure set right by the *Definitive Treaty;* yet the most important articles, relative to *cession, commerce,* and the FISHERY, remain as they were, with respect to the *French.* The proud and feeble *Spaniard* too does not RENOUNCE, but only DESISTS *from all pretensions, which he may have formed to the right of fishing*—where? Only *about the island of* NEWFOUNDLAND—till a favourouble opportunity arises of *insisting* on it, *there, as well as elsewhere.*

---

*From "Opposition to Arbitrary Power," in *American History Told by Contemporaries,* 5 vols., ed. Albert Bushnell Hart (New York: The Macmillan Company, 1914), II:378–80.

The minister cannot forbear, even in the *King's Speech,* insulting us with a dull repetition of the word *æconomy.* I did not expect so soon to hear that word again, after it had been so lately exploded, and more than once by a most numerous audience, *hissed* off the stage of our *English* theatres. It is held in derision by the *voice of the people,* and every tongue loudly proclaims the universal contempt, in which these empty professions are held by *this* nation. Let the public be informed of a single instance of *æconomy,* except indeed in the household. . . . Lord *Ligonier* is now no longer at the head of the army; but Lord *Bute* in effect is; I mean that every preferment given by the crown will be found still to be obtained by *his* enormous influence, and to be bestowed only on the creatures of the *Scottish* faction. The nation is still in the same deplorable state, while *he* governs, and can make the tools of *his* power pursue the same odious measures. Such a retreat, as he intends, can only mean the personal indemnity, which, I hope, guilt will never find from an injured nation. The negotiations of the late inglorious *peace* and the entire *excise,* will haunt him wherever he goes, and the terrors of the just resentment which he must be sure to meet from a brave and insulted people, and which must finally crush him, will be for ever before his eyes.

In vain will such a minister, or the foul dregs of his power, the tools of corruption and despotism, preach up in the speech *that spirit of concord, and that obedience to the laws, which is essential to good order.* They have sent the *spirit of discord* through the land, and I will prophecy, that it will never be extinguished, but by the extinction of their power. Is the *spirit of concord* to go hand in hand with the PEACE and EXCISE, through this nation? Is it to be expected between an insolent EXCISEMAN, and *a peer, gentleman, freeholder, or farmer,* whose private houses are now made liable to be entered and searched at pleasure? *Gloucestershire, Herefordshire,* and in general all the *cyder* counties, are not surely the *several counties* which are alluded to in the *speech.* The *spirit of concord* hath not gone forth among them, but the *spirit of liberty* has, and a noble opposition has been given to the wicked instruments of oppression. A nation as sensible as the *English,* will see that a *spirit of concord* when they are oppressed, means a tame submission to injury, and that a *spirit of liberty* ought then to arise, and I am sure ever will, in proportion to the weight of the grievance they feel. *Every* legal *attempt of a contrary tendency* to the *spirit of concord* will be deemed a justifiable resistance, warranted by the *spirit of the English constitution.*

A despotic minister will always endeavour to dazzle his prince with high-flown ideas of the *prerogative* and *honour* of the *crown,* which the minister will make a parade of *firmly maintaining.* I wish as much as any man on the kingdom to see the *honour of the crown* maintained in a manner truly becoming *Royalty.* . . .

The *Stuart* line has ever been intoxicated with the slavish doctrines of the *absolute, independent, unlimited* power of the crown. Some of the line were so weakly advised, as to endeavour to reduce them into practice; but the *English* nation was too spirited to suffer the least encroachment on the antient liberties of this kingdom. The *King of England* is only the first magistrate of this country; but is invested by the law with the whole executive power. He is, however, responsible to his people for the due execution of the royal functions, in the choice of ministers, &c. equal with the meanest of his subjects in his particular duty. The personal character of our present amiable sovereign makes us easy and happy that so great a power is lodged in such hands; but the *favourite* has given too just cause for him to escape the general odium. The *prerogative* of the crown is to exert the constitutional powers entrusted to it not of blind favour and partiality, but of wisdom and judgment. This is the spirit of our constitution. The people too have their *prerogative,* and I hope the fine words of DRYDEN will be engraved on our hearts:

Freedom *is the English Subject's* Prerogative

Harcourt Brace & Company

Parliament Responds to John Wilkes[*]

Most gracious sovereign,

WE your majesty's most dutiful and faithful subjects, the lords spiritual and temporal, and commons, in parliament assembled, having taken into our considerations a late false, scandalous and seditious libel, intituled, The North Briton, No 45, think it our indispensable duty to express our surprize and indignation at finding, that neither the public nor private virtues which so eminently intitle your majesty to the highest veneration, as well as to the most grateful and loyal attachment of all your subjects, nor the gracious expressions of your tender care and affection for your people, in your majesty's speech from the throne at the end of the last session of parliament, which has been thus infamously traduced, should have been sufficient to secure your majesty from so insolent and unexampled an indignity.

Such, indeed, has been your majesty's uniform adherence to the principles of our happy constitution, and such the uninterrupted harmony and correspondence between your majesty and your parliament, that it is no wonder to see that the same audacious hand, which hath dared thus grossly to affront your majesty, should, at the same time, violate the other sacred regards prescribed by the laws and constitution of this country, aspersing and calumniating every branch of the legislature, and endeavouring to excite, among all ranks of your majesty's subjects, such a spirit of discord and disobedience, as could end in nothing but the total subversion of all lawful government.

Permit us also to express to your majesty our firm persuasion and just confidence, that this most extravagant and outrageous attempt will prove as impotent as it is wicked; that, instead of answering those purposes for which it appears to have been calculated, it will, on the contrary, serve to excite in your faithful subjects the abhorrence of such dangerous practices, to unite them more firmly in their zealous attachment to your majesty's person and government, and in a due reverence for the authority of the legislature; and lastly, that in consequence of your majesty's directions to prosecute the authors of this infamous bill, it will bring such punishment on those who shall be found guilty of so atrocious a crime, as the laws of their country have prescribed, and as the public justice and safety shall demand.

The Proclamation of 1763[†]

King George III announced the following proclamation in an effort to organize and manage the new empire while also honoring English promises to protect Indian territory from white encroachment. The royal order established new colonial governments, and it tried to control settlement by limiting migration west of the Appalachian watershed. Many Americans deplored, and some ignored, the proclamation, because they believed that the recent war had been fought to open the west to English colonization. Prohibiting access to that land, they believed, denied them their traditional right to acquire property. Having defeated the French, they were now dismayed to realize that their own government threatened their liberty to expand.

---

[*]*The Annual Register, or a View of the History, Politicks, and Literature for the Year 1764* (London: J. Dodsley, 1765), 171.

[†]*The Annual Register, or a View of the History, Politicks, and Literature for the Year 1763,* 5th ed. (London: J. Dodsley, 1782), 208–13.

By the King. A Proclamation. George R.

Whereas we have taken into our royal consideration the extensive and valuable acquisitions in America, secured to our crown by the late definitive treaty of peace concluded at Paris the 10th day of February last; and being desirous that all our loving subjects, as well of our kingdom as of our colonies in America, may avail themselves, with all convenient speed, of the great benefits and advantages which must accrue therefrom to their commerce, manufactures, and navigation; we have thought fit, with the advice of our privy council, to issue this our royal proclamation, hereby to publish and declare to all our loving subjects, that we have, with the advice of our said privy council, granted out letters patent under our great seal of Great Britain, to erect, within the countries and islands ceded and confirmed to us by said treaty, four distinct and separate governments, stiled and called by the names of Quebec, East Florida, West Florida, and Grenada, and limited and bounded as follows, viz.

First, the government of Quebec, bounded on the Labrador coast by the river St. John, and from thence by a line drawn from the head of the river, through the like St. John, to the South end of the lake Nipissim; from whence the said line, crossing the river St. Lawrence and the lake Champlain in 45 degrees of North latitude, passes along the High Lands, which divide the rivers that empty themselves into the said river St. Lawrence, from those which fall into the sea; and also along the North coast of the Baye de Chaleurs, and the coast of the Gulph of St. Lawrence to Cape Rosieres, and from thence crossing the mouth of the river St. Lawrence by the West end of the island of Anticosti, terminates at the said river St. John.

Secondly, The government of East Florida, bounded to the Westward by the Gulph of Mexico and the Apalachicola river; to the Northward, by a line drawn from that of the said river to where the Catahouchee and Flint rivers meet, to the source of St. Mary's river, and by the course of the said river to the Atlantic Ocean; and to the East and South by the Atlantic Ocean, and the Gulph of Florida, including all islands within six leagues of the sea coast.

Thirdly, The government of West Florida, bounded to the Southward by the Gulph of Mexico, including all islands within six leagues of the coast from the river Apalachicola to lake Pontchartrain; to the Westward by the said lake, the lake Maurepas, and the river Missisippi; to the Northward, by a line drawn due East from that part of the river Missisippi which lies in thirty-one degrees North latitude, to the river Apalachicola, or Catahouchee; and to the Eastward by the said river.

Fourthly, The government of Grenada, comprehending the island of that name, together with the Grenadines, and the islands of Dominico, St. Vincent, and Tobago.

And to the end that the open and free fishery of our subjects may be extended to, and carried on upon the coast of Labrador and the adjacent islands, we have thought fit, with the advice of our said privy council, to put all that coast, from the river St. John's to Hudson's Streights, together with the islands lying upon the said coast, under the care and inspection of our governor of Newfoundland.

We have also, with the advice of our privy council, thought fit to annex the islands of St. John and Cape Breton, or Isle Royale, with the lesser islands adjacent thereto, to our government of Nova Scotia.

We have also, with the advice of our privy council aforesaid, annexed to our province of Georgia, all the lands lying between the rivers Attamaha and St. Mary's.

And whereas it will contribute greatly to the speedy settling our said new governments, that our loving subjects should be informed of our paternal care for the security of the liberty and properties of those who are, and shall become, inhabitants thereof; we have thought fit to publish and declare, by this our proclamation, that we have, in the letters patent under our great seal of Great Britain, by which the said governments are constituted, given express power and direction to our governors of our said colonies respectively, that so soon as the state and

Harcourt Brace & Company

circumstances of the said colonies will admit thereof, they shall, with the advice and consent of the members of our council, summon and call general assemblies within the said governments respectively, in such manner and form as is used and directed in those colonies and provinces in America, which are under our immediate government; and we have also given power to the said governors, with the consent of our said councils, and the representatives of the people, so to be summoned as aforesaid, to make, constitute, and ordain laws, statutes, and ordinances for the public peace, welfare, and good government of our said colonies, and of the people and inhabitants thereof, as near as may be, agreeable to the laws of England, and under such regulations and restrictions as are used in other colonies; and in the mean time, and until such assemblies can be called as aforesaid, all the persons inhabiting in, or resorting to, our said colonies, may confide in our royal protection for the enjoyment of the benefit of the laws of our realm of England; for which purpose we have given power under our great seal to the governors of our said colonies respectively, to erect and constitute, with the advice of our said councils respectively, courts of judicature and public justice within our said colonies, for the hearing and determining all causes, as well criminal as civil according to law and equity, and, as near as may be, agreeable to the laws of England, with liberty to all persons who may think themselves aggrieved by the sentence of such courts, in all civil cases, to appeal, under the usual limitations and restrictions, to us, in our privy council.

We have also thought fit, with the advice of our privy council aforesaid, to give unto the governors and councils of our said three new colonies upon the continent, full power and authority to settle and agree with the inhabitants of our said new colonies, or to any other person who shall resort thereto, for such lands, tenements, and hereditaments, as are now, or hereafter shall be, in our power to dispose of, and them to grant to any such person or persons, upon such terms, and under such moderate quit rents, services, and acknowledgments as have been appointed and settled in other colonies, and under such other conditions as shall appear to us to be necessary and expedient for the advantage of the grantees, and the improvement and settlement of our said colonies.

And whereas we are desirous, upon all occasions, to testify our royal sense and approbation of the conduct and bravery of the officers and soldiers of our armies, and to reward the same, we do hereby command and impower our governors of our said three new colonies, and other our governors of our several provinces on the continent of North America, to grant, without fee or reward, to such reduced officers as have served in North America, during the late war, and are actually residing there, and shall personally apply for the same, the following quantities of land, subject, at the expiration of ten years, to the same quit-rents as other lands are subject to in the province within which they are granted, as also subject to the same conditions of cultivation and improvement, viz.

To every person having the rank of a field officer, 5000 acres.

To every captain, 3000 acres.

To every subaltern or staff officer, 2000 acres.

To every non-commission officer, 200 acres.

To every private man 50 acres. . . .

And whereas it is just and reasonable, and essential to our interest, and the security of our colonies, that the several nations or tribes of Indians, with whom we are connected, and who live under our protection, should not be molested or disturbed in the possession of such parts of our dominions and territories as, not having been ceded to, or purchased by us, are reserved to them or any of them, as their hunting grounds; we do therefore, with the advice of our privy council, declare it to be our royal will and pleasure, that no governor, or commander in chief, in any of our colonies of Quebec, East Florida, or West Florida, do presume, upon any pretence whatever, to grant warrants of survey, or pass any patents for lands beyond the bounds of their respective governments, as described in their commissions; as also that no governor or commander in chief of our other colonies or plantations in America, do presume for the present, and until our further pleasure be known, to grant warrant of survey, or pass patents for any lands beyond the heads or sources of any of the rivers which fall into the Atlantic Ocean from the west or north-west; or upon any lands whatever, which not having been ceded to, or purchased by us, as aforesaid, are reserved to the said Indians, or any of them.

And we do further declare it to be our royal will and pleasure, for the present, as aforesaid, to reserve under our sovereignty, protection, and dominion, for the use of the said Indians, all the land and territories not included within the limits of our said three new governments, or within the limits of the territory granted to the Hudson's Bay company; as also all the land and territories lying to the westward of the sources of the rivers which fall into the sea from the west and north-west as aforesaid; and we do hereby strictly forbid, on pain of our displeasure, all our loving subjects from making any purchases or settlements whatever, or taking possession of any of the lands above referred, without our special leave and licence for that purpose first attained.

And we do further strictly forbid and require all persons whatever, who have either wilfully or inadvertently seated themselves upon any lands within the countries above described, or upon any other lands within the countries, which not having been ceded to, or purchased by us, are still reserved to the said Indians as aforesaid, forth with to remove themselves from such settlements.

And whereas great frauds and abuses have been committed in the purchasing lands of the Indians, to the great prejudice of our interests, and the great dissatisfaction of the said Indians; in order therefore to prevent such irregularities for the future, and to the end that the Indians may be convinced of our justice and determined resolution to remove all reasonable cause of discontent, we do, with the advice of our privy council, strictly enjoin and require, that no private person do presume to make any purchase from the said Indians of any lands reserved to the said Indians within those parts of our colonies where we have thought proper to allow settlement; but if at any time any of the said Indians should be inclined to dispose of the said lands, the same shall be purchased only for us, in our name, at some public meeting or assembly of the said Indians, to be held for that purpose by the governor or commander in chief of our colony respectively within which they shall lie; and in case they shall lie within the limits of any proprietaries, conformable to such directions and instructions as we or they shall think proper to give for that purpose; and we do, by the advice of our privy council, declare and enjoin, that the trade with the said Indians shall be free and open to all our subjects whatever, provided that every person who may incline to trade with the said Indians, do take out a licence for carrying on such trade, from the governor or commander in chief of any of our colonies respectively, where such persons shall reside, and also give security to, observe such regulations as we shall at any time think fit, by ourselves or commissaries, to be appointed for this purpose, to direct and appoint for the benefit of the said trade; and we do hereby authorize, enjoin, and require the governors and commanders in chief of all our colonies respectively, as well those under our immediate government, as those under the government and direction of proprietaries, to grant such licences without fee or reward, taking especial care to insert therein a condition that such licence shall be void, and the security forfeited, in case the person to whom the same is granted, shall refuse or neglect to observe such regulations as we shall think proper to prescribe as aforesaid.

And we do further expressly enjoin and require all officers whatever, as well military as those employed in the management and direction of Indian affairs, within the territories reserved, as aforesaid, for the use of the said Indians, to seize and apprehend all persons whatever, who standing charged with treasons, misprisions of treasons, murders, or other felonies or misdemeanours, shall fly from justice and take refuge in the said territory, and to send them under a proper guard to the colony where the crime was committed of which they shall stand accused, in order to take their trial for the same.

Given at the court of St. James's, the 7th day of October 1763, in the third year of our reign. GOD save the KING.

The Sugar Act*

Following the French and Indian War, Great Britain tightened trade regulations in an effort to increase imperial income. The Sugar Act of 1764 tried to end smuggling, and thereby enhance custom's collections, by making it easier for British officials to crack down on illegal trading. That effort certainly made smugglers, such as John Hancock, angry with the government, but the law had broader implications. The bold statement that the tax was designed to defray the costs of the empire by raising revenues in the colonies concerned many Americans. They questioned the necessity of huge imperial expenses. More importantly, however, the legitimacy of taxes levied without their consent became a critical issue in the debate that eventually led to rebellion.

WHEREAS it is expedient that new provisions and regulations should be established for improving the revenue of this Kingdom, and for extending and securing the navigation and commerce between Great Britain *and your Majesty's dominion in* America, *which by the peace have been so happily enlarged; and whereas it is just and necessary, that a revenue be raised, in your Majesty's said dominion in* America, *for defraying the expenses of defending, protecting and securing the same; we, your Majesty's most dutiful and loyal subjects, the commons of* Great Britain. *in parliament assembled, being desirous to make some provision, in this present session of parliament, towards raising the said revenue in* America, *have resolved to give and grant unto your Majesty the several rates and duties hereinafter mentioned;* and do most humbly beseech your Majesty, that it may be enacted; and be it enacted . . . , That from and after the twenty ninth day of *September,* one thousand seven hundred and sixty four, there shall be raised, levied, collected, and paid, unto his Majesty . . . , for and upon all white or clayed sugars of the produce or manufacture of any colony or plantation in *America,* not under the dominion of his Majesty . . . ; for and upon indigo, and coffee of foreign produce or manufacture; for and upon all wines (except *French* wine;) for and upon all wrought silks, bengals, and stuffs, mixed with silk or herba, of the manufacture of *Persia, China,* or *East India,* and all calico painted, dyed, printed, or stained there; and for and upon all foreign linen cloth called *Cambrick* and *French* Lawns; which shall be imported or brought into any colony or plantation in *America,* which now is, or hereafter may be, under the dominion of his Majesty . . . , the several rates and duties following; that is to say,

For every hundred weight avoirdupois of such foreign white or clayed sugars, one pound two shillings, over and above all other duties imposed by any former act of parliament.

For every pound avoirdupois of such foreign indigo, six pence.

For every hundred weight avoirdupois of such foreign coffee, which shall be imported from any place except *Great Britain,* two pounds, nineteen shillings, and nine pence.

For every ton of wine of the growth of the *Madeiras,* or of any other island or place from which such wine may be lawfully imported, and which shall be so imported from such islands or places, the sum of seven pounds.

For every ton of *Portugal, Spanish,* or any other wine (except *French* wine;) imported from Great Britain, the sum of ten shillings.

---

*Select Charters and Other Documents Illustrative of American History, 1606–1776, ed. William MacDonald (New York: The Macmillan Company, 1910), 272–81.

For every pound weight avoirdupois of wrought silks, bengals, and stuffs, mixed with silk or herba, of the manufacture of *Persia, China,* or *East India,* imported from *Great Britain,* two shillings.

For every piece of calico painted, dyed, printed, or stained in *Persia, China,* or *East India,* imported from *Great Britain,* two shillings and six pence.

For every piece of foreign linen cloth called *Cambrick,* imported from *Great Britain,* three shillings.

For every piece of *French lawn* imported from *Great Britain* three shillings. . . .

II. And it is hereby further enacted . . . That from and after . . . [September 29, 1764] . . . there shall also be raised, levied, collected, and paid unto his Majesty . . . , for and upon all coffee and pimento of the growth and produce of any *British* colony or plantation in *America,* which shall be there laden on any *British* ship or vessel, to be carried out from thence or any place whatsoever, except *Great Britain,* the several rates and duties following; that is to say,

III. For every hundred weight avoirdupois of such *British* coffee, seven shillings.

For every pound weight avoirdupois of such *British* pimento, one halfpenny. . . .

VI. And be it further enacted . . . , That in lieu and instead of the rate and duty imposed by the . . . act on melasses and syrups, there shall, from and after . . . [September 29, 1764] . . . , be raised, levied, collected, and paid unto his Majesty . . . , for and upon every gallon of melasses or syrups, being the growth, produce, or manufacture, of any colony or plantation in *America,* not under the dominion of his Majesty . . . , which shall be imported or brought into any colony or plantation in *America,* which now is, or hereafter may be, under the dominion of his Majesty . . . , the sum of three pence. . . .

XI. And it is hereby further enacted . . . , That all monies, from and after . . . [September 29, 1764 . . . , shall arise by the several rates and duties which, from and after the said [date], shall be raised upon sugars and panales, by virtues of the said act made in the sixth year of the reign of his said late Majesty King *George* the Second (except the necessary charges of raising, collecting, levying, recovering, answering, paying, and accounting for the same) shall be paid into the receipt of his Majesty's Exchequer, and shall be entered separate and apart from all other monies paid or payable to his Majesty . . . ; and shall there be reserved, to be, from time to time, disposed of by parliament, towards defraying the necessary expences of defending, protecting, and securing, the *British* colonies and plantations in *America.* . . .

XVIII. And be it further enacted . . . , That from and after . . . [September 29, 1764] . . . , no rum or spirits of the produce or manufacture of any of the colonies or plantations in *America,* not in the possession or under the dominion of his Majesty . . . , shall be imported or brought into any of the colonies or plantations in *America* which now are, or hereafter may be, in the possession or under the dominion of his Majesty . . . , upon forfeiture of all such rum or spirits, together with the ship or vessel in which the same shall be imported, with the tackle, apparel, and furniture thereof; to be seized by any officer or officers of his Majesty's customs, and prosecuted in such manner and form as herein after is expressed; any law, custom, or usage, to the contrary notwithstanding. . . .

XXIII. And whereas by an act of parliament made in the twelfth year of the reign of King *Charles* the Second, intituled, *An act for encouraging and increasing shipping and navigation,* and several subsequent acts of parliament which are now in force, it is, amongst other things, directed, that for every ship or vessel that shall load any commodities, in those acts particularly enumerated, at any *British* plantation, being the growth, product, or manufacture thereof, bonds shall be given with one surety, to the value of one thousand pounds, if the ship of less burthen than one hundred tons, and of the sum of two thousand pounds; if the ship be of greater burthen, that the same commodities shall be brought by such ship or vessel to some other *British* plantation, or to some port in *Great Britain;* notwithstanding which, there is great reason to apprehend such goods are frequently carried to foreign ports, and landed there; and whereas great quantities of foreign molasses and syrups are clandestinely run on shore in the *British* colonies, to the prejudice of the revenue, and the great detriment of the trade of this kingdom, and its *American* plantations; to remedy which practices for the future, be it further enacted . . . , That from and after . . . [September 29, 1764] . . . , bond and security . . . shall also be given to the collector or other principal officer of the customs at any port or place in any of the *British American* colonies or plantations, with one surety besides the master of every ship or vessel that shall lade or take on board there any goods not particularly enumerated in the said acts, being the product or manufacture of any of the said colonies or plantations, with condition, that, in case any molasses or syrups, being the produce of any of the plantations not under the dominion of his Majesty . . . , shall be laden on board such ship or vessel, the same shall (the danger of the seas and enemies excepted) be brought, without fraud or wilfull diminution, by the said ship or vessel to some of His Majesty's colonies or plantations in *America,* or to some port in *Great Britain,* or in the *British American* colonies and plantations, make a just and true report of all the goods laden on board such vessel or ship under their true and proper denominations; and if any such non-enumerated goods shall be laden on board any such ship or vessel before such bond shall be given, the goods so laden together with the ship or vessel and her furniture shall be forfeited, and shall and may be seized by any officer of the customs, and prosecuted in the manner herein after directed. . . .

XXV. And it is hereby further enacted, That if any *British* ship or vessel laden, as aforesaid, with any goods of the produce or manufacture of any *British* colony or plantation in *America,* or having on board any molasses or syrups the produce of any foreign colony or plantation, shall be discovered by any officer of his Majesty's customs within two leagues of the shore of any *British* colony or plantation in *America,* and the master or person taking charge of such ship or vessel shall not produce a certificate that bond has been given, pursuant to the directions of this or any other act of parliament, as the case may require; or if he shall not produce such certificate to the collector or other chief officer of the customs where he shall arrive, either in *Great Britain* or any *British American* colony or plantation, such ship or vessel with her tackle, apparel, and furniture, and all the goods therein laden, shall be forfeited, and shall be seized and prosecuted as herein after directed. . . .

XXVII. And it is hereby further enacted . . . , That from and after . . . [September 29, 1764] . . . , all coffee, pimento, cocoa nuts, whale fins, raw silk, hides, and skins, pot and pearl ashes, of the growth, production, or manufacture, of any *British* colony or plantation in *America,* shall be imported directly from thence into this kingdom, or some other *British* colony or plantation, under the like securities, penalties, and forfeitures, as are particularly mentioned in two acts of parliament made in the twelfth and twenty fifth years of the reign of King *Charles* the Second. . . . .

XXVIII. And it is hereby further enacted . . . , That from and after . . . [September 29, 1764] . . . , no iron, nor any sort of wood, commonly called *Lumber* . . . , of the growth, production, or manufacture, of any *British* colony or plantation in *America,* shall be there loaden on board any ship or vessel to be carried from there hence, until sufficient bond shall be given with one surety besides the master of the vessel, to the collector or other principal officer of the customs at the loading port, in a penalty of double the value of the goods, that the said goods shall not be landed in any part of *Europe* except *Great Britain.* . . .

XXIX. And for the better preventing frauds in the importation or exportation of goods that are liable to the payment of duties, or are prohibited, in the *British* colonies or plantations in *America,* it is further enacted . . . , That from and after . . . [September 29, 1764] . . . , no goods, wares, or merchandize, of any kind whatsoever shall be shipped or laden on board any ship or vessel in any of the *British* colonies or plantations in *America,* to be carried from thence to any other *British* colony or plantation, without a sufferance or warrant first had and obtained from the collector or other proper officer of the customs at the port or place where such goods shall be intended to be put on Board. . . .

XXX. And whereas *British* vessels arriving from foreign parts at several of the out ports of this kingdom, fully or in part laden abroad with goods that are pretended to be destined to some foreign plantation, do frequently take on board some small parcel of goods in this kingdom which are entered outwards for some *British* colony or plantation, and a cocket and clearance thereupon granted for such goods, under cover of which the whole cargoes of such vessels are clandestinely landed in the *British American* dominions, contrary to several acts of parliament now in force, to the great prejudice of the trade and revenues of this kingdom; for remedy whereof, be it further enacted . . . , That from and after the first day of *May* one thousand seven hundred and sixty four, no ship or vessel shall, upon any pretence whatsoever, be cleared outwards from any port of this kingdom, for any land, island, plantation, colony, territory, or place to his Majesty belonging, or which shall hereafter belong or be in the possession or under the dominion of his Majesty . . . , in *America*, unless the whole and entire cargo of such ship or vessel shall be *bona fide*, and without fraud, laden and shipped in this kingdom. . . .

XXXV. And, in order to prevent any illicit trade or commerce between his Majesty's subjects in *America,* and the subjects of the crown of *France* in the islands of *Saint Pierre* and *Miquelon,* it is hereby further enacted . . . , That from and after . . . [September 29, 1764] . . . , if any *British* ship or vessel shall be found standing into, or coming out from, either of those islands, or hovering or at anchor within two leagues of the coasts thereof, or shall be discovered to have taken any goods or merchandizes on board at either of them, or to have been there for that purpose; such ship or vessel, and all the goods so taken on board there, shall be forfeited and lost, and shall and may be seized and prosecuted by any officer of his Majesty's customs; and the master or other person having the charge of such ship or vessel, and every person concerned in taking such goods on board, shall forfeit treble the value thereof. . . .

XXXVII. And it is hereby further enacted . . . , That from and after . . . [September 29, 1764] . . . , if any goods or merchandize whatsoever, liable to the payment of duties in any *British* colony or plantation in *America* by this or any other act of parliament, shall be loaden on board any ship or vessel outward bound, or shall be unshipped or landed from any ship or vessel inward bound, before the respective duties thereon are paid, agreeable to law; or if any prohibited goods whatsoever shall be imported into, or exported out of, any of the said colonies or plantations, contrary to the true intent and meaning of this or any other act of parliament; every person who shall be assisting, or otherwise concerned, either in the loading outwards, or in the unshipping or landing inwards, such goods, or to whose hands the same shall knowingly come after the loading or unshipping thereof, shall, for each and every offence, forfeit treble the value of such goods, to be estimated and computed according to the best price that each respective commodity bears at the place where such offence was committed; and all the boats, horses, cattle, and other carriages whatsoever, made use of in the loading, landing, removing, carriage, or conveyance, of any of the aforesaid goods, shall also be forfeited and lost, and shall and may be seized and prosecuted, by any officer of his Majesty's customs, as herein after mentioned. . . .

Discussion

1. Although the Albany Plan failed to gain ratification, it served as a model for future efforts to create intercolonial cooperation. What elements of the plan address issues of power that existed in colonial America? How and to what degree is the plan a statement of American liberties?

2. In what ways do the Proclamation of 1763 and the Sugar Act express royal power? Are there ways in which those two documents express or defend English liberties?

Harcourt Brace & Company

3. Based on the documents, how might the admirers of John Wilkes have reacted to the Proclamation of 1763 and the Sugar Act? Are there specific portions of Wilkes's essay that Americans might have relied on to protest the other two declarations?

4. After 1763, Americans grew increasingly resentful of and rebellious toward royal authority. How do the documents relate to that resistance? Based on the documents presented here and in earlier chapters, what differences existed following the French and Indian War that might have encouraged resistance among Americans?

Harcourt Brace & Company

Chapter 6
Resistance, Revolution, and Independence

This famous engraving appeared the day after these "well-dressed gentlemen" were shot by British soldiers. Such propaganda fueled the anger over the Boston Massacre and promoted the popular belief that British soldiers were sent to deprive citizens of their liberties—and their lives.

*V*ictory over the French in 1763 made Great Britain the dominant power in eastern North America. Very quickly, however, Americans came to fear that British authority threatened their liberties—a fear that led to a rebellion that neither the British nor the colonists had anticipated. Beginning with the Stamp Act crisis, American patriots insisted that royal efforts to administer the new empire, and the policies designed to finance that administration, violated their rights as Englishmen. Repeal of the Stamp Act defused the situation temporarily, but Americans in the 1770s grew increasingly bolder in their resistance to royal power. Parliament responded by passing a series of intolerable acts designed to coerce Bostonians into submission. Although the First Continental Congress tried to follow a moderate course in dealing with the British, fighting broke out between the two sides in 1775. A year later, Thomas Jefferson declared that "all men are created equal," a novel concept that made the conflict a revolution as well as a war for independence.

The Stamp Act Crisis, 1765[*]

The Stamp Act of 1765 brought an unprecedented unity to the American colonies. Convinced that the tax, along with the Sugar Act, was an unconstitutional assertion of power, the Pennsylvania assembly passed the following resolutions. The document reaffirmed Americans' liberties as Englishmen, including a right to actual representation in matters of taxation. The congress also called for a boycott of British goods, while mobs violently protested the tax by rioting in several cities. In the face of such resistance, Parliament repealed the act. Patriots, jubilant over their apparent success, refused to recognize the implications of the Declaratory Act, which Parliament had approved when they withdrew the stamp tax. Thus, the Americans learned a singular lesson: when government threatened their rights, concerted and violent action could preserve liberty.

> The house taking into consideration, that an act of parliament lately passed in England, for imposing certain stamp duties, and other duties, on his Majesty's subjects in America, whereby they conceive some of their most essential and valuable rights as British subjects to be deeply affected, think it is a duty they owe to themselves and their posterity, to come to the following resolution, viz.
>
> Resolved. . . . That the assemblies of this province have from time to time, whenever requisitions have been made by his Majesty for carrying on military operations for the defence of America, most cheerfully and liberally contributed their full proportion of men and money for those services.
>
> Resolved. . . . That whenever his Majesty's services shall, for the future, require the aids of the inhabitants of this province, and they shall be called upon for that purpose in a constitutional way, it will be their indispensible duty most cheerfully and liberally to grant to his Majesty their proportion of men and money, for the defence, security and other public services of the British American colonies.

---

[*]*The Parliamentary History of England, From the Earliest Period to the Year 1803,* 36 vols. (London: T. C. Hansard, 1806–1830), XV:131–33.

Resolved. . . . That the inhabitants of this province are entitled to all liberties, rights, and privileges, of his Majesty's subjects in Great Britain or elsewhere; and that the constitution of government in this province is founded on the natural rights of mankind, and the noble principles of English liberty, and therefore is, or ought to be, perfectly free.

Resolved. . . . That it is the interest, birthright, and indubitable privilege of every British subject, to be taxed only by his consent, or that of his legal representatives, in conjunction with his Majesty, or his substitutes.

Resolved. . . . That the only legal representatives of the inhabitants of this province are the persons they annually elect, to serve as members of assembly.

Resolved therefore. . . . That the laying taxes upon the inhabitants of this province in any other manner, being manifestly subversive of public liberty, must, of necessary consequence, be utterly destructive of public happiness.

Resolved. . . . That the resting an authority in the courts of admiralty to decide in suits relating to the stamp duties, and other matters foreign to their proper jurisdiction, is highly dangerous to the liberties of his Majesty's American subjects, contrary to Magna Charta, the great charter and fountain of English liberty, and destructive of one of their most darling and acknowledged rights, that of trial by juries.

Resolved. . . . That it is the opinion of this house, that the restraints, imposed by several late acts of parliament, on the trade of this province, at a time when the people labour under an enormous debt, must, of necessity, be attended with the most fatal consequences; not only to this province, but to the trade of our mother country.

Resolved. . . . That this house think it their duty thus firmly to assert, with modesty and decency, their inherent rights, that their posterity may learn and know that it was not with their consent and acquiescence, that any taxes should be levied on them by any person, but their own representatives; and are desirous, that these their resolves should remain on their minutes, as a testimony of the zeal and ardent desire of the present house of assembly, to preserve their inestimable rights, which, as Englishmen, they have possessed ever since this province was settled, and to transmit them to their latest posterity.

A Pennsylvania Farmer, 1768*

John Dickinson, a Philadelphia lawyer who wrote a series of letters in response to the Townshend duties, struck a moderate stance in the following document. Citing the dangers of rebellion, he cautioned against those Americans advocating separation from England. The "Pennsylvania farmer" concluded, however, that, if necessary, the colonists must be prepared to take vigorous measures to protect their liberties from the misuse of royal power.

I hope, my dear countrymen, that you will in every colony be upon your guard against those who may at any time endeavour to stir you up, under pretensions of patriotism, to any measures disrespectful to our sovereign and our mother country. Hot, rash, disorderly proceedings, injure the reputation of a people as to wisdom, valour and virtue, without procuring them the least benefit. I pray God, that he may be pleased to inspire you and your posterity to the latest ages with that spirit, of which I have an idea, but find a difficulty to express; to express in the best manner I can, I mean a spirit that shall so guide you, that it will be impossible to deter-

---

*From *American History Told by Contemporaries,* 5 vols., ed. Albert Bushnell Hart (New York: The Macmillan Company, 1914), II:423–26.

mine, whether an *American's* character is most distinguishable for his loyalty to his sovereign, his duty to his mother country, his love of freedom, or his affection for his native soil.

Every government, at some time or another, falls into wrong measures; these may proceed from mistake or passion.—But every such measure does not dissolve the obligation between the governors and the governed; the mistake may be corrected; the passion may pass over.

It is the duty of the governed, to endeavour to rectify the mistake, and appease the passion. They have not at first any other right, than to represent their grievances, and to pray for redress, unless an emergenc[y] is so pressing, as not to allow time for receiving an answer to their applications which rarely happens. If their applications are disregarded, then that kind of opposition becomes justifiable, which can be made without breaking the laws, or disturbing the public peace. This consists in the prevention of the oppressors reaping advantage from their oppressions, and not in their punishment. For experience may teach them what reason did not; and harsh methods, cannot be proper, till milder ones have failed.

If at length it become undoubted, that an inveterate revolution is formed to annihilate the liberties of the governed, the English history affords frequent examples of resistance by force. What particular circumstance will in any future case justify such resistance, can never be ascertained until they happen. Perhaps it may be allowable to say, generally, that it can never be justifiable, until the people are FULLY CONVINCED, that any further submission will be destructive to their happiness.

When the appeal is made to the sword, highly probable it is, that the punishment will exceed the offence; and the calamities attending on war out weigh those preceding it. These considerations of justice and prudence, will always have great influence with good and wise men.

To these reflections on this subject, it remains to be added, and ought for ever to be remembered; that resistance in the case of colonies against their mother country, is extremely different from the resistance of a people against their prince. A nation may change their King or race of Kings, and retain[ing] their antient form of government, be gainers by changing. Thus Great-Britain, under the illustrious house of Brunswick, a house that seems to flourish for the happiness of mankind, has found a felicity, unknown in the reigns of the Stuarts. But if once we are separated from our mother country, what new form of government shall we accept, or when shall we find another Britain to supply our loss? Torn from the body to which we are united by religion, liberty, laws, affections, relations, language, and commerce, we must bleed at every vein.

In truth, the prosperity of these provinces is founded in their dependence on Great-Britain; and when she returns to "her old good humour, and old good nature," as Lord Clarendon expresses it, I hope they will always esteem their duty and interest, as it most certainly will be, to promote her welfare by all the means in their power.

We cannot act with too much caution in our disputes. Anger produces anger; and differences that might be accommodated by kind and respectful behaviour, may by imprudence be changed to an incurable rage.

In quarrels between countries, as well as those between individuals, when they have risen to a certain height, the first cause of dissention is no longer remembred, the minds of the parties being wholly engaged in recollecting and resenting the mutual expressions of their dislike. When feuds have reached that fatal point, all considerations of reason and equity vanish; and a blind fury governs, or rather confounds all things. A people no longer regards their interest, but the gratification of their wrath. The sway of the Cleon's, and Clodius's, the designing and detestable flatter[er]s of the prevailing passion, becomes confirmed.

Wise and good men in vain oppose the storm, and may think themselves fortunate, if, endeavouring to preserve their ungrateful fellow citizens, they do not ruin themselves. Their prudence will be called baseness; their moderation, guilt; and if their virtue does not lead them

Harcourt Brace & Company

to destruction, as that of many other great and excellent persons has done, they may survive, to receive from their expiring country, the mournful glory of her acknowledgment, that their councils, if regarded, would have saved her.

The constitutional modes of obtaining relief, are those which I would wish to see pursued on the present occasion, that is, by petitioning of our assemblies, or, where they are not permitted to meet, of the people to the powers that can afford us relief.

We have an excellent prince, in whose good dispositions towards us we may confide. We have a generous, sensible, and humane nation, to whom we may apply. They may be deceived: they may, by artful men, be provoked to anger against us; but I cannot yet believe they will be cruel or unjust; or that their anger will be implacable. Let us behave like dutiful children, who have received unmerited blows from a beloved parent. Let us complain to our parents; but let our complaints speak at the same time, the language of affliction and veneration.

If, however, it shall happen by an unfortunate course of affairs, that our applications to his Majesty and the parliament for the redress, prove ineffectual, let us then take another step, by witholding from Great-Britain, all the advantages she has been used to receive from us. Then let us try, if our ingenuity, industry, and frugality, will not give weight to our remonstrances. Let us all be united with one spirit in one cause. Let us invent; let us work; let us save; let us at the same time, keep up our claims, and unceasingly repeat our complaints; but above all, let us implore the protection of that infinite good and gracious Being, "by whom kings reign and princes decree justice."

"Nil desperandum."

Nothing is to be despaired of.

An Intolerable Act, 1774*

Resistance to British policies grew ever more violent during the 1770s, especially in Boston. The decade began with the "massacre" of five colonists, and in 1773 anger over the Tea Act culminated in the destruction of thousands of dollars worth of English property. Parliament reacted to the tumultuous conditions in Massachusetts by passing a series of coercive measures that Patriots referred to as the Intolerable Acts. The Administration of Justice Act, which follows, offered a response to the Boston Massacre by allowing a change of venue for officials accused of murder while carrying out their duties. Americans viewed this as an affront to justice, and in 1776 Thomas Jefferson cited the policy as one of the king's abuses of power that legitimized a declaration of independence.

Whereas in his Majesty's Province of *Massachusetts Bay,* in *New England,* an attempt hath lately been made to throw off the authority of the Parliament of *Great Britain* over the said Province, and an actual and avowed resistance, by open force, to the execution of certain Acts of Parliament, hath been suffered to take place, uncontrolled and unpunished, in defiance of his Majesty's authority, and to the utter subversion of all lawful Government; and whereas, in the present disordered state of the said Province, it is of the utmost importance to the general wel-

An Act for the Imperial Administration of Justice in the Cases of Persons Questioned for Any Acts Done by Them in Execution of the Law, or for the Suppression of Riots and Tumults in the Province of the Massachusetts Bay, in New England, in American Archives: A Documentary History of the English Colonies in North America, from the King's Message to Parliament, of March 7, 1774, to the Declaration of Independence by the United States, 2 vols., ed. Peter Force (Washington, D.C.: St. Clair Clarke and Peter Force, 1839), I:130–32.

fare thereof, and to the re-establishing of lawful authority throughout the same, that neither the Magistrates acting in support of the laws, nor any of his Majesty's subjects aiding and assisting them therein; or in the suppression of riots and tumults, raised in opposition to the execution of the laws and statutes of this realm, should be discouraged from the proper discharge of their duty, by any apprehension, that in case of their being questioned for any acts done therein, they may be liable to be brought to trial for the same before persons who do not acknowledge the validity of the laws, in the execution whereof, or the authority of the Magistrate in the support of whom, such acts had been done: in order therefore to remove every such discouragement from the minds of his Majesty's subjects, and to induce them, upon all proper occasions, to exert themselves in support of the public peace of the Province, and of the authority of the King and Parliament of *Great Britain* over the same; Be it enacted by the King's most excellent Majesty, by and with the consent of the Lords Spiritual and Temporal, and Commons, in this Parliament assembled, and by the authority of the same, that if any inquisition or indictment shall be found, or if any appeal shall be sued or preferred against any person, for murder, or other capital offence, in the Province of *Massachusetts Bay*, and it shall appear, by information given upon oath to the Governor, or, in his absence, to the Lieutenant Governor of the said Province, that the fact was committed by the person against whom such inquisition of indictment shall be found, or against whom such appeal shall be sued or preferred, as aforesaid, either in the execution of his duty as Magistrate, for the suppression of riots, or in the support of the Laws of Revenue, or in acting in his duty as an Officer of Revenue, or in the aiding and assisting in any of the cases aforesaid; and if it shall also appear, to the satisfaction of the said Governor, or Lieutenant Governor respectively, that an indifferent trial cannot be had within the said Province, in that case, it shall and may be lawful for the Governor, or Lieutenant Governor, to direct, with the advice and consent of the Council, that the inquisition, indictment, or appeal, shall be tried in some other of his Majesty's Colonies, or in *Great Britain;* and for that purpose to order the person against whom such inquisition or indictment shall be found, or against whom such appeal shall be sued or preferred, as aforesaid, to be sent under sufficient custody, to the place appointed for his trial, or to admit such person to bail, taking a recognizance, (which the said Governor, or in his absence, the Lieutenant Governor, is hereby authorized to take,) from such person, with sufficient sureties, to be approved of the said Governor, or . . . the Lieutenant Governor, in such sums of money as the said Governor, or . . . the Lieutenant Governor, shall deem reasonable, for the personal appearance of such person, if the trial shall be appointed to be had in any other Colony, before the Governor, or Lieutenant Governor, or Commander-in-Chief of such Colony; and if the trial shall be appointed to be had in *Great Britain,* then before his Majesty's Court of King's Bench, at a time to be mentioned in such recognizances, and the Governor, or Lieutenant Governor, or Commander-in-Chief of the Colony, where such trial shall be appointed to be had, or Court of King's Bench, where the trial is appointed to be had in *Great Britain,* upon the appearance of such person, according to such recognizance, or in custody, shall either commit such person, or admit him to bail, until such trial; and which the said Governor, or Lieutenant Governor, or Commander-in-Chief, and Court of King's Bench, are hereby authorized and empowered to do.

And, to prevent a failure of justice, from the want of evidence on the trial of any such inquisition, indictment, or appeal, Be it further enacted, that the Governor, or. . . Lieutenant Governor, shall, and he is hereby authorized and required, to bind in recognizances to his Majesty all such witnesses as the prosecutor or person against whom such inquisition or indictment shall be found, or appeal sued or preferred, shall desire to attend the trial of the said inquisition, indictment, or appeal, for their personal appearance, at the time and place of such trial, to give evidence: and the said Governor, or . . . Lieutenant Governor, shall thereupon appoint a reasonable sum to be allowed for the expenses of every such witness, and shall thereupon give to each witness a certificate, in writing, under his hand and seal, that such witness had entered into a recognizance to give evidence, and specifying the sum allowed for his expenses; and the Collector and Collectors of the Customs, or one of them, within the said Province, upon the delivery of such certificate, are, and is hereby authorized and required, forthwith to pay to such witness the sum specified thereupon for his expenses.

And be it further enacted by the authority aforesaid, That all prosecutors and witnesses, who shall be under recognizance to appear in any of his Majesty's Colonies, in *America,* or in *Great Britain,* in pursuance of this Act, shall be free from all arrests and restraints, in any action or suit to be commenced against them during their going to such Colony, or coming to Great Britain, and their necessary stay and abiding there, on occasion of such prosecution, and returning again to the said Province of the *Massachusetts Bay.*

And be it further enacted by the authority aforesaid, That all and every his Majesty's Justices of the Peace, and other Justices and Coroners, before whom any person shall be brought, charged with murder, or other capital crime, where it shall appear by proof, on oath, to such Justices or Coroners, that the fact was committed by such person, either in the execution of his duty as a Magistrate, for the suppression of riots, or in the support of the Laws of Revenue, or in acting under the direction of any Magistrate, for the suppression of riots, or for carrying into effect the Laws of Revenue, or in aiding and assisting in any of the cases aforesaid, are hereby authorized and required to admit every such person so brought before him or them, as aforesaid, to bail; any law, custom, or usage, to the contrary thereof in any wise notwithstanding.

And be it further enacted by the authority aforesaid, That where it shall be made to appear to the Judges or Justices of any Court, within the said Province of *Massachusetts Bay,* by any person, against whom any inquisition or indictment shall be found, or appeal sued or preferred for murder, or other capital crime, that the fact was committed by such person, either in the execution of his duty as a magistrate, for the suppression of riots, or in the support of the Laws of Revenue, or in acting in his duty as an Officer of Revenue, or in acting under the direction and order of any Magistrate, for the suppression of riots, or for carrying into effect the laws of revenue, or in aiding and assisting in any of the cases aforesaid, and that he intends to make application to the Governor, or Lieutenant Governor of said Province, that such inquisition, indictment, or appeal, may be tried in some other of his Majesty's Colonies, or in *Great Britain,* the said Judges or Justices are hereby authorized and required to adjourn or postpone the . . . trial of such inquisition, indictment, or appeal, for a reasonable time, and admit the person to bail, in order that he may make application to the Governor, or Lieutenant Governor, for the purpose aforesaid.

And be it further enacted, That the Governor or . . . Lieutenant Governor, if he shall direct the trial to be had in any other of his Majesty's Colonies, shall transmit the inquisition, or appeal, together with the recognizance's of the witnesses, and other recognizance's, under the seal of the Province, to the Governor, or Lieutenant Governor, or Commander-in-Chief, of such other Colony, who shall immediately issue a commission of Oyer and Terminer, and deliver, or cause to be delivered, the said inquisition, indictment, or appeal, with the said recognizance's, to the Chief Justice, and such other persons as have usually been Commissioners of Oyer and Terminer, Justices of Assize, or General Gaol Delivery there; who shall have power to proceed upon the said inquisition, indictment, or appeal, as if the same had been returned, found, or preferred before them; and the trial shall thereupon proceed in like manner, to all intents and purposes, as if the offence had been committed in such place; and in case the Governor or . . . Lieutenant Governor, shall direct the trial to be had in *Great Britain,* he shall

Harcourt Brace & Company

then transmit the inquisition, indictment, or appeal together with the recognizance's of the witnesses, and other recognizance's, under the seal of the Province, to one of his Majesty's principal Secretaries of State, who shall deliver, the same, to the Master of the Crown Office, to be filed of record in the Court of King's Bench, and the inquisition, indictment, or appeal, shall be tried and proceeded upon, in the next term; or at such other time as the Court shall appoint at the Bar of the Court of the King's Bench, in like manner, to all intents and purposes, as if the offence had been committed in the county of *Middlesex,* or in any other county of that part of *Great Britain* called *England*, where the Court of King's Bench shall sit, or else before such Commissioners, and in such county, in that part of *Great Britain* called *England* as shall be assigned by the King's Majesty's commission, in like manner and form, to all intents and purposes, as if such offence had been committed in the same county where such inquisition, indictment, or appeal shall be so tried.

And be it further enacted by the authority aforesaid, That in case, or on account of any error or defect in any indictment, in virtue, or under the authority of this Act, shall be transmitted to any other Colony, or to *Great Britain,* the same shall be quashed, or judgment thereon arrested, or such indictment adjudged bad on demurrer, it shall and may be lawful to prefer a new indictment, or indictments against the person or persons accused in the said Colony, to which such indictment, so quashed or adjudged bad, shall have been transmitted, or before the Grand Jury of any county in *Great Britain*, in case such former indictment shall have been transmitted to *Great Britain*, in the same manner as could be done in case the party accused should return to the place where the offence was committed; and the Grand Jury and Petty Jury of such other Colony or county in *Great Britain* shall have power to find and proceed upon such indictment or indictments, in the same manner as if the offence, by such indictment or indictments charged, had been committed within the limits of the Colony or county for which such Juries shall respectively be empannelled to serve.

And be it further enacted, by the authority aforesaid, That this Act, and every clause, provision, regulation, matter, and thing, herein contained, shall commence and take effect upon the first day of June, one thousand seven hundred and seventy-four; and be, and continue in force, for and during the term of three years.

The Galloway Motion, 1774*

In response to the Coercive Acts, delegates from twelve colonies convened in Philadelphia as the First Continental Congress. Joseph Galloway, a Pennsylvania delegate and a leading loyalist, offered the following measure as a means of easing tensions between the colonists and England. The proposal bore some resemblance to the one Benjamin Franklin had suggested in 1754, but it called for an intercolonial government that would have to approve acts of Parliament relating to the colonies. The Galloway Motion, like the Albany Plan, failed to gain approval. Some other means would have to be found for resolving disputes between Great Britain and America.

Resolved, That this Congress will apply to his Majesty for a redress of grievances, under which his faithful subjects in *America* labour, and assure him, that the Colonies hold in abhorrence the idea of being considered independent communities on the *British* Government, and

American Archives: Fourth Series. Containing a Documentary History of the English Colonies in North America, from the King's Message to Parliament, of March 7, 1774, to the Declaration of Independence by the United States, 9 vols., comp. Peter Force (Washington, D.C.: M. St. Claire and Peter Force, 1837–1853), I:905–906.

most ardently desire the establishment of a political union, not only among themselves, but with the mother state, upon those principles of safety and freedom which are essential in the constitution of all free Governments, and particularly of the *British* Legislature. And as the Colonies from their local circumstances cannot be represented in the Parliament of *Great Britain*, they will humbly propose to his Majesty, and his two Houses of Parliament, the following Plan, under which the strength of the whole Empire may be drawn together on any emergency; the interests of both countries advanced; and the rights and liberties of *America* secured:

A Plan for a proposed Union between *Great Britain* and the Colonies of *New-Hampshire*, the *Massachusetts Bay, Rhode-Island, Connecticut, New-York, New-Jersey, Pennsylvania, Maryland*, the three lower Counties on the *Delaware, Virginia, North Carolina, South Carolina, and Georgia*.

That a *British* and an *American* Legislature, for regulating the administration of the general affairs of *America*, including all the said colonies; within, and under which Government, each Colony shall retain its present Constitution and powers of regulating and governing its own internal police in all cases whatever.

That the said Government be administered by a President General to be appointed by the King, and a Grand Council to be chosen by the Representatives of the people of the several Colonies in their respective Assemblies, once in every three years. . . .

Who shall meet in the City of ★ ★ ★ ★ ★ ★ ★ ★ for the first time, being called by the President General, as soon as conveniently may be after his appointment.

That there shall be a new election of Members for the Grand Council every three years; and on the death, removal, or resignation of any Member, his place shall be supplied by a new choice at the next sitting of Assembly of the Colony he represented.

That the Grand Council shall meet once in every year if they shall think it necessary, and oftener, if occasions shall require, at such time and place as they shall adjourn to at the last preceding meeting, or as they shall be called to meet at, by the President General on any emergency.

That the Grand Council shall have power to choose their Speaker, and shall hold and exercise all the like rights, liberties, and privileges as are held and exercised by and in the House of Commons of *Great Britain*.

That the President General shall hold his office during the pleasure of the King, and his assent shall be requisite to all Acts of the Grand Council, and it shall be his office and duty to cause them to be carried into execution.

That the President General, by and with the advice and consent of the Grand Council, hold and exercise all the Legislative rights, powers, and authorities, necessary for regulating and administering all the general police and affairs of the Colonies, in which *Great Britain* and the Colonies, or any of them, the Colonies in general, or more than one Colony, are in any manner concerned, as well civil and criminal as commercial.

That the said President General and Grand Council be an inferior and distinct branch of the *British* legislature, united and incorporated with it for the aforesaid general purposes; and that any of the said general regulations may originate, and be formed and digested, either in the Parliament of *Great Britain* or in the said General Council; and being prepared, transmitted to the other for their approbation or dissent; and that the assent of both shall be requisite to the validity of all such general Acts and Statutes.

That in time of war, all Bills for granting aids to the Crown, prepared by the Grand Council, and approved by the President General, shall be valid and passed into law without the assent of the *British* Parliament.

Declaration of Rights and Grievances, 1774[*]

Most colonists in 1774 could not imagine independence from Britain, and delegates to the First Continental Congress devoted much of their efforts to defining their rights—now as Americans rather than simply as Englishmen. Events of the previous ten years had shown that substantive differences existed between Great Britain and the colonies, and Congress struggled to find the best means of expressing the grievances that they believed endangered their liberties. The following document, addressed to King George III because representatives no longer recognized parliamentary authority as legitimate in the colonies, revealed the complexity of the concerns that Americans had and the bitterness of their feelings toward England.

Whereas, since the close of the last war, the *British* Parliament, claiming a power of right to bind the people of *America,* by statute, in all cases whatsoever, both, in some Acts, expressly imposed taxes on them, and in others, under various pretences, but in fact for the purpose of raising a revenue, hath imposed rates and duties payable in these Colonies, established a Board of Commissioners, with unconstitutional powers, and extended the jurisdiction of Courts of Admiralty, not only for collecting the said duties, but for the trial of causes merely arising within the body of a County:

And whereas, in consequence of other Statutes, Judges, who before held only estates at will in their offices, have been made dependent on the Crown alone for their salaries, and Standing Armies kept in times of Peace: And it has lately been resolved in Parliament, that by force of a Statute, made in the thirty-fifth year of the reign of King *Henry,* the Eighth, Colonists may be transported to England, and tried there upon accusations of treason, and misprisions, or concealments of treason committed in the Colonies, and by a late Statute, such trials have been directed in cases therein mentioned:

And whereas, in the last session of Parliament, three Statutes were made, one entitled, "An Act to discontinue, in such manner, and for such time, as are therein mentioned, the landing and discharging, lading or shipping of Goods, Wares, and Merchandise, at the Town, and within the Harbour of *Boston,* in the Province of *Massachusetts Bay,* in *North America;*" another, entitled, "An Act for the better regulating the Government of the Province of *Massachusetts Bay,* in *New England;*" and another, entitled "An Act for the impartial administration of Justice in the cases of persons questioned for any act done by them in the execution of the law, or for the suppression of riots and tumults in the Province of *Massachusetts Bay,* in *New England;*" and another Statute was then made "for making more effectual provision of the Government of the Province of *Quebec,*" &c. All which statutes are impolitick, unjust, and cruel, as well as unconstitutional, and most dangerous and destructive of *American* rights:

And whereas, Assemblies have been frequently dissolved, contrary to the rights of the people, when they attempted to deliberate on grievances; and their dutiful, humble, loyal, and reasonable Petitions to the Crown for redress, have been repeatedly treated with contempt by his Majesty's Ministers of State:

The good people of the several Colonies of *New-Hampshire, Massachusetts Bay, Rhode-Island* and *Providence Plantations, Connecticut, New-York, New-Jersey, Pennsylvania, New-Castle, Kent,* and *Suzzex,* on *Delaware, Maryland, Virginia, North Carolina,* and *South Carolina,* justly alarmed at

---

[*]*American Archives: Fourth Series. Containing a Documentary History of the English Colonies in North America, from the King's Message to Parliament, of March 7, 1774, to the Declaration of Independence by the United States,* 9 vols., comp. Peter Force (Washington, D.C.: M. St. Claire and Peter Force, 1837–1853), I:910–12.

these arbitrary proceedings of Parliament and Administration, have severally elected, constituted, and appointed Deputies to meet and sit in General Congress, in the City of *Philadelphia*, in order to obtain and establish as that their religion, laws, and liberties may not be subverted; Whereupon the Deputies so appointed being now assembled, in a full and free representation of these Colonies, taking into their most serious consideration the best means of attaining the ends aforesaid, do, in the first place, as *Englishmen*, their ancestors in like cases have usually done, for asserting and vindicating their rights and liberties, *declare,*

That the inhabitants of the *English* Colonies in *North America*, by the immutable laws of nature, the principles of the *English* Constitution, and the several Charters or Compacts, have the following *Rights:*

Resolved, . . . 1. That they are entitled to life, liberty, and property, and they have never ceded to any sovereign power whatever a right to dispose of either without their consent.

Resolved, . . . 2. That our ancestors, who first settled these Colonies, were at the time of their emigration from the mother country, entitled to all the rights, liberties, and immunities of free and natural born subjects, within the Realm of England.

Resolved, . . . 3. That by such emigration they by no means forfeited, surrendered, or lost any of those rights, but that they were, and their descendants now are, entitled to the exercise and enjoyment of all such of them, as their local and other circumstances enable them to exercise and enjoy.

Resolved, 4. That the foundations of *English* Liberty, and of all free Government, is a right in the people to participate in their Legislative Council: and as the *English* Colonists are not represented, and from their local and other circumstances cannot be properly represented in the *British* Parliament, they are entitled to a free and exclusive power of legislation in their several Provincial Legislatures, where their right of Representation can alone be preserved, in all cases of taxation and internal polity, subject only to the negative of their Sovereign, in such manner as has been heretofore used and accustomed. But, from the necessity of the case, and a regard to the mutual interest of both Countries, we cheerfully consent to the operation of such Acts of the *British* Parliament, as are, *bona fide*, restrained to the regulation of our external commerce, for the purpose of securing the commercial advantages of the whole Empire to the mother country, and the commercial benefits of its respective members; excluding every idea of Taxation, internal or external, for raising a revenue on the subjects in *America*, without their consent.

Resolved, . . . 5. That the respective Colonies are entitled to the common law of *England,* and more especially to the great and inestimate privilege of being tried by their peers of the vicinage, according to the course of that law.

Resolved, 6. That they are entitled to the benefit of such of the English statutes as existed at the time of their Colonization; and which they have, by experience, respectively found to be applicable to their several local and other circumstances.

Resolved, . . . 7. That these, his Majesty's Colonies, are likewise entitled to all the immunities and privileges granted and confirmed to them by Royal Charters, or secured by their several codes of Provincial Laws.

Resolved, . . . 8. That they have a right peacefully to assemble, consider of their grievances, and Petition the King; and that all prosecutions, prohibitory Proclamations, and commitments of the same, are illegal.

Resolved, . . . 9. That the keeping a Standing Army in these Colonies, in times of peace, without the consent of the Legislatures of that Colony, in which such Army is kept, is against law.

Resolved, . . . 10. It is indispensably necessary to good Government, and rendered essential by the English Constitution, that the constituent branches of the Legislature be independent of each other; that; therefore, the exercise of Legislative power in several Colonies, by a Council

Harcourt Brace & Company

appointed, during pleasure, by the Crown, is unconstitutional, dangerous, and destructive to the freedom of *American* legislation.

All and each of which aforesaid Deputies, in behalf of themselves and their constituents, do claim, demand, and insist on, as their indubitable rights and liberties; which cannot be legally taken from them, altered or abridged by any power whatever, without their own consent, by their Representatives in the several Provincial Legislatures.

In the course of our injury we find many infringements and violations of the foregoing Rights, which from an ardent desire, the harmony and mutual intercourse of affection and interest may be restored, we pass over for the present, and proceed to state such Acts and measures as have been adopted since the last war, which demonstrate a system formed to enslave *America.*

Resolved, . . . That the following Acts of Parliament are infringements and violations of the rights of the Colonists; and that the repeal of them is essentially necessary in order to restore harmony between *Great Britain* and the *American Colonies,* viz:

The several Acts of 4 *George* III. ch. 15, and ch. 34. 5 *George* III. ch. 25. *George* III. ch. 52. 7 *George,* III. ch. 41, and ch. 46. 8 George III. ch. 22, which impose duties for the purpose of raising a revenue in *America,* extend the powers of the Admiralty Courts beyond their ancient limits, deprive the *American* subject of trial by jury, authorize the Judge's certificate to indemnify the prosecutor from damages, that he might otherwise be liable to, requiring oppressive security from a claimant of ships and goods seized, before he shall be allowed to defend his property, and are subversive of *American* rights.

Also the 12 *George* III. ch. 24, entitled "An Act for the better securing his Majesty's Dockyards, Magazines, Ships, Ammunitions, and Stores," which declares a new offence in America, and deprives the *American* subject of a constitutional trial by jury of the vicinage, by authorizing the trial of any persons, charged with the committing any offence described in the said Act, out of the Realm, to be indicted and tried for the same in any Shire or County within the Realm.

Also the three Acts passed in the last session of Parliament, for stopping the Port and blocking up the Harbour of *Boston,* for altering the Charter and Government of the *Massachusetts Bay*, and that which is entitled "An Act for the better administration of Justice," &C.

Also the Act passed in the same session for establishing the Roman Catholic Religion in the Province of *Quebec,* abolishing the equitable system of English Laws, and erecting a tyranny there, to the great danger, from so total a dissimilarity of Religion, Law, and Government of the neighboring *British* Colonies, by the assistance of whose blood and treasure the said country was conquered from *France.*

Also the Act passed in the same session for the better providing suitable Quarters for Officers and Soldiers in his Majesty's service in *North America.*

Also that the keeping a Standing Army in several of these Colonies, in time of peace, without the consent of the Legislature of that Colony in which such Army is kept, is against law.

To these grievous Acts and measures *Americans* cannot submit, but in hopes that their fellow-subjects in *Great Britain* will, on a revision of them, restore us to that state in which both countries found happiness and prosperity, we have for the present only resolved to pursue the following peaceable measures: 1. To enter into a Non-Importation, Non-Consumption, and Non-Exportation Agreement or Association. 2. To prepare an Address to the People of *Great Britain,* and a Memorial to the Inhabitants of *British America;* and 3. To prepare a loyal Address to his Majesty, agreeable to Resolutions already entered into.

Harcourt Brace & Company

The "Olive Branch Petition," 1775*

The following petition to King George III showed how moderate the Continental Congress remained, even after fighting had begun. This document summarized the Patriot interpretation of the events that had occurred following 1763, but it did not blame the king for the difficulties in the colonies. Instead, it called on him to find a peaceful resolution to the crisis that could ensure a lasting reconciliation between the colonies and the crown. George III refused to receive the petition; he declared the colonies in rebellion on August 23, 1775. Conflicts between British power and American liberties had become a full-scale war.

MOST GRACIOUS SOVEREIGN: We, your Majesty's faithful subjects, . . . in behalf of ourselves and the inhabitants of these Colonies, who have deputed us to represent them in General Congress, entreat your Majesty's gracious attention to this our humble petition.

The union between our Mother Country and these Colonies, and the energy of mild and just Government, produced benefits so remarkably important, and afforded such an assurance of their permanency and increase, that the wonder and envy of other nations were excited, while they beheld *Great Britain* rising to a power the most extraordinary the world had ever known.

Her rivals, observing that there was no probability of this happy connexion being broken by civil dissensions, and apprehending its future effects if left any longer undisturbed, resolved to prevent her receiving such continual and formidable accessions of wealth and strength, by checking the growth of those settlements from which they were to be deprived.

In the prosecution of this attempt, events so unfavorable to the design took place, that every friend to the interest of *Great Britain* and these Colonies, entertained pleasing and reasonable expectations of seeing an additional force and exertion immediately given to the operations of the union hitherto experienced, by an enlargement of the dominion of the Crown, and the removal of ancient and warlike enemies to greater distance.

At the conclusion, therefore, of the late war, the most glorious and advantageous that ever had been carried on by *British* arms, your loyal Colonists having contributed to its success by such repeated and strenuous exertions as frequently procured them the distinguished approbation of your Majesty, of the late King, and of Parliament, doubted not but that they should be permitted, with the rest of the Empire, to share in the blessings of peace, and the emoluments of victory and conquest.

While these recent and honourable acknowledgments of their merits remained on record on the Journals and acts of that august Legislature, the Parliament, undefaced by the imputation or even suspicion of any offence, they were alarmed by a new system of statutes and regulations adopted for the administration of the Colonies, that filled their minds with the most painful fears and jealousies; and, to their inexpressible astonishment, perceived the danger of a foreign quarrel quickly succeeded by domestick danger, in their judgment of a more dreadful kind.

Nor were these anxieties alleviated by any tendency in this system to promote the welfare of their Mother country. For though its effects were more immediately felt by them, yet its influence appeared to be injurious to the commerce and prosperity of *Great Britain.*

We shall decline the ungrateful task of describing the irksome variety of artifices practised by many of your Majesty's Ministers, the delusive pretences, fruitless terrours, and unavailing severities, that have from time to time, been dealt out by them, in their attempts to execute this

---

*American Archives: Fourth Series. Containing a Documentary History of the English Colonies in North America, from the King's Message to Parliament, of March 7, 1774, to the Declaration of Independence by the United States, 9 vols., comp. Peter Force (Washington, D.C.: M. St. Claire and Peter Force, 1837–1853), II:1870–72.

impolitick plan, or of tracing through a series of years past the progress of the unhappy differences between *Great Britain* and these Colonies, that have flowed from this fatal source.

Your Majesty's Ministers, persevering in their measures, and proceeding to open hostilities for enforcing them, have compelled us to arm in our own defence, and have engaged us in a controversy so peculiarly abhorrent to the affections of your still faithful Colonists, that when we consider whom we must oppose in this contest, and if it continues, what may be the consequences, our own particular misfortunes are accounted by us only as parts of our distress.

Knowing to what violent resentments and incurable animosities civil discords are apt to exasperate and inflame the contending parties, we think ourselves required by indispensable obligations to *Almighty God,* to your Majesty, to our fellow-subjects, and to ourselves, immediately to use all the means in our power, not incompatible with our safety, for stopping the further effusion of blood, and for averting the impending calamities that threaten the *British* Empire.

Thus called upon to address your Majesty on Affairs of such moment to *America*, and probably to all your Dominions, we are earnestly desirous of performing this office with the utmost deference to your Majesty; and we therefore pray, that your Majesty's royal magnanimity and benevolence may make the most favorable constructions of our expressions on so uncommon an occasion. Could we represent in their full force the sentiments that agitate the minds of us your dutiful subjects, we are persuaded your Majesty would ascribe any seeming deviation from reverence in our language, and even in our conduct, not to any reprehensible intention, but to the impossibility of reconciling the unusual appearances of respect with a just attention to our own preservation against those artful and cruel enemies who abuse your royal confidence and authority, for the purpose of effecting our destruction.

Attached to your Majesty's person, family, and Government, with all devotion that principle and affection can inspire; connected with *Great Britain* by the strongest ties that can unite societies, and deploring every event that tends in any degree to weaken them, we solemnly assure your Majesty, that we not only most ardently desire the former harmony between her and these Colonies may be restored, but that a concord may be established between them upon so firm a basis as to perpetuate its blessings, uninterrupted by any future dissensions, to succeeding generations in both countries, and to transmit your Majesty's name to posterity, adorned with that signal and lasting glory that has attended the memory of those illustrious personages, whose virtues and abilities have extricated states from dangerous convulsions, and, by securing happiness to others, have erected the most noble and durable monuments to their own fame.

We beg leave further to assure your Majesty, that notwithstanding the sufferings of your loyal Colonists during the course of this present controversy, our breasts retain too tender a regard for the kingdom from which we derive our origin, to request such a reconciliation as might, in any manner, be inconsistent with her dignity or her welfare. These, related as we are to her, honour and duty, as well as inclination, induce us to support and advance; and the apprehension that now oppress our hearts with unspeakable grief, being once removed, your Majesty will find your faithful subjects on this Continent, ready and willing at all times, as they have ever been, with their lives and fortunes, to assert and maintain the rights and interests of your Majesty, and of our Mother Country.

We therefore beseech your Majesty, that your royal authority and influence may be graciously interposed to procure us relief from our afflicting fears and jealousies, occasioned by the system before-mentioned, and to settle peace through every part of our Dominions, with all humility submitting to your Majesty's wise consideration, whether it may not be expedient, for facilitating those important purposes, that your Majesty be pleased to direct some mode, by which the united applications of your faithful Colonists to the Throne, in pursuance of their

Harcourt Brace & Company

common counsels, may be improved into a happy and permanent reconciliation; and that, in the mean time, measures may be taken for preventing the further destruction of the lives of your Majesty's subjects; and that such statutes as more immediately distress any of your Majesty's Colonies, may be repealed. For such arrangements as your Majesty's wisdom can form for collecting the united sense of your *American* people, we are convinced your Majesty would receive such satisfactory proofs of the disposition of the Colonists toward their Sovereign and Parent State, that the wished for opportunity would soon be restored to them, of evincing the sincerity of their professions, by every testimony of devotion becoming the most dutiful subjects, and the most affectionate Colonists.

That your Majesty may enjoy a long and prosperous reign, and that your descendants may govern your Dominions with honour to themselves and happiness to their subjects, is our sincere prayer.

Discussion

1. Between 1765 and 1775 sharp conflicts over Parliamentary power developed between Britain and the colonies. What do the documents reveal about efforts to resolve those conflicts? Do the selections suggest options other than rebellion that might have been pursued?

2. Colonists had long claimed the rights of Englishmen. According to the documents, what did Americans think constituted those rights in the mid-eighteenth century? Are those rights the same liberties revealed in the documents from previous chapters?

3. What differences, if any, exist between the Stamp Act resolution and the Declaration of Rights and Grievances and the "Olive Branch Petition"? What influence did the events of 1765–1775 have on the way Americans articulated their concerns over British power?

4. To Americans, the Administration of Justice Act posed a threat, yet the law seems to be designed to ensure, rather than deny, justice. What liberties did the law imply? Are there any liberties stated explicitly in the document? How might Americans have viewed it as an unconstitutional assertion of power?

Harcourt Brace & Company

Chapter 7
The Republican Experiment

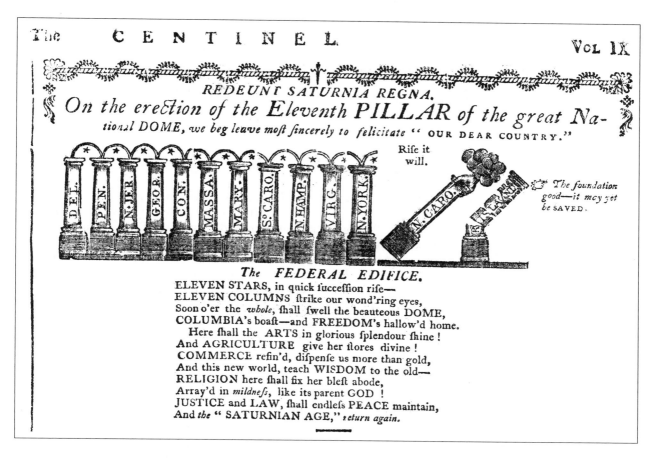

The FEDERAL EDIFICE.

ELEVEN STARS, in quick fucceffion rife—
ELEVEN COLUMNS ftrike our wond'ring eyes,
Soon o'er the *whole*, fhall fwell the beauteous DOME,
COLUMBIA's boaft—and FREEDOM's hallow'd home.
  Here fhall the ARTS in glorious fplendour fhine !
And AGRICULTURE give her ftores divine !
COMMERCE refin'd, difpenfe us more than gold,
And this new world, teach WISDOM to the old—
RELIGION here fhall fix her bleft abode,
Array'd in *mildnefs*, like its parent GOD !
JUSTICE and LAW, fhall endlefs PEACE maintain,
And *the* " SATURNIAN AGE," *return again.*

This cartoon was commissioned to celebrate New York's ratification of the new Constitution and to encourage North Carolina to do the same. The shattered pillar is Rhode Island, which refused to participate in the Philadelphia convention or to hold a ratifying convention in 1788. Rhode Island resisted ratification until May, 1790.

*A*mericans faced an enormous task as they challenged the power of the world's greatest empire. *The Revolution, however, involved more than merely overturning British authority in order to guarantee American liberties. Patriots enjoyed the opportunity to engage in an experiment in republicanism. As they wrote constitutions to create the new states, they established balanced and limited governments dedicated to protecting the rights of all citizens—that is, free adult males. In 1787, delegates applied those principles to the creation of a new central government established under the Constitution of the United States. The rhetoric of the Revolution had, on the other hand, insisted that all men are created equal. That ideal eventually made issues of equality, along with the traditional concerns over power and liberty, an important theme in the history of the American people.*

The Battle of Trenton, 1776[1]

*A*merican rebels faced the monumental task of defeating the British military—a challenge that took eight years of bloody warfare to accomplish. A critical event early in the Revolution came in December of 1776, when George Washington's army defeated a garrison of Hessian mercenaries at Trenton, New Jersey. This stunning victory, along with another at Princeton a week later, had important implications for the course of the War for Independence. British strategy in the immediate aftermath of these battles shifted from the offensive to the defensive, which gave Washington the opportunity to keep his army intact. More importantly, victory gave the Americans a crucial boost in morale as the soldiers, along with their commander in chief, realized that they could engage and defeat the enemy. In a brief letter to the Continental Congress, General Washington described that turning point in the war. The document serves as a reminder of the extreme hardships and severe dangers that soldiers faced in order to win independence.

Head-Quarters, Newtown, 27 December, 1776

Sir,

I have the pleasure of congratulating you upon the success of an enterprise, which I had formed against a detachment of the enemy lying in Trenton, and which was executed yesterday morning. The evening of the 25th I ordered the troops intended for this service to parade back of McKonkey's Ferry, that they might begin to pass as soon as it grew dark, imagining we should be able to throw them all over, with the necessary artillery, by twelve, o'clock, and that we might easily arrive at Trenton by five in the morning, the distance being about nine miles. But the quantity of ice, made that night, impeded the passage of the boats so much, that it was three o'clock before the artillery could all be got over; and near four, before the troops took up the line of march. This made me despair of surprising the town, as well I knew we could not reach

---

[1]From Jared Sparks, *The Writings of George Washington, Being His Correspondence, Addresses, Messages, and Other Papers, Official and Private, Selected and Published from the Original Manuscripts; with a Life of the Author,* 12 vols. (Boston: Little, Brown, and Company, 1855), IV:246–49.

Harcourt Brace & Company

it before the day was fairly broke. But as I was certain there was no making a retreat without being discovered and harassed on repassing the river, I formed my detachment into two divisions, one to march by the lower or river road, the other by the upper or Pennington road. As the divisions had nearly the same distance of march, I ordered each of them, immediately upon forcing the out-guards, to push directly into the town, that they might charge the enemy before they had time to form.

The upper division arrived at the enemy's advanced post exactly at eight o'clock; and in three minutes after, I found from the fire on the lower road, that that diversion had also got up. The out-guards made but small opposition, though, for their numbers, they behaved very well, keeping up a constant retreating fire from behind houses. We presently saw their main body formed; but, from their motions, they seemed undetermined how to act. Being hard pressed by our troops, who had already got possession of their artillery, they attempted to file off by a road on their right, leading to Princeton. But, perceiving their intention, I threw a body of troops in their way, which immediately checked them. Finding from our disposition, that they were surrounded, and that they must inevitably be cut to pieces if they made any further resistance, they agreed to lay down their arms. The number that submitted in this manner was twenty-three officers, and eight hundred and eighty-six men. Colonel Rahl, the commanding officer, and seven others were found wounded in the town. I do not exactly know how many were killed; but I fancy not above twenty or thirty, as they never made any regular stand. Our loss was trifling indeed, only two officers and one or two privates wounded.

I find that the detachment of the enemy consisted of three Hessian regiments of Anspach, Knyphausen, and Rahl, amounting to about fifteen hundred men, and a troop of British light-horse; but, immediately upon the beginning of the attack, all those, who were not killed or taken, pushed directly down the road towards Bordentown. These would likewise have fallen into our hands, could my plan have been completely carried into execution. General Ewing was to have crossed before day at Trenton Ferry, and taken possession of the bridge leading out of town; but the quantity of ice was so great, that, though he did every thing in his power to effect it, he could not get over. This difficulty also hindered General Cadwalader from crossing with the Pennsylvania militia from Bristol. He got part of his foot over; but, finding it impossible to embark his artillery, he was obliged to desist. I am fully confident, that, could the troops under Generals Ewing and Cadwalader have passed the river, I should have been able with their assistance to drive the enemy from all their posts below Trenton. But the numbers I had with me being inferior to theirs below me, and a strong battalion of light infantry being at Princeton above me, I thought it most prudent to return the same evening with the prisoners and artillery we had taken. We found no stores of any consequence in the town.

In justice to the officers and men, I must add, that their behaviour upon this occasion reflects the highest honor upon them. The difficulty of passing the river in a very severe night, and their march through a violent storm of snow and hail, did not in the least abate their ardor; but, when they came to the charge, each seemed to vie with the other in pressing forward; and were I to give a preference to any particular corps, I should do great injustice to the others. Colonel Baylor, my first aid-de-camp, will have the honor of delivering this to you; and from him you may be made acquainted with many other particulars. His spirited behaviour upon every occasion requires me to recommend him to your particular notice. . . .

Harcourt Brace & Company

The Virginia Bill of Rights, 1776*

Establishing constitutions for new state governments was one of the first steps taken by Americans experimenting with republicanism. Virginia representatives began their effort by preparing a declaration of rights, indicating the importance that they placed on a written guarantee of liberty. The following document, drafted mostly by George Mason, served as a model for numerous bills of rights, including that of the national constitution. It enumerated the rights and liberties that Americans held most dear and for which they had proven willing to fight.

A declaration of rights made by the representatives of the good people of Virginia, assembled in full and free convention; which rights do pertain to them and their posterity, as the basis and foundation of government.

SECTION 1. That all men are by nature equally free and independent, and have certain inherent rights, of which, when they enter into a state of society, they cannot, by any compact, deprive or divest their posterity; namely, the enjoyment of life and liberty, with the means of acquiring and possessing property, and pursuing and obtaining happiness and safety.

Sec. 2. That all power is vested in, and consequently derived from, the people; that all magistrates are their trustees and servants, and at all times amenable to them.

Sec. 3. That government is, or ought to be, instituted for the common benefit, protection, and security of the people, nation, or community; of all the various modes and forms of government, that is best which is capable of producing the greatest degree of happiness and safety, and is most effectually secured against the danger of maladministration; and that, when any government shall be found inadequate or contrary to these purposes, a majority of the community hath an indubitable, inalienable, and indefeasible right to reform, alter, or abolish it, in such manner as shall be judged most conducive to the public weal.

Sec. 4. That no man, or set of men, are entitled to exclusive or separate emoluments or privileges from the community, but in consideration of public services; which, not being descendible, neither ought the offices magistrate, legislator, or judge to be hereditary.

Sec. 5. That the legislative and executive powers of the State should be separate and distinct from the judiciary; and that the members of the two first may be restrained from oppression, by feeling and participating the burdens of the people, they should, at fixed periods, be reduced to a private station, return into that body from which they were originally taken, and the vacancies be supplied by frequent, certain, and regular elections, in which all, or any part of the former members, to be again eligible, or ineligible, as the laws shall direct.

Sec. 6. That elections of members to serve as representatives of the people, in assembly, ought to be free; and that all men, having sufficient evidence of permanent common interest with, and attachment to, the community, have the right of suffrage, and cannot be taxed or deprived of their property for public uses, without their own consent, or that of their representatives so elected, nor bound by any law to which they have not, in like manner, assembled, for the public good.

Sec. 7. That all power of suspending laws, or the execution of laws, by any authority, without consent of the representatives of the people, is injurious to their rights, and ought not to be exercised.

Sec. 8. That in all capital or criminal prosecutions a man hath a right to demand the cause and the nature of his accusation, to be confronted with the accusers and witnesses, to call for

---

*From the *Constitution of Virginia, 1776,* in *The Federal and State Constitutions , Colonial Charters , and Other Organic Laws of the State Territories, and Colonies Now or Heretofore Forming the United States of America,* 7 vols., ed. Francis N. Thorpe (Washington, D.C.: U.S. Government Printing Office, 1909), VII:3812–14.

Harcourt Brace & Company

evidence in his favor, and to a speedy trial by an impartial jury of twelve men of his vicinage, without whose unanimous consent he cannot be found guilty; nor can he be compelled to give evidence against himself; that no man be deprived of his liberty, except by the law of the land or the judgment of his peers.

Sec. 9. That excessive bail ought not to be required, nor excessive fines imposed, nor cruel and unusual punishment be inflicted.

Sec. 10. That general warrants, whereby an officer or messenger may be commanded to search suspected places without evidence of a fact committed, or to seize any person or persons, not named, or whose offence is not particularly described and supported by evidence, are grievous and oppressive, and ought not to be granted.

Sec. 11. That in controversies respecting property, and in suit between man and man, the ancient trial by jury is preferable to any other, and ought to be held sacred.

Sec. 12. That the freedom of the press is one of the great bulwarks of liberty, and can never be restrained but by despotic governments.

Sec. 13. That a well-regulated militia, composed of the body of the people, trained to arms, is the proper, natural, and safe defence of a free State; that standing armies, in time of peace, should be avoided, as dangerous to liberty; and that in all cases the military should be under strict subordination to, and governed by, the civil power.

Sec. 14. That the people have a right to uniform government; and, therefore, that no government separate from, or independent of the government of Virginia, ought to be erected or established within the limits thereof.

Sec. 15. That no free government, or the blessings of liberty, can be preserved to any people, but by a firm adherence to justice, moderation, temperance, frugality, and virtue, and by frequent recurrence to fundamental principles.

Sec. 16. That religion, or the duty which we owe to our Creator, and the manner of discharging it, can be directed only by reason and conviction, not by force or violence; and, therefore all men are equally entitled to the free exercise of religion, according to the dictates of conscience; and that it is the mutual duty of all to practise Christian forbearance, love, and charity towards each other.

"Remember the Ladies," 1776*

The American Revolution grew out of the conflict between British power and American liberties, but the movement for independence institutionalized the ideal of equality in the United States. Over the past two centuries, consequently, egalitarianism has become a major force in the nation's history. During the revolutionary era, artisans and yeomen worked to enhance their status, while many Americans urged the abolition of slavery. Women, too, hoped to improve their lot. In the following letters to her husband, Abigail Adams revealed her revolutionary understanding of the place of women in a republican society. Abigail and John Adams enjoyed a refreshingly forthright communication in their correspondence, and the documents reveal the powerful personality and incisive intellect of the future First Lady.

Braintree, 31 March, 1776

I wish you would ever write me a letter half as long as I write you, and tell me, if you may, where your fleet are gone; what sort of defense Virginia can make against our common enemy; whether it is so situated as to make an able defense. Are not the gentry lords, and the common

*From Charles Francis Adams, *Familiar Letter of John Adams and His Wife Abigail Adams, during the Revolution. With a Memoir of Mrs. Adams* (New York: Hurd and Houghton, 1876), 148–50, 212–14.

Harcourt Brace & Company

people vassals? Are they not like the uncivilized vassals Britain represents us to be? I hope their riflemen, who have shown themselves very savage and even blood-thirsty, are not a specimen of the generality of the people. I am willing to allow the colony great merit for having produced a Washington; but they have been shamefully duped by a Dunmore.

I have sometimes been ready to think that the passion for liberty cannot be equally strong in the breasts of those who have been accustomed to deprive their fellow creatures of theirs. Of this I am certain, that it is not founded upon the generous and Christian principle of doing to others as we would that others should do unto us.

Do not you want to see Boston? I am fearful of the small-pox, or I should have been in before this time. I got Mr. Crane to go to our house and see what state it was in. I find it has been occupied by one of the doctors of a regiment; very dirty, but no other damage has been done to it. The few things which were left in it are all gone. I look upon it as a new acquisition of property—a property which one month ago I did not value at a single shilling, and would with pleasure have seen it in flames.

The town in general is left in a better state than we expected; more owing to the precipitate flight than any regard to the inhabitants; though some individuals discovered a sense of honor and justice, and have left the rent of the houses in which they were, for the owners, and the furniture unhurt, or, if damaged, sufficient to make it good. Others have committed abominable ravages. The mansion-house of your President is safe, and the furniture unhurt; while the house and furniture of the Solicitor General have fallen a prey to their own merciless party. Surely the very fiends feel a reverential awe for virtue and patriotism, whilst they detest the patricide and traitor.

I feel very differently at the approach of spring from what I did a month ago. We knew not then whether we could plant or sow with safety, whether where we had tilled we could reap the fruits of our own industry, whether we could rest in our own cottages or whether we should be driven from the seacoast to seek shelter in the wilderness; but now we feel a temporary peace, and the poor fugitives are returning to their deserted habitations.

Though we felicitate ourselves, we sympathize with those who are trembling lest the lot of Boston should be theirs. But they cannot be in similar circumstances unless pusillanimity and cowardice should take possession of them. They have time and warning given them to see the evil and shun it.

I long to hear that you have declared an independency. And, by the way, in the code of laws which I suppose it will be necessary for you to make, I desire you would remember the ladies and be more generous and favorable to them than your ancestors. Do not put such unlimited power into the hands of the husbands. Remember, all men would be tyrants if they could. If particular care and attention is not paid to the ladies, we are determined to foment a rebellion, and will not hold ourselves bound by any laws in which we have no voice or representation.

That your sex are naturally tyrannical is a truth so thoroughly established as to admit of no dispute; but such of you as wish to be happy willingly give up the harsh title of master for the more tender and endearing one of friend. Why, then, not put it out of the power of the vicious and the lawless to use us with cruelty and indignity with impunity? Men of sense in all ages abhor those customs which treat us only as the vassals of your sex; regard us then as being placed by Providence under your protection, and in imitation of the Supreme Being make use of that power only for our happiness. . . .

————————

14 August, 1776

Your letter of August 3 came by this day's post. I find it very convenient to be so handy. I can receive a letter at night, sit down and reply to it, and send it off in the morning.

Harcourt Brace & Company

You remark upon the deficiency of education in your countrymen. It never, I believe, was in a worse state, at least for many years. The college is not in the state one could wish. The scholars complain that their professor in philosophy is taken off by public business, to their great detriment. In this town I never saw so great a neglect of education. The poorer sort of children are wholly neglected, and left to range the streets, without schools, without business, given up to all evil. There is either too much business left upon the hands of a few, or too little care to do it. We daily see the necessity of a regular government.

You speak of our worthy brother. I often lament it, that a man so peculiarly formed for the education of youth, and so well qualified as he is in many branches of literature, excelling in philosophy and the mathematics, should not be employed in some public station. I know not the person who would make half so good a successor to Dr. Winthrop. He has a peculiar, easy manner if communicating his ideas to youth; and the goodness of his heart and the purity of his morals, without an affected austerity, must have a happy effect upon the minds of pupils.

If you complain of neglect of education in sons, what shall I say with regard to daughters, who every day experience the want of it? With regard to the education of my own children, I find myself soon out of my depth, destitute and deficient in every part of education.

I most sincerely wish that some more liberal plan might be laid and executed for the benefit of the rising generation, and that our new Constitution may be distinguished for encouraging learning and virtue. If we mean to have heroes, statesmen, and philosophers, we should have learned women. The world perhaps would laugh at me and accuse me of vanity, but you, I know, have a mind too enlarged and liberal to disregard the sentiment. If much depends, as is allowed, upon the early education of youth, and the first principles which are instilled take the deepest root, great benefit must arise from literary accomplishments in women.

Excuse me. My pen has run away with me. I have no thought of coming to Philadelphia. The length of time I have and shall be detained here would have prevented me, even if you had no thoughts of returning till December; but I live in daily expectation of seeing you here. Your health, I think, requires your immediate return. I expected Mr. G_____ would have set off before now, but he perhaps finds it very hard to leave his mistress. I won't say harder than some do to leave their wives. Mr. Gerry stood very high in my esteem. What is meat for one is not for another. No accounting for fancy. She is a queer dame and leads people [on?] wild dances.

But hush! Post, don't betray your trust and lose my letter.

Federalist Number Ten, 1787*

During the 1780s, the experiment in republicanism endured trying times. The removal of British authority cleared the way for rivalries between different elements of American society—struggles profoundly shaped by the ancient tradition of liberty as well as the new faith in equality. Economic and political turmoil led to the Philadelphia Convention of 1787, which proposed the Constitution of the United States. Strong opposition to the constitution caused Alexander Hamilton, James Madison, and John Jay to write a series of articles to gain support for the new central government. The following essay addressed the antifederalist fear that a large republic would be inherently unstable and that "factions" posed a dire threat to all republics. Rather, argued Madison, in a large nation like the United States no group or coalition would ever be able to assert the power that could destroy the rights that Americans deemed sacred.

---

*From *The Federalist: A Collection of Essays by Alexander Hamilton, John Jay, and James Madison* (New York: P. F. Collier & Son, 1901), 44–51.

Among the numerous advantages promised by a well-constructed union, none deserves to be more accurately developed than its tendency to break and control the violence of faction. The friend of popular governments never finds himself so much alarmed for their character and fate as when he contemplates their propensity to this dangerous vice. He will not fail, therefore, to set a due value on any plan which, without violating the principles to which he is attached, provides a proper cure for it. The instability, injustice, and confusion introduced into the public councils have, in truth, been the mortal diseases under which popular government have everywhere perished; as they continue to be the favorite and fruitful topics from which the adversaries to liberty derive their most specious declamations. The valuable improvements made by the American constitutions on the popular models, both ancient and modern, cannot certainly be too much admired; but it would be an unwarrantable partiality, to contend that they have as effectually obviated the danger on this side as was wished and expected. Complaints are everywhere heard from our most considerable and virtuous citizens, equally the friends of public and private faith and of public and personal liberty, that our governments are too unstable; that the public good is disregarded in the conflict of rival parties; and that measures are too often decided, not according to the rules of justice, and the rights of the minor party, but the superior force of an interested and overbearing majority. However anxiously we may wish that these complaints had no foundation, the evidence of known facts will not permit us to deny that they are in some degree true. It will be found, indeed, on a candid review of our situation, that some of the distresses under which we labor have been erroneously charged on the operation of our governments; but it will be found, at the same time, that other causes will not alone account for many of our heaviest misfortunes; and particularly, for that prevailing and increasing distrust of public engagements, and alarm for private rights, which are echoed from one end of the continent to the other. These must be chiefly, if not wholly, effects of the unsteadiness and injustice with which a factious spirit has tainted our public administrations.

By a faction, I understand a number of citizens, whether amounting to a majority or a minority of the whole, who are united and actuated by some common impulse of passion, or of interest, adverse to the rights of other citizens or to the permanent and aggregate interests of the community.

There are two methods of curing the mischiefs of faction: the one, by removing its cause; the other, by controlling its effects.

There are again two methods of removing the causes of faction: the one, by destroying the liberty which is essential to its existence; the other, by giving to every citizen the same opinions, the same passions, and the same interests.

It could never be more truly said than of the first remedy, that it is worse than the disease. Liberty is to faction what air is to fire, an [element] without which it instantly expires. But it could not be less folly to abolish liberty, which is essential to political life, because it nourished faction, than it would be to wish the annihilation of air, which is essential to animal life, because it imparts to fire its destructive agency.

The second expedient is as impracticable as the first would be unwise. As long as the reason of man continues fallible, and he is at liberty to exercise it, different opinions will be formed. As long as the connection subsists between his reason and his self-love, his opinions and his passions will have a reciprocal influence on each other; and the former will be objects to which the latter will attach themselves. The diversity in the faculties of men, from which the rights of property originate, is not less an insuperable obstacle to a uniformity, of interests. The protection of these faculties is the first object of government. From the protection of different and unequal faculties of acquiring property, the possession of different degrees and kinds of property immediately results; and from the influence of these on the sentiments and views of the respective proprietors, ensues a division of the society into different interests and parties.

Harcourt Brace & Company

The latent causes of faction are thus sown in the nature of man; and we see them everywhere brought into different degrees of activity, according to the different circumstances of civil society. A zeal for different opinions concerning religion, concerning government and many other points, as well of speculation as of practice; an attachment to different leaders ambitiously contending for pre-eminence and power, or to persons of other descriptions whose fortunes have been interesting to the human passions, have, in turn, divided mankind into parties, inflamed them with mutual animosity, and rendered them much more disposed to vex and oppress each other, than to co-operate for their common good. So strong is this propensity of mankind to fall into mutual animosities, that where no substantial occasion presents itself, the most frivolous and fanciful distinctions have been sufficient to kindle their unfriendly passions and excite their most violent conflicts. But the most common and durable source of factions has been the various and unequal distribution of property. Those who are creditors and those who are debtors fall under a like discrimination. A landed interest, a manufacturing interest, a mercantile interest, a moneyed interest, with many lesser interests, grow up of necessity in civilized nations, and divide them into different classes, actuated by different sentiments and views. The regulation of these various and interfering interests forms the principle task of modern legislation, and involves the spirit of party and faction in the necessary and ordinary operations of the government.

No man is allowed to be a judge in his own cause; because his interest would certainly bias his judgment and, not improbably, corrupt his integrity. With equal, nay, with greater reason, a body of men are unfit to be both judges and parties at the same time; yet what are many of the most important acts of legislation, but so many judicial determinations, not indeed concerning the rights of single persons, but concerning the rights of large bodies of citizens. and what are the different classes of legislators, but advocates and parties to the causes which they determine? Is a law proposed concerning private debts?—it is a question to which the creditors are parties on one side, and the debtors on the other. Justice ought to hold the balance between them. Yet the parties are, and must be, themselves the judges; and the most numerous party, or, in other words, the most powerful faction, must be expected to prevail. Shall domestic manufacturing be encouraged, and in what degree, by restrictions on foreign manufactures? are questions which would be differently decided by the landed and the manufacturing classes, and probably neither with a sole regard to justice and the public good. The apportionment of taxes on the various descriptions of property is an act which seems to require the most exact impartiality; yet there is, perhaps, no legislative act in which greater opportunity and temptation are given to a predominant party, to trample on the rules of justice. Every shilling with which they overburden the inferior number is a shilling saved to their own pockets.

It is vain to say that enlightened statesmen will be able to adjust these clashing interests and render them all subservient to the public good. Enlightened statesmen will not always be at the helm; nor, in many cases, can such an adjustment be made at all, without taking into view indirect and remote considerations, which will rarely prevail over the immediate interest which one party may find in disregarding the rights of another or the good of the whole.

The inference to which we are brought is that the causes of faction cannot be removed, and that relief is only to be sought in the means of controlling its effects.

If a faction consist of less than a majority, relief is supplied by the republican principle, which enables the majority to defeat its sinister views by regular vote. It may clog the administration, it may convulse the society; but it will be unable to execute and mask its violence under the forms of the Constitution. When a majority is included in a faction, the form of popular government, on the other hand, enables it to sacrifice to its ruling passion of interest both the public good and the rights of other citizens. To secure the public good, and private rights, against the danger of such a faction, and at the same time to preserve the spirit and the form of pop-

Harcourt Brace & Company

ular government, is then the great object to which our inquiries are directed. Let me add that it is the great desideratum, by which alone this form of government can be rescued for the opprobrium under which it has too long labored, and be recommended to the esteem and the adoption of mankind.

By what means is this object attainable? Evidently by one of two only. Either the existence of the same passions or interest in a majority, at the same time, must be prevented; or the majority, having such coexistent passion or interest, must be rendered, by their number and local situation, unable to concert and carry into effect schemes of oppression. If the impulse and the opportunity be suffered to coincide, we well know that neither moral nor religious motives can be relied on as an adequate control. They are not found to be such on the injustice and violence of individuals, and lose their efficacy in proportion to the number combined together; that is, in proportion as their efficacy becomes needful.

From this view of the subject it may be concluded that a pure democracy, by which I mean a society consisting of a small number of citizens, who assemble and administer the government in person, can admit of no cure for the mischiefs of faction. A common passion or interest will, in almost every case, be felt by a majority of the whole; a communication and concert results from the form of government itself; and there is nothing to check the inducements to sacrifice the weaker party or an obnoxious individual. Hence it is that such democracies have ever been spectacles of turbulence and contention; have ever been found incompatible with personal security, or the rights of property, and have in general been as short in their lives as they have been violent in their deaths. Theocratic politicians, who have patronized this species of government, have erroneously supposed that by reducing mankind to a perfect equality in their political rights, they would at the same time be perfectly equalized and assimilated in their possessions, their opinions, and their passions.

A republic, by which I mean a government in which the scheme of representation takes place, opens a different prospect, and promises the cure for which we are seeking. Let us examine the points in which it varies from pure democracy, and we shall comprehend both the nature of the cure and the efficacy which it must derive from the union.

The two great points of difference between a democracy and a republic are: First, the delegation of the government, in the latter, to a small number of citizens elected by the rest; secondly, the greater number of citizens, and greater sphere of country, over which the latter may be extended.

The effect of the first difference is, on the one hand, to refine and enlarge the public views, by passing them through the medium of a chosen body of citizens, whose wisdom may best discern the true interest of their country, and whose patriotism and love of justice will be least likely to sacrifice it to temporary or partial considerations. Under such a regulation, it may well happen that the public voice, pronounced by the representatives of all the people, will be more consonant to the public good than if pronounced by the people themselves, convened for that purpose. On the other hand, the effect may be inverted. Men of factious tempers, of local prejudices, or the sinister designs, may by intrigue, by corruption, or by other means, first obtain the suffrages, and then betray the interests of the people. The question resulting is, whether small or extensive republics are most favorable to the election of proper guardians of the public weal; and it is clearly decided in favor of the latter by two obvious considerations.

In the first place, it is to be remarked that, however small the republic may be, the representatives must be raised to a certain number, in order to guard against the cabals of a few; and that, however large it may be, they must be limited to a certain number, in order to guard against the confusion of a multitude. Hence, the number of representatives in the two cases not being in proportion to that of the constituents, and being proportionally greatest in the small republic, it follows that if the proportion of fit characters be not less in the large than in the small republic, the former will present a greater option, and consequently a greater probability of a fit choice.

In the next place, as each representative will be chosen by a greater number of citizens in the large than in the small republic, it will be more difficult for unworthy candidates to prac-tise with success the vicious arts, by which elections are too often carried; and the suffrages of the people, being more free, will be more likely to centre in men who possess the most attrac-tive merits and the most diffusive and established characters.

It must be confessed that in this as in most other cases, there is a mean, on both sides of which inconveniences will be found to lie. By enlarging too much the number of electors, you render the representative too little acquainted with all their local circumstances and lesser inter-ests; as by reducing it too much, you render him unduly attached to these, and too little fit to comprehend and pursue great and national objects. The federal Constitution forms a happy combination in this respect; the great and aggregate interests being referred to the national, the local and particular to the State, legislatures.

The other point of difference is, the greater number of citizens and extent of territory which may be brought within the compass of republican than of democratic government; and it is this circumstance principally which renders factious combinations less to be dreaded in the former, than in the latter. The smaller the society, the fewer probably will be the distinct parties and interests composing it; the fewer the distinct parties and interests, the more frequently will a majority be found of the same party; and the smaller the number of individuals composing a majority, and the smaller the compass within which they are placed, the more easily will they concert and execute their plans of oppression. Extend the sphere, and you take in a greater vari-ety of parties and interests; you make it less probable that a majority of the whole will have a common motive to invade the rights of other citizens; or if such a common motive exists, it will be more difficult for all who feel it to discover their own strength, and to act in unison with each other. Besides other impediments, it may be remarked that where there is a consciousness of unjust or dishonorable purposes, communication is always checked by distrust, in proportion to the number whose concurrence is necessary.

Hence it clearly appears that the same advantage which a republic has over a democracy, in controlling the effects of faction, is enjoyed by a large over a small republic—is enjoyed by the Union over the States composing it. Does the advantage consist in the substitution of repre-sentatives, whose enlightened views and virtuous sentiments render them superior to local prej-udices, and to schemes of injustice? It will not be denied that the representation of the Union will be most likely to possess these requisite endowments. Does it consist in the greater securi-ty afforded by a greater variety of parties, against the event of any one party being able to out-number and oppress the rest? In an equal degree does the increased variety of parties, comprised within the Union, increase this security? Does it, in fine, consist in the greater obstacles opposed to the concert and accomplishment of the secret wishes of an unjust and interested majority? Here, again, the extent of the Union gives it the most palpable advantage.

The influence of factious leaders may kindle a flame within their particular States, but it will be unable to spread a general conflagration through the other States. A religious sect may degenerate into a political faction in a part of the confederacy; but the variety of sects dispersed over the entire face of it must secure the national councils against any danger from that source. A rage for paper money, for an abolition of debts, for an equal division of property, or for any other improper or wicked project will be less apt to pervade the whole body of the Union than a particular member of it; in the same proportion as such a malady is more likely to taint a par-ticular country or district than an entire State.

In the extent and proper structure of the Union, therefore, we behold a republican reme-dy for the diseases most incident to republican government. And according to the degree of pleasure and pride we feel in being republicans, ought to be our zeal in cherishing the spirit and supporting the character of federalists.

Discussion

1. To gain independence, Americans had to defeat a major military power. What does George Washington's letter suggest about his ability to meet that task? Does the document reveal any of Washington's leadership qualities? Does the selection indicate something about Washington's attitudes toward liberty or equality?

2. How do the Virginia Bill of Rights and *Federalist Number Ten* address issues of liberty, equality, and power? What liberties did Americans hold dear, and how did they propose to protect them?

3. In her call for her husband to "remember the ladies," do you think Abigail Adams was advocating gender equality? What liberties does she seem to think women deserve? What do her letters suggest about issues of power within American families at the time of the Revolution?

4. In *Federalist Number Ten*, James Madison authored an insightful political analysis. Does his essay reflect ideals presented in documents from earlier chapters? How does the article incorporate previously held concepts? In what way does it introduce new perceptions of liberty and power?

Harcourt Brace & Company

Chapter 8
The Democratic Republic, 1790–1820

VENERATE THE PLOUGH

*The ideal of the yeoman farmer, an independent citizen free from domination
by business or government, has been popular since Jefferson's time, when
most Americans had independent family farms. This plate links the farmer
with a female America figure who combines mythical ideas of Mother Earth,
husbandry, and the thirteen stars of the original states, suggesting that the
yeoman farmer is the strength of the republic.*

*D*uring the thirty years following ratification of the Constitution of the United States, Americans created a vibrant economy and a dynamic society. The United States remained largely rural, with farmers and frontiersmen often claiming a special status in the agrarian democratic republic, but in the young nation, all property-owning white fathers enjoyed power and liberty, along with a certain degree of equality. Their position, however, was based on the dependent condition of women and children and the subordinate roles of Indians and slaves. These disfranchised Americans held little or no power, they often did not share in the blessings of liberty, and they never obtained equality.

What Is an American, 1782*

French-born J. Hector St. John de Crèvecoeur considered America a heaven compared to Europe, and for many property-holding males like Crèvecoeur the young country did indeed seem to be utopia. The essay below offered some of the reasons he believed in the inherent superiority of the agrarian republic. His description of the United States affirmed the notion that liberty had made equality possible, and that this new breed—these American people—need not suffer the abuses of power that burdened Europeans.

I wish I could be acquainted with the feelings and thoughts which must agitate the heart and present themselves to the mind of an enlightened Englishman, when he first lands on this continent. He must greatly rejoice that he lived at a time to see this fair country discovered and settled; he must necessarily feel a share of national pride, when he views the chain of settlements which embellishes these extended shores. When he says to himself, this is the work of my countrymen, who, when convulsed by factions, afflicted by a variety of miseries and wants, restless and impatient, took refuge here. They brought along with them their national genius, to which they principally owe what liberty they enjoy, and what substance they possess. Here he sees the industry of his native country displayed in a new manner, and traces in their works the embryos of all the arts, sciences, and ingenuity which flourish in Europe. Here he beholds fair cities, substantial villages, extensive fields, an immense country filled with decent houses, good roads, orchards, meadows, and bridges, where an hundred years ago all was wild, woody, and uncultivated! What a train of pleasing ideas this fair spectacle must suggest; it is a prospect which must inspire a good citizen with the most heartfelt pleasure. The difficulty consists in the manner of viewing so extensive a scene. He is arrived on a new continent; a modern society offers itself to his contemplation, different from what he had hitherto seen. It is not composed, as in Europe, of great lords who possess everything, and of a herd of people who have nothing. Here are no aristocratical families, no courts, no kings, no bishops, no ecclesiastical dominion, no invisible power given to a few very visible one[s]; no great manufacturers employing thousands, no great refinements of luxury. The rich and the poor are not so removed from each other as they are in Europe. Some few towns excepted, we are all tillers of the earth, from Nova Scotia to West Florida. We are a people of cultivators, scattered over an immense territory, communicating with

---

*From J. Hector St. John de Crèvecoeur, *Letters from an American Farmer* (New York: E. P. Dutton & Company, 1912), 39–41, 56–58.

each other by means of good roads and navigable rivers, united by the silken bands of mild government, all respecting the laws, without dreading their power, because they are equitable. We are all animated with the spirit of industry, which is unfettered and unrestrained, because each person works for himself. If he travels through our rural district he views not the hostile castle, and the haughty mansion, contrasted with the clay-built and miserable cabin, where cattle and men help to keep each other warm, and dwell in meanness, smoke, and indigence. A pleasing uniformity of decent competence appears throughout our habitations. The meanest of our log-houses is a dry and comfortable habitation. Lawyer or merchant are the fairest titles our towns afford; that of a farmer is the only appellation of the rural inhabitants of our country. It must take some time ere he can reconcile himself to our dictionary, which is but short in words of dignity, and names of honour. There, on a Sunday, he sees a congregation of respectable farmers and their wives, all clad in neat homespun, well mounted, or riding in their own humble waggons. There is not among them an esquire, saving the unlettered magistrate. There he sees a parson as simple as his flock, a farmer who does not rot on the labour of others. We have no princes, for whom we toil, starve, and bleed: we are the most perfect society now existing in the world. Here man is as free as he ought to be; nor is this pleasing equality so transitory as many others are. Many ages will not see the shores of our great lakes replenished with inland nations, nor the unknown bounds of North America entirely peopled. Who can tell the millions of men whom it will feed and contain? for no European foot has yet travelled half the extent of this mighty continent. . . .

There is no wonder that this country has so many charms, and presents to Europeans so many temptations to remain in it. A traveller in Europe becomes a stranger as soon as he quits his own kingdom; but it is otherwise here. We know, properly speaking, no strangers; this is every person's country; the variety of our soils, situations, climates, governments, and produce, hath something which must please everybody. No sooner does an European arrive, no matter of what condition, than his eyes are opened upon the fair prospect; he hears his language spoke, he retraces many of his own country manners, he perpetually hears the names of families and towns with which he is acquainted; he sees happiness and prosperity in all places disseminated; he meets with hospitality, kindness, and plenty everywhere; he beholds hardly any poor, he seldom hears of punishments and executions; and he wonders at the elegance of our towns those miracles of industry and freedom. He cannot admire enough our rural districts, our convenient roads, good taverns, and our many accommodations; he involuntarily loves a country where everything is so lovely. When in England, he was a mere Englishman; here he stands on larger portion of the globe, not less than its fourth part, and may see the production of the north, in iron and naval stores; the provisions of Ireland, the grain of Egypt, the indigo, the rice of China. He does not find, as in Europe, a crowded society, where every place is over-stocked; he does not feel the perpetual collision of parties, that difficulty of beginning, that contention which oversets so many. There is room for everybody in America; has he any particular talent of industry? he exerts it in order to procure a livelihood, and it succeeds. Is he a merchant? the avenues of trade are infinite; is he eminent in any respect? he will be employed and respected. Does he love a country life? pleasant farms present themselves; he may purchase what he wants, and thereby become an American farmer. Is he a labourer, sober and industrious? he need not go many miles, nor receive many informations before he will be hired, well fed at the table of his employer, and paid four or five times more than he can get in Europe. Does he want uncultivated lands? thousands of acres present themselves, which he may purchase cheap. Whatever be his talents or inclinations, if they are moderate he may satisfy them. I do not mean that every one who comes here will grow rich in a little time; no, but he may procure an easy, decent maintenance, by his industry. Instead of starving, he will be fed, instead of being idle he will have employment; and these are riches enough for such men as come over here. The rich stay in

Harcourt Brace & Company

Europe, it is only the middling and the poor that emigrate. Would you wish to travel in independent idleness, from north to south, you will find easy access, and the most cheerful reception at every house; society without ostentation, good cheer without pride, and every decent diversion which the country affords, with little expense. It is no wonder that the European who has lived here a few years, is desirous to remain; Europe with all its pomp, is not to be compared with this continent, for men of middle stations, or labourers.

An European, when he first arrives, seems limited in his intentions, as well as in his views; but he very suddenly alters his scale; two hundred miles formerly appeared a very great distance, it is now but a trifle; he no sooner breathes our air than he forms schemes, and embarks in designs he never would thought of in his own country. There the plenitude of society confines many useful ideas, and often extinguishes the most laudable schemes which here ripen into maturity. Thus Europeans become Americans. . . .

On Motherhood*

The patriarchal society of the early nineteenth century assigned very specific roles to women. This so-called cult of domesticity increasingly insisted that women should remain at home and that raising children should be their primary responsibility. Mothers bore a special obligation toward sons. Young men needed to know how to empower themselves and how to preserve liberty in order for the nation to survive. As time passed and the United States embraced egalitarianism, women taught their sons to consider themselves the equals of all other men. For the most part, however, these republican mothers could not empower themselves, economically or socially. Ironically, although they played a key part in ensuring that liberty flourished in America, women were not equal to men. The following selection summarizes the thinking of John Abbott, one of the more influential advocates of the ideals that so profoundly shaped the lives of women in the democratic republic.

Mothers have as powerful an influence over the welfare of future generations as all other causes combined.—Thus far the history of the world has been composed of the narrations of oppression and blood. War has scattered its unnumbered woes. The cry of the oppressed has unceasingly ascended to heaven. Where are we to look for the influence which shall change this scene, and fill the earth with the fruits of peace and benevolence? It is to Christianity as taught from a mother's lips. In nine cases out of ten, the first six or seven years decide the character of the man. If a boy leaves the paternal roof uncontrolled, turbulent and vicious, he will, in all probability, rush on in the mad career of self-indulgence. There are exceptions. But these exceptions are rare. If, on the other hand, your son goes from home accustomed to control himself, he will most undoubtedly retain that habit through life. If he has been taught to make sacrifices of his own enjoyment, that he may promote the happiness of those around him, he will continue to practise benevolence, and consequently he will be respected and useful and happy. If he has adopted firm resolutions to be faithful in all the relations of life, he in all probability will be a virtuous man, and an estimable citizen, and a benefactor of his race.

When our land is filled with virtuous and patriotic mothers, then will it be filled with virtuous and patriotic men. She who was first in the transgression, must be yet the principal earthly instrument in the restoration. Other causes may greatly aid. Other influences must be ready to receive the mind as it comes from the mother's hand, and carry it onward in its improve-

---

*From John S. C. Abbott, *The Mother at Home; or, The Principles of Maternal Duty,* revised and corrected by Daniel Walton (London: John Mason, 1834), 165–67, 182–84.

ment. But the mothers of our race must be the chief instruments in its redemption. The brightest rays of the millennial morn must come from the cradle. This sentiment will bear examining; and the more it is examined the more manifestly true will it appear. It is alike the dictate of philosophy and experience. The mother who is neglecting personal effort, and relying upon other influences for the formation of virtuous character in her children, will find, when it is too late, that she has fatally erred. The patriot who hopes that schools, and lyceums, and the general diffusion of knowledge, will promote the good order and happiness of the community, while family government is neglected, will find that he is attempting to purify the streams which are flowing from a corrupt fountain. It is maternal influence, after all, which must be the great agent, in the hands of God, in bringing back our guilty race to duty and happiness. O that mothers could feel this responsibility as they ought! then would the world assume a different aspect. Then should we less frequently behold unhappy families and brokenhearted parents. A new race of men would enter upon the busy scene of life, and cruelty and crime would pass away. O mothers! reflect upon the power your Maker has placed in your hands. There is no earthly influence to be compared with yours. There is no combination of causes so powerful, in promoting the happiness of the misery of our race, as the instructions of home. In a most particular sense, God has constituted you the guardians and the controllers of the human family. . . .

There is an impression upon the minds of many, that skill in governing must be instinctive; that it is an original and native talent, and not to be acquired by information or thought. But look at those parents who have been most successful in family government, and they will be found to be those who have most diligently and uniformly attended to the subject. You may go into the family of some man of celebrity in one of the learned professions, and, as you look upon his lawless children, you are perhaps discouraged. You say, If this man, with his powerful and highly-cultivated mind, cannot succeed in family government, how can I expect success? But a little observation will satisfy you that this man is giving his time and attention to other pursuits. He is neglecting his children; and they are forming precisely those characters we should expect from the influences to which they are exposed.

There is no absolute certainty that any procedure will result in the piety of the child. But if we go on in our attempts to govern without system or thought, or care, we shall undoubtedly reap most bitter consequences. The mother must study her duty. She must carefully observe the effect produced by her mode of discipline. There is but little advantage to be derived from books, unless we revolve their contents in our minds. Others may suggest the most valuable ideas. But we must take those ideas and dwell upon them, and trace out their effects, and incorporate them into our minds, by associating them with others of our own. We must accustom ourselves to investigation and thought. The mother who will do this will most certainly grow in wisdom. She will daily perceive that she is acquiring more facility in forming her children the character she desires. And the increasing obedience and affection she will receive will be her constant reward. Care and labour are necessary in training up a family. But no other cares are rewarded with so rich a recompence; no other labours ensure such permanent and real enjoyment. You, O mothers, have immortal souls entrusted to your keeping. Their destiny is in a great degree in your hands. Your ignorance or unfaithfulness may sink them to the world of woe: your fidelity, under the divine blessing, which will not be withheld, may elevate them to the mansions of heaven.

Indian Relations

Women held a dependent role in America, but at least they had a place in the young republic. Indians, on the other hand, did not. Consequently, the history of Indian relations in the United States is generally one of assertions of power that deprived Native Americans of their lands, their freedom, and their culture. The following documents offer two examples of treaties between the federal government and various Indian tribes. The first, the Treaty of Greenville, followed the victory of troops under General "Mad" Anthony Wayne at the Battle of Fallen Timbers in 1794. This treaty opened up much of the Northwest Territory for American settlement. The second treaty resulted from General Andrew Jackson's success at the Battle of Horseshoe Bend. The Creek Treaty made available millions of acres that became the southern "Cotton Belt." Both documents, then, helped make possible the agrarian society that served as a foundation for the rapid growth of the new nation.

Treaty with the Wyandot, Etc., 1795*

A treaty of peace between the United States of America and the Tribes of Indians, called the Wyandots, Delawares, Shawnees, Ottawas, Chipewas, Putawatimes, Miamis, Eel-River, Weea's Kickapoos, Piankashaws, and Kaskaskias.

To put an end to a destructive war, to settle all controversies, and to restore harmony and a friendly intercourse between the said United States, and Indian tribes; Anthony Wayne, major-general, commanding the army of the United States, and sole commissioner for the good purposes above-mentioned, and the said tribes of Indians, by their Sachems, chiefs, and warriors, met together at Greenville, the head quarters of the said army, have agreed on the following articles, which, when ratified by the President, with the advice and consent of the Senate of the United States, shall be binding on them and the said Indian tribes.

ARTICLE I.

Henceforth all hostilities shall cease; peace is hereby established, and shall be perpetual; and a friendly intercourse shall take place, between the said United States and Indian tribes.

ARTICLE II.

All prisoners on both sides shall be restored. The Indians, prisoners to the United States, shall be immediately set at liberty. The people of the United States, still remaining prisoners among the Indians, shall be delivered up in ninety days, . . . and ten chiefs of the said tribes shall remain at Greenville as hostages, until the delivery of the prisoners shall be effected.

ARTICLE III.

The general boundary lines between the United States, and the lands of the . . . tribes, shall begin at the Cayahoga River, and run thence up the same to the portage between that and the Tuscarawas branch of the Muskingum; thence down that branch to the crossing place above Fort Lawrence; thence westerly to a fork of that branch of the great Miami River running into the Ohio, at or near which fork stood Loromie's store, and whence commences the portage between the Miami and Ohio, and St. Mary's river, which is a branch of the Miami, which runs into Lake Erie; thence a westerly course to Fort Recovery, which stands on a branch of the Wabash; then south-westerly in a direct line to the Ohio, so as to intersect that river opposite the mouth of the Kentucke or Cuttawa river. And in consideration of the peace now established; of the goods formerly received from the United States; of those now to be delivered, and of the yearly delivery of goods . . . to be made hereafter, and to indemnify the United States of the injuries and expenses they have sustained during the war; the . . . tribes do hereby cede and

---

*From *Indian Affairs. Laws and Treaties,* 7 vols., comp. and ed. Charles J. Kappler (Washington, D.C.: U.S. Government Printing Office, 1904–1979), II:39–43.

relinquish forever, all their claims to the lands lying eastwardly and southwardly of the general boundary line now described; and these lands, or any part of them, shall never hereafter be made a cause or pretence, on part of the said tribes . . . , of war or injury to the United States. . . .

And for the same considerations, and as an evidence of the returning friendship of the . . . tribes, . . . [they] do also cede to the United States the following pieces of land; to-wit. [Eleven specific pieces of land totaling 408 square miles, plus] . . . (12.) The post of Detroit and all the land to the north, the west, and south of it, of which the Indian title has been extinguished by gifts or grants to the French or English governments; and so much more of the land to be annexed to the district of Detroit as shall be comprehended between the river Rosine on the south, lake St. Clair on the north, and a line . . . six miles distant from the west end of lake Erie, and Detroit river. (13.) The post of Michillimackinac, and all the land on the island, on which that post stands, and the main land adjacent . . . ; and a piece of land on the main to the north of the island, to measure six miles on lake Huron, of the strait between lakes Huron and Michigan, and to extend three miles back from the water of the lake or strait, and also the island De Bois Blanc, being an extra and voluntary gift of the Chipewa nation. (14.) One piece of land six miles square at the mouth of the Chikago river, emptying into the south-west end of Lake Michigan. . . . (15.) One piece twelve miles square at or near the mouth of the Illinois river, emptying into the Mississippi. (16.) One piece six miles square at the old Piorias fort and village, near the south end of the Illinois lake on said Illinois river: And whenever the United States shall think proper to survey and mark the boundaries of the land hereby ceded to them, they shall give timely notice thereof to the . . . Indians, that they may appoint some of their wise chiefs to attend and see that the lines are run according to the terms of this treaty.

And the . . . tribes will allow the people of the United States a free passage by land and by water . . . through their country, along the chain of posts herein before mentioned. . . . And the . . . tribes will also allow to the people of the United States the free use of the harbors and mouths of the rivers along the lakes adjoining Indian lands, for sheltering vessels and boats, and liberty to land their cargoes where necessary for their safety.

ARTICLE IV.

In consideration of the peace now established . . . , and to manifest the liberality of the United States, as the great means of rendering this peace strong and perpetual; the United States relinquish their claims to all other Indian lands northward of the river Ohio, eastward of the Mississippi, and westward and southward of the Great Lakes and the waters uniting them, according to the boundary line agreed on by the United States and the king of Great-Britain, in the treaty of peace made between them in the year 1783. But from this relinquishment by the United States, the following tracts of land, are explicitly excepted. 1st. The tract of one hundred and fifty thousand acres near the rapids of the river Ohio, which has been assigned to General Clark. . . . 2d. The post of St. Vincennes on the river Wabash, and the lands adjacent, of which the Indian title has been extinguished. 3d. The lands at all other places in possession of the French people and other white settlers among them, of which the Indian title has been extinguished. . . ; and 4th. The post of fort Massac towards the mouth of the Ohio. . . .

And for the same considerations and with the same views as above mentioned, the United States now deliver to the . . . tribes a quantity of goods to the value of twenty thousand dollars . . . ; and henceforth every year forever the United States will deliver . . . like useful goods, suited to the circumstances of the Indians, of the value of nine thousand five hundred dollars. . . .

Provided, That if either of the said tribes shall hereafter . . . desire that a part of their annuity should be furnished in domestic animals, implements of husbandry, and other utensils convenient for them, . . . and [to] be employed for their benefit, the same shall at the subsequent annual deliveries be furnished accordingly.

Harcourt Brace & Company

ARTICLE V.

To prevent any misunderstanding about the Indian land relinquished by the United States . . . , it is now explicitly declared, that the meaning of relinquishment is this: The Indian tribes who have a right to those lands, are quietly to enjoy them, hunting, planting, and dwelling thereon as long as they please, without any molestation from the United States; but when those tribes . . . shall be disposed to sell their lands . . . they are to be sold only to the United States; and until such sale, the United States will protect all the . . . tribes. . . . And the . . . tribes again acknowledge themselves to be under the protection of the said United States and no other power whatever.

ARTICLE VI.

If any citizen of the United States, or any other white person or persons, shall presume to settle upon lands now relinquished by the United States, such . . . person shall be out of the protection of the United States; and the Indian tribe, on whose lands the settlement shall be made, may drive off the settler, or punish him in such manner as they shall think fit; and . . . the United States shall be at liberty to . . . remove and punish the settlers as they shall think proper, and so effect the protection of the Indian lands herein before stipulated.

ARTICLE VII.

The . . . Indians, parties to this treaty, shall be at liberty to hunt within the territory . . . they have now ceded to the United States, without hindrance or molestation, so long as they demean themselves peaceably, and offer no injury to the people of the United States.

ARTICLE VIII.

Trade shall be opened with the . . . tribes; and they do hereby respectfully engage to afford protection to such persons . . . as shall be duly licensed to reside among them for the purpose of trade . . . ; but no person shall be permitted to reside at any of their towns or hunting camps as a trader, who is not furnished with a license for that purpose. . . . And if any licensed trader shall abuse his privilege by unfair dealing, upon complaint and proof thereof, his license shall be taken away from him, and he shall be further punished according to the laws of the United States. . . . And to prevent impositions by forged licenses, the said Indians shall at least once a year give information to the superintendent or his deputies, of the names of the traders residing among them.

ARTICLE IX.

Lest the firm peace and friendship now established should be interrupted by the misconduct of individuals, the United States, and the . . . tribes agree, that for injuries done by individuals on either side, no private revenge or retaliation shall take place; but instead thereof, complaint shall be made by the party injured, to the other . . . : and such prudent measures shall then be pursued as shall be necessary to preserve the said peace and friendship. . . . Should any Indian tribes mediate a war against the United States or either of them, and the same shall come to the attention of the . . . tribes, . . . they do hereby engage to give immediate notice thereof to the . . . officer commanding the troops of the United States, at the nearest post. . . . In like manner, the United States shall give notice to the . . . tribes of any harm that may be meditated against them . . . ; and do all in their power to hinder and prevent the same. . . .

ARTICLE X.

All other treaties heretofore made between the United States and the . . . tribes . . . since the treaty of 1783, between the United States and Great Britain, that come within the purview of this treaty, shall henceforth cease and become void.

Harcourt Brace & Company

Treaty with the Creeks, 1814*

Articles of agreement and capitulation, made and concluded this ninth day of August, one thousand eight hundred and fourteen, between major general Andrew Jackson, on behalf of the President of the United States of America, and the chiefs, deputies, and warriors of the Creek Nation.

WHEREAS an unprovoked, inhuman, and sanguinary war, waged by the hostile Creeks against the United States, hath been repelled, prosecuted, and determined, successfully, on the part of the said States, in conformity with principles of national justice and honorable warfare— And whereas consideration is due to the rectitude of proceeding dictated by instructions relating to the re-establishment of peace: be it remembered, that prior to the conquest of that part of the Creek nation hostile to the United States, numberless aggressions had been committed against the peace, property, and the lives of citizens of the United States, and those of the Creek nation in amity with her, at the mouth of Duck river, Fort Mimms, and elsewhere, contrary to national faith, and the regard due to an article of the treaty concluded at New-York, in the year seventeen hundred ninety, between the two nations: That the United States, previously to the perpetration of such outrages did, in order to ensure future amity and concord between the Creek nation and the said states, in conformity with the stipulations of former treaties, fulfil, with punctuality and good faith, her engagements to the said nation: that more than two-thirds of the whole number of chiefs and warriors of the Creek nation, disregarding the genuine spirit of existing treaties, suffered themselves to be instigated to violations of their national honor, and the respect due to a part of their own nation faithful to the United States and the principles of humanity, by impostures [impostors,] denominating themselves Prophets, and by the duplicity and misrepresentations of foreign emissaries, whose governments are at war, open and understood, with the United States. Wherefore,

1st—The United States demand an equivalent for all expenses incurred in prosecuting the war to its termination, by a cession of all the territory belonging to the Creek nation within the territories of the United States, lying west, south, and south-eastwardly, of a line to be run and described by persons duly authorized by the President of the United States—Beginning at a point on the eastern bank of the Coosa river, where the south boundary line of the Cherokee nation crosses the same; running from thence . . . to a point one mile above the mouth of Cedar creek, at Fort Williams, thence . . . to a point opposite the upper end of the great falls, (called by the natives Woetumka,) thence east . . . to a point due north of the mouth of Ofucshee, thence south . . . to the mouth of Ofucshee on the south side of the Tallapoosa river, thence up the same . . . to a point where a direct course will cross the same at the distance of ten miles from the mouth thereof, thence a direct line to the mouth of Summochico creek, . . . thence east . . . to a point which shall intersect the line now dividing the lands claimed by the said Creek nation from those owned and claimed by the state of Georgia; Provided, nevertheless, that where any possession of any chief or warrior of the Creek nation, who shall have been friendly to the United States during the war, and taken an active part therein, shall be within the territory ceded by these articles to the United States, every person shall be entitled to a reservation of land within the said territory of one mile square, to include his improvements as near the centre thereof as may be, which shall inure to the said chief or warrior, and his descendants, so long as he or they shall continue to occupy the same, who shall be protected by and subject to the laws of the United States; but upon the voluntary aban-

---

[4]From *Indian Affairs. Laws and Treaties,* 7 vols., comp. and ed. Charles J. Kappler (Washington, D.C.: U.S. Government Printing Office, 1904–1979), II:107–109.

Harcourt Brace & Company

donment thereof . . . the right of occupancy or possession of said lands shall devolve to the United States. . . .

2nd—The United States will guarantee to the Creek nation, the integrity of all their territory eastwardly and northwardly of the said line to be run and described as mentioned in the first article.

3d—The United States demand, that the Creek nation abandon all communication, and cease to hold any intercourse with any British or Spanish post, garrison, or town; and that they shall not admit among them, any agent or trader, who shall not derive authority to hold commercial, or other intercourse with them, by licence from the President or authorized agent of the United States.

4th—The United States demand an acknowledgment of the right to establish military posts and trading houses, and to open roads within the territory, guaranteed to the Creek nation by the second article, and a right to free navigation of all its waters.

5th—The United States demand, that a surrender be immediately made, of all the persons and property taken from the citizens of the United States, the friendly part of the Creek nation, the Cherokee, Chickasaw, and Choctaw nations, to the respective owners; and the United States will cause to be immediately restored to the formerly hostile Creeks, all the property taken from them since their submission, either by the United States, or by any Indian nation in amity with the United States, together with all the prisoners taken from them during the war.

6th—The United States demand the caption and surrender of all the prophets and instigators of the war, whether foreigners or natives, who have not submitted to the arms of the United States, and become party to these articles of capitulation, if ever they shall be found within the territory guaranteed to the Creek nation. . . .

7th—The Creek nation being reduced to extreme want, and not at present having the means of subsistence, the United States, from motives of humanity, will continue to furnish gratuitously the necessaries of life, until the crops of corn can be considered competent to yield the nation a supply, and will establish trading houses in the nation . . . to enable the nation, by industry and economy, to procure clothing.

8th—A permanent peace shall ensue from the date of these presents forever, between the Creek nation and the United States, and between the Creek nation and the Cherokee, Chickasaw, and Choctaw nations. . . .

The parties to these presents, after due consideration, for themselves and their constituents, agree to ratify and confirm the preceding articles, and constitute the basis of a permanent peace between the two nations. . . .

Davy Crockett*

David Crockett was a frontier entrepreneur who served as a scout during the Creek campaign and sat in the Tennessee legislature as well as the national Congress before his death at the Battle of the Alamo immortalized him as an American hero. Early in his career, Crockett had created an alter ego—"Davy"—that helped ensure his fame. Davy Crockett epitomized that archetypical rugged individualist who helped make egalitarianism a key theme in American history. The following selection, taken from his autobiography, shows how he created his image as a dauntless fron-

*From *Life of Col. David Crockett, Written by Himself. Comprising His Early Life, Hunting Adventures, Services Under General Jackson in the Creek War, Electioneering Speeches, Career in Congress, Triumphal Tour in the Northern States, and Services in the Texan War. To Which is Added An Account of Colonel Crockett's Glorious Death at the Alamo, While Fighting in Defence of Texan Independence. By the Editor* (Philadelphia: G. G. Evans, 1859), 125–29, 135–37.

tiersman and as a simple populist representative of the people. A dedicated husband and father who could meet extraordinary challenges, a fearless man who refused to suffer defeat, and an intrepid hunter who could "grin a bear out of a tree," Crockett was also an astute observer who understood well the nature of politics in a democratic society.

I gathered my corn, and then set out for my Fall's hunt. This was in the last of October 1822. I found bear very plenty, and, indeed, all sorts of game and wild varments, except buffalo. There was none of them. I hunted on till Christmas, having supplied my family very well all along with wild meat, at which time my powder gave out; and I had none either to fire Christmas guns, which is very common in that country, or to hunt with. I had a brother-in-law who had now moved out and settled about six miles west of me, on the opposite side of Rutherford's fork of the Obion river, and he had brought me a keg of powder, but I had never gotten it home. There had just been another of Noah's freshes, and the low grounds were flooded all over with water. I know'd the stream was at least a mile wide which I would have to cross, as the water was from hill to hill, and yet I determined to go on over in some way or another, so as to get my powder. I told this to my wife, and she immediately opposed it with all her might. I still insisted, telling her that we had no powder for Christmas, and, worse than all, we were out of meat. She said, we had as well starve as for me to freeze to death or to get drowned, and one or the other was certain if I attempted to go.

But I didn't believe the half of this; and so I took my woolen wrappers, and a pair of moccasins, and put them on, and tied up some dry clothes, and a pair of shoes and stockings, and started. But I didn't before know how much anybody could suffer and not die. This, and some of my other experiments in water, learned me something about it, and I therefore relate them.

The snow was about four inches deep when I started; and when I got to water, which was only about a quarter of a mile off, it looked like an ocean. I put in, and waded on till I come to the channel, where I crossed that on a high log. I then took water again, having my gun and all my hunting tools along, and waded till I came to a deep slough, that was wider than the river itself. I had crossed it often on a log; but behold, when I got there, no log was to be seen. . . . I then felt my way along with my feet, in the water, about waist deep, but it was a mighty ticklish business. However, I got over, and by this time I had very little feeling in my feet and legs, as I had been all the time in the water. . . .

I went but a short distance before I came to another slough, over which there was a log, and it was floating on the water. I thought I could walk it, and so I mounted on it; but when I had got about the middle of the deep water, somehow or somehow else, it turned over, and in I went up to my head. I waded out of this deep water, and went ahead until I came to a highland, where I stopp'd to pull of my wet clothes, and put on the others, which I had held up with my gun, above the water, when I fell in. I got them on, but my flesh had no feeling in it, I was so cold. I tied up the wet ones, and hung them up in a bush. I now thought I would run, so as to warm myself a little, but I couldn't raise a trot for some time; indeed, I couldn't step more than half the length of my foot. After awhile I got better, and went on five miles to the house of my brother-in-law, having not even smelt fire from the time I started. I got there late in the evening, and he was much astonished at seeing me at such a time. I staid all night, and the next morning was most piercing cold, and so they persuaded me not to go home that day. I agreed, and turned out and killed him two deer; but the weather still got worse and colder, instead of better. I staid that night, and in the morning they still insisted I couldn't get home. I knowed the water would be frozen over, but not hard enough to bear me, and so I agreed to stay that day. I went out hunting again, and pursued a big *he-bear* all day, but didn't kill him. The next morning was bitter cold, but I knowed my family was without meat, and I determined to get home to them, or die a-trying.

I took my keg of powder, and all my hunting tools, and cut out. When I got to the water, it was a sheet of ice as far as I could see. I put on to it, but hadn't got far before it broke through with me; and so I took out my tomahawk, and broke my way along before me for a considerable distance. At last I got to where the ice would bear me for a short distance, and I mounted on it, and went ahead; but it soon broke again, and I had to wade on. . . . By this time I was nearly frozen to death, but I saw all along before me, where the ice had been fresh broke, and I thought it might be a bear straggling about in the water. I, therefore, fresh primed my gun, and, cold as I was, I was determined to make war on him, if we met. But I followed the trail till it led me home, and I then found it had been made by a young man that lived with me, who had been sent out by my distressed wife to see, if he could, what had become of me, for they all believed that I was dead. When I got home, I wasn't quite dead, but mighty nigh it; but had my powder, and that was what I went for. . . .

I had on hand a great many skins, and so, in the month of February, I packed a horse with them, and taking my eldest son with me, cut out for a little town called Jackson, situated about forty miles off. We got there well enough, and I sold my skins, and bought me some coffee, and sugar, powder, lead, and salt. I packed them all up in readiness for a start, which I intended to make early the next morning. Morning came, but I concluded, before I started, I would go and take a horn with some of my old fellow-soldiers that I had met with at Jackson.

I did so; and while we were engaged in this, I met with three candidates for the Legislature. A Doctor Butler, who was, by marriage, a nephew to General Jackson, a Major Lynn, and a Mr. McEver, all first-rate men. We all took a horn together, and some person present said to me, "Crockett, you must offer for the Legislature." I told him I lived at least forty miles from any white settlement; and had no thought of becoming a candidate at that time. So we all parted, and I and my little boy went on home.

It was about a week or two after this, that a man came to my house, and told me I was a candidate. I told him not so. But he took out a newspaper from his pocket, and showed me where I was announced. I said to my wife that this was all a burlesque on me, but I was determined to make it cost the man who had put it at least the value of the printing, and of the fun he wanted at my expense. So I hired a young man to work in my place on the farm, and turned out myself electioneering. I hadn't been out long, before I found the people began to talk very much about the bear hunter, the man from the cane; and the three gentlemen, who I have already named, soon found it necessary to enter into an agreement to have a sort of caucus at their March court, to determine which of them was the strongest, and the other two was to withdraw and support him. As the court came on, each one of them spread himself, to secure the nomination; but it fell on Dr. Butler, and the rest backed out. The doctor was a clever fellow, and I have often said he was the most talented man I ever run against for any office. His being related to General Jackson also helped him on very much; but I was in for it, and I was determined to push ahead and go through, or stick. Their meeting was held in Madison county, which was the strongest in the representative district, which was composed of eleven counties, and they seemed bent on having the member from there.

At the time Colonel Alexander was a candidate for Congress, and attending one of his public meetings one day, I walked to where he was treating the people, and he gave me an introduction to several of his acquaintances, and informed them that I was out electioneering. In a little time my competitor, Doctor Butler, came along; he passed by without noticing me, and I supposed, he did not recognize me. But I hailed him, as I was for all sorts of fun; and when he turned to me, I said to him, "Well, doctor, I suppose they have weighed you out to me; but I should like to know why they fixed your election for *March* instead of *August*? This is," said I, "a branfire new way of doing business, if a caucus is to make a representative of the people!" He now discovered who I was, and cried out, "D___n it, Crockett, is that you?" "Be sure it is," said I, "but I don't want it understood that I have come electioneering. I have just crept out of the cane, to see what discoveries I could make among the white folks." I told him that when I set out electioneering, I would go prepared to put every man on as good a footing as when I found him on. I would therefore have me a large buckskin hunting-shirt made, with a couple of pockets holding about a peck each; and that in one I would carry a great big twist of tobacco, and in the other my bottle of liquor; for I knowed when I met a man and offered him a dram, he would throw out his quid of tobacco to take one, and after he had taken his horn, I would out with my twist, and give him another chew. And in this way he would not be worse off than when I found him; and I would be sure to leave him in a first-rate good humor. He said I could beat him electioneering all hollow. I told him I would give him better evidence of that before August, notwithstanding he had many advantages over me, and particularly in the way of money; but I told him I would go on the products of the country; that I had industrious children, and the best of coondogs; and they would hunt every night till midnight to support my election; and when the coon fur wasn't good, I would myself go a wolfing, and shoot down a wolf, and skin his head, and his scalp would be good to me for three dollars, in our State Treasury money; and in this way I would get along on the big string. He stood like he was both amused and astonished, and the whole crowd was in a roar of laughter. From this place I returned home, leaving the people in a first-rate way, and I was sure I would do a good business among them. At any rate, I was determined to stand up to my lick-log, salt or no salt.

In a short time there came out two other candidates, a Mr. Shaw and a Mr. Brown. We all ran the race through; and when the election was over, it turned that I had beat them all by a majority of two hundred and forty-seven votes, and was again returned as a member of the Legislature from a new region of the country, without losing a session. This reminded me of the old saw—"A fool for luck, and a poor man for children."

The Slave Trade, 1817*

Slavery in the United States was always a complex concern. A nation founded on liberty, and one becoming more dedicated to equality, enslaved millions of African Americans. That paradox caused intense debates over slavery, in both the North and the South. The following document, originally published in a New Orleans newspaper and reproduced in a leading national periodical, revealed that the slave trade, like many elements of the peculiar institution, did not enjoy unmitigated support in the slave states.

SLAVE TRADE—The legislatures of several of the southern states have passed very severe laws to check the late infamous trade that has been carried on in negroes. Of that enacted by *Georgia,* the Journal observes—"A section of our new penal code interdicts, under very severe penalties, the introduction of slaves into this state by negro traders for speculation—subjecting to a fine of a thousand dollars and to five years imprisonment in the penitentiary, the person who shall bring into the state a slave, and sell or offer for sale, such slave *within one year thereafter,* with the exception only of emigrants from the other states, who are allowed to bring with them, and dispose of as they think proper, slaves who are their *bona fide* property. It will be observed, that the section above alluded to, does not prevent residents of this state or others, from bringing negroes into it *for their own use,* but subjects them to the severe penalties of the act, *if they sell or offer them for sale within a specified time.*"

---

*From *Niles' Weekly Register* (Baltimore: H. Niles, 1817), XI:399–400.

Harcourt Brace & Company

By the law of *South Carolina,* it is made felony to introduce a slave into the state except by express permission of the legislature. This will seriously interfere with the business of many a scoundrel kidnapper and dealer in Maryland and elsewhere.

An increased vigilance is also manifested in *North Carolina*—some kidnappers have been caught there and imprisoned, we hope for life.

Louisiana appears alarmed at being made the depot of the very worst class of slaves, vomitings of the jails and penitentiaries and the refuse of all the rest of the states; and seems about to take measures to check the trade.

This business of negro slavery is much easier deprecated than removed, even if all were consenting to it. It is to the praise of the American people that slaves were originally introduced against their consent and that they, first of all, enacted laws to abolish the trade. It is a great grievance—and how we are to be relieved of it has never yet been satisfactorily proposed—except in the gradual amelioration of their condition, preparatory to gradual emancipation. In the first stage of this mighty work, we are happy to believe that very considerable progress is making.

Negro convicts.—Some inhuman speculator at New York, has disburthened the prisons of that city of seventy or eighty negroes, by procuring their imprisonment to be committed for transportation, and shipping them for this place—where they arrived a few days ago. But he has been disappointed in his expectation of profit, and we doubt if he will clear even the freight of his cargo. The corporation has very properly ordered the vessel containing this gang of thieves and ruffians, to proceed without the limits of the city. We hope their exertions will not stop here: but that they will endeavour to bring to signal punishment every person concerned in this most villainous traffic.

[From] *New Orleans paper.*

Discussion

1. Based on the documents, how might various members of American society, such as male farmers, women, Indians, and slaves, have viewed liberty, equality, and power between 1790 and 1820?

2. The selection by J. Hector St. John de Crèvecoeur is different from many of the previously presented documents because he discusses neither power nor liberty. Why are these topics not discussed? How does his description of the early republic show the growing importance of equality to Americans?

3. Compare the preface and opening paragraph of the Treaty of Greenville with that of the Treaty with the Creeks. What do the two documents suggest about the nature of national power in 1795 and in 1814? What do they suggest about perceptions of power by the people who wrote the treaties? Is there anything in the selections that indicates prospects of liberty or equality for the Indians? If so, what? If not, why?

4. Based on the passage from Davy Crockett's autobiography, what might you conclude that Crockett thought about equality? Did he consider himself the equal of others? Did he embrace political egalitarianism? Were liberty and power important matters to him?

5. How do you think Mrs. Crockett might have reacted to the advice John Abbott gave to mothers? How might the women who read Abbott's books and frontier wives like Crockett have differed or been similar in their views of liberty, equality, and power?

6. What do you think led to the laws that curtailed the slave trade in different southern states? Does the document reveal concern for the liberties or equality of slaves? Does it deal with issues of power, and if so, whose?

Chapter 9
Completing the Revolution

*Disagreements between Federalists and Republicans took many forms.
Newspapers practiced character assassination, opposing factions fought in the streets,
and violence spread to the hallowed floor of the House of Representatives.
The pictured fight took place on February 15, 1798, between Republican
Matthew Lyon (with the fire tongs) and Federalist Roger Griswold.*

War gained America its independence, and the Constitution created a government for the new republic, but the country still faced tremendous challenges. Domestic programs had to be enacted and a vision for the nation articulated. Moreover, foreign powers seemed to dismiss the United States, and many Americans believed that they had to gain the respect of Europe before the Revolution would be complete. Between 1790 and 1815, the executive branch of the government played a critical role in accomplishing those tasks. Although coequal with the legislature and the judiciary, the president and the cabinet took a dynamic part in defining the relationship of liberty, equality, and power in the United States. Alexander Hamilton and George Washington proved to be particularly important in the development of the nation, but Jeffersonians believed that the Federalists assumed too much authority and that the policies they established imperiled liberty and equality. Beginning with Jefferson's election to the presidency in 1800, consequently, Republicans worked to dismantle state power in order to preserve revolutionary ideals. They found, however, that the agrarian republic they so admired was undergoing a transformation—one that in some ways would be as significant as the changes that occurred between 1775 and 1790.

Manufactures, 1791*

Alexander Hamilton, who as secretary of the treasury ensured the financial strength of the nation, often advanced almost prerevolutionary attitudes toward power and liberty. He viewed property rights, especially as they related to commerce and manufacturing, as the fundamental source of liberty. He also believed that governments had to exercise power in order to protect and expand those essential rights. Many of his policies, therefore, dealt with matters of economic power and with the nature of the government's ability to deal with such issues. His 1791 Report on Manufactures revealed his economic insight, and it profoundly defined the debate over financial programs in the early years of the republic. In addition, his principles have continued to influence national policy for more than two hundred years. The following selection suggested ways in which the government might use its authority to encourage the growth of industry.

The expediency of encouraging manufactures in the United States, which was not long since deemed very questionable, appears at this time to be pretty generally admitted. The embarrassments which have obstructed the progress of our external trade, have led to serious reflections on the necessity of enlarging the sphere of our domestic commerce. The restrictive regulations, which, in foreign markets, abridge the vent of the increasing surplus of our agricultural produce, serve to beget an earnest desire that a more extensive demand for that surplus may be created at home; and the complete success which has rewarded manufacturing enterprise in some valuable branches, conspiring with the promising symptoms which attend some less mature essays in others, justify a hope that the obstacles to the growth of the species of industry are less formidable than they were apprehended to be, and that it is not difficult to find,

*From *The Works of Alexander Hamilton,* 12 vols., ed. Henry Cabot Lodge (New York: G. P. Putnam's Sons, 1904), IV:70–71, 138–59.

in its further extension, a full indemnification for any external disadvantages, which are or may be experienced, as well as an accession of resources, favorable to national independence and safety. . . .

It is not uncommon to meet with an opinion, that, though the promoting of manufactures may be the interest of a part of the Union, it is contrary to that of another part. The Northern and Southern regions are sometimes represented as having adverse interests in this respect. Those are called manufacturing, these agricultural States; and a species of opposition is imagined to subsist between the manufacturing and agricultural interests.

The idea of an opposition between those two interests is the common error of the early periods of every country; but experience gradually dissipates it. Indeed, they are perceived so often to succor and befriend each other, that they come at length to be considered as one—a supposition which has been frequently abused, and is not universally true. Particular encouragements of particular manufactures may be of a nature to sacrifice the interests of landholders to those of manufacturers; but it is nevertheless a maxim, well established by experience, and generally acknowledged, where there has been sufficient experience, that the aggregate prosperity of manufactures and the aggregate prosperity of agriculture are intimately connected. . . .

Ideas of a contrariety of interests between the Northern and Southern regions of the Union are, in the main, as unfounded as they are mischievous. The diversity of circumstances, on which such contrariety is usually predicated, authorizes a directly contrary conclusion. Mutual wants constitute one of the strongest links of political connection; and the extent of these bears a natural proportion to the diversity in the means of mutual supply. . . .

In proportion as the mind is accustomed to trace the intimate connection of interest which subsists between all the parts of a society united under the same government, the infinite variety of channels will serve to circulate the prosperity of each, to and through the rest,—in that proportion will be little apt to be disturbed by solicitudes and apprehensions which originate in local discriminations. . . .

But there are more particular considerations which serve to fortify the idea that the encouragement of manufactures is the interest of all parts of the Union. If the Northern and Middle States should be the principal scenes of such establishments, they would immediately benefit the more Southern, by creating a demand for productions, some of which they have in common with the other States, and others, which are either peculiar to them, or more abundant, or of better quality, than elsewhere. . . .

If, then, it satisfactorily appears, that it is the interest of the United States, generally, to encourage manufactures, it merits particular attention, that there are circumstances which render the present a critical moment for entering, with zeal, upon the important business. The effort cannot fail to be materially seconded by a considerable and increasing influx of money, in consequence of foreign speculations in the funds, and by the disorders which exist in different parts of Europe. . . .

There is, at the present juncture, a certain fermentation of mind, a certain activity of [foreign] speculation which, if properly directed, may be made subservient to useful purposes; but which, if left entirely to itself, may be attended with pernicious effects.

The disturbed state of Europe inclining its citizens to emigration, the requisite workmen will be more easily acquired than at another time; and the effect of multiplying the opportunities of employment to those who emigrate, may be an increase of the number and extent of valuable acquisitions to the population, arts, and industry of the country.

To find pleasure in the calamities of other nations should be criminal; but to benefit ourselves, by opening an asylum to these who suffer in consequence of them, is as justifiable as it is politic. . . .

Harcourt Brace & Company

[I]t is proper . . . to consider the means by which [the promotion of manufactures] may be effected, as introductory to a specification of the objects, which, in the present state of things, appear the most fit to be encouraged, and of the particular measures which it may be advisable to adopt, in respect to each.

In order to a better judgment of the means proper to be resorted to by the United States, it will be of use to advert to those which have been enjoyed with success in other countries. The principal of these are:

1. *Protecting duties—or duties on those foreign articles which are the rivals of the domestic ones intended to be encouraged*

    Duties of this nature evidently amount to a virtual bounty on the domestic fabrics; since, by enhancing the charges of foreign articles, they enable the national manufactures to undersell all their foreign competitors. . . . [I]t has the additional recommendation of being a source of revenue. Indeed, all the duties imposed on imported articles, have . . . a beneficent aspect toward the manufactures of the country.

2. *Prohibitions of rival articles, or duties equivalent to prohibitions*

    This is another and an efficacious mean of encouraging national manufactures; but, in general, it is only fit to be employed when a manufacture has made such progress, and is in so many hands, as to insure a due competition, and an adequate supply on reasonable terms. . . .

    Considering a monopoly of the domestic market to its own manufactures as the reigning policy of manufacturing nations, a similar policy, on the part of the United States, in every proper instance, is dictated, it might almost be said, by the principles of distributive justice; certainly, by the duty if endeavoring to secure to their own citizens a reciprocity of advantages.

3. *Prohibitions of the exportation of the materials of manufacture*

    The desire of securing a cheap and plentiful supply for the national workmen, and where the article is either peculiar to the country, or of a peculiar quality there, the jealousy of enabling foreign workmen to rival those of the nation with its own materials, are the leading motives to this species of regulation. It ought not to be affirmed that it is no instance proper; but is, certainly, one that ought to be adopted with great circumspection, and only in very plain cases. It is seen at once, that its immediate operation is to abridge the demand, and keep down the price of the produce of some other branch of industry—generally speaking, of agriculture—to the prejudice of those who carry it on; and . . . prudence seems to dictate that the expedient in question ought to be indulged with a sparing hand.

4. *Pecuniary bounties*

    This has been found one of the most efficacious means of encouraging manufactures, and is, in some views, the best. Though it has not yet been practised upon by the Government of the United States . . . , and though it is less favored by public opinion than some other modes, its advantages are these:

    1. It is a species of encouragement more positive and direct than any other, and, for that very reason, has a more immediate tendency to stimulate and uphold new enterprises. . . .
    2. It avoids the inconvenience of a temporary augmentation of price, which is incident to some other modes; or it produces it to a less degree, either by making no addition to the charges of the rival foreign articles, as is the case of protecting duties, or by making a smaller addition. . . . Indeed the bounty . . . is calculated to promote a reduction of price; because without laying any new charge on the foreign article, it serves to introduce a competition with it, and to increase the total quantity of the article in the market.

3. Bounties have not, like high protecting duties, a tendency to produce scarcity. . . .

4. Bounties are, sometimes, not only the best but the only proper expedient for uniting the encouragement of a new object of agriculture with that of a new object of manufacture. . . .

Except the simple and ordinary kinds of household manufacture or those for which there are very commanding local advantages, pecuniary bounties are, in most cases, indispensable to the introduction of a new branch. A stimulus and a support, not less powerful and direct, is, generally speaking, essential to the overcoming of the obstacles which arise from the competitions of a superior skills and maturity elsewhere. . . .

The continuance of bounties on manufactures long established must always be of questionable policy; because a presumption would arise, in every such case, that there were natural and inherent impediments to success. But, in new undertakings, they are justifiable as they are oftentimes necessary. . . .

5. *Premiums*

These are of a nature allied to bounties, though distinguishable from them in some important features.

Bounties are applicable to the whole quantity of an article produced, or manufactured, or exported, and involve a correspondent expense. Premiums serve to reward some particular excellence or superiority, some extraordinary exertion or skill, and are dispensed only in a small number of cases. But their effect is to stimulate general effort. . . . They are, accordingly, a very economical means of exciting the enterprise of a whole community. . . .

6. *The exemption of the materials of manufactures from duty*

The policy of that exemption, . . . particularly in reference to new establishments, is obvious. It can hardly ever be advisable to add the obstructions of fiscal burthens to the difficulties which naturally embarrass a new manufacture; and where it is matured, in condition to become an object of revenue, it is . . . better that the fabric, than the material, should be the subject of taxation. . . .

7. *Drawbacks of the duties which are imposed on the materials of manufactures*

It has already been observed, as a general rule, that duties on those materials ought, with certain exceptions, to be forborne. Of these exceptions, three cases occur, which may serve as examples. One, where the material is itself an object of general or extensive consumption, and a fit and productive source of revenue. Another, where a manufacture of a simpler kind, the competition of which, with a like domestic article, is desired to be restrained, partakes of the nature of the raw material, from being capable, by a further process, to be converted into a manufacture of a different kind, the introduction or growth of which is desired to be encouraged. A third, where the material itself is a production of the country, and in sufficient abundance to furnish a cheap and plentiful supply to the national manufactures. . . .

8. *The encouragement of new inventions and discoveries at home, and of the introduction into the United States of such as may have been made in other countries; particularly those that relate to machinery*

This is among the most useful and unexceptionable of the aids which can be given to manufactures. The usual means of that encouragement are pecuniary rewards, and, for a time, exclusive privileges. . . . But it is desirable, in regard to improvements, and secrets of extraordinary value, to be able to extend the same benefits to introducers, as well as authors and inventors; a policy which has been practised with advantage in other countries. . . .

9. *Judicious regulations for the inspection of manufactured commodities*

This is not among the least important of the means by which prosperity of manufactures may be promoted. It is, indeed, in many cases, one of the most essential. Contributing to prevent frauds upon consumers at home and exporters to foreign countries, to improve

Harcourt Brace & Company

the quality and preserve the character of the national manufactures, it cannot fail to aid the expeditious and advantageous sale of them, and to serve as a guard against successful competition from other quarters.

10. *The facilitating of pecuniary remittances from place to place—*

It is a point of considerable moment to trade in general, and to manufactures in particular, by rendering more easy the purchase of raw materials and provisions, and the payment for manufacturing supplies. A general circulation of bank money, which is to be expected from the institution lately established, will be a most valuable means to this end. But much good would also accrue from some additional provisions regarding inland bills of exchange. If those drawn in one State, payable in another, were made negotiable everywhere, . . . it would greatly promote negotiations between the citizens of different States, by rendering them more secure, and with it the convenience and advantage of the merchants and manufacturers of each.

11. *The facilitating of transportation of commodities*

Improvements favoring this object intimately concern all the domestic interests of a community; but they may, without impropriety, be mentioned as having an important relation to manufactures. There is, perhaps, scarcely anything which has been better calculated to assist the manufacturers of Great Britain than the melioration of the public roads of that kingdom, and the great progress which has been made of late in opening canals. Of the former, the United States stand much in need; for the latter, they present uncommon facilities.

The symptoms of attention to the improvement of inland navigation which have lately appeared in some quarters . . . must fill with pleasure every breast warmed with a true zeal for the prosperity of the country. These examples, it is to be hoped, will stimulate the exertions of the government and citizens of every State. There can certainly be no object more worthy of the cares of the local administration; and it were to be wished there was no doubt of the power of the National Government to lend its direct aid on a comprehensive plan. This is one of those improvements which could be prosecutes with more efficacy by the whole than by any part or parts of the Union. . . .

Washington's Farewell Address, 1796*

President George Washington used his farewell address to share with the nation his vision of, and concerns for, the United States. Like many citizens, he feared the danger that partisanship posed to liberty, and he sternly warned against the perils that might occur with the rise of the new political parties. As a former general, Washington also felt grave concern for the threat that foreign struggles might present to the country; in his speech he advised the American people on how the United States might best meet its responsibilities as an international power.

. . . I have already intimated to you the dangers of parties in the state, with particular reference to the founding of them on geographical discriminations. Let me now take a more comprehensive view, and warn you in the most solemn manner against the baneful effects of the spirit of party, generally.

This spirit, unfortunately, is inseparable from our nature, having its root on the strongest passion of the human mind. It exists under different shapes in all governments, more or less stifled,

---

*From *Messages of the Presidents of the United States,* comp. Jonathan Phillips (Columbus, Ohio: Jonathan Phillips, 1841), 74–79.

controlled, or repressed; but, in those of the popular form, it is seen in its greatest rankness, and is truly their worst enemies.

The alternate domination of one faction over another, sharpened by the spirit of revenge, natural to party dissension, which in different ages and countries has perpetrated the most horrid enormities, is itself a frightful despotism. The disorders and miseries, which result, gradually incline the minds of men to seek security and repose in the absolute power of an individual; and sooner or later the chief of some prevailing faction, more able or more fortuitous than his competitors, turns this disposition to the purposes of his own elevation, and the ruins of Public Liberty.

Without looking forward to an extremity of this kind (which nevertheless ought not to be entirely out of sight,) the common and continual mischiefs of the spirit of party are sufficient to make the interest and the duty of a wise people to discourage and restrain it. . . .

There is an opinion, that parties in free countries are useful checks upon the administration of the Government, and serve to keep alive the spirit of Liberty. This within certain limits is probably true; and in Government of a Monarchical cast, Patriotism may look with indulgence, if not with favor, upon the spirit of party. But in those of the popular character, in Governments purely elective, it is a spirit not to be encouraged. From their natural tendency, it is certain there will always be enough of that spirit for every salutary purpose. And, there being constant danger of excess, the effort ought to be, by force of public opinion, to mitigate and assuage it. A fire not to be quenched, it demands a uniform vigilance to prevent it bursting into a flame, lest, instead of warming, it should consume.

It is important, likewise, that the habits of thinking in a free country should caution, in those intrusted with its administration, to confine themselves within their respective constitutional spheres, avoiding in the exercise of the powers of one department to encroach upon another. The spirit of encroachment tends to consolidate the powers of all the departments in one, and thus to create, whatever the form of government, a real despotism. A just estimate of the love of power, and proneness to abuse it, which predominates in the human heart, is sufficient to satisfy us of the truth of this position. . . .

Of all the dispositions and habits which lead to political prosperity, religion and morality are indispensable supports. In vain would that man claim the tribute of patriotism, who should labor to subvert these great pillars of human happiness—these finest props of the duties of men and citizens. . . . And let us with caution indulge the supposition, that morality can be maintained without religion. Whatever may be conceded to the influence of refined education on minds of peculiar structure, reason and experience both, forbid us to expect that national morality can prevail in exclusion of religious principle.

It is substantially true, that virtue or morality is a necessary spring of popular government. The rule indeed extends with more or less force to every species of free government. Who, that is a sincere friend to it, can look with indifference upon attempts to shake the foundations of the fabric?

Promote, then, as an object of primary importance, institutions for the general diffusion of knowledge. In proportion as the structure of a government gives force to public opinion, it is essential that public opinion should be enlightened.

As a very important source of strength and security, cherish public credit. One method of preserving it is to use it as sparingly as possible; avoiding occasions of expense, by cultivating peace, but remembering also that timely disbursements to prepare for danger, frequently prevent much greater disbursements to repel it; avoiding, likewise, the accumulation of debt; not only by shunning occasions of expense, but by vigorous exertions, in time of peace, to discharge the debts which unavoidable wars may have occasioned, not ungenerously throwing upon posterity the burthen which we ourselves ought to bear. The execution of these maxims belongs

Harcourt Brace & Company

to your representatives, but it is necessary that public opinion should co-operate. To facilitate to them the performance of their duty, it is essential that you should practically bear in mind, that, towards the payment of debt, there must be revenue; that to have revenue, there must be taxes; that no taxes can be devised which are not more or less inconvenient and unpleasant. . . .

Observe good faith and justice towards all nations; cultivate peace and harmony with all. Religion and morality enjoin this conduct; and can it be that good policy does not equally enjoin it? It will be worthy of a free, enlightened, and, at no distant period, a great nation, to give to mankind the magnanimous and too novel example of a people always guided by an exalted justice and benevolence. . . .

In the execution of such a plan, nothing is more essential than that permanent inveterate antipathies against particular nations, and passionate attachments for others should be excluded; and that in place of them, just and amicable feelings towards all should be cultivated. The nation which indulges towards another an habitual hatred, or an habitual fondness, is, in some degree, a slave. . . .

Excessive partiality for one foreign nation, and excessive dislike of another, cause those whom they actuate to see danger only on one side, and serve to veil and even second the arts of influence on the other. Real patriots, who may resist the intrigues of the favorite, are liable to become suspected and odious, while its tools and dues usurp the applause and confidence of the people, to surrender their interests.

The great rule of conduct for us, in regard to foreign nations, is, in extending our commercial relations, to have with them as little *political* connexion as possible. So far as we have already formed engagements, let them be fulfilled with perfect good faith. Here let us stop.

Europe has a set of primary interests, which to us have none, or a very remote relation. Hence she must be engaged in frequent controversies, the causes of which are essentially foreign to our concerns. Hence, therefore, it must be unwise in us to implicate ourselves, by artificial ties, in the ordinary vicissitudes of her politics, or the ordinary combinations and collisions of her friendships or enmities.

Our detached and distant situation invites and enables us to pursue a different course. If we remain one people, under an efficient government, the period is not far off, when we may defy material injury from external annoyance; when we may take such an attitude as will cause the neutrality, we may at any time resolve upon, to be scrupulously respected; when belligerent nations, under the impossibility of making acquisitions upon us, will not lightly hazard the giving us provocation; when we may choose peace or war, as our interest, guided by justice, shall counsel. . . .

It is our true policy to steer clear of permanent alliances with any portion of the foreign world; so far, I mean, as we are now at liberty to do it; for let me not be understood as capable of patronizing infidelity of existing engagements. I hold the maxim no less applicable to public than to private affairs, that honesty is always the best policy. I repeat, therefore, let those engagements be observed in their genuine sense. But, in my opinion, it is unnecessary, and would be unwise to extend them.

Taking care always to keep ourselves, by suitable establishments, on a respectable defensive posture, we may safely trust to temporary alliances for extraordinary emergencies. . . .

In offering to you, my countrymen, these counsels of an old and affectionate friend, I dare not hope they will make the strong and lasting impression I could wish; that they will control the usual current of the passions, or prevent any nation from running the course, which hitherto has marked the destiny of nations. But, if I may even flatter myself, that they may be productive of some partial benefit, some occasional good; that they may now and then recur to moderate the fury of party spirit, to warn against the mischiefs of foreign intrigue, to guard against the impostures of pretended patriots; this hope will be a full recompense for the solicitude for your welfare, by which they have been dictated. . . .

Jefferson's First Inaugural Address, 1801*

Thomas Jefferson emphasized egalitarian ideals throughout his life, and he understood how vulnerable liberty could be. He viewed the Federalists, particularly President John Adams, as tyrannical advocates of power, and Jefferson recognized the "Revolution of 1800" as an opportunity to restore liberty and equality to the United States. In his first inaugural address, he called for a reconciliation between the two parties, but he also used the speech to define his understanding of the emerging agrarian republic that would ensure equality for all men.

Called upon to undertake the duties of the first executive office of our country, I avail myself of the presence of that portion of my fellow-citizens which is here assembled to express my grateful thanks for the favor with which they have been pleased to look toward me, to declare a sincere consciousness that the task is above my talents, and that I approach it with those anxious and awful presentiments which the greatness of the charge and the weakness of my powers to justly inspire. A rising nation, spread over a wide and fruitful land, traversing all the seas with the rich productions of their industry, engaged in commerce with nations who feel power and forget right, advancing rapidly to destinies beyond the reach of mortal eye—when I contemplate these transcendent objects, and see the honor, the happiness, and the hopes of this beloved country committed to the issue and auspices of the day, I shrink from the contemplation, and humble myself before the magnitude of the undertaking. Utterly, indeed, should I despair did not the presence of many whom I here see remind me that in the other high authorities provided by our Constitution shall I find resources of wisdom, of virtue, and of zeal on which to rely under all difficulties. . . .

During the contest of opinion through which we have passed the animation of discussions and of exertions has sometimes worn an aspect which might impose on strangers unused to think freely and to speak and to write what they think; but this being now decided by the voice of the nation, announced according to the rules of the Constitution, all will, of course, arrange themselves under the will of the law, and unite in common effort for the common good. All, too, will bear in mind this sacred principle, that though the will of the majority is in all cases to prevail, that will to be rightful must be reasonable; that the minority possess their equal rights, which equal law must protect, and to violate would be oppression. Let us, then, fellow-citizens, unite with one heart and one mind. Let us restore to social intercourse the harmony and affection without which liberty and even life itself are but dreary things. And let us reflect that, having banished from our land that religious intolerance under which mankind so long bled and suffered, we have yet gained little if we countenance a political intolerance as despotic, as wicked, and capable of as bitter and bloody persecutions. . . . But every difference of opinion is not a difference of principle. We have called by different names brethren of the same principle. We are all Republicans, we are all Federalists. If there is any among us who would wish to dissolve this Union or to change its republican form, let them stand undisturbed as monuments to the safety with which error of opinion may be tolerated where reason is left free to combat it. I know, indeed, that some honest men fear that a republican government can

---

*From *A Compilation of the Messages and Papers of the Presidents, 1789–1897,* 10 vols., comp. James D. Richardson (Washington, D.C.: U.S. Government Printing Office, 1896–1899), I:321–24.

not be strong, that this Government is not strong enough; but would the honest patriot, in the full tide of successful experiment, abandon a government which has so far kept us free and firm on the theoretic and visionary fear that this Government, the world's best hope, may by possibility want energy to preserve itself? I trust not. I believe this, on the contrary, the strongest Government of earth. I believe it the only one where every man, at the call of the law would fly to the standard of the law, and would meet invasions of the public order as his own personal concern. . . .

Let us, then, with courage and confidence pursue our own Federal and Republican principles, our attachment to union and representative government. Kindly separated by nature and a wide ocean from the exterminating havoc of one quarter of the globe; too high-minded to endure the degradations of the others; possessing a chosen country, with room enough for our descendants to the thousandth and thousandth generation; entertaining a due sense of our equal right to the use of our own faculties, to the acquisitions of our own industry, to honor and confidence from our fellow-citizens, resulting not from birth, but from our actions and their sense of them; enlightened by a benign religion, professed, indeed, and practiced in various forms, yet all of them inculcating honesty, truth, temperance, gratitude, and the love of man; acknowledging and adoring an overruling Providence, which by all its dispensations proves that it delights in the happiness of man here and his greater happiness hereafter—with all these blessings, what more is necessary to make us a happy and a prosperous people? Still one thing more, fellow-citizens—a wise and frugal Government, which shall restrain men from injuring one another, shall leave them otherwise free to regulate their own pursuits of industry and improvement, and shall not take from the mouth of labor bread it has earned. This is the sum of good government. . . .

About to enter, fellow-citizens, on the exercise of duties which comprehend everything dear and valuable to you, it is proper you should understand what I deem the essential principles of our Government, and consequently those which ought to shape its Administration. . . . Equal and exact justice to all men, of whatever state or persuasion, religious or political; peace, commerce, and honest friendship with all nations, entangling alliances with none; the support of the State governments in all their rights, as the most competent administrations of our domestic concerns and the surest bulwarks against antirepublican tendencies; the preservation of the General Government in its whole constitutional vigor, as the sheet anchor of our peace at home and safety abroad; a jealous care of the right of election by the people—a mild and safe corrective of abuses which are lopped by the sword of revolution when peaceable remedies are unprovided; absolute acquiescence in the decisions of the majority, the vital principle of republics, from which is no appeal but to force, the vital principle and immediate parent of despotism; a well-disciplined militia, our best reliance in peace and for the first moments of war, till regulars may relieve them; the supremacy of the civil over the military authority; economy in the public expense, that labor may be lightly burthened; the honest payment of our debts and sacred preservation of the public faith; encouragement of agriculture, and of commerce as its handmaid; the diffusion of information and arraignment of all abuses at the bar of the public reason; freedom of religion; freedom of the press, and freedom of person under the protection of the habeas corpus, and trial by juries impartially selected. These principles form the bright constellation which has gone before us and guided our steps through an age of revolution and reformation. . . .

Relying, then, on the patronage of your good will, I advance with obedience to the work, ready to retire from it whenever you become sensible how much better choice it is in your power to make. And may the Infinite Power which rules the destinies of the universe lead our councils to what is best, and give them a favorable issue for your peace and prosperity.

Harcourt Brace & Company

James Madison's War Message, 1812*

The War of 1812 broke out for numerous reasons. To many people, however, English arrogance and disdain for American rights stood as the critical issues. In his war message to Congress, President James Madison emphasized the importance of British maritime policies in forcing the United States to fight. In a sense, the conflict was a continuation of the American Revolution. That War for Independence, which had erupted because Americans believed that Great Britain wanted to curtail their liberties, resulted in the removal of British power and a guarantee of those rights. Yet, until the English recognized the United States as an international power and respected its rights as one, the Revolution remained unfinished.

Without going back beyond the renewal in 1803 of the war in which Great Britain is engaged, and omitting unrepaired wrongs of inferior magnitude, the conduct of her Government presents a series of acts hostile to the United States as an independent and neutral nation.

British cruisers have been in the continued practice of violating the American flag on the great highway of nations, and of seizing and carrying off persons sailing under it, not in the exercise of a belligerent right founded on the law of nations against an enemy, but of a municipal prerogative over British subjects. British jurisdiction is thus extended to neutral vessels in a situation where no laws can operate but the law of nations and the laws of the country to which the vessels belong, and a self-redress is assumed, which if British subjects were wrongfully detained and alone concerned, is that substitution of force . . . which falls within the definition of war. Could the seizure of British subjects in such cases be regarded as within the exercise of a belligerent right, the acknowledged laws of war . . . would imperiously demand the fairest trial where the sacred rights of persons were at issue. In place of such a trial these rights are subjected to the will of every petty commander.

The practice, hence, is so far from affecting British subjects alone that, under the pretext of searching for these, thousands of American citizens, under the safeguard of public law and of their national flag, have been torn away from everything dear to them; have been dragged on board ships of war of a foreign nation and exposed, under the severities of their discipline, to be exiled to the most distant and deadly climes, to risk their lives in the battles of their oppressors, and to be the melancholy instruments of taking away those of their own brethren.

Against this crying enormity, which Great Britain would be so prompt to avenge if committed against herself, the United States have in vain exhausted remonstrances and expostulations, and that no proof might be wanting of their conciliatory dispositions, and no pretext left for a continuance of the practice, the British Government was formally assured of the readiness of the United States to enter into arrangements such as could not be rejected if the recovery of British subjects were the real and sole object. The communication passed without effect.

British cruisers have been in practice also of violating the rights and the peace of our coasts. They hover over and harass our entering and departing commerce. To the most insulting pretensions they have added the most lawless proceedings in our very harbors, and have wantonly spilt American blood within the sanctuary of our territorial jurisdiction. The principles and rules enforced by that nation, when a neutral nation, against armed vessels of belligerents hovering near coasts and disturbing her commerce are well known. When called on, nevertheless, by the United States to punish the greater offenses committed by her own vessels, her Government has bestowed on their commanders additional marks of honor and confidence.

---

*From *A Compilation of the Messages and Papers of the Presidents, 1789–1897,* 10 vols., comp. James D. Richardson (Washington, D.C.: U.S. Government Printing Office, 1896–1899), I:499–505.

Harcourt Brace & Company

Under pretended blockades, without the presence of an adequate force and sometimes without the practicability of applying one, our commerce has been plundered in every sea, the great staples of our country have been cut off from their legitimate markets, and a destructive blow aimed at our agricultural and maritime interests. . . .

Not content with these occasional expedients for laying waste our neutral trade, the cabinet of Britain resorted at length to the sweeping system of blockades, under the name of orders in council, which has been molded and managed as might best suit its political views, its commercial jealousies, or the avidity of British cruisers.

To our remonstrances against the complicated and transcendent injustice of this innovation the first reply was that the orders were reluctantly adopted by Great Britain as a necessary retaliation on decrees of her enemy proclaiming a general blockade of the British Isles at a time when the naval force of that enemy dared not issue from his own ports. She was reminded without effect that her own prior blockades, unsupported by an adequate naval force actually applied and continued, were a bar to this plea; that executed edicts against millions of our property could not be retaliation on edicts confessedly impossible to be executed; that retaliation, to be just, should fall on the party setting the guilty example, not on an innocent party which was not even chargeable with an acquiescence in it.

When deprived of this flimsy veil for a prohibition of our trade with her enemy by the repeal of his prohibition of our trade with Great Britain, her cabinet, instead of a corresponding repeal or a practical discontinuance of its orders, formally avowed a determination to persist in them against the United States until the markets of her enemy should be laid open to British products, thus . . . contradicting her own practice toward all nations, in peace as well as war, and betraying the insincerity of those professions which inculcated a belief that, having resorted to her orders with regret, she was anxious to find an occasion for putting an end to them.

Abandoning still more all respect for the neutral rights of the United States and for its own constituency, the British Government now demands as prerequisites to a repeal of its orders as they relate to the United States that a formality should be observed in the repeal of the French decrees . . . and that the French repeal . . . should not be a single and special repeal in relations to the United States, but should be extended to whatever other neutral nations unconnected with them may be affected by those decrees. And as an additional insult, they are called on for a formal disavowal of conditions and pretensions advanced by the French Government for which the United States are so far from having made themselves responsible that . . . such a responsibility was explicitly and emphatically disclaimed.

It has become, indeed, sufficiently certain that the commerce of the United States is to be sacrificed, not as interfering with the belligerent rights of Great Britain; not as supplying the wants of her enemies, which she herself supplies; but as interfering with the monopoly which she covets for her own commerce and navigation. . . .

Anxious to make every experiment short of the last resort of injured nations, the United States have withheld from Great Britain . . . the benefits of a free intercourse with their market. . . . And to entitle these experiments to the more favorable consideration they were so framed as to enable her to place her adversary under the exclusive operation of them. To these appeals her Government has been equally inflexible, as if willing to make sacrifices of every sort rather than yield to the claims of justice or renounce the errors of a false pride. Nay, so far were the attempts carried to overcome the attachment of the British cabinet to its unjust edicts that it received every encouragement within the competency of the executive branch of our Government to expect that a repeal of them would be followed by a war between the United States and France, unless the French edicts should be repealed. Even this communication . . . received no attention. . . .

Harcourt Brace & Company

There was a period when a favorable change in the policy of the British cabinet was justly considered as established. The minister plenipotentiary of His Britannic Majesty here proposed an adjustment of the differences more immediately endangering the harmony of the two countries. The proposition was accepted with the promptitude and cordiality corresponding with the invariable professions of this Government. A foundation appeared to be laid for a sincere and a lasting reconciliation. The prospect, however, quickly vanished. The whole proceeding was disavowed by the British Government, without any explanations which could at that time repress the belief that the disavowal proceeded from a spirit of hostility to the commercial rights and prosperity of the United States; and . . . at the very moment when the public minister was holding the language of friendship and inspiring confidence in the sincerity of the negotiations with which he was charged a secret agent of his Government was employed in intrigues having for their object a subversion of our Government and a dismemberment of our happy union.

In reviewing the conduct of Great Britain towards the United States our attention is necessarily drawn to the warfare just renewed by the savages on one of our extensive frontiers—a warfare which is known to spare neither age nor sex and to be distinguished by features peculiarly shocking to humanity. It is difficult to account for the activity and combinations which have for some time been developing themselves among tribes in constant intercourse with British traders and garrisons without connecting their hostility with that influence and without recollecting the authenticated examples of such interpositions heretofore furnished by the officers and agents of that Government.

Such is the spectacle of injuries and indignities which have been heaped on our country. . . . It might have least been expected that an enlightened nation . . . would have found in its true interest alone a sufficient motive to respect [the] rights [of the United States] and their tranquillity on the high seas; that an enlarged policy would have favored that free and general circulation of commerce in which the British nation is at all times interested, and which in times of war is the best alleviation of its calamities to herself . . . .

Other counsels have prevailed. Our moderation and conciliation have had no other effect than to encourage perseverance and to enlarge pretensions. We behold our seafaring citizens still the daily victims of lawless violence, committed on the great common and highway of nations, even within sight of the country which owes them protection. We behold our vessels, freighted with the products of our soil and industry, or returning with the honest proceeds of them, wrested from their lawful destinations, confiscated by prize courts no longer the organs of public law but the instruments of arbitrary edicts, and their unfortunate crews dispersed and lost, or forced or inveigled in British ports into British fleets. . . .

We behold, in fine, on the side of Great Britain a state of war against the United States, and on the side of the United States a state of peace toward Great Britain.

Whether the United States shall continue passive under these progressive usurpations and these accumulating wrongs, or, opposing force to force in defense of their natural rights, shall commit a just cause into the hands of the Almighty Disposer of Events, avoiding all connections which might entangle it in the contest or views of other powers, and preserving a constant readiness to concur in an honorable reestablishment of peace and friendship, is a solemn question which the Constitution wisely confides to the legislative department of the Government. In recommending it to their early deliberations I am happy in the assurance that the decision will be worthy the enlightened and patriotic councils of a virtuous, a free, and a powerful nation. . . .

Harcourt Brace & Company

Discussion

1. The documents presented in this chapter all had a significant influence on the early history of the United States, and they all emanated from the executive branch. What does this suggest about political power between 1790 and 1815? What does it reveal about the power of the government? Are there any implications about the long-term power of the presidency?

2. Based on Alexander Hamilton's Report on Manufactures, what elements of society would gain power through his policies? Who would lose power? Is there anything in the document to suggest that Hamilton believed in liberty or equality?

3. Based on George Washington's Farewell Address, what do you think Washington feared posed the gravest threat to liberty? What do you think he believed were the best ways to preserve liberty? Are there any issues of equality in the speech? If so, what; if not, why not?

4. After reading Jefferson's inaugural address, how do you think Jefferson viewed liberty, equality, and power? How would you compare Jefferson's principles as he expressed them in the speech to the ideals Hamilton presented in his report?

5. In his war message, how does President Madison describe assertions of British power and English threats to American liberties? Exactly what liberties did the English endanger? Does anything about the speech suggest Madison viewed the War of 1812 as an extension or continuation of the Revolution? How did the war relate to issues of liberty, equality, and power?

Chapter 10
The Market Revolution, 1815–1860

Part of the Lowell appeal for young New England women was the mill owners' claim that they could improve themselves. The Lowell Offering, originally sponsored by a local minister, published work by members of a working woman's self-improvement society. This title page from the 1845 collection shows the supposed glamour of mill life.

A period of unprecedented development followed the War of 1812 as the United States experienced yet another revolution—this one economic. Between 1815 and 1860 the United States changed from a society based primarily on subsistence agricultural households to a large, expanding market economy. This transition had important implications for families and the organization of labor, but the shift also rearranged the distribution of economic power and altered concepts of liberty. The advent of the market economy, for example, raised issues concerning the government's authority to increase tariffs and to fund internal improvements. The market revolution also posed concerns for the role of workers and the liberties they would enjoy in an emerging factory system. By 1860, much of the economic growth had occurred in the North, exacerbating questions of sectional power that had existed from the earliest years of the republic. Although the South remained mostly agrarian, increased cotton production played a crucial role in the growth of the American economy. Ironically, a tremendous amount of the wealth in the United States was drawn from the labor of slaves who had no power, liberty, or equality.

In Defence of the American System, 1832*

Henry Clay of Kentucky, in what he referred to as the "American system," advanced many of the principles that Alexander Hamilton had proposed. In the following excerpt from one of his speeches, Clay defends the use of protective tariffs to ensure a vibrant economy. Such tariffs posed several questions of power. For one thing, they helped increase the profits of American manufacturers, giving them economic strength that could be translated into political and social influence. In addition, increased revenues from high tariffs enhanced the power of the national government. In the following selection, Clay raised still another concern by addressing the increasing sectional fears associated with the tariff question.

> . . . I stand here as the humble but zealous advocate, not of the interests of one state, or of seven states only, but of the whole union. And never before have I felt, more intensely, the overpowering weight of that share of responsibility which belongs to me in these deliberations. Never before have I had more occasion than I now have, to lament my want of those intellectual powers, the possession of which might enable me to unfold to this senate and to illustrate to this people great truths, intimately connected with the lasting welfare of my country. I should, indeed, sink overwhelmed and subdued beneath the appalling magnitude of the task which lies before me, if I did not feel myself sustained and fortified by a thorough consciousness of the justness of the cause which I have espoused, and by a persuasion, I hope not presumptuous, that it has the approbation of that Providence who has so often smiled upon these United States.
>
> Eight years ago, it was my painful duty to present to the other house of congress an unexaggerated picture of the general distress pervading the whole land. We must all yet remember

---

*From *The Life and Speeches of the Honorable Henry Clay*, 2 vols., ed. Daniel Mallory (Hartford: Silas Andrus & Son, 1855), II:6–9, 13, 17–18, 23–24, 27–31, 37–38, 41–43, 46.

some of its frightful features. We all know that the people were then oppressed, and borne down by an enormous load of debt; that the value of property was at the lowest point of depression; that ruinous sales and sacrifices were every where made of real estate; that stop laws, and relief laws, and paper money were adopted, to save the people from impending destruction; that a deficit in the public revenue existed, which compelled government to seize upon, and divert from its legitimate object, the appropriations to the sinking fund, to redeem the national debt; and that our commerce and navigation were threatened with a complete paralysis. In short, sir, if I were to select any term of seven years since the adoption of the present constitution which exhibited a scene of the most wide-spread dismay and destruction, it would be exactly that term of seven years which immediately preceded the establishment of the tariff of 1824.

I have now to perform the more pleasing task of exhibiting an imperfect sketch of the existing state of the unparalleled prosperity of the country. On a general survey, we behold cultivation extended, the arts flourishing, the face of the country improved, our people fully and profitably employed, and the public countenance exhibiting tranquillity, contentment, and happiness. And if we descend into particulars, we have the agreeable contemplation of a people out of debt; land rising slowly in value, but in a secure and salutary degree; a ready though not extravagant market for all the surplus productions of our industry; innumerable flocks and herds browsing and gamboling on ten thousand hills and plains, covered with rich and verdant grasses; our cities expanded, and whole villages springing up, as it were, by enchantment; our exports and imports increased and increasing; our tonnage, foreign and coastwise, swelling and fully occupied; the rivers of our interior animated by the perpetual thunder and lightening of countless steamboats; the currency sound and abundant; the public debt of two wars nearly redeemed; and, to crown all, the public treasury overflowing, embarrassing congress, not to find subjects of taxation, but to select the objects which shall be liberated from the impost. If the term of seven years were to be selected, of the greatest prosperity which this people have enjoyed since the establishment of their present constitution, it would be exactly that period of seven years which immediately followed the passage of the tariff of 1824. . . .

It is now proposed to abolish the system, to which we owe so much of the public prosperity. . . .

If the system of protection be founded on principle erroneous in theory, pernicious in practice, above all, if it be unconstitutional, as is alleged, it ought to be forthwith abolished, and not a vestige of it suffered to remain. But, before we sanction this sweeping denunciation, let us look a little at this system, its magnitude, its ramifications, its duration, and the high authorities which have sustained it. . . . Why, sir, there is scarcely an interest, scarcely a vocation in society, which is not embraced by the beneficence of this system. . . .

The question, therefore, which we are now called upon to determine, is . . . whether we shall break down and destroy a long established system, patiently and carefully built up and sanctioned, during a series of years, again and again, by the nation and by its highest and most revered authorities. . . .

When gentlemen have succeeded in their design of an immediate or gradual destruction of the American system, what is their substitute? Free trade! Free trade! The call for free trade is as unavailing, as the cry of a spoiled child in its nurse's arms, for the moon, or the stars that glitter in the firmament of heaven. It never has existed, it never will exist. Trade implies at least two parties. To be free, it should be fair, equal, and reciprocal. But if we throw our ports wide open to the admission of foreign productions, free of all duty, what ports of any other foreign nation shall we find to be open to the free admission of our surplus produce? We may break down all barriers to free trade on our part, but the work will not be complete, until foreign powers shall have removed theirs. There would be freedom on one side, and restrictions, prohibitions, and exclusions on the other. . . .

Harcourt Brace & Company

Gentlemen deceive themselves. It is not free trade that they are recommending to our acceptance. It is, in effect, the British colonial system that we are invited to adopt; and, if their policy prevail, it will lead substantially to the recolonization of these states, under the commercial dominion of Great Britain. . . .

I will now . . . proceed to a more particular consideration of the arguments urged against the protective system, and an inquiry into its practical operation, especially on the cotton-growing industry. . . . It is alleged, that the system operates prejudicially to the cotton planter, by diminishing the foreign demand for his staple; that we cannot sell to Great Britain unless we buy from her; that the import duty is equivalent to an export duty, and falls upon the cotton grower; that South Carolina pays a disproportionate quota of the public revenue, that an abandonment of the protective policy would lead to an augmentation of our exports . . . ; and, finally, that the south cannot partake of the advantages of manufacturing, if there be any. Let us examine these various propositions in detail. First, that the foreign demand for cotton is diminished, and we cannot sell to Great Britain unless we buy from her. The demand of both our great foreign customers is constantly and annually increasing. It is true, that the ratio of the increase may not be equal to that of production; but this is owing to the fact, that the power of producing the raw material is much greater, and is, therefore, constantly in advance of the power of consumption. . . .

Second, that the import duty is equivalent to an export duty, and falls on the producer of cotton.

The framers of our constitution, by granting the power to congress to lay imports, and prohibiting that of laying an export duty, manifested that they did not regard them as equivalent. Nor does the common sense of mankind. An export duty fastens upon, and incorporates itself with, the article on which it is laid. The article cannot escape from it—it pursues and follows it, wherever the article goes; and if, in the foreign market, the supply is above or just equal to the demand, the amount of the export duty will be a clear deduction to the exporter from the price of the article. But an import duty on a foreign article leaves the exporter of the domestic article free, first to import specie; secondly, goods which are free from the protecting duty; or, thirdly, such goods as, being chargeable with the protecting duty, he can still sell at home, and throw the duty on the consumer. . . .

Third. The next objection to the American system is, that it subjects South Carolina to the payment of an undue proportion of the public revenue. The basis of this objection is the assumption, shown to have been erroneous, that the producer of the exports from this country pays the duty on its imports, instead of the consumer of those imports. . . .

Fourth. An abandonment of the American system, it is urged, would lead to an addition to our export of one hundred and fifty millions of dollars. The amount of one hundred and fifty millions of cotton in the raw state, would produce four hundred and fifty millions in the manufactured state. . . . Now . . . , where would markets be found for this vast addition to the supply? Not in the United States, certainly, nor in any other quarter of the globe, England having already everywhere pressed her cotton manufactures to the utmost point of repletion. We must look for new worlds, seek for a new and unknown race of mortals, to consume this immense increase of cotton fabrics. . . .

Fifth. But it is contended, in the last place, that the south cannot, from physical and other causes, engage in the manufacturing arts. I deny the premises, and I deny the conclusion. I deny the fact of inability; and, if it existed, I deny the conclusion, that we must, therefore break down our manufactures, and nourish those of foreign countries. The south possesses in an extraordinary degree, two of the most important elements of manufacturing industry—water-power and labor. The former gives to our whole country a decided advantage over Great Britain. But a single experiment . . . in which a faithless slave put the torch to a manufacturing establishment, has discouraged similar enterprises. We have in Kentucky the same description of population, and we employ them almost exclusively, in many of our hemp manufactories. A neighbor of mine, one of our most opulent and respectable citizens, has had one, two, if not three, manufactories burnt by incendiaries; but he persevered, and his perseverance has been rewarded with wealth. . . .

I pass . . . from this . . . topic, to two general propositions which cover the entire ground of debate. The first is, that, under the operation of the American system, the objects which it protects and fosters are brought to the consumer at cheaper prices, than they commanded prior to its introduction, or, than they would command if it did not exist. . . .

This brings me to consider what I apprehend to be the most efficient of all causes in the reduction of the prices of manufactured articles, and that is COMPETITION. By competition, the total amount of the supply is increased, and by increase of the supply, a competition in the sale ensues, and this enables the consumer to buy at lower rates. . . .

The great law of *price* is determined by supply and demand. Whatever affects either, affects the price. If the supply is increased, the demand remaining the same, the price declines; if the demand is increased, the supply remaining the same, the price advances; if both supply and demand are undiminished, the price is stationary, and the price is influenced exactly in proportion to the degree of the disturbance to the demand or supply. It is, therefore, a great error to suppose that an existing or new duty *necessarily* becomes a component element to its exact amount of price. If the proportions of demand and supply are varied by the duty, either in augmenting the supply, or diminishing the demand, or *vice versa,* price is affected to the extent of that variation. But the duty never becomes an integral part of the price, except in the instances where the demand and the supply remain after the duty is imposed, precisely what they were before, or the demand is increased, and the supply remains stationary.

Competition, therefore, wherever existing, whether at home or abroad, is the parent cause of cheapness. If a high duty excites production at home, and the quantity of the domestic article exceeds the amount which had been previously imported, the price will fall. . . .

I have now to consider the remaining of the two propositions which I have already announced. That is,

Second, that under the operation of the American system, the products of our agriculture command a higher price than they would do without it, by the creation of a home market; and by the augmentation of wealth produced by manufacturing industry, which enlarges our powers of consumption both of domestic and foreign articles. The importance of the home market is among the established maxims which are universally recognized by all writers and all men. . . .

What would be the condition of the farming country of the United States . . . if a home market did not exist for this immense amount of agricultural produce? Without that market, where could it be sold? In foreign markets? If their restrictive laws did not exist, their capacity would not enable them to purchase and consume this vast addition to their present supplies, which must be thrown in, or thrown away, but for the home market. . . .

I conclude this part of the argument with the hope that my humble exertions have not been altogether unsuccessful in showing,

First, that the policy which we have been considering ought to continue to be regarded as the genuine American system.

Secondly, that the free trade system, which is proposed as its substitute, ought really to be considered as the British colonial system.

Thirdly, that the American system is beneficial to all parts of the union, and absolutely necessary to much the larger portion.

Fourthly, that the price of the great staple cotton, and of all our chief productions of agriculture, has been sustained and upheld, and a decline averted, by the protective system.

Fifthly, that if the foreign demand for cotton has been at all diminished, by the operation of that system, the diminution has been more than compensated, in the additional demand created at home.

Sixthly, that the constant tendency of the system, by creating competition among ourselves, and between American and European industry, reciprocally acting upon each other, is to reduce prices of manufactured objects.

Seventhly, that, in point of fact, objects within the scope of the policy of protection, have greatly fallen in price. . . .

President James Monroe Vetoes the National Road, 1822*

A viable market economy depended on the transportation revolution that made possible the large-scale movement of people and commodities. The need for good roads attracted strong popular support for what were called "internal improvements," President James Monroe believed that a federal role in building highways violated the Constitution. He presented his opinions on the matter in a veto message delivered in 1822. The document raises two interesting points regarding power. One of those points involved the authority of the national government to construct roads, which Madison clearly rejected. The second significant point involves the use of presidential power in the early republic. Presidents initially believed that the veto power could be exercised only over questions of constitutional authority, as Madison does here. Later presidents assumed a different power, often rejecting acts of Congress for partisan or political, rather than for constitutional, reasons.

Having duly considered the bill entitled "An act for the preservation and repair of the Cumberland road," it is with deep regret, approving as I do the policy, that I am compelled to object to its passage and to return the bill to the House of Representatives, in which it originated, under a conviction that Congress do not possess the power under the Constitution to pass such a law.

A power to establish turnpikes with gates and tolls, and to enforce the collection of tolls by penalties, implies a power to adopt and execute a complete system of internal improvement. A right to impose duties to be paid by all persons passing a certain road, and on horses and carriages, as is done by this bill, involves the right to take the land from the proprietor on a valuation and pass laws for the protection of the road from injuries, and if it exists as to one road it exists as to any other, and to as many roads as Congress may think proper to establish. A right to legislate for one of these purposes is a right to legislate for the others. It is a complete right of jurisdiction and sovereignty for all the purposes of internal improvement, and not merely the right of applying money under the power vested in Congress to make appropriations, under which power, with the consent of the States through which the road passes, the work was originally commenced, and has been so far executed. I am of opinion that Congress do not possess this power; that the States individually can not grant it, for although they may assent to the appropriation of money within their limits for such purposes, they can grant no power of jurisdiction or sovereignty by special compacts with the United States. This power can be granted only by an amendment to the Constitution and in the mode prescribed by it.

If the power exist, it must be either because it has been specifically granted to the United States or that it is incidental to some power which has been specifically granted. If we examine the specific grants of power we do not find it among them, nor is it incidental to any power which has been specifically granted.

*From *A Compilation of the Messages and Papers of the Presidents, 1789–1897,* 10 vols., comp. James D. Richardson (Washington, D.C.: U.S. Government Printing Office, 1896–1899), II:142–43.

It has never been contended that the power was specifically granted. It is claimed only as being incidental to some one or more of the powers which are specifically granted. The following are powers from which it is said to be derived:

First, from the right to establish post-offices and post-roads; second, from the right to declare war; third, to regulate commerce; fourth, to pay debts and provide for the common defense and general welfare; fifth, from the power to make all laws necessary and proper for carrying into execution all the powers vested by the Constitution in the Government of the United States or in any department or officer thereof; sixth and lastly, from the power to dispose of and make all needful rules and regulations respecting the territory and other property of the United States.

According to my judgment it can not be derived from either of those powers, nor from all of them united, and in consequence it does not exist.

Having stated my objections to the bill, I should now cheerfully communicate at large the reasons on which they are founded if I had time to reduce them to such form as to include them in this paper. The advanced stage of the session renders that impossible. Having at the commencement of my service in this high trust considered it a duty to express the opinion that the United States do not possess the power in question, and to suggest for the consideration of Congress the propriety of recommending to the States an amendment to the Constitution to vest the power in the United States, my attention has been often drawn to the subject since, in consequence whereof I have occasionally committed my sentiments to paper respecting it. The form which this exposition has assumed is not such as I would have given it had it been intended for Congress, nor is it included. Nevertheless, as it contains my views on this subject, being one which I deem of very high importance, and which in many of its bearings has now become peculiarly urgent, I will communicate it to Congress, if in my power, in the course of the day, or certainly on Monday next.

The Lowell System

The growth of factories created the need for an industrial working class, a prospect that alarmed many people who feared that a permanent proletariat would create class differences dangerous to American liberties and equality. The Lowell system hoped to avert that threat by using unmarried young women as workers who after temporary employment in the factories would return to their homes to establish their own families. The following documents provide some insight into the lives of those "factory girls." In the first selection, a male observer gives a favorable view of several of the key elements that characterized the Lowell system. The second selection, from the memoirs of a former employee, offers an additional perspective on working in the factories.

Moral Police*

. . . The productiveness of these works depends on one primary and indispensable condition—the existence of an industrious, sober, orderly, and moral class of operatives. Without this, the mills in Lowell would be worthless. Profits would be absorbed by cases of irregularity, carelessness, and neglect; while the existence of any great moral exposure in Lowell would cut off the supply of help from the virtuous homesteads of the country. Public morals and private interests, identical in all places, are here to be linked together in an indissoluble connection. Accordingly, the sagacity of self-interest, as well as more disinterested considerations, has led to the adoption of a strict system of moral police.

---

[3]Henry A. Miles, *Lowell, As It Was, And As It Is,* 2d ed. (Lowell: Merrill & Heywood, 1846), 128–46.

Before we proceed to notice the details of this system, there is one consideration bearing upon the character of the operatives, which must be all the while borne in mind. *We have no permanent factory population.* This is the wide gulf which separates the English manufacturing town from Lowell. Only a very few of our operatives have their homes in this city. The most of them come from the distant interior of the country. . . .

To the general fact, here noticed, should be added another, of scarcely less importance to a just comprehension of this subject,—*the female operatives in Lowell do not work, on average, more than four and a half years in the factories.* They then return to their homes, and their places are taken by their sisters, or other female friends from their neighborhood. . . .

Here, then, we have two important elements of the difference between English and American operatives. The former are resident operatives, and are operatives for life, and constitute a permanent, dependent factory caste. The latter comes from distant homes, to which in a few years they return, to be the wives of the farmers and the mechanics of the country towns and villages. The English visitor to Lowell, when he finds it so hard to understand why American operatives are so superior to those of Leeds and Manchester, will do well to remember what a different class of females we have here to *begin* with—girls well educated in virtuous rural homes; nor must the Lowell manufacturer forget, that we forfeit the distinction, from that moment, when we cease to obtain such girls as the operatives of the city.

To obtain this constant importation of female hands from the country, it is necessary to secure *the moral protection of their characters while they are resident in Lowell.* This, therefore, is the chief object of that moral police referred to, some details of which will now be given.

It should be stated, in the outset, that no persons are employed on the Corporations who are addicted to intemperance, or who are known to be guilty of any immoralities of conduct. As the parent of all other vices, intemperance is most carefully excluded. Absolute freedom from intoxicating liquors is understood, throughout the city, to be a prerequisite to obtaining employment in the mills, and any person known to be addicted to their use is at once dismissed. This point has not received the attention, from writers upon the moral conditions of Lowell, which it deserves; and we are surprised that the English traveler and divine, Dr. Scoresby, in his recent book upon Lowell, has given no more notice to this subject. A more strictly and universally temperate class of persons cannot be found, than the nine thousand operatives of this city; and the fact is well known to all others living here, as it is of some honest pride among themselves. In relation to other immoralities, it may be stated, that the suspicion of criminal conduct, association with suspected persons, and general and habitual light behavior and conversation, are regarded as sufficient reasons for dismissions, and for which delinquent operatives are discharged.

In respect to discharged operatives, there is a system observed, of such an effectual and salutary operation, that it deserves to be minutely described.

Any person wishing to leave a mill, is at liberty to do so, at any time, after giving a fortnight's notice. The operative so leaving, if of good character, and having worked a year, is entitled, as a matter of right, to an honorable discharge, made out after a printed form, with which every counting-room is supplied. . . .

This letter of discharge is a letter of recommendation to any other mill in the city, and not without its influence in procuring employment in any other mill in New England. A record of all such discharges is made in each counting-room, in a book kept for that purpose.

So much for honorable discharges. Those dishonorable have another treatment. The names of all persons dismissed for bad conduct, or who leave the mill irregularly, are also entered in a book kept for that purpose, and these names are sent to all counting-rooms of the city, and are there entered upon *their* books. Such persons obtain no more employment throughout the city.

The question is put to each applicant, "Have you worked before in the city, and if so, where is your discharge? If no discharge be presented, an inquiry of the applicant's name will enable the superintendent to know whether that name stands on his book of dishonorable discharges, and he is thus saved from taking in a corrupt or unworthy hand. This system, which has been in operation in Lowell from the beginning, is of great important effect in driving unworthy persons from our city, and in preserving the high character of our operatives. . . .

Any description of the moral care, studied by the Corporations, would be defective if it omitted a reference to the overseers. Every room in every mill has its first and second overseers. The former, or, in his absence, the latter, has the entire care of the room, taking in such operatives as he wants for the work of the room, assigning them to their employment, superintending each process, directing the repairs of disordered machinery, giving answers to questions of advice, and granting permissions of absence. At his small desk, near the door, where he can see all who go out or come in, the overseer may generally be found; and he is held responsible for the good order, propriety of conduct, and attention to business, of the operatives of that room. Hence, this is a post of most importance, and the good management of the mill is almost wholly dependent upon the character of the overseers. It is for this reason that peculiar care is exercised in their appointment. Raw hands, and of unknown characters, are never placed in this office. It is attained only by those who have either served a regular apprenticeship as machinists in the Repair Shop, or have become well known and well tried, as third hands, and assistant overseers. It is a post for which there are always many applicants, the pay being two dollars a day, with a good house, owned by the company, and rented at . . . reduced charge. . . . The overseers are almost universally married men, with families; and as a body, numbering about one hundred and eighty, in all, are among the most permanent residents, and most trustworthy and valuable citizens of the place. A large number of them are members of our churches, and are often chosen as council men in the city government, and representatives in the State legislature. The guiding and salutary influence which they exert over the operatives, is one of the most essential parts of the moral machinery of the mills. . . .

Still another source of trust which a Corporation has, for the good character of its operatives, is the moral control which they have over one another. Of course this control would be nothing among a generally corrupt and degraded class. But among virtuous and high-minded young women, who feel that they have the keeping of their characters, and that any stain upon their associates brings reproach upon themselves, the power of opinion becomes an ever-present, and ever-active restraint. A girl, *suspected* of immoralities, or serious improprieties of conduct, at once loses caste. Her fellow-boarders will at once leave the house, if the keeper does not dismiss the offender. In self-protection, therefore, the matron is obliged to put the offender away. Nor will her former companions walk with, or work with her; till at length, finding herself everywhere talked about, and pointed at, and shunned, she is obliged to relieve her fellow-operatives of a presence which they feel brings disgrace. From this power of opinion, there is no appeal; and as long as it is exerted in favor of propriety of behavior and purity of life, it is one of the most active and effective safeguards of character.

It may not be out of place to present here the regulations, which are observed alike on all the Corporations, which are given to the operatives when they are first employed, and are posted up conspicuously in all the mills. They are as follows:—

"*Regulations to be observed by all persons employed by the _____ Manufacturing Company, in the Factories.*

Every overseer is required to be punctual himself, and to see that those employed under him are so.

The overseers may, at their discretion, grant leave of absence to those employed under them, when there are sufficient spare hands in the room to supply their place; but when there are not sufficient spare hands, they are not allowed to grant leave of absence unless in cases of absolute necessity.

All persons are required to observe the regulations of the room in which they are employed. They are not allowed to be absent from their work without the consent of their overseer, except in the case of sickness, and then they are required to send him word for the cause of their absence.

All persons are required to board in one of the boarding houses belonging to the company, and conform to the regulations of the house in which they board.

All persons are required to be constant in attendance on public worship, at one of the regular places of worship in this place.

Persons who do not comply with the above regulations will not be employed by the company.

Persons entering the employment of the company, are considered as engaging to work one year.

All persons intending to leave the employment of the company, are required to give notice of the same to their overseer, at least two weeks previous to the time of leaving.

Any one who shall take from the mills, or the yard, any yarn, cloth, or other article belonging to the company, will be considered guilty of STEALING—and prosecuted accordingly.

The above regulations are considered part of the contract with all persons entering the employment of the _____MANUFACTURING COMPANY. All persons who shall have complied with them, on leaving the company, shall be entitled to an honorable discharge, which will serve as a recommendation to any of the factories in Lowell. No one who shall not have complied to them will be entitled to such a discharge."

Lucy Larcom Remembers the Mills*

. . . The printed regulations forbade us to bring books into the mill, so I made my window-seat into a small library of poetry, pasting its side all over with newspaper clippings. In those days we had only weekly papers, and they had always a "poet's corner," where standard writers were well represented, with anonymous ones also. . . . I chose my verses for their sentiment, and because I wanted to commit them to memory. . . .

Some of the girls could not believe that the Bible was meant to be counted among forbidden books. We all thought that the Scriptures had a right to go wherever we went, and that if we needed them anywhere, it was at our work. I evaded the law by carrying some leaves from a torn Testament in my pocket.

The overseer, caring more for the law than gospel, confiscated all he found. He had his desk full of Bibles. It sounded oddly to hear him say to the most religious girl in the room, when he took hers away, "I always did think you had more conscience than to bring that book here." But we had some close ethical questions to settle in those days. It was a rigid code of morality under which we lived. Nobody complained of it, however, and we were doubtless better off for its strictness, in the end. . . .

I do not believe that any Lowell mill-girl was ever absurd enough to wish to be known as a "factory-lady," although most of them knew that "factory-girl" did not represent a high type of womanhood in the Old World. But they themselves belonged to the New World, not to the Old; and they were making their own traditions, to hand down to their Republican descen-

---

*Lucy Larcom, *A New England Girlhood, Outlined from Memory* (Boston: Houghton Mifflin Company, 1889), 175–76, 180–83, 201–202, 233.

dants,—one of which was and is that honest work has no need to assert itself or to humble itself in a nation like ours, but simply to take its place as one of the foundation stones of the Republic.

The young women who worked at Lowell had the advantage of living in a community where character alone commanded respect. They never, at their work or away from it, heard themselves contemptuously spoken of on account of their occupation, except by the ignorant or weak-minded, whose comments they were of course too sensible to heed. . . .

We were allowed to have books in the cloth-room. The absence of machinery permitted that privilege. Our superintendent, who was a man of culture and a Christian gentleman of the Puritan-school, dignified and reserved, used often to stop at my desk in his daily round to see what book I was reading. . . . It was a satisfaction to have a superintendent like him, whose granite principles, emphasized by his stately figure and bearing, made him a strength in the church and in the community. He kept a silent, kindly, rigid watch over the corporation life of which he was the head; and only those of us who were incidentally admitted to his confidence knew how carefully we were guarded. . . .

The Cotton South, 1835*

Harriet Martineau, a visitor from England, traveled extensively through the United States early in the 1830s, and she wrote an excellent account of life in America. Martineau made the following comments based on a visit to the booming "cotton belt" of Alabama. Although southerners often mistrusted industrialization, and although they came to fear the growing power of the manufacturing North, Martineau's comments left little doubt that cotton growers were as attracted as Yankee factory owners to the wealth of the market economy. The Englishwoman's observations, in addition, touched briefly on the conditions of the slaves who served as the labor foundation for the cotton economy.

We saw to-day, the common sight of companies of slaves travelling westwards; and the very uncommon one of a party returning to South Carolina. When we overtook such a company proceeding westwards, and esked where they were going, the answer commonly given by the slaves was, "Into Yellibama."—Sometimes these poor creatures were encamped, under the care of a slave-trader, on the banks of a clear stream, to spend a day in washing their clothes. Sometimes they were loitering along the road; the old folks and infants mounted on top of a wagon-load of luggage; the able-bodied, on foot, perhaps silent, perhaps laughing; the prettier of the girls, perhaps with a flower in her hair, and a lover's arm around her shoulder. There were wide differences in the air and gait of these people. It is usual to call the most depressed of them brutish in appearance. In some sense, they are so; but I never saw in any brute an expression of countenance so low, so lost, as in the most degraded class of negroes. There is some life and intelligence in the countenance of every animal; even in that of the "silly sheep," nothing so dead as the vacant, unheeding look of the depressed slaves is to be seen. To-day there was a spectacle by the roadside which showed that this has nothing to do with negro nature; though no such proof is needed by those who have seen negroes in favorable circumstances, and know how pleasant an aspect those grotesque features may wear. To-day we passed, in the Creek Territory, an establishment of Indians who held slaves. Negroes are anxious to be sold to Indians, who give them moderate work, and accommodations as good as their own. Those seen today among the Indians, were sleek, intelligent, and cheerful-

---

*Harriet Martineau, *Society in America,* 3 vols. (London: Saunders and Otley, 1837), I:291–92, 297–98, 300–301, 307–309.

looking, like the most favoured house-slaves, or free servants of colour, where the prejudice is least strong. . . .

Our friends, now residing seven miles from Montgomery, were from South Carolina; and the lady, at least, does not relish living in Alabama. It was delightful to me to be a guest in such an abode as theirs. They were about to build a good house: meantime, they were in one which I liked exceedingly: a log-house, with the usual open passage in the middle. Roses and honey-suckles, to which humming-birds resort, grew before the door. Abundance of books, and hand-some furniture and plate, were within the house, while daylight was to be seen through its walls. In my well furnished chamber, I could see through the chinks between the logs. During the summer, I should be sorry to change this primitive kind of abode for a better.

It is not difficult to procure the necessaries and comforts of life. Most articles are provided on the plantation. Wine and groceries are obtained from Mobile or New Orleans; and clothing and furniture come from the north. Tea is twenty shillings English per lb.; brown sugar, three-pence-halfpenny; white sugar, sixpence-halfpenny. A gentlemen's family, where there are chil-dren to be educated, cannot live for less than from seven hundred pounds to one thousands pounds per annum. The sons take land and buy slaves very early; and the daughters marry almost in childhood; so that education is less thought of, and sooner ended, than in almost any part of the world. The pioneers of civilisation, as the settlers in these new districts may be regarded, care for other things more than for education; or they would not come. They are, from whatever motive, money-getters; and few but money-getting qualification are to be looked for in them. It was partly amusing, and partly sad, to observe the young people of these regions; some, fit for a better mode of life, discontented; some youths pedantic, some maidens romantic, to a degree which makes the stranger almost doubt the reality of the scenes and personages before his eyes. The few better educated who come to get money, see the absurdity, and feel the wearisome-ness of this kind of literary cultivation; but the being in such society is the tax they must pay for making haste to be rich.

I heard in Montgomery of a wealthy old planter in the neighborhood, who has amassed millions of dollars, while his children can scarcely write their names. Becoming aware of their deficiencies, as the place began to be peopled from the eastward, he sent a son of sixteen to school, and a younger one to college; but they proved "such gawks," that they were unable to learn, or even to remain in the society of others who were learning; and their old father has bought land in Missouri, whither he was about to take his children, to remove them from the contempt of their neighbors. They are doomed to the lowest office of social beings; to be the mechanical, unintelligent pioneers of man in the wilderness. Surely such a warning as this should strike awe into the whole region, lest they should also perish to all the best purposes of life, by getting to consider money, not as a means, but an end. . . .

We saw several plantations while we were in this neighborhood. Nothing can be richer than the soil of one to which we went, to take a lesson in cotton-growing. It will never want more than to have the cotton seed returned to it. We saw the plough, which is very shallow. Two throw up a ridge, which is wrought by hand into little mounds. After these are drilled, the seed is put in by hand. This plantation consists of nine hundred and fifty acres, and is flourishing in every way. The air is healthy, as the situation is high prairie land. The water is generally good; but, after rain, so impregnated with lime, as to be disagreeable to the smell and taste. . . . Another griev-ance is, that no trees can be allowed to grow near the house for fear of mosquitoes. Everything else is done for coolness; there are wide piazzas on both sides of the house; the rooms are lofty, and amply provided with green blinds; but all this does not compensate to the eye for the want of the shade of trees. . . . But the plague of mosquitoes is a sufficient warrant for the pleasures of the eye; for they allow but little enjoyment of anything in their presence. . . .

Harcourt Brace & Company

The profits of cotton-growing, when I was in Alabama, were thirty-five per cent. One planter whom I knew had bought fifteen thousand dollars worth of land within two years, which he could then have sold for sixty-five thousand dollars. He expected to make, that season, fifty or sixty thousand dollars of his growing crop. It is certainly the place to become rich in; but the state of society is fearful. One of my hosts, a man of great good-nature, as he shows in the treatment of his slaves, and in his family relations, had been stabbed in the back in the reading-room of the town, two years before, and no prosecution was instituted. Another of my hosts carried loaded pistols . . . knowing that he was lain in wait for by persons against whose illegal practices he had given information to a magistrate. . . . It will be understood that I describe this region as presenting an extreme case of the material advantages and moral evils of a new settlement, under the institution of slavery. The most prominent relief is the hospitality,— the virtue of a young society. It is so remarkable, and to the stranger so grateful, that there is danger of its blinding him to the real state of affairs. In the drawing-rooms, the piazza, the barouche, all is so gay and friendly, there is such a prevailing hilarity and kindness, that it seems positively ungrateful and unjust to pronounce, even in one's heart, that all this way of life is full of wrong and peril. . . .

Discussion

1. How might the policies that Henry Clay defended have influenced the distribution of economic powers in the United States? How do you think Clay perceived liberty and equality? How do the policies he advanced compare to those outlined in Hamilton's Report on Manufactures in Chapter 9? How does Clay's vision of the United States compare to that of Thomas Jefferson as expressed in his first inaugural address?

2. What does President Madison's veto message suggest about his understanding of national power? Why do you think Madison considered subsidizing roads to be unconstitutional? What does the message reveal about the nature of presidential power?

3. Based on the documents describing the Lowell system, how do you think that factory girls might have understood liberty, equality, and power? To what degree did the Lowell workers enjoy power? Did they have any liberties? If so, what; if not, why not? How does the Lowell system relate to the American faith in equality?

4. Would you describe Harriet Martineau as being sympathetic toward or critical of the American South? Who held power in the South, and how was that power manifested? Did Southerners believe in equality or liberty?

5. How might a factory girl or a white Southerner have responded to Henry Clay's proposals?

Harcourt Brace & Company

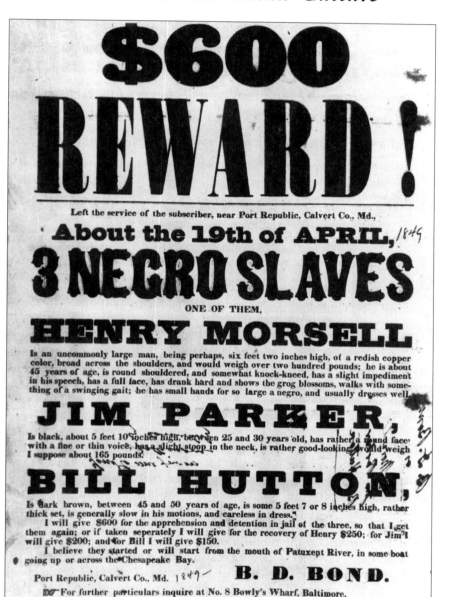

Blacks resisted slavery in many ways, from destroying equipment and work slow-downs to the extreme of slave revolts. Running away was another extreme, but seldom successful, response to the system. Notice in this 1849 handbill the detailed descriptions of the runaways, as well as the size of the reward. $600 was more than most workers earned in a year.

*A*ttitudes toward liberty, equality, and power shaped the politics as well as the economics of the early republic, but those three forces also profoundly influenced the development of an American culture. In the years following the War of 1812, the nation underwent a religious and intellectual transformation that affected all sectional, social, and racial groups. Certain groups came to hold power in the United States, and since that concentration of power had deep implications for liberty and equality, cultural differences became apparent. On one hand, "core" groups of middle-class northerners and commercially minded southerners generally supported the traditional American ideals of republicanism and capitalism promoted by men such as Alexander Hamilton and Henry Clay. On the other hand, poorer and more marginal Americans advanced a different vision of popular government and property by insisting on a democratic society that stressed equality—especially for white male adults.

American Revivalism, 1835*

Charles G. Finney played a critical role in the religious experience known as the Second Great Awakening, and in the following selection he summarized his views on revivals. In the selection, taken from an introduction to a book, he stressed the dynamic part that human beings should assume in carrying out God's will. Finney placed a strong emphasis on individuals, because each person had the opportunity to choose between good and evil. That egalitarianism reflected the growing democratic character of the nation. His message of "free agency," which called for active human intervention to improve the moral universe, also fit nicely with the emerging middle-class values of material progress built upon sobriety and industriousness. Finney's theology, then, helped provide a moral imperative to the economic and political power that many Americans were gaining as a result of the market revolution, and his ideas served as a foundation for the middle-class culture that emerged in the 1830s.

1.   Revivals were formerly regarded as miracles. And it has been so by some even in our day. And others have ideas on the subject so loose and unsatisfactory, that if they would only *think,* they would see their absurdity. For a long time, it was supposed by the church, that a revival was a miracle, an interposition of Divine power which they had nothing to do with, and which they had no more agency in producing, than they had in producing thunder, or a storm of hail, or an earthquake. It is only within a few years that ministers generally have supposed revivals were to be *promoted,* by the use of means designed and adapted specially to that object. Even in New England, it has been supposed that revivals came just as showers do, sometimes in one town, and sometimes in another, and that ministers and churches could do nothing more to produce them, than they could to make showers of rain come on their own town, when they are falling on a neighboring town.

It used to be supposed that a revival would come about once in fifteen years, and all would be converted that God intended to save, and then they must wait until another crop came for-

---

*Charles G. Finney, "What a Revival of Religion Is," in *Lectures on Revivals of Religion* (New York: Leavitt, Lord & Company, 1835), 17–20.

Harcourt Brace & Company

ward on the stage of life. Finally, the time got shortened down to five years, and they supposed there might be a revival about as often as that.

I have heard a fact in relation to one of these pastors, who supposed revival might come about once in five years. There had been a revival in his congregation. The next year, there was a revival in a neighboring town, and he went there to preach, and staid several days, till he got his soul all engaged in the work. He returned home on Saturday, and went into his study to prepare for the Sabbath. And his soul was in an agony. He thought how many adult persons there were in his congregation at enmity with God—so many still unconverted—so many persons *die* yearly—such a portion of them unconverted—if a revival does not come under five years, so many adult heads of families will be in hell. He put down his calculations on paper, and embodied them in his sermon for the next day, with his heart bleeding at the dreadful picture. As I understood it, he did not do this with any expectation of a revival, but he felt deeply, and poured out his heart to his people. And that sermon awakened *forty heads of families,* and a powerful revival followed; and so his theory about a revival once in five years was all exploded.

Thus God has overthrown, generally, the theory that revivals are miracles.

2. Mistaken notions concerning the sovereignty of God, have greatly hindered revivals. Many people have supposed God's sovereignty to be something very different from what it is. They have supposed it to be such an arbitrary disposal of events, and particularly of the gift of his Spirit, as precluded a rational employment of means for promoting a revival of religion. But there is no evidence from the Bible, that God exercises any such sovereignty as that. There are no facts to prove it. But every thing goes to show, that God has connected means with the end through all the departments of his government—in nature and in grace. There is no *natural* event in which his own agency is not concerned. He has not built the creation like a vast machine, that will go on alone without his further care. He has not retired from the universe, to let it work for itself. This is mere atheism. He exercises a universal superintendence and control. And yet every event in nature has been brought about by means. He neither administers providence nor grace with that sort of sovereignty, that dispenses with the use of means. There is no more sovereignty in one than in the other.

And yet some people are terribly alarmed at all direct efforts to promote a revival, and they cry out, "you are trying to get up a revival in your own strength. Take care, you are interfering with the sovereignty of God. Better keep along in the usual course, and let God give a revival when he thinks it is best. God is a sovereign, and it is very wrong for you to attempt to get up a revival, just because *you think* a revival is needed." This is just such preaching as the devil wants. And men cannot do the devil's work more effectually, than by preaching up the sovereignty of God, as a reason why we should not put forth efforts to produce a revival.

3. You see the error of those who are beginning to think that religion can be better promoted in the world without revivals, and who are disposed to give up all efforts to produce religious excitements. Because there are evils arising in some instances out of great excitements on the subject of religion, they are of an opinion that it is best to dispense with them altogether. This cannot, and must not be. True, there is danger of abuses. In cases of great *religious* as well as other excitements, more or less incidental evils may be expected of course. But this is no reason why they should be given up. The best things are always liable to abuses. Great and manifold evils have originated in the providential and moral government of God. But these *foreseen* perversions and evils were not considered a sufficient reason for giving them up. For the establishment of these governments was on the whole the best that could be done for the production of the greatest amount of happiness. So in revivals of religion, it is found by experience, that in the present state of the world, religion cannot be promoted to any considerable extent without them. The evils which are sometimes complained of, when they are real, are incidental, and of small importance when compared with the amount of good produced by revivals.

Harcourt Brace & Company

The sentiment should not be admitted by the church for a moment, that revivals may be given up. It is fraught with all that is dangerous to the interests of Zion, is death to the cause of missions, and brings in its train the damnation of the world.

FINALLY—I have a proposal to make to you who are here present. I have not commenced this course of Lectures on Revivals to get up a curious theory of my own on the subject. I would not spend my time and strength merely to give you instructions, to gratify your curiosity, and furnish you something to talk about. I have no idea preaching *about* revivals. It is not my design to preach so as to have you able to say at the close, "We *understand* all about revivals now," while you do *nothing*. But I wish to ask you a question. What do you hear lectures on revivals for? Do you mean that whenever you are convinced what your duty is in promoting a revival, you will go to work and practise it?

Will you follow the instructions I shall give you from the word of God, and put them in practice in your own hearts? Will you bring them to bear upon your families, your acquaintance, neighbors, and through the city? Or will you spend the winter in learning *about* revivals, and do nothing *for* them? I want you, as fast as you learn anything on the subject of revivals, to put it in practice, and go to work and see if you cannot promote a revival among sinners here. If you will not do this, I wish you to let me know at the beginning, so that I need not waste my strength. You ought to decide *now* whether you will do this or not. You know that we call sinners to decide on the spot whether *they* will obey the gospel. And we have no more authority to let you take time to deliberate whether *you* will obey God, than we have to let sinners do so. We call on you to unite now in a solemn pledge to God, that you will do your duty as fast as you learn what it is and to pray that He will pour out his Spirit upon this church and upon all the city this winter.

Uncle Tom's Cabin, 1852*

*U*ncle Tom's Cabin was an incredibly popular novel, and in the following passage there occurred one of the most dramatic moments in nineteenth-century American literature—the death of Little Eva St. Clare. The melodrama that Harriet Beecher Stowe described in her novel certainly revealed the sentimentalism of the mid-1800s. The story also stressed the importance of evangelical religion, and it is striking in its presentation of a female as the moral agent of Christianity. In addition, the book dealt with some of the issues of power and liberty that marked the era. The dependent status of the slaves is apparent, and Stowe clearly hoped to attract attention to the plight of the people she referred to as the "lowly." She addressed gender relations as well, with three women providing the most powerful characters in the scene presented here. Like most cultural works, then, *Uncle Tom's Cabin* reflected much of the society out of which it emerged.

Eva lay back on her pillows; her hair hanging loosely about her face, her crimson cheeks contrasting painfully with the intense whiteness of her complexion and the thin contour of her limbs and features, and her large soul-like eyes fixed earnestly on every one.

The servants were struck with a sudden emotion. The spiritual face, the long locks of hair cut off and lying by her, her father's averted face, and Marie's sobs, struck at once upon feelings of a sensitive and impressible race; and as they came in, they looked at one another, sighed, and shook their heads. There was a deep silence, like that of a funeral.

Eva raised herself, and looked long and earnestly round at every one. All looked sad and apprehensive. Many of the women hid their faces in their aprons.

---

*From Harriet Beecher Stowe, *Uncle Tom's Cabin, or, Life Among the Lowly,* 2 vols. (Boston: J. P. Jewett, 1852), II:102–105, 107–108, 110–13.

"I sent for you all, my dear friends," said Eva, "because I love you. I love you all; and I have something to say to you, which I want you always to remember. . . . I am going to leave you. In a few more weeks, you will see me no more—"

Here the child was interrupted by bursts of groans, sobs, and lamentations, which broke from all present, and in which her slender voice was lost entirely. She waited a moment, and then, speaking in a tone that checked the sobs of all, she said

"If you love me, you must not interrupt me so. Listen to what I say. I want to speak to you about your souls. . . .Many of you, I am afraid, are very careless. You are thinking only about this world. I want you to remember that there is a beautiful world, where Jesus is. I am going there, and you can go there. It is for you, as much as me. But, if you want to go there, you must not live idle, careless, thoughtless lives. You must be Christians. You must remember that each one of you can become angels and be angels forever. . . .If you want to be Christians, Jesus will help you. You must pray to him; you must read—"

The child checked herself, looked piteously at them, and said, sorrowfully,

"O, dear! you *can't* read,—poor souls!" and she hid her face in the pillow and sobbed, while many a smothered sob from those she was addressing, who were kneeling on the floor, aroused her.

"Never mind," she said, raising her face and smiling brightly through her tears, "I have prayed for you; and I know Jesus will help you, even if you can't read. Try all to do the best you can; pray every day; ask Him to help you, and get the Bible read to you whenever you can; and I think I shall see you all in heaven."

"Amen," was the murmured response from the lips of Tom and Mammy, and some of the elder ones, who belonged to the Methodist church. The younger and more thoughtless ones, for the time completely overcome, were sobbing, with their heads bowed upon their knees.

"I know" said Eva, "you all love me."

"Yes; oh, yes! indeed we do! Lord bless her!" was the involuntary answer of all.

"Yes, I know you do! There is n't one of you that has n't always been very kind to me; and I want to give you something that, when you look at, you shall always remember. I'm going to give all of you a curl of my hair; and when you look at it, think that I loved you and am gone to heaven, and that I want to see all of you there."

It is impossible to describe the scene, as, with tears and sobs, they gathered round the little creature, and took from her hands what seemed to them a last mark of her love. They fell on their knees; they sobbed, and prayed, and kissed the hem of her garment; and the elder ones poured forth words of endearment, mingled in prayers and blessings, after the manner of their susceptible race.

As each one took their gift, Miss Ophelia, who was apprehensive for the effect of the excitement on her little patient, signed to each one to pass out of the apartment.

At last, all were gone but Tom and Mammy.

"Here, Uncle Tom," said Eva, "is a beautiful one for you. O, I am so happy, Uncle Tom, to think I shall see you in heaven,—for I'm sure I shall; and Mammy, —dear, good, kind Mammy!" she said, fondly throwing her arms round her old nurse,—"I know you'll be there, too."

"O, Miss Eva, don't see how I can live without ye, no how!" said the faithful creature. "'Pears like it's just taking everything off the place to oncet" and Mammy gave way to a passion of grief.

Miss Ophelia pushed her and Tom gently from the apartment. . . .

Eva, after this, declined rapidly; there was no more any doubt of the event; the fondest hope could not be blinded. Her beautiful room was avowedly a sick room; and Miss Ophelia day and night performed the duties of a nurse,—and never did her friends appreciate her value more than in that capacity. With so well-trained a hand and eye, such perfect adroitness and practice in every art which could promote neatness and comfort, and keep out of sight every disagreeable incident of sickness,—with such a perfect sense of time, such a clear, untroubled head, such exact accuracy in remembering every prescription and direction of the doctors,—she was everything to him. They who had shrugged their shoulders at her little peculiarities and set-nesses, so unlike the careless freedom of southern manners, acknowledged that now she was the exact person that was wanted.

Uncle Tom was much in Eva's room. The child suffered much from nervous restlessness, and it was a relief to her to be carried; and it was Tom's greatest delight to carry her little frail form in his arms, resting on a pillow, now up and down her room, now out into the verandah; and when the fresh sea-breezes blew from the lake,—and the child felt freshest in the morning,—he would sometimes walk with her under the orange-trees in the garden, or, sitting down in some of their old seats, sing to her their favorite old hymns.

Her father often did the same thing; but his frame was slighter, and when he was weary, Eva would say to him,

"O, papa, let Tom take me. Poor fellow! it pleases him; and you know it's all he can do for now, and he wants to do something!"

"So do I, Eva!" said her father.

"Well, papa, you can do everything, and are everything to me. You read to me,—you sit up nights,—and Tom has only this one thing, and his singing; and I know, too, he does it easier than you can. He carries me so strong!"

. . . Eva had been unusually bright and cheerful, that afternoon, and had sat raised in her bed, and looked all over her little trinkets and precious things, and designated the friends to whom she would have them given; and her manner was more animated, and her voice more natural, than they had known it for weeks. Her father had been in, in the evening, and had said that Eva appeared more like her former self than ever she had done since her sickness; and when he kissed her for the night, he said to Miss Ophelia,—"Cousin, we may keep her with us, after all; she is certainly better;" and he had retired with a lighter heart in his bosom than he had had there for weeks.

But at midnight,—strange, mystic hour!—when the veil between the frail present and the eternal future grows thin,—then came the messenger!

There was a sound in that chamber, first of one who stepped quickly. It was Miss Ophelia, who had resolved to sit up all night with her little charge, and who, at the turn of the night, had discerned what experienced nurses significantly call "a change." The outer door was quick-ly opened, and Tom, who was watching outside, was on the alert, in a moment.

"Go for the doctor, Tom! lose not a moment," said Miss Ophelia. . . .

On the face of the child, however, there was no ghastly imprint,—only a high and almost sublime expression,—the overshadowing presence of spiritual natures, the drawing of immortal life in that childish soul.

They stood there so still, gazing upon her, that even the ticking of the watch seemed too loud. In a few moments, Tom returned, with the doctor. He entered, gave one look, and stood silent as the rest.

"When did this change take place?" said he, in a low whisper, to Miss Ophelia.

"About the turn of night," was the reply.

Marie, roused by the entrance of the doctor, appeared, hurriedly, from the next room.

"Augustine! Cousin!—O!—what!" she hurriedly began.

"Hush!" said St. Clare, hoarsely; "*she is dying!*"

Mammy heard the words, and flew to awaken the servants. The house was soon roused,—lights were seen, footsteps heard, anxious faces thronged the verandah, and looked tearfully through the glass doors; but St. Clare heard and said nothing,—he saw only *that look* on the face of the little sleeper.

"O, if she would only wake, and speak once more!" he said; and, stooping over her, he spoke in her ear,—"Eva, darling!"

The large blue eyes unclosed,—a smile passed over her face;—she tried to raise her head, and to speak.

"Do you know me, Eva?"

"Dear papa," said the child, with a last effort, throwing her arms about his neck. In a moment they dropped again; and, as St. Clare raised his head, he saw a spasm of mortal agony pass over the face,—she struggled for breath, and threw up her little hands.

"O, God, this is dreadful!" he said, turning away in agony, and wringing Tom's hand, scarce conscious what he was doing. "O, Tom, my boy, it is killing me!"

Tom had his master's hands between his own; and, with tears streaming down his dark cheeks, looked up for help where he had always been used to look.

"Pray that this may be cut short!" said St. Clare,—"this wrings my heart."

"O, bless the Lord! it's over.—it's over, dear Master!" said Tom; "look at her."

The child lay panting on her pillows, as one exhausted,—the large clear eyes rolled up and fixed. Ah, what said those eyes, that spoke so much of heaven? Earth was past, and earthly pain; but so solemn, so mysterious, was the triumphant brightness of that face, that it checked even the sobs of sorrow. They pressed around her, in breathless stillness.

"Eva," said St. Clare, gently.

She did not hear.

"O, Eva, tell us what you see! What is it?" said her father.

A bright, a glorious smile passed over her face, and she said brokenly.—"O! love,—joy,—peace!" gave one sigh, and passed from death unto life!

"Farewell, beloved child! the bright, eternal doors have closed after thee; we shall see thy sweet face no more. O, woe for them who watched the entrance into heaven, when they shall wake and find only the cold gray sky of daily life, and thou gone forever!"

Henry David Thoreau, 1854*

In *Walden,* Henry David Thoreau espoused the lessons to be taken from living close to nature. In the selection presented below, he warned against the conventional belief that wealth created power and happiness. Thoreau insisted instead that real power, and hence true liberty and equality, came from an internal moral wealth rather than from any profits that might be made in the market economy. Consequently, much of what Thoreau learned during his sojourn at Walden Pond appeared out of step with the middle-class values that influenced many of his contemporaries. For numerous people, however, especially those outside the mainstream, his reflections have become an integral part of their American culture.

I left the woods for as good a reason as I went there. Perhaps it seemed to me that I had several more lives to live, and could not spare any more time for that one. It is remarkable how easily and insensibly we fall into a particular route, and make a beaten track for ourselves. I had not lived there for a week before my feet wore a path from my door to the pond-side; and though it is five or six years since I trod it, it is still quite distinct. It is true, I fear that others may have fallen into it, and so helped to keep it open. The surface of the earth is soft and impressible by the feet of men; and so with the paths which the mind travels. How worn and dusty, then, must the highways of the world, how deep the ruts of tradition and conformity! I

---

*From Henry David Thoreau, *Walden* (New York: Grosset & Dunlap, 1910), 426–27, 430, 433–34.

Harcourt Brace & Company

did not wish to take a cabin passage, but rather to go before the mast and on the deck of the world, for there I could best see the moonlight amid the mountains. I do not wish to go below now.

I learned this, at least, by my experiment: that if one advances confidently in the direction of his dreams, and endeavors to live the life which he has imagined, he will meet with a success unexpected in the common hours. He will put some things behind, will pass on an invisible boundary; new, universal, and more liberal laws will begin to establish themselves around and within him; or the old laws be expanded, and interpreted in his favor in a more liberal sense, and he will live with the license of a higher order of beings. In proportion as he simplifies his life, the laws of the universe will appear less complex, and solitude will not be solitude, nor poverty poverty, nor weakness weakness. If you have built castles in the air, your work need not be lost; that is where they should be. Now put the foundations under them. . . .

Some are dinning in our ears that we Americans, and moderns generally, are intellectual dwarfs compared with ancients, or even the Elizabethan men. But what is that to the purpose? A living dog is better than a dead lion. Shall a man go and hang himself because he belongs to the race of pygmies, and not be the biggest pygmy that he can? Let every one mind his own business, and endeavor to be what he was made.

Why should we be in such desperate haste to succeed, and in such desperate enterprises? If a man does not keep pace with his companions, perhaps it is because he hears a different drummer. Let him step to the music which he hears, however measured or far away. It is not important that he should mature as soon as an apple tree or an oak. Shall he turn his spring into summer? If the condition of things which we were made for is not yet, what were any reality which we can substitute? We will not be shipwrecked on a vain reality. Shall we with pains erect a heaven of blue grass over ourselves, though when it is done we shall be sure to gaze still at the true ethereal heaven far above, as if the former were not? . . .

However mean your life is, meet it and live it; do not shun it and call it hard names. It is not so bad as you are. It looks poorest when you are richest. The faultfinder will find faults even in paradise. Love your life, poor as it is. You may perhaps have some pleasant, thrilling, glorious hours, even in a poorhouse. The setting sun is reflected from the windows of the almshouse as brightly as from the rich man's abode; the snow melts before its door as early in the spring. I do not see but a quiet mind may live as contentedly there, and have as cheering thoughts, as in a palace. The town's poor seem to me often to live the most independent life of any. Maybe they are simply great enough to receive without misgiving. Most think that they are above being supported by the town; but it oftener happens that they are not above supporting themselves by dishonest means, which should be more disreputable. Cultivate poverty like a garden herb, like sage. Do not trouble yourself much to get new things, whether clothes or friends. Turn the old; return to them. Things do not change; we change. Sell your clothes and keep your thoughts. God will see that you do not want society. If I were confined to a corner of a garret all my days, like a spider, the world would be just as large to me while I had my thoughts about me. The philosopher said: "From an army of three divisions one can take away its general, and put it in disorder; from the man the most abject and vulgar one cannot take away his thought." Do not seek so anxiously to be developed, to subject yourselves to so many influences to be on; it is all dissipation. Humility like darkness reveals the heavenly lights. The shadows of poverty and meanness gather around us, "and lo! creation widens to our view." We are often reminded that if there were bestowed on us the wealth of Croesus, our aims must still be the same, and our means essentially the same. Moreover, if you are restricted in your range by poverty, if you cannot buy books and newspapers, for instance, you are but confined to the most significant and vital experiences; you are compelled to deal with the material which yields the most sugar and the most starch. It is life near the bone where it is sweetest. You are defended from being a tri-

Harcourt Brace & Company

fler. No man loses ever on a lower level by magnanimity on a higher. Superfluous wealth can buy superfluities only. Money is not required to buy one necessary of the soul. . . .

Astor Place Riot, 1849*

As the United States grew and the market economy expanded, some poorer Americans came to believe that an unequal distribution of wealth threatened their liberty as surely as the British had threatened the rights of an earlier generation. Such powerful social tensions led to a number of violent urban demonstrations, including the famous Astor Place Riot. That disturbance, sparked by a theatrical performance by English actor William Charles Macready, revealed the depth of the anger that many people felt toward the wealthy aristocracy that they believed endangered the egalitarian principles of the democratic republic. The following material provided one of the first accounts of the brutal incident that took place in New York City in 1849.

[May 16, 1849] RIOT IN NEW YORK.—The city of New York has become the scene of a terrible riot, arising from a private quarrel between two actors, Forrest and Macready. The details of it are too voluminous for our columns, and we confine ourselves to some leading particulars. On Monday, 7th inst. Macready, who is an Englishman, attempted to play, but the disturbance was so great that it was impossible to proceed. At the advice of leading play-goers he attempted it again on Thursday, the 10th inst. at the Aster Place Opera House. A mob soon assembled, and a strong police force was assembled to preserve the peace. The national guards were called out to aid the police. At the commencement of the performance rioters inside of the house raised a disturbance, and were immediately seized by the police.

The leading rioters having been taken out, a mob outside—about five thousand persons having gathered around the house—commenced throwing stones at the windows. Some of these missiles, weighing from one to three pounds, passed into the building, and fell among the audience, knocking off hats and inflicting injuries. Nobody was seriously hurt.

During these proceedings, a number of policemen, headed by their chief, remained inside, picking out the rioters from the various parts of the building, while outside a troop of cavalry and a body of police were kept at bay by the mob.

The cavalry, from some cause or other, did not arrive on the ground until near 9 o'clock, when the police conquered the rioters inside.

All the doors were guarded by police and strongly barred inside, which prevented the mob from breaking in, although some uneasiness prevailed, lest an attempt be made to fire the building.

Between eight and nine o'clock the mob outside was increasing each moment in numbers and ferocity. Several of the policemen had been brought in severely wounded, one or two of the entrances were forced, and as imminent danger was apprehended, Mayor Woodhall, who was present, gave orders to Gen. Sanford to bring the military into the melee. The order was promptly obeyed, and in a few minutes several companies of the National Guard were placed in position around the theatre.

They were at first greeted with hisses and groans, but in a short time, just after the curtain fell on Macbeth, the paving-stones began to be hurled at them, and many of them were very severely, if not fatally injured. They stood this pelting, however, like veterans, nearly half an hour, only removing their comrades inside the theatre, as fast as they were struck down. At the solicitation of the Chief of Police, Mr. Recorder Tallmadge, amid a shower of missiles ventured his

*Niles' National Register, LXXV (1849), 319, 368.

life to warn them off. The caution was unheeded, and the Mayor and Sheriff Westervelt being called to the scene, the order was finally given to *fire!*

A platoon of the National Guard instantly answered the summons! a number of the mob fell, and among them a noted convict from the State Prison. The rioters then retreated in confusion, but soon rallying, they came on more determined than ever, and it was only until three more volleys had been discharged into the crowd, that they were induced to retire. Probably two hundred balls were fired, of which twenty took effect.

The whole number killed and who have since died of their wounds, is *twenty-one;* and the number of wounded, including the military, is *thirty-three.* Several persons were killed and wounded who were attracted to the scene by mere foolish curiosity. The city was in a high state of excitement; many citizens approving of the course adopted by the authorities to suppress the mob, and others condemning it. Attempts by the lawless and reckless have happily failed to renew the scenes of violence; many arrests have been made, and the law has regained supremacy. Thus a whole community has been inflamed, and blood has been profusely shed, and all about a couple of worthless players. The coroner's inquest on the dead is awaited with some anxiety and supprehension.

The Coroner's jury have brought in a verdict in relation to those killed in the late riot, "that *the circumstances existing at the time justified the authorities in giving the order to fire upon the mob.* We further believe that if a larger number of the police had been ordered out, the necessity of a resort to the use of the military might have been avoided."

[May 30, 1949] DAMAGES BY THE ASTER PLACE RIOTS.—Mr. Hackett, Manager of the Astor Place Theatre, has presented to the city of New York, a claim of $5,005.20, for the damages sustained during the late riot. The bill for meals and refreshments to the police is $754.50; and the aggregate will be about $6,000.

Concerning Slaves, 1842*

Charles Colcock Jones, who encouraged the religious instruction of slaves, hoped to bring Christianity to them—unquestionably to ensure their salvation but also to obtain absolute obedience to their masters. The government and economy of the United States empowered many people, but the presence of millions of slaves posed a dilemma for American society. A republic founded on concepts of freedom and equality denied all hope of liberty to a vast segment of its population. As the country matured, therefore, questions concerning the "peculiar institution" took on increasing significance, and the place of African Americans in the national culture became one of the important themes in the history of the American people. In the passage below, Jones, who was not a "typical" southerner, leveled sharp criticisms at slave owners. At the same time, his description of the slaves mirrored many of the white attitudes toward African Americans during the antebellum period.

The character of a people may be gathered from their circumstances. A consideration therefore of the circumstances in which we find our Negro population, is a necessary and preparatory step to the inquiry we have in hand.

1.   *The circumstances of the Slave Population.*

As habits of virtue and vice are formed, and character shaped, at a very early age, I shall begin with—

---

*Charles C. Jones, *The Religious Instruction of the Negroes in the United States* (Savannah: Thomas Purse, 1842), 112–19.

The Negro in his Childhood.—The formation of good character depends upon family government and training; upon religious instruction, private and public; access to the Scriptures and other sources of intellectual and moral improvement; the character of associates; modesty of clothing, and general mode of living.

If we take the mass of the slave population, properly speaking, we shall find but little *family government,* and for the reason that parents are not qualified, neither are they so circumstanced as to fulfil perfectly the duties devolving upon them as such.

In the more intellectual and pious families, the children are taught to say their prayers, to go to church on the Sabbath, to attend evening prayers on the plantation, and a few simple rules of good conduct and manners. The majority of church members, come short of this. The moral training of their children forms but a small part of their effort in the family. There is not one family in a thousand in which family prayer is observed morning and evening. Prayers are held in some families morning and evening on the Sabbath day; in others in the evening of every day. But a general meeting of all the members of the church as well as of worldly persons, for prayer in the evening on the plantations, conducted by some prominent person among them, takes the place of family worship—the plantation is considered one large family. To this meeting children are required to come or not, as the case may be. The hour is usually so late that most of the children have retired for the night. If such is the state of religious families what must be the state of those who are irreligious? In multitudes of families, both by precept and example, the children are trained up in iniquity; taught by their parents to steal, to lie, to deceive; nor can the rod of correction induce a confession or revelation of their clearly ascertained transgressions. Virtue is not cherished nor protected in them. Parents put their children to use as early as it is possible, and their discipline mainly respects omissions of duty in the household; moral delinquencies are passed by; and that discipline owes its chief efficiency to excited passion, and consequently exists in the extreme of laxity or severity. They ofttimes when under no restraint, beat their children unmercifully.

As to the direct *religious instruction*, we have seen that the amount communicated *in families* is small. The Negroes on plantations sometimes appoint one of their number, commonly the old woman who minds the children during the day, to teach them to say prayers, repeat a little catechism and a few hymns, every evening. The instances are however not frequent, and it is the only approximation I have ever known to systematic instruction for their children, adopted by the Negroes themselves.

But how much religious instruction do the young Negroes receive from their *Masters*, who sustain very much the relation of parents to them? What is the number of planters who have established plantation schools? In other words, who have commenced a system of regular instruction for their Negro children; conducting themselves that instruction daily or weekly, or engaging the services of members of their own families, or even going to the expense of employing missionaries for the purpose?

Push the inquiry still further. How may *ministers* assemble at stated seasons, the colored children of their congregations for catechetical instruction, exhortation, and prayer? How many *churches* have established Sabbath schools at convenient stations in the country, or in towns and villages for colored children and youth, and do maintain them from year to year? To all of these questions, it must in candor be replied that the numbers are small compared to the whole.

Shall we speak of *public instruction* such as is communicated by a *preached* Gospel? Negro children do not enjoy the advantages of a preached Gospel; for the custom is, where no effort is made to alter it, for the children to remain at home on the Sabbath. Multitudes never having been taught to "remember the Sabbath day to keep it holy," consider it in the light, purely, of a holyday;—a day of rest, of sports, and plays. The distance to the house of worship is frequently considerable, too considerable for the attendance of small children; and, in short, should the chil-

Harcourt Brace & Company

dren accompany them, the service being conducted for the most part for the special benefit of masters, do them no good, being above not only their comprehension, but even that of their parents.

Shall we speak of *access to the Scriptures?* The *statutes* of our respective slave States forbid all knowledge of letters to the Negroes; and where the statutes do not *custom does.* It is impossible to form an estimate of the number of Negroes that *read.* My belief is that the proportion would be expressed by an almost inconceivable fraction. The greatest number of readers is found in and about towns and cities, and among the free Negro population, some two or three generations removed from servitude. There are perhaps in all of the larger cities in the South, schools for the education of colored children, supported chiefly by the *free* Negroes, and kept generally in the shade. On the one hand, therefore, the Negro children cannot be "hearers of the law," for oral instruction is but sparingly afforded to the mass of them; and on the other, they cannot "search the Scriptures," for a knowledge of letters they have not, and legally, they cannot obtain.

With whom is the young Negro *associated?* With children no better instructed and disciplined than himself, and the whole subjected to the pernicious examples of the adults. They are favored with no association calculated to elevate and refine.

Negroes, especially the children, are exceedingly inattentive to the preservation of their *clothing.* The habits, in the particular of dress, of their forefathers from Africa still cleave to them, especially in the warmer seasons of the year, when they are left to themselves. This very improvidence on the part of the Negroes presents an increase of expenditure on the part of owners for clothing. The waste is great. And indeed, once for all, I will here say, that the wastes of the system are so great, as well as the fluctuations in the price of staple articles for market, that it is difficult, nay, impossible, to indulge in large expenditures on plantations and make them savingly profitable.

Their general *mode of living* is coarse and vulgar. Many Negro houses are small, low to the ground, blackened with smoke, often with dirt floors, and the furniture of the plainest kind. On some estates the houses are framed, weather-boarded, neatly white-washed, and made sufficiently large and comfortable in every respect. The improvements in the size, material, and finish of Negro houses is extending. Occasionally they may be found constructed of tabby or brick.

A room is partitioned off for a sleeping apartment and store-room, though houses are found destitute of the convenience. In such dwellings privacy is impossible, and we may in a manner say that families live, sleep, and grow up together; their habits and manners being coarse and rude. Some owners make additions to the house according to the number and age of the children of families.

Having now considered the circumstances of the Negro during his childhood, we may proceed and consider the circumstances of—

The Negro at Adult Age.—he lives in a house similar to the ones in which he passed his childhood and youth. He has the necessary and annual provision made for his wants; associates with fellow-servants of like character to his own. The seeds of virtue or vice sown in his youth, now blossom and bear fruit. He marries and settles in life, his children grow up around him and tread in his footsteps, as he did in the footsteps of his father before him.

The remarks on the *religious instruction of children* apply with equal correctness to *adults.* Religious instruction of adults *on plantations,* communicated by masters, ministers, or missionaries employed for the purpose, taking the slave States together, is not of frequent occurrence. The chief privilege enjoyed by thousands on plantations is *evening prayers,* conducted by themselves. If the individuals upon whom the conduct of the evening meeting devolves are able to *read,* a chapter in the Bible is read; a hymn is read and given out and sung; followed with prayer. If they cannot read, then a brief exhortation in place of the Scriptures founded, it may be, on some remembered passage, then a hymn from memory and prayer. There are thousands also, who, although freely allowed the privilege, do not embrace it, either from want of inclination, or of suitable persons to conduct the meetings. It is a matter of thankfulness that the owners are few in number, indeed, who forbid religious meetings on their plantations, held either by their servants themselves, or by competent and approved white instructors or ministers. "All men have not faith." I have never known servants forbidden to attend the worship of God *on the Sabbath day,* except as a restraint temporarily laid, for some flagrant misconduct.

On special occasions, such as fast days, communion seasons, and protracted meetings, a day or more is allowed servants by many masters. Throughout the slave-holding States the rest of the Sabbath is secured to the Negroes, and on this day they have extensive opportunities of attending divine worship, in town and country. But it is well known to those who have attentively observed the habits of this people, that large numbers of adults remain at home or spend the day in visiting or in ways still more exceptionable. Various causes conspire to produce the effect. For instance; it is their day of rest; the distance which they must walk to church is considerable; the accommodations for seats, in certain cases, are limited; the services of the sanctuary are too elevated for them; they are not required or encouraged to go; they have no exalted ideas of the importance of religion, and in common with all men, are naturally disinclined to it; and other causes which might be mentioned. Many, in settlements that are and that are not supplied with Gospel ministrations, live and die without an adequate knowledge of the way of salvation.

Nor can the adult Negro acquaint himself with duty and the way of salvation *through the reading of the Scriptures,* any more than can the child. Of those that do read, but few read well enough for the edification of the hearers. Not all the colored *preachers* read.

Two other circumstances which have considerable bearing on the moral and religious character of the Negro deserve attention. The first is that the *marriage state is not protected by law.* Whatever of protection it enjoys is to be attributed to custom, to the conscientious efforts of owners, and the discipline and doctrines of the churches; and also the correct principle and virtue of the contracting parties. But the relation is liable to disruption in a variety of forms, for some of which there is no remedy. The second is that *the government* to which they are subjected is *too much physical* in its nature. To discard an appeal to the principle of fear—the fear of punishment of *the person* of the transgressor in some form or other, would be running contrary to all governments in existence, both human and divine. While the necessity is admitted, yet the appeal should be made as seldom as possible and in the mildest form consistent with the due support of authority and the reformation of the transgressor. Man has a *spiritual* as well as an animal nature, and corrective influences, should be brought to bear upon that *directly* and in the *first instance,* as soon as he is able to discern between good and evil.

Such then are the circumstances of the slave population, which have an unfavorable influence upon their moral and religious condition. These circumstances only have been referred to which prominently assist us in our inquiry. In conclusion it may be added that servants have neither intellectual nor moral intercourse with their masters generally, sufficient to redeem them from the adverse influence of the circumstances alluded to; for the two classes are distinct in their association, and it cannot well be otherwise. Nor have servants any redeeming intercourse with any other persons. On the contrary in certain situations there is intercourse had with them, and many temptations laid before them against they have little or no defence, and the effect is deplorable. . . .

Harcourt Brace & Company

Discussion

1. In the documents by Charles G. Finney, Harriet Beecher Stowe, Henry David Thoreau, and Charles Colcock Jones, who do you think the authors believed held power in the United States? Which of the documents discuss liberty, and how do they do so? Which of the selections raise issues of equality, and how are they presented?

2. Why do you think Charles G. Finney expressed so much excitement over the conversions of heads of households? What does his enthusiasm over their conversion suggest about American culture in the 1830s? Do his comments have any significance regarding gender relations during the era?

3. Both Harriet Beecher Stowe and Charles Colcock Jones stress the illiteracy of slaves. What are the implications concerning power when one social group refuses to allow another group to read? What are the implications for liberty and for equality?

4. Compare the ideas that Henry David Thoreau expressed with the selection from the previous chapter on Moral Police. How do the two documents reveal different understandings of power and liberty in the United States? How do you think Thoreau would have reacted to the rules the mill owners imposed?

5. How do you think that different people in the United States might have responded to the Astor Place Riot? What groups might have feared the demonstrations? What groups might have seen the riots as an expression of patriotism? How do you think Charles G. Finney or Charles Colcock Jones might have reacted to the report on the riot?

Chapter 12
Jacksonian Democracy

Calhoun was roundly criticized for his nullification doctrine. Here he steps from nullification, past treason and civil war, to despotism, as both the Constitution and the Union lie dead where he slew them. Off to the right, President Jackson restrains one of Calhoun's supporters and threatens to hang them all.

*T*he years from 1819 to 1840 marked a time of growing interest in politics, and conse quently the period is often regarded as the beginning of American democracy. Concern over important issues, such as slavery and monetary policy, helped spark the high voter turnout that accompanied the creation of a new party system in the United States. Those Americans who hoped to use government power to establish an integrated commercial republic became known as Whigs, a name they adopted because of their opposition to what they saw as the reign of King Andrew Jackson. Jackson's supporters, the Democrats, argued that the Whigs' concept of government threatened liberty and the equality of adult white males. As a result of those party differences, the new power relationships that had developed with the rise of the market economy profoundly influenced American political institutions.

The Missouri Question, 1819*

Virulent debate over Missouri statehood in 1819 focused attention on the expansion of slavery— a matter that assumed increasing importance during the subsequent decades. The issue raised few concerns over equality, since most white Americans had little interest in, or compassion for, the status of African Americans. The Missouri question did, however, raise grave concerns over power. Admitting another slave state to the Union would increase southern strength in the national government, while, to southerners, prohibiting slavery would be an assertion of power that threatened their liberty. When New York Congressman James Tallmadge, Jr., proposed eliminating slavery in Missouri gradually, he was surprised at the vicious attacks the proposal brought. In the following speech, he responded to those attacks and defended his proposal to limit slavery in the new state. His comments touched on some of the important topics that shaped the argument over slavery; they also revealed the bitterness that the matter generated and that so terrorized Thomas Jefferson and many other Americans.

Mr. Tallmadge, of New York, rose.—Sir, said he, it has been my desire and my intention to avoid any debate on the present painful and unpleasant subject. When I had the honor to submit to this House the amendment now under consideration, I accompanied it with a declaration, that it was intended to confine its operation to the newly acquired territory across the Mississippi; and I then expressly declared that I would in no manner intermeddle with the slaveholding States, nor attempt manumission in any of the original States in the Union. Sir, I even went further, and stated that I was aware of the delicacy of the subject, and that I had learned from Southern gentlemen the difficulties and the dangers of having free blacks intermingle with slaves; and, on that account, and with a view to the safety of the white population of the adjoining States, I would not even advocate the prohibition of slavery in the Alabama Territory; because, surrounded as it was by slaveholding States, and with only imaginary lines of division, the intercourse between slaves and free blacks could not be prevented, and a *servile* war might be the result. While we deprecate and mourn over the evil of slavery, humanity and good morals require us to wish its abolition, under circumstances consistent with the safety of the white pop-

---

*From *Debates and Proceedings of the Congress of the United States . . . ,* 15th Congress, 2d Session (Washington, D.C.: Gales and Seaton, 1855), 1203–1205.

ulation. Willingly, therefore, will I submit to an evil which we cannot safely remedy. I admitted all that had been said of the danger of having free blacks visible to slaves, and therefore did not hesitate to pledge myself that I would neither advise nor attempt coercive manumission. But, sir, all these reasons cease when we cross the banks of the Mississippi, a newly acquired territory, never contemplated in the formation of our Government, not included within the compromise or mutual pledge in the adoption of our Constitution, a new territory acquired by our common fund, and ought justly to be subject to our common legislation.

Sir, when I submitted the amendment now under consideration, accompanied with these explanations, and with these avowals of my intentions and my motives, I did expect that gentlemen who might differ from me in opinion would appreciate the liberality of my views, and would meet with moderation, as upon a fair subject for general legislation. Sir, I did expect at least that the frank declaration of my views would protect me from harsh expressions, and from the unfriendly imputations which have been cast out on this occasion. But, sir, such has been the character and the violence of this debate, and expressions of so much intemperance, and of an aspect so threatening have been used, that continued silence on my part would ill become me, who had submitted to this House the original proposition. While this subject was under debate before the Committee of the Whole, I did not take the floor, and I avail myself of this occasion to acknowledge my obligations to my friends, (Mssrs. Taylor and Mills,) for the manner in which they supported my amendment, at a time when I was unable to partake in the debate. I had only on that day returned from a journey long in its extent, and painful in its occasion; and, from an affection of my breast, I could not then speak; I cannot yet hope to do justice to the subject; but I do hope to say enough to assure my friends that I have not *left* them in the controversy, and to convince the opponents of the measure, that their violence has not driven me from the debate.

Sir, the honorable gentleman from Missouri, (Mr. Scott,) who has just resumed his seat, has told us of the *ides of March,* and has cautioned us to *"beware of the fate of Caesar and of Rome."* Another gentleman, (Mr. Cobb,) from Georgia, in addition to other expressions of great warmth, has said, "that, if we persist, the Union will be dissolved;" and, with a look fixed on me, has told us, "we have kindled a fire which all the waters of the ocean cannot put out, which seas of blood can only extinguish."

Sir, language of this sort has no effect on me; my purpose is fixed, it is interwoven with my existence, its durability is limited with my life, it is a great and glorious cause, setting bounds to a slavery the most cruel and debasing the world ever witnessed; it is the freedom of man; it is the cause of unredeemed and unregenerated human beings.

Sir, if a dissolution of the Union must take place, let it be so! If civil war, which gentlemen so much threaten, must come, I can only say, let it come! My hold on life is probably as frail as that of any man who now hears me; but, while that hold lasts, it shall be devoted to the service of my country—to the freedom of man. If blood is necessary to extinguish any fire which I have assisted to kindle, I can assure gentlemen, while I regret the necessity, I shall nor forbear to contribute my mite. Sir, the violence to which gentlemen have resorted on this subject will not move my purpose, nor drive me from my place. I have the fortune and the honor to stand here as the representative of freemen, who possess intelligence to know their rights, who have the spirit to maintain them. Whatever might be my own private sentiments on this subject, standing here as the representatives of others, no choice is left me. I know the will of my constituents, and, regardless of consequences, I will avow it; as their representative, I will proclaim their hatred to slavery in every shape; as their representative, here will I hold my stand, until this floor, with the Constitution of my country which supports it, shall sink beneath me. If I am doomed to fall, I shall at least have the painful consolation to believe that I fall, as a fragment, in the ruins of my country. . . .

Harcourt Brace & Company

Inaugural Address of John Quincy Adams, 1825*

In his inaugural address, John Quincy Adams provided a thoughtful survey of the country's history. The Revolution, according to Adams, had been completed successfully because Americans had gained the fruits of liberty. In addition, the United States had survived the dangers that domestic partisanship and international rivalries had posed to the young republic. The nation had indeed enjoyed a period of peace and "an era of good feelings," but Adams's critics would be quick to point out that many white men had yet to gain the economic or political equality they deserved. In addition, the grand concepts he expressed concerning internal improvements frightened many Americans who saw the new president as a usurper in the office and who remembered that the glory of the Roman Republic had given way to the tyranny of Caesar.

In compliance with an usage coeval with the existence of our Federal Constitution, and sanctioned by the example of my predecessors in the career upon which I am about to enter, I appear, my fellow-citizens, in your presence and in that of Heaven to bind myself by the solemnities of religious obligation of the faithful performance of the duties allotted to me in the station to which I have been called.

In unfolding to my countrymen the principles by which I shall be governed in the fulfillment of those duties my first resort will be to that Constitution which I shall swear to the best of my ability to preserve, protect, and defend. That revered instrument enumerates the powers and prescribes the duties of the Executive magistrate, and in its first words declares the purposes to which these and the whole action of the Government instituted by it should be invariably and sacredly devoted—to form a more perfect union, establish justice, insure domestic tranquillity, provide for the common defense, promote the general welfare, and secure the blessings of liberty to the peoples of this Union in their successive generations. Since the adoption of this social compact one of these generations has passed away. It is the work of our forefathers. Administered by some of the most eminent men who contributed to its formation, through a most eventful period in the annals of the world, and through all the vicissitudes of peace and war incidental to the conditions of associated man, it has not disappointed the hopes and aspirations of those illustrious benefactors of their age and nation. It has promoted the lasting welfare of that country so dear to us all; it has to an extent far beyond the ordinary lot of humanity secured the happiness and freedom of this people. We now receive it as a precious inheritance from those to whom we are indebted for its establishment, doubly bound by the examples which they have left us and by the blessings which we have enjoyed as the fruits of their labors to transmit the same unimpaired to the succeeding generation.

In the compass of thirty-six years since this great national covenant was instituted a body of laws enacted under its authority and in conformity with its provisions has unfolded its powers and carried into practical operation its effective energies. Subordinate departments have distributed the executive functions in their various relations to foreign affairs, to the revenue and expenditures, and to the military force of the Union by land and sea. A coordinate department of the judiciary has expounded the Constitution and the laws, setting in harmonious coincidence with the legislative will numerous weighty questions of construction which the imperfection of human language had rendered unavoidable. The year of jubilee since the first formation of our Union has just elapsed; that of the declaration of independence is at hand. The consummation of both was effected by this Constitution.

---

*From "Inaugural Address," *A Compilation of the Messages and Papers of the Presidents, 1789–1897,* 10 vols., comp. James D. Richardson (Washington, D.C.: U.S. Government Printing Office, 1896–1899), II:294–99.

Since that period a population of four millions has multiplied to twelve. A territory bounded by the Mississippi has been extended from sea to sea. New states have been admitted to the Union in numbers nearly equal to those of the first Confederation. Treaties of peace, amity, and commerce have been concluded with the principal dominions of the earth. The people of other nations, inhabitants of regions acquired not by conquest, but by compact, have been united with us in the participation of our rights and duties, of our burdens and blessings. The forest has fallen by the ax of the woodsman; the soil has been made to teem by the tillage of our farmers; our commerce has whitened every ocean. The dominion of man over physical nature has been extended by the invention of our artists. Liberty and law have marched hand in hand. All the purposes of human association have been accomplished as effectively as under any other government on the globe, and at a cost little exceeding in a whole generation the expenditure of other nations in a single year.

Such is the unexaggerated picture of our conditions under a Constitution founded upon the republican principle of equal rights. To admit that this picture has its shades is but to say that it is still the condition of men upon earth. From evil—physical, moral, and political—it is not our claim to be exempt. We have suffered sometimes by the visitation of heaven through disease; often by the wrongs and injustice of other nations, even to the extremities of war; and, lastly, by dissensions among ourselves—dissensions perhaps inseparable from the enjoyment of freedom, but which have more than once appeared to threaten the dissolution of the Union, and with it the overthrow of all the enjoyments of our present lot and all our earthly hopes of the future. The causes of these dissensions have been various, founded upon differences of speculation in the theory of republican government; upon conflicting views of policy in our relations with foreign nations; upon jealousies of partial and sectional interests, aggravated by prejudices and prepossessions which strangers are ever apt to entertain.

It is a source of gratification and of encouragement to me to observe that the great result of this experiment upon the theory of human rights has at the close of that generation by which it was formed been crowned with success equal to the most sanguine expectations of its founders. Union, justice, tranquillity, the common defense, the general welfare, and the blessings of liberty—all have been promoted by the Government under which we have lived. Standing at this point of time, looking back to that generation which has gone by and forward to that which is advancing, we may at once indulge in grateful exultation and in cheering hope. From the experience of the past we derive instructive lessons for the future. Of the two great political parties which have divided the opinions and feelings of our country, the candid and the just will now admit that both have contributed splendid talents, spotless integrity, ardent patriotism, and disinterested sacrifices to the formation and administration of this Government, and both have required a liberal indulgence for a portion of infirmity and error. The revolutionary wars of Europe, commencing precisely at the moment when the Government of the United States first went into operation under this Constitution, excited a collision of sentiments and of sympathies which kindled all the passions and imbittered the conflict of parties till the nation was involved in war and the Union was shaken to its center. This time of trial embraced a period of five and twenty years, during which the policy of the Union in its relations with Europe constituted the principal basis of our political divisions and the most arduous part of the action of our Federal Government. With the catastrophe in which the wars of the French Revolution terminated, and our own subsequent peace with Great Britain, this baneful weed of party strife was uprooted. From that time no difference of principle, connected either with the theory of government or with our intercourse with foreign nations, has existed or been called forth in force sufficient to sustain a continued combination of parties or to give more than the wholesome animation to public sentiment or legislative debate. Our political creed is, without a dissenting voice that can be heard, that the will of the people is the source and the happiness of the people is the end of all legitimate government upon earth; that the best security for the beneficence and the best guaranty against the abuse of power consists in the freedom, the purity, and the frequency of popular elections; that the General Government of the Union and the separate governments of the States are all sovereignties of limited powers, fellow-servants of the same masters, uncontrolled within their respective spheres, uncontrollable by encroachments upon each other; that the firmest security of peace is the preparation during peace of the defenses of war; that a rigorous economy and accountability of public expenditures should guard against the aggravation and alleviate when possible the burden of taxation; that the military should be kept in strict subordination to the civil power; that the freedom of the press and of religious opinion should be inviolate; that the policy of our country is peace and the ark of our salvation union are articles of faith upon which we are all now agreed. If there have been those who doubted whether a confederated representative democracy were a government competent to the wise and orderly management of the common concerns of a mighty nation, those doubts have been dispelled; if there have been projects of partial confederacies to be erected upon the ruins of the Union, they have been scattered to the winds; if there have been dangerous attachments to one foreign nation and antipathies against another, they have been extinguished. Ten years of peace, at home and abroad, have assuaged the animosities of political contention and blended into harmony the most discordant elements of public opinion. There still remains one effort of magnanimity, one sacrifice of prejudice and passion, to be made by the individuals throughout the nation who have heretofore followed the standards of political party. It is that of discarding every remnant of rancor against each other, of embracing as countrymen and friends, and of yielding to talents and virtue alone that confidence which in times of contention for principle was bestowed only upon those who bore the badge of party communion.

The collisions of party spirit which originate in speculative opinions or in different views of administrative policy are in their nature transitory. Those which are founded on geographical divisions, adverse interests of soil, climate, and modes of domestic life are more permanent, and therefore, perhaps more dangerous. It is this which gives inestimable value to the character of our Government, at once federal and national. It holds out to us a perpetual admonition to preserve alike and with equal anxiety the rights of each individual State in its own government and the rights of the whole nation in that of the Union. Whatsoever is the domestic concernment, unaccounted with the other members of the Union or with foreign lands, belongs exclusively to the administration of the State governments. Whatsoever directly involves the rights and interests of the federal fraternity or of foreign powers is of the resort of this General Government. The duties of both are obvious in the general principle, though sometimes perplexed with difficulties in the detail. To respect the rights of the State governments is the inviolable duty of that of the Union; the government of every State will feel its own obligation to respect and preserve the rights of the whole. The prejudices everywhere too commonly entertained against distant strangers are worn away, and the jealousies of jarring interests are allayed by the composition and functions of the great national councils annually assembled from all quarters of the Union at this place. Hence the distinguished men from every section of our country, while meeting to deliberate upon the great interests of those by whom they are deputed, learn to estimate the talents and do justice to the virtues of each other. The harmony of the nation is promoted and the whole Union is knit together by the sentiments of mutual respect, the habits of social intercourse, and the ties of personal friendship formed between the representatives of its several parts in the performance of their service at this metropolis.

Passing from this general review of the purposes and injunctions of the Federal Constitution and their results as indicating the first traces of the path of duty in the discharge of my public trust, I turn to the Administration of my immediate predecessor as the second. It has passed away in a period of profound peace, how much to the satisfaction of our country and to the honor of our country's name is known to you all. The great features of its policy, in general concurrence with the will of the Legislature, have been to cherish peace while preparing for defensive war; to yield exact justice to other nations and maintain the rights of our own; to cherish the principles of freedom and of equal rights wherever they were proclaimed; to discharge with all possible promptitude the national debt; to reduce within the narrowest limits of efficiency the military force; to improve the organization and discipline of the Army; to provide and sustain a school of military science; to extend equal protection to all the great interests of the nation; to promote the civilization of the Indian tribes, and to proceed in the great system of internal improvements within the limits of the constitutional power of the Union. Under the pledge of these promises, made by that eminent citizen at the time of his first induction to this office, in his career of eight years the internal taxes have been repealed; sixty millions of the public debt have been discharged; provision has been made for the comfort and relief of the aged and indigent among the surviving warriors of the Revolution; the regular armed force has been reduced and its constitution revised and perfected; the accountability for the expenditure of public moneys has been made more effective; the Floridas have been peaceably acquired, and our boundary has been extended to the Pacific Ocean; the independence of the southern nations of this hemisphere has been recognized, and recommended by example and by counsel to the potentates of Europe; progress has been made in the defense of the country by fortifications and the increase of the Navy, toward the effectual suppression of the African trade in slaves, in alluring the aboriginal hunters of our land to the cultivation of the soil and of the mind, in exploring the interior regions of the Union, and in preparing by scientific researches and surveys for the further application of our national resources to the internal improvement of our country.

In this brief outline of the promise and performance of my immediate predecessor the line of duty for his successor is clearly delineated. To pursue to their consummation those purposes of improvement in our common condition instituted or recommended by him will embrace the whole sphere of my obligations. To the topic of internal improvement, emphatically urged by him at his inauguration, I recur with peculiar satisfaction. It is that from which I am convinced that the unborn millions of our posterity who are in future ages to people this continent will derive their most fervent gratitude to the founders of the Union; that in which the beneficent action of its Government will be most deeply felt and acknowledged. The magnificence and splendor of their public works are among the imperishable glories of the ancient republics. The roads and aqueducts of Rome have been the admiration of all after ages, and have survived thousands of years after all her conquests have been swallowed up in despotism or become the spoil of barbarians. Some diversity of opinion has prevailed with regard to the powers of Congress for legislation upon subjects of this nature. The most respectful deference is due to doubts originating in pure patriotism and sustained by venerated authority. But nearly twenty years have passed since the construction of the first national road was commenced. The authority for its construction was then unquestioned. To how many thousands of our countrymen has it proved a benefit? To what single individual has it ever proved an injury? Repeated, liberal, and candid discussions in the Legislature have conciliated the sentiments and approximated the opinions of enlightened minds upon the question of constitutional power. I can not but hope that by the same process of friendly, patient, and persevering deliberation all constitutional objections will ultimately be removed. The extent and limitation of the powers of the General Government in relation to this transcedently important interest will be settled and acknowledged to the common satisfaction of all, and every speculative scruple will be solved by a practical public blessing.

Fellow-citizens, you are acquainted with the peculiar circumstances of the recent election, which have resulted in affording me the opportunity of addressing you at this time. You have heard the expositions of the principles which will direct me in the fulfillment of the high and

Harcourt Brace & Company

solemn trust imposed upon me by this station. Less possessed of your confidence in advance than any of my predecessors, I am deeply conscious of the prospect that I shall stand more and oftener in need of your indulgence. Intentions upright and pure, a heart devoted to the welfare of our country, and the unceasing application of all the faculties allotted to me to her service are all the pledges that I can give for the faithful performance of the arduous duties I am to undertake. To the guidance of the legislative councils, to the assistance of the executive and subordinate departments, to the friendly cooperation of the respective State governments, to the candid and liberal support of the people so far as it may be deserved by honest industry and zeal, I shall look for whatever success may attend my public service; and knowing that "except the Lord keep the city the watchman waketh but in vain," with fervent supplications for His favor, to His overruling providence I commit with humble but fearless confidence my own fate and the future destinies of my country.

Andrew Jackson's First Inaugural Address, 1829*

The selection below serves to contrast John Quincy Adams and Andrew Jackson. Brief, even laconic, the speech differed noticeably from the eloquence that characterized the intellectual discourse of Adams. Jackson was in mourning over the recent death of his wife Rachel when he presented the address, and his immense grief surely affected the tone of the speech. On the other hand, in his diminution of internal improvements and his adulation of the militia, Jackson disclosed a substantive divergence between his political philosophy and that of his predecessor. With Jackson's terse comments a new era—an age of democracy—began in the United States.

FELLOW-CITIZENS: About to undertake the arduous duties that I have been appointed to perform by the choice of a free people, I avail myself of this customary and solemn occasion to express the gratitude which their confidence inspires and to acknowledge the accountability which my situation enjoins. While the magnitude of their interests convinces me that no thanks can be adequate to the honor they have conferred, it admonishes me that the best return I can make is the zealous dedication of my humble abilities to their service and their good.

As the instrument of the Federal Constitution it will devolve on me for a stated period to execute the laws of the United States, to superintend their foreign and their confederate relations, to manage their revenue, to command their forces, and, by communications to the Legislature, to watch over and promote their interests generally. And the principles of action by which I shall endeavor to accomplish this circle of duties it is now proper for me briefly to explain.

In administering the laws of Congress, I shall keep steadily in view the limitations as well as the extent of the Executive power, trusting thereby to discharge the functions of my office without transcending its authority. With foreign nations it will be my study to preserve peace and to cultivate friendship on fair and honorable terms, and in the adjustment of any differences that may exist or arise to exhibit the forbearance becoming a powerful nation rather than the sensibility belonging to a gallant people.

In such measures as I may be called on to pursue in regards to the rights of the separate States I hope to be animated by a proper respect for those sovereign members of our Union,

---

*From "First Inaugural Address," *A Compilation of the Messages and Papers of the Presidents, 1789–1897,* 10 vols., comp. James D. Richardson (Washington, D.C.: U.S. Government Printing Office, 1896–1899), II:436–38.

taking care not to confound the powers they have reserved to themselves with those they have granted to the Confederacy.

The management of the public revenue—that searching operation in all governments—is among the most delicate and important trusts in ours, and it will, of course, demand no inconsiderable share of my official solicitude. Under every aspect in which it can be considered it would appear that advantage must result from the observance of a strict and faithful economy. This I shall aim at the more anxiously both because it will facilitate the extinguishment of the national debt, the unnecessary duration of which is incompatible with real independence, and because it will counteract the tendency to public and private profligacy which a profuse expenditure of money by the Government is but too apt to engender. Powerful auxiliaries to the attainment of this desirable end are to be found in the regulations provided by the wisdom of Congress for the specific appropriations of public money and the prompt accountability of public officers.

With regard to the proper selection of the subjects of impost with a view to revenue, it would seem to me that the spirit of equity, caution, and compromise in which the Constitution was formed requires that the great interests of agriculture, commerce, and manufactures should be equally favored, and that perhaps the only exception to this rule should consist in the peculiar encouragement of any products of either of them that may be found essential to our national independence.

Internal improvements and the diffusion of knowledge, so far as they can be promoted by the constitutional acts of the Federal Government, are of high importance.

Considering standing armies as dangerous to free governments in time of peace, I shall not seek to enlarge our present establishment, nor disregard that salutary lesson of political experience which teaches that the military should be held subordinate to the civil power. The gradual increase of our Navy, whose flag has displayed in distant climes our skill in navigation and our fame in arms; the preservation of our forts, arsenals, and dockyards, and the introduction of progressive improvements in the discipline and science of both branches of our military service are so plainly prescribed by prudence that I should be excused for omitting their mention sooner than for enlarging on their importance. But the bulwark of our defense is the national militia, which in the present state of our intelligence and population must render us invincible. As long as our Government is administered for the good of the people, and is regulated by their will; as long as it secures to us the rights of person and of property, liberty of conscience and of the press, it will be worth defending; and so long as it is worth defending a patriotic militia will cover it with an impenetrable aegis. Partial injuries and occasional mortifications we may be subjected to, but a million of armed freemen, possessed of the means of war, can never be conquered by a foreign foe. To any just system, therefore, calculated to strengthen this natural safeguard of the country I shall cheerfully lend all the aid in my power.

It will be my sincere and constant desire to observe toward the Indian tribes within our limits a just and liberal policy, and to give that humane and considerable attention to their rights and their wants which is consistent with the habits of our Government and the feelings of our people.

The recent demonstration of public sentiment inscribes on the list of Executive duties, in characters too legible to be overlooked, the task of *reform*, which will require particularly the correction of those abuses that have brought the patronage of the Federal Government into conflict with the freedom of elections, and the counteraction of those causes which have disturbed the rightful course of appointment and have placed or continued power in unfaithful or incompetent hands.

In the performance of a task thus generally delineated I shall endeavor to select men whose diligence and talents will insure in their respective stations able and faithful cooperation, depending for the advancement of the public service more on the integrity and zeal on the public officer than on their numbers.

A diffidence, perhaps too just, in my own qualifications will teach me to look with reverence to the examples of public virtue left by my illustrious predecessors, and with veneration to the lights that flow from the mind that founded and the mind that reformed the system. The same diffidence induces me to hope for instruction and aid from the coordinate branches of the Government, and for the indulgence and support of my fellow-citizens generally. And a firm reliance on the goodness of that Power whose providence mercifully protected out national infancy, and has since upheld our liberties in various vicissitudes, encourages me to offer my ardent supplications that He will continue to make our beloved country the object of His divine care and gracious benediction.

Principles of the American Banking System, 1833*

Andrew Jackson faced the considerable challenge of reconciling the market revolution with the ideals of agrarian egalitarianism that the Democrats considered to be the legacy of the American Revolution. Among his gravest concerns was the conviction that the Bank of the United States empowered a corrupt economic aristocracy that embraced greed and privilege to the detriment of liberty and equality. Consequently, the bank's existence threatened the very foundation of the republic. That fear led to the Bank War of 1832, which in turn helped spawn the Whig opposition to the Democrats. In the following document, economist William Gouge severely criticized the American banking system, and in so doing he summarized the views of anti-bank Jacksonians. The following passage focused primarily on the differences between "real wealth" and the "false wealth" that the bank created.

We have maintained:

1. That real money is that valuable by a reference to which the value of other articles is estimated, and by the instrumentality of which they are circulated. It is a *commodity,* done up in a particular form to serve a particular use, and does not differ *essentially* from other items of wealth.

2. That silver, owing to its different physical properties, the universal and incessant demand for it, and the small proportion the annual supply bears to the stock on hand, is as good a practical standard of value as can reasonably be desired. It has no variations except such as *necessarily* arise from the nature of the value.

3. That real money diffuses itself through different countries, and through different parts of a country, in proportion to the demands of commerce. No prohibitions can prevent its departing from countries where wealth and trade are declining; and no obstacle, except spurious money, can prevent its flowing into countries where wealth and trade are increasing.

4. That money is the tool of all trades, and is, as such, one of the most useful of productive instruments, and one of the most valuable of labor saving machines.

5. That bills of exchange and promissory notes are a *mere commercial medium,* and are, as *auxiliaries* of gold [and] silver money, very useful: but they differ from metallic money in having no inherent value, and in being evidence of debt. The expression of value in bills of

---

*From William M. Gouge, *A Short History of Paper Money and Banking in the United States* . . . (Philadelphia: T. W. Ustick, 1833), Part I, 135–40.

exchange and promissory notes, are according to the article which law or custom has made the standard; and the failure to pay bills of exchange and promissory notes, does not affect the value of the currency, or the standard by which all contracts are regulated.

6. That Bank notes are *mere evidence of debt* due by the Banks, and in this respect differ not from the promissory notes of the merchants; but, being received in full of all demands, they become to all intents and purposes the money of the country.

7. That Banks owe their credit to their charters; for, if these were taken away, not even their own stockholders would trust them.

8. That the circulating quality of Bank notes is in part owing to their being receivable in payment of dues to government; in part to the interest which the debtors to Banks and Bank stockholders have in keeping them in circulation; and in part to the difficulty, when the system is firmly established, of obtaining metallic money.

9. That so long as specie payments are maintained, there is a limit on Bank issues; but this is not sufficient to prevent successive "expansions" and "contractions," which produce ruinous fluctuations of prices; while the means by which Bank medium is kept "convertible" inflict great evils on the community.

10. That no restriction which can be imposed on Banks, and no discretion on the part of the Directors, can prevent these fluctuations; for, Bank credit, as a branch of commercial credit, is affected by all causes, natural and political, that affect trade, or that affect the confidence man has in man.

11. That the "flexibility" or "elasticity" of Bank medium is not an excellence, but a defect, and that "expansions" and "contractions" are not made to suit the wants of the community, but from a simple regard to the profits and safety of the Banks.

12. That the uncertainty of trade produced by these successive "expansions" and "contractions," is but *one* of the evils of the present system. That the Banks cause credit dealings to be carried to an extent that is highly pernicious—that they cause credit to be given to men who are not entitled to it, and deprive others of credit to whom it would be useful.

13. That the granting of exclusive privileges to companies, or the exempting of companies from liabilities to which individuals are subject, is repugnant to the fundamental principles of American Government; and that the Banks, inasmuch as they have exclusive privileges and exemptions and have the entire control of credit and currency, are the most pernicious of money corporations.

14. That a *nominal* responsibility may be imposed on such corporations, but that it is impossible to impose on them effective responsibility. They respect the laws and public opinion so far only as to promote their own interest.

15. That on the supposition most favorable to the friends of the Banking system, the whole amount gained by the substitution of Bank medium for gold and silver coin, is equal only to about 40 cents per annum for each individual in the country; but that it will be found that nothing is in reality gained *by the nation,* if due allowance be made for the expense of supporting three or four hundred Banks, and for the fact that Bank-medium is a machine which performs its work badly.

16. That some hundreds of thousands of dollars are annually extracted from the people of Pennsylvania, and some millions from the people of the United States, for the support of the Banks, insomuch as through Banking the natural order of things is reversed, and interest paid to the Banks on evidence of debt due by them, instead of interest being paid to those who part with commodities in exchange for bank notes.

Harcourt Brace & Company

17. That into the formation of the Bank capital of the country very little substantial wealth has ever entered, that capital having been formed principally out of the promissory notes of the original subscribers, or by other means which the operations of the Banks themselves have facilitated. They who have bought the script of the Banks at second hand, may have honestly paid cent. per cent. for it; but what they have paid has gone to those from whom they bought the script, and does not form any part of the capital of the Banks.

18. That if it was the wish of the Legislature to promote usurious dealings, it could not well devise any more efficient means than incorporating paper money Banks. That these Banks, moreover, give rise to many kinds of stock-jobbing, by which the simple-minded are injured and the crafty benefited.

19. That many legislators have, in voting for Banks, supposed that they were promoting the welfare of their constituents; but the prevalence of false views in legislative bodies in respect to money corporations and paper money, is to be attributed chiefly to the desire certain members have to make money for themselves, or to afford their political partisans and personal friends opportunities for speculation.

20. That the banking interests has a pernicious influence on the periodical press, on public elections, and the general course of legislation. This interest is so powerful, that the establishment of a system of sound currency and sound credit is impracticable, except one or the other of the political parties into which the nation is divided, makes such an object its primary principle of action.

21. That through the various advantages which the system of incorporated paper money Banking has given to some men over others, the foundation has been laid of an *artificial* inequality of wealth, which kind of inequity is, when once laid, increased by all the subsequent operations of society.

22. That this artificial inequality of wealth, adds nothing to the substantial happiness of the rich, and detracts much from the happiness of the rest of the community. That its tendency is to corrupt one portion of society, and debase another.

23. That the sudden dissolution of the Banking system, without suitable preparation, would put an end to the collection of debts, destroy private credit, break up many productive establishments, throw most of the property of the industrious into the hands of speculators, and deprive laboring people of employment.

24. That the system can be got rid of, without difficulty, by prohibiting, after a certain day, the issue of small notes, and proceeding gradually to those of the highest denomination.

25. That the feasibility of getting rid of the system, is further proven by the fact, that the whole amount of Bank notes and Bank credits, is, according to Mr. Gallatin's calculation, only about one hundred and nine million dollars. By paying ten or eleven millions a year, the whole can be liquidated in the term of ten years. If, however, twenty or thirty years should be required for the operation, the longest of these is but a short period in the life time of a nation.

26. That it has not been through the undervaluation of gold at the mint, that eagles and half-eagles have disappeared; but from the free use of Bank notes. Nevertheless, a new coinage of pieces containing four and eight, or five and ten dollars worth of gold is desirable, to save the trouble of calculating fractions. The dollar being the money of contract and account, no possible confusion or injustice can be produced by an adjustment of the gold coinage to the silver standard.

27. That incorporating a paper money Bank is not the "necessary and proper," or "natural and appropriate" way of managing the fiscal concerns of the Union; but that the "necessary and proper," or "natural and appropriate" way, is by sub-treasury offices.

28. That incorporating a paper money Bank is not "the necessary and proper," or "natural and appropriate" way of correcting the evils occasioned by the State Banks, inasmuch as a National Bank, resting upon the same principles as the State Banks, must produce similar evils.

29. That "convertible" paper prevents the accumulation of such a stock of the precious metals as will enable the country to bear transitions from peace to war, and insure the punctual payment of war taxes, and that the "necessary and proper," or "natural and appropriate" way of providing for all public exigencies, is, by making the Government *a solid money Government*, as was intended by the framers of the Constitution.

30. That if Congress should, from excessive caution, or some less commendable motive, decline passing the acts necessary to insure the gradual withdrawal of Bank notes, they may greatly diminish the evils of the system, by declaring that nothing but gold and silver shall be received in payment of duties, and by making the operations of the Government entirely distinct from those of the Bank.

31. That, on the abolition of incorporated paper money Banks, private Bankers will rise up, who will receive money on deposit, and allow interest on the same, discount promissory notes, and buy and sell bills of exchange. Operating on sufficient funds, and being responsible for their engagements in the whole amount of their estates, these private Bankers will not by sudden and great "expansions" and "curtailments" derange the whole train of mercantile operations. In each large city, an office of deposit and transfer, similar to the Bank of Hamburgh, will be established, and we shall thus secure all the good of the present Banking system, and avoid all its evils.

32. That, if the present system of Banking and paper money shall continue, the wealth and population of the country will increase from natural causes, till they shall be equal for each square mile to the wealth and population of Europe. But, with every year, the state of society in the United States will more nearly approximate the state of society in Great Britain. Crime and pauperism will increase. A few men will be inordinately rich, some comfortable, and a multitude in poverty. This condition of things will naturally lead to the adoption of that policy which proceeds on the principle that a legal remedy is to be found for each social evil, and nothing left for the operations of nature. This kind of legislation will increase the evils it is intended to cure.

33. That there is reason to *hope* that, on the downfall of monied corporations, and the substitution of gold and silver for Bank medium, sound credit will take the place of unsound, and legitimate enterprize the place of wild speculation. That the moral and intellectual character of the people will be sensibly though gradually raised, and the causes laid open of a variety of evils under which society is now suffering. That the source of legislation will, to a certain extent, be purified, by taking from members of legislative bodies inducements to pass laws for the special benefits of themselves, their personal friends and political partisans. That the operation of the natural and just causes of wealth and poverty, will no longer be inverted, but that each cause will operate in its natural and just order, and produce its natural and just effect—wealth becoming the reward of industry, frugality, skill, prudence, and enterprise, and poverty and punishment of few except the indolent and prodigal.

Harcourt Brace & Company

Discussion

1. Which of the preceding documents express fears that liberty and equality in the United States are being threatened by power? What seems to be the basis of those fears? Are the concerns given here similar to those expressed by Americans prior to, or just after, the Revolution? How so, and why or why not?

2. Based on the speech by James Tallmadge, what do you think he meant to achieve by ending slavery in Missouri? Does he seem motivated by concerns for liberty or equality? Why or why not? What does the vehement tone of the address and the threats of civil war it contains suggest about political power struggles in the United States during this era?

3. What social groups does it appear that John Quincy Adams believed should hold power in society? How do you think Adams defined liberty and equality? What elements of the speech reveal Adams's attitudes toward the power of government, and what are those powers?

4. What expressions of democratic egalitarianism did Andrew Jackson make in his inaugural address? Does Jackson seem to be concerned with liberty? If so, how? How does Jackson appear to view the power of government, and how do his perceptions compare to those of Adams?

5. Based on the selection by William Gouge, how did Democrats believe that the Bank of the United States created "false wealth"? To what social groups did such paper wealth give power? What are the implications of the bank for liberty and equality, according to Gouge? Did he provide an accurate assessment?

Harcourt Brace & Company

Chapter 13
Society, Culture, and Politics

Temperance supporters wished to save the family, promote industry, create a reliable work force, and "Americanize" Irish and German immigrants. Using easily understood, lividly illustrated texts, they spread their message of the personal demise and family ruin caused by drink.

During the antebellum period, intense moral fervor spawned a wide-spread reform movement in the United States. Whigs, showing the influence of the Christian evangelicalism of the period, wanted to use the power of the government to ensure moral progress as well as economic opportunity. These crusaders turned their attention to a variety of causes, including the plight of criminals, the fate of alcoholics, the suffering of slaves, and the place of women. Democrats, who clung to the traditional faith that power destroyed liberty, often resisted such reform efforts because they endangered the status and equality of adult white males. In addition to shaping politics by creating a new party system, then, differences between Democrats and Whigs also had significant ramifications for American culture and society.

Prisons, 1838*

Reformers, beginning in the 1820s, sought ways to impose the authority of the state against criminals while still preserving the ideals of freedom and equality. Penitentiaries, where convicts could reflect on the errors of their ways and grow penitent, seemed to offer an effective means of reconciling power and liberty. New York established a prison at Auburn that relied on solitary confinement at night and strictly controlled labor during the day to create an environment in which prisoners could be rehabilitated. The "Auburn system" attracted international attention, and in the following selection Englishwoman Harriet Martineau discussed the relative merits of "congregate" incarceration as practiced at the Auburn Prison and the solitary confinement employed in Pennsylvania.

I have shown in my account of Society in America that, after visiting several prisons in the United States, I was convinced that the system of solitary confinement at Philadelphia is the best that has yet been adopted. So much has been heard in England of the Auburn prison, its details look so complete and satisfactory on paper, and it is so much a better system than the English have been accustomed to see followed at home, that it has a high reputation among us. But I think a careful survey of the institution on the spot must lessen the admiration entertained for this mode of punishment.

The convicts are, almost without exception, pale and haggard. As their work is done either in the open air or in well-ventilated shops, and their diet is good, their unhealthy appearance is no doubt owing to the bad construction of their night-cells. These cells are small and ill-ventilated, and do not even answer the purpose of placing the prisoners in solitude during the night. The convicts converse with nearly as much ease, through the air-pipes or otherwise, at night, as they do by speaking behind their teeth, without moving the lips, while at work in the day. In both cases they feel that they are transgressing the laws of the prison by doing an otherwise innocent and almost necessary act; a knowledge and feeling most unfavourable to reformation; and destructive of any conscientiousness which retribution may be generating in them. Their anxious and haggard looks may easily be accounted for. They are denied the forgetfulness of themselves and their miseries which they might enjoy in free conversation; and also the repose and the shelter from shame which are the privileges of solitary confinement. Every movement

*From Harriet Martineau, *Retrospect of Western Travel,* 2 vols. (London: Saunders and Otley, 1838), I:123–39.

reminds them that they are in disgrace; a multitude of eyes (the eyes of the wicked, too) is ever upon them; they can live neither to themselves nor to society, and self-respect is rendered next to impossible. A man must be either hardened, or restless and wretched under such circumstance; and the faces at Auburn are no mystery.

The finishing of the day's work and the housing for the night are sights barely endurable. The governor saw my disgust, and explained that he utterly disapproved of strangers being allowed to be present at all this; but that the free Americans would not be debarred from beholding the operation of anything which they have decreed. This is right enough; the evil is in there being such a spectacle to behold. The prisoners are ranged in companies for the march from the workshops into the prison. Each fills his pail and carries it, and takes up the can with his supper as he passes the kitchen; and, when I was there, this was done in the presence of staring and amused strangers, who looked down smiling from the portico. Some of the prisoners turned their heads every possible way to avoid meeting our eyes, and were in an agony of shame. . . .

The arrangements for the women were extremely bad at that time; but the governor needed no convincing of this, and hoped for a speedy rectification. The women were all in one large room, sewing. The attempt to enforce silence was soon given up as hopeless; and the gabble of tongues among the few who were there was enough to paralyze any matron. . . . There was an engine in sight which made me doubt the evidence of my own eyes; stocks of a terrible construction; a chair, with a fastening for the head and for all of the limbs. Any lunatic asylum ought to be ashamed of such an instrument. The governor liked it no better that we; but he pleaded that it was his only means of keeping his refractory female prisoners quiet while he was allowed only one room to put them all into. I hope these stocks have been used for firewood before this.

The first principle in the management of the guilty seems to me to be to treat them as men and women; which they were before they were guilty, and will always be when they are no longer so; and which they are in the midst of all of it. Their humanity is the principal thing about them; their guilt is a temporary state. The insane are first men, and secondarily diseased men; and in a due consideration of this order of things lies the main secret of the successful treatment of such. The drunkard is first a man, and secondarily a man with a peculiar weakness. The convict is, in like manner, first a man, and then a sinner. Now, there is something in the isolation of the convict which tends to keep this order of consideration right in the mind of his guardians. The warden and his prisoner converse like two men when they are face to face; but when the keeper watches a hundred men herded together in virtue of the one common characteristic of their being criminals, the guilt becomes the prominent circumstance, and there is an end of the brotherly faith in each, to which each must mainly owe his cure. This, in our human weakness, is the great evil attendant upon the good of collecting together sufferers under any particular physical or moral evil. Visitors are shy of the blind, the deaf and dumb, and insane, when they see them all together, while they would feel little or nothing of this shyness if they met each sufferer in the bosom of his own family. In the one case, the infirmity, defying sympathy, is the prominent circumstance; in the other, not. It follows from this, that such an association of prisoners as that at Auburn must be more difficult to reform, more difficult to do the state's duty by, than any number or kind of criminals who are classed by some other characteristic, or not classed at all. . . .

The greatest advantage of solitary confinement is that it presents the best part of a prisoner's mind to be acted upon by his guardians; and the next is, that the prisoner is preserved from the evil influences of vicious companionship, of shame within the prison walls, and of degradation when he comes out. I am persuaded that no system of secondary punishment has yet been devised that can be compared with this. I need not, at this time of day, explain that I mean solitary confinement with labour, and with frequent visits from the guardians of the prisoner.

Harcourt Brace & Company

Without labour, the punishment is too horrible and unjust to be thought of. The reflective man would go mad, and the clown would sleep away his term, and none of the purposes of human existence could be answered. Work is, in prison as out of it, the grand equalizer, stimulus, composer, and rectifier; the prime obligation and the prime privilege. It is delightful to see how soon its character is recognized there. In the Philadelphia penitentiary work is forbidden to the criminal for two days subsequent to his entrance; he petitions for it before the two days are out, however doggedly he may have declared that he will never work. . . .

On his entrance the convict is taken to the bathroom, where he is well cleansed, and his state of health examined into and recorded by the physician and warden. A hood is then put over his head, and he is led to his apartment. I never met with one who could in the least tell what the form of the central part of the prison was, or which of the radii his cell was placed in, though they make very accurate observances of the times at which the sun shines in. At the end of two days, during which the convict has neither book nor work, the warden visits him, and has a conversation with him about the mode of life in the institution. If he asks for work, he is offered a choice of three or four kinds, of which weaving and shoemaking are the chief. He is told that if he does a certain amount of work, he will have the full diet provided for hard labourers; if less, he will have what is sufficient for a moderate worker; if more, the price of it will be laid by to accumulate, and paid over to him on his leaving the prison. He is furnished with a Bible; and other books, provided by the friends to the institution, circulate among the convicts. Some who have books at home are allowed to have them brought. . . .

As the system of imprisonment gains ground, I trust that the practice of prison-visiting will gain ground too. It is most desirable that it should not be left wholly in the hands of proselyting religionists, but be shared by those who better understand human nature and command a greater variety of influences. For the sake of religion itself this is desirable, to rescue it from becoming a mere prison solace; an excitement seized when no other can be had, and to be laid aside when old pursuits offer themselves for resumption. Kind-hearted persons will have an opportunity of doing extensive and unquestionable good by keeping up the social affections of the prisoners, giving them new ideas, making them cheerful, and investing with pleasant associations whatever things are honest, pure, lovely, and of good report.

In other prisons much might thus be done, though not, I think, with such extraordinary affect as under the system of solitary confinement. I was struck with something I saw at the Charlestown prison (Massachusetts). Several convicts, black and white, who had behaved well, were practising singing, which is allowed as an indulgence. It seemed strange to hear "The heavens are telling" from such lips; but I listened to it with more pleasure than in some finer places. Any kind person who can introduce a new innocent pursuit into a prison as a solace to its inmates cannot fail to be doing an important good. . . .

I saw at the Charleston prison a sight more impressive to me than all else that the walls contained; a man of might, but whose power has taken a wrong direction; his hand being against every man, and every man's against him. He is a prison-breaker so formidable as to be regarded and treated as if he were of Satanic race, and not as made up of flesh and blood, and emotions that may be roused, and affections subject to touch. He seems, indeed, to have become somewhat of the Satanic kind, for now he is piqued to do all the harm he can. His pride is in for it; his reputation stands upon it. I was shown an enormous block of stone which he had displaced by the aid of a "gentleman" outside, who, for fear of the prison-breaker's blabbing, committed suicide on his recapture. The strong man was heavily fettered, confined in a different cell every night, and conducted to it by a procession of turnkeys. As we stood aside in the echoing passage to let the array go by, there was something really grand in the air of a man who had virtually said to himself, "Evil, be thou my good!" He stepped slowly, clanking his chains, and looking us full in the face as he passed. He cannot but have a calm sense of power when he nightly sees the irons, the bars and locks, and the six fellow-men, all in requisition to keep him from working his will. As we saw him slowly turn into his cell, and heard lock after lock shot behind him, I could not help thinking that there was much true monarchical feeling within those four narrow walls. . . .

Reflections on Prohibition, 1852*

The use of alcohol has been one of the most widely discussed social concerns in the history of the United States. In the antebellum period, Democrats and Whigs often had substantial differences of opinion over the issue. As time passed and Americans continued to drink, reformers came to believe that they would have to use the power of the government to compel individuals to behave properly. Democrats, for the most part, feared that such coercion threatened American liberties. The Democratic attitudes are clearly evident in the following document, an editorial condemning the Maine Law of 1851 that was the first comprehensive effort to prohibit the manufacture and sale of liquor.

Intemperance is an evil; but for a free government to violate, for any cause, the plainest, most vital and fundamental principles of civil liberty, is also an evil, and one with which the first may not at all be compared.

A majority of the people of Maine, not liking, themselves, to drink, have forbidden the minority to do so. Our downeast friends have discovered, that the old theory of the fall of man, and the true plan of his redemption, was a gross error. According to them, the way of it was thus: when the first pair bit the first apple, they sucked the juice, and thereby acquired a relish for cider, which, transmitted to their progeny, became a taste for wine, and finally, in later times and colder climates, grew into a thirst for downright rum. This, they say, is original sin, the veritable, original article specified in Genesis. And the deduction they draw is, that the salvation of the race is to be found neither in sacramental wine nor sprinkled water, but in stringent anti-liquor laws, and internal applications of the baptismal fluid; a plan which, to their minds, loses not a whit of its plausibility from having never been so much as dreamed of by the leaders, prophets, and judges of Israel, the Savior and his apostles, the bishops, priests, and deacons of the church, all of whom came eating and drinking—and, of course, all signally failed.

This new sect, pursuing their idea with the zeal common to all such propagandists, and urging their measures through thousands of affiliated organizations, whose special business it has been to disseminate fallacies, which, however unsound, it has been no one's particular vocation to refute, and politic enough to scorn none of the tricks of the stump, none of the arts of lobbying, "log rolling," and electioneering intrigue, have succeeded at length, in one state, to get their theory of morals and dietetics actualized in the form of a statute law, which, though it does not honestly and boldly prohibit *buying* or *drinking,* puts its penalty upon *selling* or *keeping to sell,* "flogging the demon of intemperance" round the rum barrel, as it were, in the fashion of the most noted despot of the season, who, not venturing to prohibit the mere *use* of printing-presses, makes it penal to sell them except for special uses. And now, flushed with this success, the same sort of means and meanness are being put into play to extend this law into other states.

We claim to be a free people, and are accustomed to find the sanction for the continuance of our liberties, not in the chance good-will or unguided discretion of our rulers, but in those fundamental principles which every commonwealth in the true confederacy has adopted, as well for the enlightenment of legislators as the protection of the undelegated or unprescriptable rights of the citizen. But really such doings as this admonish us that those principles are either

---

*From "The Maine Liquor Law," *The Democratic Review* 30 (March 1852), 271–73.

not comprehensible, or else are a miserably insufficient shield against the strong arm of a rampant majority, and render a short explanation of the meaning of free principles not all impertinent.

It is to be hoped that the greater number of our people will accuse us of uttering a self-evident proposition, when we say, that a free government is something more than a despotism administered by a benevolent despot; something more than a constitution under which the majority rules, for it may rule with a rod of iron; something more than an equal government, for their may be equality in slavery. A state can be called free only while the power of the rulers is restrained, and their judgment controlled, by certain well-understood, constantly referred to, and inviolably kept, *principles;* broad enough for all circumstances, and superior to all expediency; guarantying to the citizen that freedom which, coming from any other source, is accidental and precarious, and unworthy the acceptance of an intelligent people.

And what is freedom? The only definition which does not define away all meaning is, that *it is the absence of restraint.* The right to make laws, results solely from necessity. "The best government is that which governs least." And since even the most arbitrary rulers usually permit all such actions as *they* conceive to be right, we aver that the only criterion for knowing how far a government is free, is the extent to which *bad* actions are allowed, and that civil liberty may be termed the constitutional right to do wrong. What is the freedom of the press—but the power to punish wicked and pernicious doctrines? or freedom of speech, but the power to speak them? What is religious freedom, but the power to follow a false worship—freedom of locomotion, but the power to go to the wrong place—freedom of occupation but the power to choose the wrong trade? And yet the proposition remains true, that the right to do wrong in all these, and as many other respects as possible, is the essential condition of all true development, real happiness, and healthful progress.

Let it not, however, be thought important, that a very wide definition of civil liberty need be laid down, in order to show the grossness of a Maine liquor law. There are few governments, even of those the most arbitrary in their constitution, which do not recognize principles, with which such legislation as this is utterly inconsistent. Narrow down the word "freedom" to its scantiest limit, and it still retains a meaning that forbids a thing like this, for it is the very centre and core of it that is now attacked: it is the liberty of the person that is here struck down, and the contents of its inward parts to which these notion-mongers apply their chemical test.

It may not be easy precisely to define the limits of the law-making power. A wide range of human activity must ever remain guarded only by the best discretion of the legislature. But political philosophy has been able to set up, here and there, a few positive land-marks, and it must be true, that in the very nature and fitness of things, there does somewhere exist a sphere of right, quite apart and distinct from the limits of legislation, within which the individual may repose, unmolested by civil law.

The power wielded in the passage of the law we are considering, is so tremendous, that it is difficult to conceive it. Legislation, so overwhelming upon private action, is startling to the minds of the best balance, and the most favorably disposed towards the needed restraints of law.

Nothing could be more cheering to the mind, than the prospect of society redeemed from vice of every kind. But like children, brought up under the rod only, we shall find that prohibitory enactments, acting upon ill-regulated character, only lead to evasion and deceit. The frightful relief of opium will be sought by many who see their external independence thus abruptly checked, while, notwithstanding, the fires of uncontrolled license are burning within. It is known that the effects of indulgence in this drug, are more debasing mentally and physically, than even those of drunkenness from liquor, revolting as they are. Unhappily, this experience begins to obtain even in respectable families, and—pale be the ink that writes it—among women, refined and cultivated!

Harcourt Brace & Company

We believe, then, that moral means, which have lately, we are sorry to say, come to be sneered at, will, in the end, as they have progressively, heretofore, prove to be the true corrective. It is unjust to the efforts of that respectable class of our citizens, who have been so long and so faithfully presenting this subject to the moral consideration of mankind, to say that their efforts have had no effect. Every one who reflects, knows better. We do not wish to see the cause injured by substituting physical force for moral influence. Without this immense reach of legislation, means more justifiable, more profitable, more wholesome, and really effective may be discovered and applied.

We do not wish the community to stand still, or go back on this, any more than on any other great measure; but we desire to see it go forward well. We want the step to be an advance, and not a retrogression.

With this in view, we say, then, that we condemn the principle involved in this measure, as regards its expediency. We have, moreover, no faith in its final moral success, and we are constrained to declare unconstitutional the attempt thus to lay the iron hand of a gigantic governmental control upon the conscience and habits of a whole people. This last objection with us is final.

On the *policy* of entire restraint, apart from other considerations, we will say that we are in favor of the use of light wines. The experience of Europe is favorable as to the temperance of those nations, with whom wine is a daily beverage. Our own country promises most favorably for the cultivation of the vine, and we anticipate its success with hope and pleasure; believing that this itself will be a powerful auxiliary aid in the suppression of the gross taste for coarse and strong drink. We are opposed, however, to the negative policy of all kinds; we admit also that when a scheme has been proposed for the accomplishment of a great good, and those who oppose it should feel themselves in justice bound to suggest at least the elements of some substitute.

We propose, then, that stringent laws be put into practical effect against drunkenness. That it should be punished as a crime—as it is.

A man found drunk upon the street should be regarded as having forfeited his personal liberty, in having invaded the safety of society. The police should be required to seize, fine, and imprison him.

An habitual drunkard, having surrendered his reason, may justly be deprived of the dignity of a citizen, and should not be allowed to vote.

The carrying of a secret weapon is forbidden by law—not the sale of them, however; and this is a fair parallel. The public sense is against the carrying of private weapons, the law is against it, and they are seldom carried. We think the same good effect will result from public decision in the other case, especially joined with stringent laws which will be in accordance with the Federal Constitution, and will attack the evil in the right place.

Scientific Racism, 1861*

Prior to the 1850s, most white Americans believed that historical and environmental circumstances accounted for the differences between the various human races. New ways of thinking, however, insisted that biological forces had made Africans a subhuman race; to the most extreme proponents of this view, Africans were members of an inferior species. John Van Evrie, a doctor and

---

*From J. H. Van Evrie, *Negroes and Negro "Slavery": The First an Inferior Race: The Latter Its Normal Condition* (New York: Van Evrie, Horton & Company, 1861), v–vii, 336–39.

leading advocate of this "scientific" racism, summarized his opinions in the introduction and conclusion to a book he published in 1861. Those opinions, presented in the following document, influenced countless Americans and had grave implications for the liberty of slaves and the equality of blacks and other minorities well into the twentieth century.

TO THE WHITE MEN OF AMERICA—

There are now thirty millions of white men, twelve millions of negroes, and perhaps twelve millions of Indians or Aborigines, in America.

God has made these white men, Indians, and negroes just what we see they are—just what our senses, as well as our instincts and our reason show us they are—different creatures, different *species* of men, with different bodies, and different minds, and different natures, exactly as we witness all about us in all other forms of life. Why, or when, or how the Creator saw fit, in His infinite wisdom and almighty power, to thus order things, we can never know, nor need to know, any thing further or beyond the fixed and indestructible *facts* thus presented to us. And it certainly needs but a moment's reflection to convince any *American* mind that a universal equality or affiliation with these Indians and negroes would, of necessity, result in the universal degradation and destruction of the white blood of America, with the consequent overthrow of republican institutions, and, indeed, the civilization and Christianity of the New World. The great men of the Revolutionary era, therefore, with a wise instinct and that lofty perception of the superiority of their race which always distinguishes the true America, laid the foundations of a white republic, and organized a government of white men, which, as they declared in the preamble to the Constitution, should secure the blessings of liberty to *themselves* and *their* posterity forever.

The enemies of this glorious fabric of freedom, unable to beat it down by the strong hand of physical force, have resorted to fraud, and originated an imposture—the most disgusting, the most impious, the most irrational—and yet strange indeed, the most extensive and powerful that has ever stultified the reason or perverted the moral instincts of the race. They set up the dogma or assumption of a single human species—that the negro had the same nature, and therefore was naturally entitled to the same liberty or rights as the white man—and the governments of Europe, with American dependencies, have labored together, and constantly, for more than half a century past, to apply this monstrous assumption to the unfortunate people subject to their rule.

England alone has expended five hundred millions, and mortgaged the bodies and souls of unborn generations of white men and women at home, to abolish the natural supremacy of the white man over the negro in America—to blot out the distinctions of nature and equalize races—to thrust aside the Almighty and make those equal He has eternally decreed shall remain unequal. This monstrous policy is now applied to the whole of tropical America save Cuba, and is designed to pen up our negro population within its present limits, when, with free negroism in front, backed by European governments, and as they hope an "anti-slavery" party in our midst in its rear, the ultimate result must be the abolition of white supremacy, as in Jamaica, etc., with the consequent affiliation with negroes.

The time, therefore, has come when the truth must be laid before the people, and the millions at the North made to understand that this "anti-slavery" policy which, in their blindness they have regarded as philanthropy, is treason to themselves, to their posterity, to their country, and to American civilization.

The author has attempted to perform this great work for the benefit of his countrymen, and indeed, for the civilized and master race of America; and if the time and labor, patient investigation, and unfaltering devotion to truth, and the cause of real freedom deserve success, then he shall have succeeded. And, indeed, however much he may fail, from want of ability, to do justice to a subject so vast, and involving such stupendous consequences, and which no one hitherto has ever ventured to discuss from the stand-point of scientific fact, he can not be mistaken or doubt for a moment the final triumph of the great fundamental truths embodied in the title of this work, for while the first of these traits is fixed forever by the hand of God himself, the latter is an unavoidable induction that can no longer be disregarded without involving the destruction of our institutions, and, finally the ruin of our civilization.

In conclusion, the author begs to say to those who have read the introductory chapter of this work, published several years ago in pamphlet form, that the publication of the entire work has been protracted by unavoidable consequences; but however much it may be regretted in some respects, it has given the author time and reflection to thoroughly examine the facts at its basis, and to test the soundness of his own reasonings on this great subject, while the widespread excitement and fearful danger now impending over the country may perhaps induce some to inquire into it who at another time, and under other circumstances, might remain indifferent. . . .

It has been shown in the foregoing pages of this work how that providential arrangement of human affairs, in which the negro is placed in natural juxtaposition with the white man, has resulted in the freedom of the latter and the general well-being of both. It has been seen how a subordinate and widely different social element in Virginia and other States, naturally gave origin to new ideas and new modes of thought, which, thrusting aside the mental habits and political notions brought from the Old World, naturally culminated in the grand idea of 1776, and the establishment of a new political existence, based on the natural, organic, and everlasting equality of the race. It has been seen, moreover, how the great civil revolution of 1800, which, under the lead of Mr. Jefferson, restored the purity and simplicity of republican principles, saved the Northern laboring and producing classes from the rule of an oligarchy, otherwise unavoidable, however it might have been disguised by republican formulas.

It is scarcely necessary to appeal to the political history of the country since 1800 to demonstrate the vital importance—indeed, the measureless benefit—of what, by an absurd perversion of terms, has been called negro slavery, to the freedom, progress, and posterity of the laboring classes of the North, and indeed, to all mankind. It is seen that the existence of an inferior race—the presence of a natural substratum in the political society of the New World—has resulted in the creation of a new political and social order, and relieved the producing classes from that abject dependence on capital which in Europe, and especially in England, renders them mere beasts of burthen to a fraction of their brethren. The simple but transcendent fact, that capital and labor are united at the South—that the planter, or so-called slaveholder, is, *per se* and of necessity, the defender of the rights of the producing classes—this simple fact is the key to our political history, and the hinging-point of our party politics for half a century past.

The Southern planter and the Northern farmer—the producing classes—a Southern majority and a Northern minority—have governed the country, fought all its battles, acquired all its territories, and conducted the nation step by step to its present position of strength, power, and grandeur. Just as steadily a Northern majority and a Southern minority have opposed this progress, and labored blindly, doubtless, to return to the system of the federalists, indeed to the European idea of class distinctions, and to render the government an instrument for the benefit of the few at the expense of the many.

They have sought to create national banks; demanded favors for those engaged in manufactures; for others engaged in Northern fisheries; for the benefit of bands of jobbers and speculators, under pretence of internal improvements; in short, the Northern majority have labored continually to render the government, as in England, an instrument for benefiting classes at the expense of the great body of people.

Harcourt Brace & Company

All these efforts, however, have been defeated by the union of Northern and Southern producers, and mainly by the latter. A large majority of the votes in Congress against special legislation and schemes of corruption have been those of so-called slaveholders; and in those extraordinary instances when Northern representatives of agricultural constituencies have proved faithless, and those schemes "worked" through Congress, "slaveholders" in the Presidential chair have interposed the veto, and saved the laboring and producing classes from this dangerous legislation, and the government from being perverted into an instrument of mischief.

Such has been our political and current party history, and from the nature and necessity of things, every "extension of slavery," or every expansion of territory, must in the future, as it has in the past, strengthen the cause of the producing classes, and give greater scope and power to the American idea of government.

The acquisition of Louisiana, of Florida, of Texas, etc., of those great producing States on the Gulf Coast, has nearly overwhelmed the anti-republican tendencies of the North, and rendered almost powerless those combinations of capital and speculation which have always endangered the purity and simplicity of our republican system, and thus the rights and safety of the laboring and producing millions everywhere.

Indeed, it is a truth, a simple fact, that can not be too often repeated, that in precise proportion to the amount or extent so-called "slaveholding"—of the number of negroes in their normal condition—is freedom rendered secure to the white millions of the North. And when in the progress of time Cuba and Central America, and the whole tropical center of the continent is added to the Union, and placed in the same relation to New York and Ohio that Mississippi, Alabama, etc., are now, then it is evident that the democratic or American idea of government will be securely established forever, and the rights and interests of the producing millions who ask nothing from government but its protection, will be no longer endangered by those anti-republican tendencies which in the North have so long conflicted with the natural development of our system, and struggled so long and fiercely against its existence.

If this freedom and prosperity of the white man rested on wrong or oppression of the negro, then it would be valueless, for the Almighty has evidently designed that all His creatures should be permitted to live out the life to which He has adapted them. But when all the facts are considered, and the negro population of the South contrasted with any similar number of their race now or at any other time in human experience, then it is seen that, relatively considered, they are, perhaps, benefited to even a greater extent than the white population themselves.

The efforts, as it has been shown, to reverse the natural order of things—to force the negro into the position of the white man—are not merely failures, but frightful cruelties—cruelties that among ourselves end in the extinction of those poor creatures, while in the tropics it destroys the white man and impels the negro into barbarian.

In conclusion, therefore, it is clear, or will be clear to every mind that grasps the facts of this great question, with the inductive facts, of the unavoidable inferences that belong to them, that any American citizen, party, sect, or class among us, so blinded, bewildered, and besotted by foreign theories and false mental habits as to labor for negro "freedom"—to drag down their own race, or to thrust the negro from his normal condition, is alike the enemy of both, a traitor to his blood and at war with the decrees of the Eternal.

Immediate Emancipation, 1831*

Not all Americans accepted the inherent inferiority of blacks that Van Evrie believed he had proven. Abolitionists insisted that slaves were human beings who deserved to be free, and the

---

*From Wendell Phillips Garrison, *William Lloyd Garrison, 1805–1879: The Story of His Life, Told by His Children* , 4 vols. (New York: The Century Company, 1885–1892), I:224–25.

Harcourt Brace & Company

more radical members of the movement championed full equality for African Americans. Among the most vocal of the abolitionists was William Lloyd Garrison. Disenchanted with the failure to end slavery through gradual emancipation, he began publishing *The Liberator* in 1831 to demand immediate abolition. His efforts helped impassion the debate over the slavery issue, and he played a critical part in turning the effort to free the slaves into an overwhelming crusade. In his introductory editorial, presented here, he displayed the fervor that characterized his efforts to destroy slavery in the United States.

In the month of August, I issued proposals for publishing "THE LIBERATOR" in Washington City; but the enterprise, though hailed in different sections of the country, was palsied by public indifference. Since that time, the removal of the *Genius of Universal Emancipation* to the seat of government has rendered less imperious the establishment of a similar periodical in that quarter.

During my recent tour for the purpose of exciting the minds of the people by a series of discourses on the subject of slavery, every place that I visited gave fresh evidence of the fact, that a greater revolution in public sentiment was to be effected in the free States—*and particularly in New-England*—than at the South. I found contempt more bitter, opposition more active, detraction more relentless, prejudice more stubborn, and apathy more frozen, than among the slave-owners themselves. Of course, there were individual exceptions to the contrary. This state of things afflicted, but did not dishearten me. I determined, at every hazard, to lift up the standard of emancipation in the eyes of the nation, *within sight of Bunker Hill and in the birthplace of liberty*. That standard is now unfurled; and long may it float, unhurt by the spoliations of time or the missiles of a desperate foe—yea, till every chain be broken, and every bondsman set free! Let Southern oppressors tremble—let their secret abettors tremble—let their Northern apologists tremble—let all the enemies of the persecuted blacks tremble.

I deem the publication of my original Prospectus unnecessary, as it has obtained a wide circulation. The principles therein inculcated will be steadily pursued in this paper, excepting that I shall not array myself as the political partisan of any man. In defending the great cause of human rights, I wish to derive the assistance of all religions and of all parties.

Assenting to the "self-evident truth" maintained in the American Declaration of Independence, "that all men are created equal, and endowed by their Creator with certain inalienable rights—among which are life, liberty and the pursuit of happiness," I shall strenuously contend for the immediate enfranchisement of our slave population. In Park-Street Church, on the Fourth of July, 1829, in an address on slavery, I unreflectingly assented to the popular but pernicious doctrine of *gradual* emancipation. I seize this opportunity to make a full and unequivocal recantation, and thus publicly to ask pardon of my God, of my country, and of my brethren the poor slaves, for having uttered a sentiment so full of timidity, injustice, and absurdity. A similar recantation, from my pen, was published in the *Genius of Universal Emancipation* at Baltimore, in September, 1829. My conscience is now satisfied.

I am aware that many object to the severity of my language; but is there not cause for severity? I *will be* as harsh as truth, and as uncompromising as justice. On this subject, I do not wish to think, or speak, or write, with moderation. No! no! Tell a man whose house is on fire to give a moderate alarm; tell him to moderately rescue his wife from the hands of the ravisher; tell the mother to gradually extricate her babe from the fire into which it has fallen;—but urge me not to use moderation in a cause like the present. I am in earnest—I will not equivocate—I will not excuse—I will not retreat a single inch—AND I WILL BE HEARD. The apathy of the people is enough to make every statue leap from his pedestal, and to hasten the resurrection of the dead.

It is pretended, that I am retarding the cause of emancipation by the coarseness of my invective and the precipitancy of my measures. *The charge is not true.* On this question my influence,—

humble as it is,—is felt at this moment to a considerable extent, and shall be felt in coming years—not perniciously, but beneficially—not as a curse, but as a blessing; and posterity will bear witness that I was right. I desire to thank God, that he enables me to disregard "the fear of man which bringeth a snare," and to speak his truth in its simplicity and power. . . .

Women's Rights, 1843*

The enthusiasm for reform during the antebellum years spawned a movement for women's rights. Despite the republican rhetoric of the Revolution, and despite Abigail Adams's plea that the Founding Fathers "remember the ladies," many women believed that they had not gained the blessings of liberty that white males possessed. The place of women in society changed after 1776, but they resented their lack of social, economic, and political rights. Indeed, women faced fierce resistance in their efforts to be empowered, and their struggle to gain liberty and equality has been a significant issue throughout the history of the American people. In the following letter, author and reformer Lydia Maria Child touched upon some of the concerns she had as a woman—concerns that in some ways seem as relevant at the end of the twentieth century as they were one hundred and fifty years ago.

You ask what are my opinions about "Women's Rights." I confess, a strong distaste to the subject, as it has been generally treated. On no other theme, probably, has there been uttered so much of false, mawkish sentiment, shallow philosophy, and sputtering, farthing-candle wit. If the style of its advocates has often been offensive to taste, and unacceptable to reason, assuredly that of its opponents have been still more so. College boys have amused themselves with writing dreams, in which they saw women in hotels, with their feet hoisted, and chairs tilted back, or growling and bickering at each other in legislative halls, or fighting at the polls, with eyes blackened by fisticuffs. But it never seems to have occurred to these facetious writers, that the proceedings which appear so ludicrous and improper in *women,* are also ridiculous and disgraceful in *men.* It were well that *men* should learn not to hoist their feet above their heads, and tilt their chairs backward, nor to growl and snap in the halls of legislation, or give each other black eyes at the polls. . . .

It would seem . . . as if men were willing to give women the exclusive benefit of gospel-teaching. "*Women* should be gentle," say the advocates of subordination; but when Christ said, "Blessed are the meek," did he preach to women only? "*Girls* should be modest," is the language of common teaching, continually uttered in words and customs. Would it not be an improvement for men, also, to be scrupulously pure in manners, conversation, and life? Books addressed to young married people abound with advice to the *wife,* to control her temper, and never to utter wearisome complaints, or vexatious words, when the husband comes home fretful or unreasonable, from his out-of-door conflicts with the world. Would not the advice be as excellent and appropriate, if the husband were advised to conquer *his* fretfulness, and forbear his complaints, in consideration of his wife's ill-health, fatiguing cares, and the thousand disheartening influences of domestic routine? In short, whatsoever, can be named as loveliest, best, and most graceful in women, would likewise be good and graceful in man. You will perhaps remind me of courage. If you use the word in its highest signification, I answer that women, above others, has abundant need of it, in her pilgrimage; and the true woman wears it with quiet grace. If you mean mere animal courage, *that* is not mentioned in the Sermon on the Mount, among those

---

*From L. Maria Child, *Letters from New-York* (New York: Charles S. Francis and Company, 1843), 232–40.

qualities which enable us to inherit the earth, or become the children of God. That the feminine ideal approaches much nearer to the gospel standard, than the prevalent idea of manhood, is shown by the universal tendency to represent the Saviour and his most beloved disciples with mild, meek expression, and feminine beauty. None speak of the bravery, the might, or the intellect of Jesus; but the devil is always imagined as being of acute intellect, political cunning, and the fiercest courage. These universal and instinctive tendencies of the human mind reveal much.

That the present position of women in society is the result of physical force, is obvious enough; whosoever doubts it, let her reflect why she is afraid to go in the evening without the protection of a man. What constitutes the danger of aggression? Superior physical strength, uncontrolled by the moral sentiments. If physical strength were in complete subjection to moral influence, there would be no need of outward protection. That animal instinct and brute force now govern the world, is painfully apparent in the conditions of women everywhere; from the Morduan Tartars, whose ceremony of marriage consists of placing the bride on a mat, and consigning her to the bridegroom, with the words, "Here, wolf, take thy lamb,"—to the German remark, that "stiff ale, stinging tobacco, and a girl in her smart dress, are the best things." The same thing, softened by the refinements of civilization, peeps out in Stephen's remark, that "women never look so interesting, as when leaning on the arm of a soldier:" and in Hazlitt's complaint that "it is not easy to keep up a conversation with women in company. It is thought a piece of rudeness to differ from them; it is not quite fair to ask them a *reason* for what they say."

This sort of politeness to women is what men call gallantry; an odious word to every sensible woman, because she sees that it is merely the flimsy veil which foppery throws over sensuality, to conceal its grossness. So far is it from indicating sincere esteem and affection for women, that the profligacy of a nation may, in general, be fairly measured by its gallantry. This taking away *rights,* and *condescending* to *great privileges,* is an old trick of the physical force principle; and with the immense majority, who only look on the surface of things, this mask effectually disguises an ugliness, which would otherwise be abhorred. The most inveterate slaveholders are probably those who take most pride in dressing their household servants handsomely, and who would be most ashamed to have the name of being *unnecessarily* cruel. And profligates, who form the lowest and most sensual estimate of women, are the very ones who treat them with an excess of outward deference. . . .

I have said enough to show that I consider prevalent opinions and customs highly unfavorable to the moral and intellectual development of women; and I need not say, that, in proportion to their true culture, women will be more useful and happy, and domestic life more perfected. True culture, in them, as in men, consists in the full and free development of individual character, regulated by their *own* perception of what is true, and their *own* love of what is good. . . .

Discussion

1. Harriet Martineau stressed equality throughout her essay. What are some examples of her focus, and what do they suggest about the relationship of criminal justice and liberty? Do prisoners deserve to be treated as equals, and do they deserve the blessings of liberty? What do you think of Martineau's assertion that prisons can empower convicts?

2. In the editorial on the Maine Law, how does *The Democratic Review* reveal the party's definitions of liberty, equality, and power? How do the Democrats differ from the Whigs? Do you agree that liberty is the "right to do wrong"? If so, why; if not, why not?

3. Who do you think John Van Evrie believed held power in the United States? Do you think that Van Evrie believed that all white people were equal? Why or why not? If not, who is superior? How does Van Evrie argue that slavery had guaranteed liberty in the United States?

Harcourt Brace & Company

4. Who do you think William Lloyd Garrison believed held power in the United States? Why might northerners and New Englanders have been more opposed to Garrison than the slave-owners? What are the implications in the editorial for the liberty of slaves and the equality of African Americans?

5. Compare the letter of Lydia Maria Child to those of Abigail Adams presented in Chapter 7. What do the documents reveal about similarities or differences in the status of women in 1776 and in the 1840s? What do you think Lydia Maria Child believed constituted liberty and equality for women? How might Child have hoped to see women empowered politically and socially? Which of her concerns, if any, are still relevant today?.

Chapter 14

Manifest Destiny:
An Empire for Liberty—or Slavery?

"This is the house that Polk built." This c. 1846 anti-Polk cartoon protests his expansionist goals and the Mexican War. Polk sits on a nest hatching his plans under the walls of territorial expansion and tariff reduction. His flimsy house of cards cannot last.

*D*uring the 1830s and 1840s, the national faith that the United States should expand across the continent became more and more apparent. This Manifest Destiny, which in many ways was the legacy of John Winthrop's hope for creating a "city upon a hill," encouraged emigration to western states and sparked interest in gaining additional territories. By 1850, the nation reached to the Pacific Ocean and stretched from Canada to the southwestern deserts. American power, and American concepts of liberty and equality, spread from sea to sea. Expansion, however, deepened the already existing sectional differences over slavery. The debate over Texas statehood, for instance, brought into sharp focus the growing animosity between northerners and southerners. War with Mexico only served to exacerbate the problem, because the status of slavery in newly acquired territory became an overriding, and extremely divisive, political issue. To northerners, expanding slavery threatened the economic prospects and the equality of white men. Southerners feared just as strongly that limiting slavery endangered their rights and liberties. Ironically, just as the United States seemed to have achieved an unprecedented power, it appeared that questions of liberty and equality might destroy the Union.

Overland Trails, 1859*

In the years prior to the Civil War, thousands of Americans headed west hoping to find new and better prospects. Those pioneers, motivated by a variety of personal reasons, carried across the continent with them the republican principles of the nation. Most of the emigrants had never been to the West, and they had not experienced the rigors of the overland trails. For help, they turned to the many available guide books that offered advice and suggestions to travelers. Randolph B. Marcy, who explored vast regions of the American West as an officer in the United States Army, wrote one of the most popular of the emigrant's guides. In his book he outlined a method for governing overland expeditions—a system that underscored the cooperative and democratic nature of westward expansion. His essay also pointed out some of the hardships and dangers the settlers might face on their journey west.

> After a particular route has been selected to make the journey across the plains, and the requisite number have arrived at the eastern terminus, their first business should be to organize themselves into a company and elect a commander. The company should be of sufficient magnitude to herd and guard animals, and for protection against Indians.
>
> From 50 to 70 men, properly armed and equipped, will be enough for these purposes, and any greater number only makes the movements of the party more cumbersome and tardy.
>
> In the selection of a captain, good judgment, integrity of purpose, and practical experience are the essential requisites, and these are indispensable to the harmony and consolidation of the association. His duty should be to direct the order of march, the time of starting and halting, to

---

*From Randolph B. Marcy, *A Hand-book for Overland Expeditions, with Maps, Illustrations, and Itineraries of the Principal Routes between the Mississippi and the Pacific* (New York: Harper & Brothers, 1859), 22–25, 46–54.

select the camps, detail and give orders, and, indeed, to control and superintend all the movements of the company.

An obligation should then be drawn up and signed by all the members of the association, wherein each one should bind himself to abide in all cases by the orders and decisions of the captain, and to aid him by every means in his power in the execution of his duties; and they should also obligate themselves to aid each other, so as to make the individual interest of each member the common concern of the whole company. To insure this, a fund should be raised for the purchase of extra animals to supply the places of those which may give out or die on the road; and if the wagons or team of a particular member should fail and have to be abandoned, the company should obligate themselves to transport his luggage, and the captain should see that he has his share of transportation equal with any other member. Thus it will be made the interest of every member of the company to watch over and protect the property of others as well as his own.

In case of failure on the part of any one to comply with the obligations imposed by the articles of agreement after they have been duly executed, the company should of course have the power to punish the delinquent member, and, if necessary, to exclude him from all the benefits of the association.

On such a journey as this, there is much to interest and amuse one who is fond of picturesque scenery, and of wild life in its most primitive aspect, yet no one should attempt it without anticipating many rough knocks and much hard labor; every man must expect to do his share of any duty faithfully and without a murmur.

On long and arduous expeditions men are apt to become irritable and ill-natured, and oftentimes fancy they have more labor imposed on them than their comrades, and that person who directs the march is partial to his favorites, etc. That man who exercises the greatest forbearance under such circumstances, who is cheerful, slow to take up quarrels, and endeavors to reconcile difficulties among his companions, is deserving of all praise, and will, without doubt, contribute largely to the success and comfort of an expedition.

The advantages of an association such as I have mentioned are manifestly numerous. The animals can be herded and guarded by the different members of the company in rotation, thereby securing to all the opportunities of sleep and rest. Besides this, this is the only way to resist depredations of the Indians, and to prevent their stampeding and driving off animals; and much more efficiency is secured in every respect., especially in crossing streams, repairing roads, etc., etc.

Unless a systematic organization be adopted, it is impossible for a party of any magnitude to travel in company for any great length of time, and for all the members to agree upon the same arrangements in marching, camping, etc. I have several times observed, where this has been attempted, that discords and dissensions sooner or later arose which invariably resulted in breaking up and separating the company.

When a captain has once been chosen, he should be sustained in all his decisions unless he commit some manifest outrage, when a majority of the company can always remove him, and put a more competent man in his place. Sometimes men may be selected who, upon trial, do not come up to the anticipations of those who have placed him in power, and other men will exhibit, during the course of the march, more capacity. Under these circumstances it will not be unwise to make a change, the first election having been distinctly provisional. . . .

The scarcity of water upon some of the routes across the plains occasionally exposes the traveler to intense suffering, and renders it a matter of much importance for him to learn the best methods of guarding against the disasters liable to occur to men and animals in the absence of this most necessary element.

In mountainous districts water can generally be found either in springs, the dry beds of streams, or in holes in the rocks, where they are sheltered from rapid evaporation. . . .

Harcourt Brace & Company

During a season of the year when there are occasional showers, water will generally be found in low places where there is a substratum of clay, but after the dry season has set in these pools evaporate, and it is necessary to dig wells. The lowest spots should be selected for this purpose when the grass is green and the surface earth moist.

In searching for water along the dry sandy beds of streams, it is well to try the earth with a stick or ramrod, and if this indicates moisture water will generally be obtained by excavation. Streams often sink in light and porous sand, and sometimes make their appearance again lower down, where the bed is more tenacious; but it is a rule with prairie travelers, in searching for water in a sandy country, to ascend the streams, and the nearer their sources are approached the more water will be found in a dry season.

When it becomes necessary to sink a well in a stream bed of which is quicksand, a flour-barrel, perforated with small holes, should be used as a curb, to prevent the sand from caving in. The barrel must be forced down as the sand is removed; and when, as is often the case, there is an undercurrent through the sand, the well will be continually filled with water. . . .

The use of water is a matter of habit, very much within our control, as by practice we may discipline ourselves so as to require but a small amount. Some persons, for example, who place no restraint upon their appetites, will, if they can get it, drink water twenty times a day, while others will not perhaps drink more than once or twice during the same time. I have found a very effectual preventative to thirst by drinking a large quantity of water before breakfast, and, on feeling thirsty on the march, chewing a small green twig or leaf.

Water taken from stagnant pools, charged with putrid vegetable matter and animalculae, would be very likely to generate fevers and dysentaries if taken into the stomach without purification. It should therefore be thoroughly boiled, and all the scum removed from the surface as it rises; this clarifies it, and by mixing powdered charcoal with it the disinfecting process is perfected. Water may also be purified by placing a piece of alum in the end of a stick that has been split, and stirring it around in a bucket of water. Charcoal and the leaves of the prickly pear are also used for the same purpose. . . . Water may be partially filtered in a muddy pond by taking a barrel and boring the lower half full of holes, then filling it up with grass or moss above the upper holes, after which it is placed in the pond with the top above the surface. The water filters through the grass or moss, and rises in the barrel to a level with the pond. Travelers often drink muddy water by placing a cloth or handkerchief over the mouth of a cup to catch the larger particles of dirt and animalculae.

Water may be cooled so as to be quite palatable by wrapping cloths around the vessels containing it, wetting them and hanging them in the air, where rapid evaporation will be produced. Some of the frontier-men use a leathern sack for carrying water: this is porous, and allows the necessary evaporation without wetting.

No expedition should ever set out into the plains without being supplied with the means of carrying water, especially in an unknown region. If wooden kegs are used they must frequently be looked after, and soaked, in order that they my not shrink and fall to pieces. Men, in marching in a hot climate, throw off a great amount of perspiration from the skin, and require a corresponding quantity of water to supply the deficiency, and unless they get this they suffer greatly. When a party makes an expedition into a desert section, where there is a probability of finding no water, and intend to return over the same track, it is well to carry water as far as convenient, and bury it in the ground for use on the return trip. . . .

In some localities 50 or 60 miles, and even greater distances, are frequently traversed without water; these long stretches are called by the Mexicans *"journadas,"* or day's journey. There is one in New Mexico called *Journada del Muerto* ["Journey of Death"], which is 78 1/2 miles in length, where, in a dry season, there is not a drop of water; yet, with proper care, this drive can be made with ox or mule teams, and without loss or injury to the animals. . . .

Female Life Among the Mormons, 1855*

Although most pioneers headed west as individuals, single families, or small groups, the Church of Jesus Christ of Latter-Day Saints organized a massive immigration of thousands of people from Illinois to the Great Basin. The Mormons had suffered violent persecution—especially for their practice of polygamy—and they moved west to find a haven far from the Gentile animosity they had faced in the past. Their efforts were successful for many reasons, including the powerful leadership of Brigham Young. Maria Ward, the wife of a church elder, wrote a memoir in which she expressed strong admiration for founder Joseph Smith but showed less devotion to Brigham Young. The following selection, noticeably critical, presented one woman's view of Mormon polygamy. She also discussed the pervasive influence that Young had on church members.

It is scarcely necessary to remark that with the demise of Smith, Mormonism took a new aspect in many particulars. This is chiefly to be attributed to the differences in the characters of the leaders. B_____m, though professing to believe in miracles, rarely attempted the exhibition of them, and finally, ceased to talk of any such thing. Smith had introduced spiritual-wifery, under the pretence of a pure platonic, or rather spiritual affection; B_____m openly advocated polygamy; and, in order that his precepts and practices might coincide, he espoused three wives in one day. Before the demise of Smith, however, polygamy was slowly coming into practice, though the sentiments of the ladies were divided on the subject. It was decided by the latter to be not simply a privilege, but a duty, and the virtues of the believers were estimated very much by the numbers of their wives. During the journey, however, they had little time for marrying, or giving in marriage. . . .

It was the general policy of B_____m to encourage preaching mostly, in those who were well off in temporal affairs. This obviated any necessity of assistance on the part of the Church. The rich men likewise monopolized the women, to a great extent, consequently, while one man enjoyed the honor of being a preacher and a rich man, with a house full of women, all loveable and lovely, waiting to do his bidding, another, quite as good, or better probably better in mind and heart, though with less of this world's goods, was doomed to the cold and joyless trials of celibacy.

In this respect, however, it cannot be denied that some of the women were culpable, and that their conduct contributed, in a small degree, to the continuance of polygamy. Not a few preferred a rich man, with a dozen wives, to a poor without any, and, though repentance might inevitably ensue, it would be too late. The Prophet encouraged this state of things, for various reasons; indeed, he seemed to consider poverty as little short of crime, whose punishment consisted in the deprivation of social and domestic comforts.

It seemed the policy of B_____m, to give the Mormon creed a consistency, or rather a systematized form, such as it had never taken under the administration of Smith. Besides the wonders of millennial glory, on which the preachers loved to descant, they were fond of expatiating on spiritual life. They professed to believe, and they certainly taught, that God had constantly on a hand a multitude of little spirits, who want to come, and whom he has ordained shall come, and assume mortal bodies, and sojourn on earth for a time; human bodies being earthly tabernacles, temporary dwelling-houses for spirits. Yet, conjugal intercourse is necessary to accomplish the work, and hence, as God is very anxious that these spirits should be provided with bodies, and as the spirits themselves are very anxious to get down here, it became the duty of all true believers to lend their aid and produce the bodies as fast as possible. . . .

---

*From Maria Ward, *Female Life Among the Mormons; A Narrative of Many Years' Personal Experience* (New York: G. H. Wooten, 1855), 165, 318–19, 321–22.

As the principles of Mormonism developed, it became evident that the females were to be regarded as an inferior order of beings. One by one the rights to which they had been accustomed, as well as the courtesies generally conceded to them were taken away. When the husband died, his property reverted to the church, instead of going to support his bereaved family, a regulation which occasioned an infinite amount of trouble and difficulty. However, if the husband and father was particularly interested in making provision of the future support of his family, he could do so, by paying the church during his life-time a certain extra stipend, which would release its claim.

Many widows were thus actually necessitated to take husbands on the first opportunity, and many young girls, not exceeding the ages of twelve and fourteen years, became the wives of men old enough to be their grandfathers, to save them from the streets.

No family in Utah ever hires household service. Some few have slaves, but generally speaking when one wife is insufficient to perform the labor, another is taken, perhaps a third, or fourth, and so on, for the number is only limited by the discretion and desire of the husband.

In all cases where the father was living, his consent was necessary to the marriage of a daughter, even though that daughter was a widow and a mother. In the case of his death, the head of the church acted in the capacity of guardian, and his consent was indispensable. The fathers, from the instruction they constantly received, and other causes, paid little attention to the inclinations of their children, but were greatly influenced by the size of the nominal gift. . . . These bargains were not unfrequently the subjects of much chicanery and intrigue, as if the object for sale was a horse, and the contracting parties two regular jockies. . . .

An Anti-Slavery Protest, 1837*

When the new Republic of Texas petitioned to join the Union, the request initiated a long, bitter national debate that became known as the "Texas question." Concern centered on the addition of such a large slave territory to the Union, particularly since Texas would have the right to divide into as many as five states. Unitarian Reverend William E. Channing wrote a powerful statement of opposition to annexation, and his essay mirrored many of the contemporary attitudes. He began his essay with a discussion of the political power the South would gain with the addition of Texas—the traditional argument against expanding slavery. He next advanced a relatively new contention that slave labor threatened the rights of free labor. Finally, he made clear his belief that slavery was an evil that had to be, and would be, destroyed. Channing, like William Lloyd Garrison, helped turn the issue into a moral concern that gained intensity over the following two decades. Beginning with the Texas question, issues of liberty, power, and equality in the United States increasingly involved the matter of slavery.

> . . . I proceed now to a consideration of what is to me the strongest argument against annexing Texas to the United States. This measure will extend and perpetuate slavery. . . .
>
> . . . On this point there can be no doubt. As far back as the year 1829, the annexation of Texas was agitated in the Southern and Western States; and it was urged on the ground of the strength and extension it would give to the slaveholding interest. In a series of essays ascribed to a gentleman, now a senator in Congress, it was maintained, that five or six slaveholding states by this measure could be added to the Union; and he even intimated that as many as nine states as large as Kentucky might be formed within the limits of Texas. In Virginia, about the same

---

*From *American History Told by Contemporaries,* 5 vols., ed. Albert Bushnell Hart (New York: The Macmillan Company, 1914), IV:642–45.

time, calculations were made as to the increased value which would thus be given to slaves, and it was said, that this acquisition would raise the price fifty per cent. Of late the language on this subject is most explicit. The great argument for annexing Texas, that it will strengthen "the peculiar institution" of the South and open a new and vast field for slavery.

By this act, slavery will spread over regions to which it is now impossible to set limits. Texas, I repeat it, is but the first step of aggressions. I trust, indeed, that Providence will beat back and humble our cupidity and ambition. But one guilty success is often suffered to be crowned, as men call it, with greater; in order that a more awful retribution may at length vindicate the justice of God, and the rights of the oppressed. Texas, smitten with slavery, will spread the infection beyond herself. We know that the tropical regions have been found most propitious to this pestilence; nor can we promise ourselves, that its expulsion from them for a season forbids its return. By annexing Texas, we may send this scourge to a distance, which, if now revealed, would appal us, and through these vast regions every cry of the injured will invoke wrath on our heads.

By this act, slavery will be perpetuated in the old states as well as spread over new. It is well known, that the soil of some of the old states have become exhausted by slave cultivation. Their neighborhood to communities, which are flourishing under free labor, forces on them perpetual arguments for adopting the better system. They now adhere to slavery, not on account of the wealth which it extracts from the soil, but because it furnishes men and women to be sold in newly settled and more southern districts. It is by slave breeding and slave selling that these states subsist. Take away from them a foreign market, and slavery would die. Of consequence, by opening a new market, it is prolonged and invigorated. By annexing Texas, we shall not only create it where it does not exist, but breathe new life into it, where its end seemed to be near. States, which might and ought to throw it off, will make the multiplication of slaves their great aim and chief resource.

Nor is the worst told. As I have before intimated, and it cannot be too often repeated, we shall not only quicken the domestic slave trade; we shall give new impulse to the foreign. This indeed we have pronounced in our laws to be felony; but we make our laws cobwebs, when we offer to rapacious men strong motives for their violation. Open a market for slaves in an unsettled country, with a sweep of sea-coast, and at such distance from the seat of government that laws may be evaded with immunity, and how can you exclude slaves from Africa? It is well known that cargoes have been landed in Louisiana. What is to drive them from Texas? In incorporating this region with the Union to make it a slave country, we send the kidnapper to prowl through the jungles, and to dart, like a beast of prey, on the defenceless villages of Africa. We chain the helpless despairing victims; crowd them into the fetid, pestilential slave ship; expose them to the unutterable cruelties of the middle passage, and, if they survive it, crush them with perpetual bondage.

I now ask, whether as a people, we are prepared to seize on a neighboring territory for the end of extending slavery? I ask, whether, as a people, we can stand forth in the sight of God, in the sight of the nations, and adopt this atrocious policy? Sooner perish! Sooner be our name blotted out from the record of nations! . . .

Whoever studies modern history with any care, must discern in it a steady growing movement towards one most interesting result, I mean, towards the elevation of the laboring class of society. . . .

It is the great mission of this country, to forward this revolution, and never was a sublimer work committed to a nation. Our mission is to elevate society through all its conditions, to secure every human being the means of progress, to substitute the government of equal laws for that of irresponsible individuals, to prove that, under popular institutions, the people may be carried forward, that the multitude who toil are capable of enjoying the noblest blessings of the social state. The prejudice, that labor is a degradation, one of the worst prejudices handed down

Harcourt Brace & Company

from barbarous ages, is to receive here, a practical refutation. The power of liberty to raise up the whole people, this is the great Idea, on which our institutions rest, and which is to be wrought out in our history. Shall a nation having such a mission abjure it, and even fight against the progress which it is specially called to promote?

The annexation of Texas, if it should be accomplished, would do much to determine the future history and character of this country. It is one of those measures, which call a nation to pause, reflect, look forward, because their force is not soon exhausted.... The chief interest of a people lies in measures, which, making, perhaps little noise, go far to fix its character, to determine its policy for ages, to decide its rank among other nations. A fearful responsibility rests on those who originate or control these pregnant acts. The destiny of millions is in their hands. The execration of millions may fall on their heads. Long after present excitements have passed away, long after they and their generation shall have vanished from the earth, the fruits of their agency will be reaped. Such is a measure that of which I now write. It will commit us to a degrading policy, the issues of which lie beyond human foresight. In opening to ourselves vast regions, through which we may spread slavery, and in spreading it for this, among other ends, that the slaveholding states may bear rule in the national councils, we make slavery the predominant interest of the state. We make it the basis of power, the spring or guide of public measures, the object for which revenues, strength, and wealth of the country, are to be exhausted. Slavery will be branded on our front, as the great Idea, the prominent feature of the country. We shall renounce our high calling as a people, and accomplish the lowest destiny to which a nation can be bound.

And are we prepared for this degradation? Are we prepared to couple with the name of our country the infamy of deliberately spreading slavery? and especially of spreading it through regions from which the wise and humane legislation of a neighboring republic had excluded it? We call Mexico a semi-barbarous people; and yet we talk of planting slavery where Mexico would not suffer it to live. What American will not blush to lift his head in Europe, if this disgrace shall be fastened on his country? Let other calamities, if God so will, come on us. Let us be steeped in poverty. Let pestilence stalk through our land. Let famine thin our population. Let the world join hands against free institutions, and deluge our shores with blood. All this can be endured. A few years of industry and peace will recruit our wasted numbers, and spread fruitfulness over our desolated fields. But a nation devoting itself to the work of spreading and perpetuating slavery, stamps itself with a guilt and shame, which generations will not be able to efface. The plea on which we have rested, that slavery was not our choice, but a sad necessity bequeathed to us by our fathers, will avail us no longer. The whole guilt will be assumed by ourselves.

It is very lamentable, that among the distinguished men of the South, any should be found so wanting to their own fame, as to become advocates of slavery.... Have they nothing of that prophetic instinct, by which truly great men read the future? Can they learn nothing from the sentence now passed on men, who fifty years ago, defended the slave trade? ...

I have expressed my fears, that by the annexation of Texas, slavery is to be continued and extended. But I wish not to be understood, as having the slightest doubt as to the approaching fall of the institution. It may be prolonged to our reproach and greater ultimate suffering. But fall it will and must.... Moral laws are as irresistible as physical. In the most enlightened countries of Europe, a man would forfeit his place in society, by vindicating slavery. The slaveholder must not imagine, that he has nothing to do but fight with a few societies. These, of themselves, are nothing. He should not waste on them one fear. They are strong, only as representing the spirit of the Christian and civilized world. His battle is with the laws of human nature and the irresistible tendency of human affairs. These are not to be withstood by artful strokes of policy, or by daring crimes. The world is against him, and the world's Maker. Every day the sympathies of the world are forsaking him. Can he hope to sustain slavery against the moral feeling, the solemn sentence of the human race?

President Polk on Texas and Oregon, 1845*

Despite the strong resistance to Texas statehood that forced the Lone Star Republic to remain independent for almost ten years, Manifest Destiny proved too alluring for most Americans. The dream of national expansion outweighed the fear of a slaveowners' conspiracy, especially since the free Oregon territory could counterbalance Texas. In 1844, Democratic presidential candidate James K. Polk won the election with a platform to re-annex Texas, which many people felt already belonged to the United States as part of the Louisiana Purchase, and the acquisition of Oregon. President Polk used his inaugural address to set forth his reasons for claiming vast new holdings for the republic. The United States would have its continental empire; it remained to be determined whether it would be an empire for liberty or an empire for slavery.

The Republic of Texas has made known her desire to come into our Union, to form a part of our Confederacy and enjoy with us the blessings of liberty secured and guaranteed by our Constitution. Texas was once a part of our country—was unwisely ceded away to a foreign power—is now independent, and possesses an undoubted right to dispose of a part of the whole of her territory and to merge her sovereignty as a separate and independent state in ours. I congratulate my country that by an act of the late Congress of the United States the assent of this government has been given to the reunion, and it only remains for the two countries to agree upon terms to consummate an object so important to both.

I regard the question of annexation as belonging exclusively to the United States and Texas. They are independent powers competent to contract, and foreign nations have no right to interfere with them or to take exceptions to their reunion. Foreign powers do not seem to appreciate the true character of our Government. Our Union is a confederation of independent States, whose policy is peace with each other and all the world. To enlarge its limits is to extend the dominions of peace over additional territories and increasing millions. The world has nothing to fear from military ambition in our Government. While the Chief Magistrate and the popular branch of Congress are elected for short terms by the suffrages of those millions who must in their own persons bear all the burdens and miseries of war, our Government can not be otherwise than pacific. Foreign powers should therefore look on the annexation of Texas to the United States not as the conquest of a nation seeking to extend her dominions by arms and violence, but as the peaceful acquisitions of a territory once her own, by adding another member to our confederation, with the consent of that member, thereby diminishing the chances of war and opening to them new and ever-increasing markets for their products.

To Texas the reunion is important, because the strong protecting arm of our Government would be extended over her, and the vast resources of her fertile soil and genial climate would be speedily developed, while the safety of New Orleans and our whole southwestern frontier against hostile aggression, as well as the interests of the whole Union, would be promoted by it. . . .

None can fail to see the danger to our safety and future peace if Texas remains an independent state or becomes an ally or dependency of some foreign nation more powerful than

---

*From "Inaugural Address of James K. Polk," in *A Compilation of the Messages and Papers of the Presidents, 1789–1897,* 10 vols., comp. James D. Richardson (Washington, D.C.: U.S. Government Printing Office, 1896–1899), IV:379–81.

herself. . . . Whatever is good or evil in the local institutions of Texas will remain her own whether annexed to the United States or not. None of the present States will be responsible for them any more than they are the local institutions of each other. They have confederated together for certain specified objects. Upon the same principle that they would refuse to form a perpetual union with Texas because of her local institutions our forefathers would have been prevented from forming our present Union. Perceiving no valid objection to the measure and many reasons for its adoption vitally affecting the peace, the safety, and the prosperity of both countries, I shall on the broad principle which formed the basis and produced the adoption of our Constitution, and not in any narrow spirit of sectional policy, endeavor all constitutional, honorable, and appropriate means to consummate the expressed will of the people and Government of the United States by the reannexation of Texas to our Union at the earliest practicable period.

Nor will it become in a less degree my duty to assert and maintain by all constitutional means the right of the Untied States to that portion of our territory which lies beyond the Rocky Mountains. Our title to the country of the Oregon is "clear and unquestionable," and already are our people preparing to perfect that title by occupying it with their wives and children. But eighty years ago our population was confined on the west by the ridge of the Alleghanies. Within that period—within the lifetime, I might say, of some of my hearers—our people, increasing to many millions, have filled the eastern valley of the Mississippi, adventurously ascended the Missouri to its headsprings, and are already engaged in establishing the blessings of self-government in valleys of which the rivers flow to the Pacific. The world beholds the peaceful triumphs of the industry of our emigrants. To us belongs the duty of protecting them adequately wherever they may be upon our soil. The jurisdiction of our laws and the benefits of our republican institutions should be extended over them in the distant regions which they have selected for their homes. The increasing facilities of intercourse will easily bring the States, of which the formation in that part of our territory can not be long delayed, within the sphere of our federative Union. In the meantime, every obligation imposed by treaty or conventional stipulations should be sacredly respected. . . .

David Wilmot Opposes the Extension of Slavery, 1847[*]

While war raged between the United States and Mexico, Representative David Wilmot of Pennsylvania proposed prohibiting the expansion of slavery into any territory taken during the conflict. In the following speech, he elaborated on his position. His statements clearly revealed the growing northern conviction that since the founding of the country, national power had been used to expand slavery. He also touched upon the immorality of the institution, and he suggested the inherent superiority of a free society to a slave culture. The Pennsylvania congressman articulated the feelings of many northerners, and the Wilmot Proviso became the focal point of the debate over slavery for the next fifteen years. Wilmot was prescient indeed when he recognized that the issue posed a "difficult and dangerous problem" for the nation.

. . . Sir, the issue now presented is not whether slavery shall exist unmolested where it now is, but whether it shall be carried to new and distant regions, now free, where the footprint of a slave cannot be found. This, sir, is the issue. Upon it I take my stand, and from it I cannot be frightened or driven by idle charges of abolitionism. I demand that this Government preserve the integrity of *free territory* against the aggressions of slavery—against its wrongful usurpations.

---

[*]From *Appendix to the Congressional Globe,* 29th Congress, 2d Session, 1847, 315, 317, 318.

Sir, I was in favor of the annexation of Texas. I supported it with my whole influence and strength. I was willing to take Texas as she was. I sought not to change the character of her institutions. Slavery existed in Texas—planted there, it is true, in defiance of law; still it existed. It gave character to the country. True, it was held out to the North, that at least two of the five States to be formed out of Texas would be free. Yet, sir, the whole of Texas has been given up to slavery. The Democracy of the North, almost to a man, went for annexation. Yes, sir, here was an empire larger than France given up to slavery. Shall further concessions be made by the North? Shall we give up free territory, the inheritance of free labor? Must we yield this also? Never, sir, never, until we ourselves are fit to be slaves. The North may be betrayed by her Representatives, but upon this great question she will be true to herself—true to posterity. Defeat! Sir, there can be no defeat. Defeat to-day will but arouse the teeming millions of the North, and lead to a more decisive and triumphant victory to-morrow.

But, sir, we are told, that the joint blood and treasure of the whole country being extended in this acquisition, therefore it should be divided, and slavery allowed to take its share. Sir, the South has her share already; the instalment for slavery was paid in advance. We are fighting this war for Texas and for the South. I affirm it—every intelligent man knows it—Texas is the primary cause of the war. For this, sir, northern treasure is being exhausted, and northern blood poured out upon the plains of Mexico. We are fighting this war cheerfully, not reluctantly—cheerfully fighting this war for Texas; and yet we seek not to change the character of her institutions. Slavery is there; there let it remain. Sir, the whole history of this question is a history of concessions on the part of the North. The money of the North was expended in the purchase of Louisiana, two-thirds of which was given up to slavery. Again, in the purchase of Florida, did slavery gain new acquisitions. Slavery acquired an empire in the annexation of Texas. Three slave states have been admitted out of the Louisiana purchase. The slave State of Florida has been received into the Union; and Texas annexed, with the privilege of making five States out of her territory. What has the North obtained from these vast acquisitions, purchased by the joint treasure and defended by the common blood of the Union? One State, sir—one: young Iowa, just admitted to the Union, and not yet represented on the floor of the Senate. This, sir, is a history of our acquisitions since we became a nation. A history of northern concessions—of southern triumphs. . . .

Sir, I have said before, that I have no morbid sympathies upon the subject of slavery; still, I regard it as a great social and political evil—a blight and deadly mildew upon any country or State in which it exists. I regard it as the most difficult and dangerous problem which we will have to work out in this free Government. If we go back to the period of the establishment of the Constitution, we find there were six slave and seven free States; the slave States containing an area of some fifty thousand square miles more than the free, with about an equal population. Now, these free States have double the population of the slave. Why is this? In the Revolution, Massachusetts furnished more men for carrying on the war than the entire slave States. How happened this? Not from any want of patriotism on the part of the South, but from the want of ability, growing out of this institution. Where the men who labor are slaves, you cannot place arms in their hands; and it is the free laboring man who constitutes the strength and defence of his country on the field of battle. If this war continues, Pennsylvania will, if permitted, I believe, send more men into the field than the original six slave States. Not that Pennsylvania would be more forward than they in the vindication of the honor of the country, but because she has the men; and, owing to this peculiar institution of the South, they have them not. Their laborers cannot take up arms; indeed, they dare not form them into military organizations, and teach them the use of the weapons of war. Why is it that Virginia, the "mother of States"—that State which has ever been foremost in the vindication of the rights of the States, and of the liberties of the people—why is it that the sun of the glorious "Old Dominion" is not still in the ascen-

Harcourt Brace & Company

dant? She stood first—before New York, before Pennsylvania—and now she is out-stripped by States that have grown up within the memory of the present generation. Why is it? Can any doubt that slavery is the cause? . . . .

Viewing slavery as I do, I must resist its further extension and propagation on the North American continent. It is an evil, the magnitude and the end of which, no man can see. . . .

Fugitive Slave Law, 1850*

The slavery question reached an apparent resolution with the Compromise of 1850, which included a new Fugitive Slave Law. Instead of easing tensions between the sections, however, the law increased them dramatically. Slaveholders wanted to use the power of the national government to ensure the return of runaways. At the same time, abolitionists and many other northerners saw the law, which denied a jury trial for accused fugitives, as an imposition on American liberty and an affront to human dignity. Efforts to enforce the law resulted in numerous violent demonstrations in the North and helped strengthen the anti-slavery movement. Northern reluctance to obey the law and return slaves convinced southerners that their fundamental economic and social institution had at last become truly vulnerable.

Be it enacted . . . , That the persons who have been, or may hereafter be, appointed commissioners . . . by the Circuit Courts of the United States . . . shall be, and hereby are, authorized and required to exercise and discharge all the powers and duties conferred by this act.

SEC. 2. . . . That the Superior Court of each organized Territory of the United States shall have the same power to appoint commissioners . . . for similar purposes. . . .

SEC. 3. . . . That the Circuit Courts of the United States, and the Superior Courts of each organized Territory, shall from time to time enlarge the number of commissioners, with a view to afford reasonable facilities to reclaim fugitives from labor, and to the prompt discharge of the duties imposed by this act. . . .

SEC. 5. . . . That it shall be the duty of all marshals and deputy marshals to obey and execute all warrants and precepts issued under the provisions of this act, . . . and after arrest of such fugitive, by such marshal or his deputy, or whilst at any time in his custody under the provision of this act, should such fugitive escape, whether with or without the assent of the marshal or his deputy, such marshal shall be liable, on his official bond to be prosecuted for the benefit of such claimant, for the full value of the service or labor of said fugitive . . . ; and the better to enable the said commissioners . . . to execute their duties . . . , they are hereby authorized . . . to appoint . . . any one or more suitable persons . . . to execute all such warrants and other process as many be issued by them . . . ; with authority to said commissioners . . . to summon and call to their aid the bystanders, or *posse comitatus* of the proper county, when necessary to ensure a faithful observance of the . . . Constitution . . . , in conformity with the provisions of this act; and all good citizens are hereby commanded to aid and assist in the prompt and efficient execution of this law, whenever their services may be required. . . .

SEC. 6. . . . That when a person held to service or labor in any State or Territory of the United States, has heretofore or shall hereafter escape into another State of Territory . . . , the person or persons to whom such service or labor may be due, or his, or her, or their agent or attorney, duly authorized, by power of attorney, in writing, . . . may pursue and reclaim such fugitive person, either by procuring a warrant from some one of the courts, judges, or commissioners aforesaid . . . for the apprehension of such fugitive . . . , or by seizing and arresting

*From *United States Statutes at Large,* 31st Congress, 1st Session, Chapter 60, 1850, 462–65.

such fugitive, where the same can be done without process, and by taking, or causing such person to be taken, forthwith before such court, judge, or commissioner, whose duty it shall be to hear and determine the case of such claimant in a summary manner; and upon satisfactory proof being made, . . . in writing, . . . of the identity of the person [and] . . . that the person so arrested does in fact owe service to the person or persons claiming him or her, . . . to make out and deliver to such claimant . . . a certificate setting forth the substantial facts as to the service or labor due from such fugitive . . . , with authority to such claimant . . . to use such reasonable force and restraint as may be necessary . . . to take and remove such fugitive person back to the State or Territory whence he or she may have escaped. . . . In no trial or hearing under this act shall the testimony of such alleged fugitive be admitted in evidence; and the certificates in this . . . section mentioned, shall be conclusive of the right of the person or persons in whose favor granted, to remove such fugitive . . . , and shall prevent all molestation of such person or persons by any process issued by any court, judge, magistrate, or other persons whomever.

SEC. 7. . . . That any person who shall knowingly and willingly obstruct, hinder, or prevent such claimant, . . . or any person or persons lawfully assisting him . . . from arresting such fugitive . . . , either with or without process as aforesaid, or shall rescue, or attempt to rescue, such fugitive . . . from the custody of such claimant . . . ; or shall aid or abet, or assist such person so owing labor or service . . . , directly or indirectly, to escape from such claimant . . . ; or shall harbor or conceal such fugitive, so as to prevent the discovery and arrest of such person, after notice or knowledge of the fact that such person was a fugitive . . . , shall, for either of said offences, be subject to a fine not exceeding one thousand dollars, and imprisonment not exceeding six months. . . ; and shall moreover forfeit and pay, by way of civil damages to the party injured by such illegal conduct, the sum of one thousand dollars, for each fugitive so lost. . . .

SEC. 8. . . . That the marshals, their deputies, and the clerks of the said District and Territorial Courts, shall be paid . . . by such claimant, his agent or attorney; and in all cases where the proceedings are before a commissioner, he shall be entitled to a fee of ten dollars in full for his services in each case, upon the delivery of the said certificate to the claimant . . . ; or a fee of five dollars in cases where the proof shall not, in the opinion of such commissioner, warrant such certificate and delivery, . . . to be paid, in either case, by the claimant. . . . The . . . persons authorized to execute the process . . . for the arrest and detention of fugitives . . . shall also be entitled to a fee of five dollars each for each person . . . they may arrest . . . , with such others fees as may be deemed reasonable . . . for such additional services as may be necessarily performed by . . . them; . . . paid by such claimants . . . whether such supposed fugitives . . . be ordered to be delivered to such claimants by the final determination of such commissioners or not.

SEC. 9 . . . That, upon affidavit made by the claimant of such fugitive, . . . that he has reason to apprehend that such fugitive will be rescued by force . . . before he can be taken beyond the limits of the State in which the arrest was made, it shall be the duty of the officer making the arrest to retain such fugitive in his custody, and to remove him to the State whence he fled, and there to deliver him to said claimant. . . . And to this end, the officer aforesaid is hereby authorized and required to employ so many persons as he may deem necessary to overcome such force, and to retain them in his service as long as circumstances may require. . . .

SEC. 10. . . . That when any person held to service or labor . . . , shall escape. . . , the party to whom such service or labor shall be due, . . . may apply to any court of record . . . and make satisfactory proof to such court . . . of the escape aforesaid. . . . Whereupon the court shall cause a record to be made of the matters so proved, and also a general description of the person so escaping, . . . and a transcript of such record, . . . being produced in any other State, Territory, or district, in which the person so escaping may be found, and being exhibited to any judge, commissioner, or other officer authorized by the law of the United States . . . , shall be held and taken to be full and conclusive evidence of the fact of escape. . . . *Provided*, That nothing herein contained shall be construed as requiring the production of a transcription of such record as evidence as aforesaid. But in its absence the claim shall be heard and determined upon other satisfactory proofs. . . .

Discussion

1. The document by Randolph B. Marcy reveals the strong democratic feelings he held. What are some of the expressions of liberty and equality in the selection? Why might an army officer suggest that expeditions elect their leaders?

2. How similar are the concerns that Maria Ward expressed about women's rights to those of Lydia Maria Child in the previous chapter? Why do you think Ward is so critical of the power of the church? Do you think the situation she described was particularly unique to the Mormons?

3. Who do you think William E. Channing believed held power in the United States? Whose liberty did he think that slavery threatened, and why? Does Channing seem very concerned with equality? If so, whose and how?

4. The address by President James Polk presented his reasons for wanting to gain Texas and Oregon for the United States. What do you think about his arguments? Was it the Manifest Destiny of the United States to acquire territory across the entire continent? Why or why not? What does his message imply about the power of the nation? Are there any implications for the principles of liberty and equality?

5. Who do you think David Wilmot believed held power in the United States? How do his comments compare to those of William Channing? What do the differences or similarities between the two passages suggest about the slave question in the 1830s and 1840s? What concerns does Wilmot express for liberty or equality?

6. How might southerners have believed that the Fugitive Slave Law protected their liberty? How might abolitionists have believed that it threatened liberty?

Harcourt Brace & Company

Chapter 15
The Gathering Tempest, 1853–1860

This cartoon, drawn by a John Bell supporter, graphically illustrates the feared dissolution of the Union. On the left, Lincoln and Douglas fight over the United States. In the center Breckenridge rips away the South, while Bell tries futilely to paste the nation together again.

*M*ost Americans hoped that the Compromise of 1850 had resolved the slavery issue, but sectional differences grew even more pronounced during the subsequent years. Those differences, especially as manifested in Kansas, led to the creation of the Republican party and further hardening of the divisions between the North and the South. The Republicans established an anti-slavery coalition made up of several northern factions that stood adamantly against the expansion of slavery, and they hoped to gain enough power in Congress to implement the Wilmot Proviso. Proslavery forces obviously insisted on the right to extend slavery, and they gained the support of the Supreme Court when it ruled that Congress could not exclude the institution from any territory. The Dred Scott decision only helped fan the passions on both sides, and as the decade ended almost every national issue was tied to the slavery question. By the time John Brown was executed in 1859 for his attack on Harpers Ferry, emotions ran so high and bitterness so deep that, in effect, the nation had already divided.

Nativism, 1835*

Samuel F. B. Morse, who gained fame as the inventor of the telegraph, wrote a series of nativist essays in the 1830s just as a new wave of immigration to the United States began. In the following selection, Morse revealed the virulent anti–Catholicism that characterized the nativist movement. Hatred of Catholics had a long tradition in America, and in some ways Morse was merely repeating centuries-old feelings. Fears of conspiratorial threats to liberty were also a part of the nation's heritage, and Morse directed his anger toward the Pope and the Jesuits in much the same manner that an earlier generation had attacked King George III and the British Redcoats. In the 1850s, Republicans increased their political strength by channeling northerners' anxieties about immigrants into a campaign against the power of the slave aristocracy in the South. Consequently, many people came to believe that the gravest danger to freedom and equality was not a foreign state or a religious leader. The threat came from fellow Americans.

I have shown that a Society, (the "St. Leopold Foundation") is organized in a Foreign Absolute government, having its central direction in the capital of that government in Vienna, under the patronage of the Emperor of Austria, and the other Despotic Rulers,—a Society for the purpose of spreading Popery in this country. Of this fact there is no doubt. This "St. Leopold Foundation" has its ramifications through the whole of the Austria empire. It is not a small private association, but a great and extensive combination. It embraces in its extent, as shown by their own documents, not merely the wide Austrian Empire, Hungary, and Italy, but it includes Piedmont, Savoy, and Catholic France; it embodies the civil and ecclesiastical authorities of all these countries. And is such an extensive combination in foreign countries for the avowed purpose of operating in this country, (no matter for what purpose,) so trivial an affair, that we may safely dismiss it with a sneer? Have these foreign Rulers so much sympathy with our system of

*From Samuel F. B. Morse, *Imminent Dangers to the Free Institutions of the United States through Foreign Immigration, and the Present State of the Naturalization Laws* (New York: E. B. Clayton, 1835), 9–11.

government, that we may trust them safely to meddle with it, in any way? Are they so impotent in combination as to excite in us no alarm? May they send money, and agents, and a system of government wholly at variance with our own, and spread it through all our borders with impunity from our search, because it is nick-named Religion? There was a time when American sensibilities were quick on the subject of foreign interference. What has recently deadened them?

Let us examine the operation of this Austrian Society, for it is hard at work all around us; yes, here in this country, from one end to the other, at our very doors, in this city. From a machinery of such a character and power, we shall doubtless be able to see already some effect. With its head-quarters at Vienna, under the immediate direction and inspection of Metternich, the well-known great managing general of the diplomacy of Europe, it makes itself already felt through the republic. Its emissaries are here. And who are these enemies? They are JESUITS. The society of men, after exerting their tyranny for upwards of 200 years, at length became so formidable to the world, threatening the entire subversion of all social order, that even the Pope, whose devoted subjects they are, and must be, by the vow of their society, was compelled to dissolve them. They had not been suppressed, however, for 50 years, before the waning influence of Popery and Despotism required their useful labours, to resist the spreading light of Democratic liberty, and the Pope, (Pius VII,) simultaneously with the formation of the Holy Alliance, revived the order of the Jesuits in all their power. From the vow of "unqualified submission to the Sovereign Pontiff," they have been appropriately called the Pope's body guard. It should be known, that Austrian influence elected the present Pope; his body guard are therefore at the service of Austria, and these are the soldiers that the Leopold Society has sent to this country, and they are agents of this society, to execute its designs, whatever these designs may be. And do Americans need to be told what Jesuits are? If any are ignorant, let them inform themselves of their history without delay; no time is to be lost: their workings are before you in every day's events: they are a secret society, a sort of Masonic order, with superadded features of most revolting odiousness, and a thousand times more dangerous. They are not confined to one class in society; they are not merely priests, or priests of one religious creed, they are merchants, and lawyers, and editors, and men of any profession. and no profession, having no outward badge, (in this country,) by which to be recognized; they are about in all your society. They can assume any character, that of angels of light, of ministers of darkness, to accomplish their one great end, the service upon which they are sent, whatever that service may be. "They are all educated men, prepared, and sworn to start at any moment, in any direction, and for any service, commanded by the general of their order, bound to no family, to community, or country, by the ordinary ties which bind men; and sold for life to the cause of the Roman Pontiff."

These are the men at this moment ordered to America. And can they do nothing, Americans, to derange the free workings of your democratic institutions? Can they not, and do they not fan the slightest embers of discontent into a flame, those thousand little differences which must perpetually occur in any society, into riot, and quell its excess among their own people as it suits their policy and the establishment of their own control? Yes, they can be the aggressors, and contrive to be the aggrieved. They can do the mischief, and manage to be publicly lauded for their praiseworthy forbearance and their suffering patience. They can persecute, and turn away from the popular indignation, ever roused by the cry of persecution from themselves, and make it fall upon their victim. They can control the press in a thousand secret ways. They can write under the signature of "Whig," to-day, and if it suits their turn, "Tory," to-morrow. They can be Democrat to-day, and Aristocrat to-morrow. They can out-American Americans in admiration of American institutions to-day, and "condemn them as unfit for any people" to-morrow. These are the men that Austria has sent here, that she supplies with money, with whom she keeps up an active correspondence, and whose officers (the Bishops) are passing back and forth between Europe and America, doubtless to impart that information orally which not be so safe committed to writing.

Is there no danger to the Democracy of the country from such formidable foes arrayed against it? Is Metternich its friend? Is the Pope its friend? Are his official documents, now daily put forth, Democratic in their character?

O there is no danger to the Democracy; for those most devoted to the Pope, the Roman Catholics, especially the Irish Catholics, are all on the side of Democracy. Yes; to be sure they are on the side of Democracy. They are just where I should look for them. Judas Iscariot joined with the true disciples. Jesuits are not fools. They would not startle our slumbering fears, by bolting out their monarchical designs, directly in our teeth, and by joining the opposing ranks, except so far as to cover their designs. This is a Democratic country, and the Democratic party is and ever must be the strongest party, unless ruined by traitors and Jesuits in the camp. Yes; it is in the ranks of Democracy I should expect to find them, and for no good purpose be assured. Every measure of Democratic policy in the least exciting will be pushed to ultraism, so soon as it is introduced for discussion. Let every real Democrat guard against this common Jesuitical artifice of tyrants, an artifice which there is much evidence to believe is practicing against them at this moment, an artifice which if not heeded will surely be the ruin of Democracy: it is founded on the well-known principle that "extremes meet." The writer has seen it pass under his own eyes in Europe, in more than one instance. When in despotic governments popular discontent, arising from the intolerable oppressions of the tyrants of the people, has manifested itself by popular outbreakings, to such a degree as to endanger the throne, and the people seemed prepared to shove their masters from their horses, and are likely to mount, and seize the reins themselves; then, the popular movement, unmanageable any longer by resistance, is pushed to the extreme. The passions of the ignorant and vicious are excited to outrage by pretended friends of the people. Anarchy ensues; and then the mass of the people, who are always lovers of order and quiet, unite at once in support of the strong arm of force for protection; and despotism, perhaps, in another, but preconcerted shape, resumes its iron reign. Italy and Germany are furnishing examples every day. If an illustration is wanted on a larger scale, look at France in her late Republican revolution, and in her present relapse into despotism.

He who would prevent you from mounting his horse, has two ways of thwarting your design. If he finds your efforts to rise too strong for his resistance, he has but to add a little more impulse to them, and he shoves you over on the other side. In either case you are on the ground.

The Crime Against Kansas, 1856*

In 1856, Congressman Preston Brooks walked into the Senate chamber and soundly whipped Senator Charles Sumner of Massachusetts. The violence that had plagued Kansas was replayed on the Senate floor. Perhaps no single incident revealed the intensity of the slavery issue as vividly as the Brooks-Sumner Affair. Sumner had attracted wide attention with a speech on conditions in Kansas. In the opening portion of his lengthy address, he harshly criticized Senators Andrew Butler of South Carolina and Stephen Douglas of Illinois. Representative Preston Brooks of South Carolina took exception to the comments regarding Butler, who was a cousin, and he replied with vigor. The portion of the Sumner speech presented here includes the comments that infuriated Brooks.

Mr. President, you are now called to redress a great transgression. Seldom in the history of nations has such a question been presented. Tariffs, Army bills, Navy bills, Land bills, are impor-

---

*From *Appendix to the Congressional Globe,* 34th Congress, 1st Session, *1856,* 529–31.

Harcourt Brace & Company

tant, and justly occupy your care; but these all belong to the course of ordinary legislation. As means and instruments only, they are necessarily subordinate to the conservation of Government itself. Grant them or deny them, in greater or less degree, and you will inflict no shock. The machinery of Government will continue to move. The State will not cease to exist. For otherwise it is with the eminent question now before you, involving, as it does, Liberty in a broad Territory, and also involving the peace of the whole country with our good name in history for evermore. . . .

But, before entering upon the argument, I must say something of a general character, particularly in response to what has fallen from Senators who have raised themselves to eminence on this floor in championing human wrongs; I mean the Senator from South Carolina, [Mr. Butler,] and the Senator form Illinois, [Mr. Douglas,] who, though unlike as Don Quixote and Sancho Panza, yet, like this couple, sally forth together in the same adventure. I regret much to miss the elder Senator from his seat; but the cause, against which he has run a tilt, with such activity of animosity, demands that the opportunity of exposing him should not be lost; and it is for the cause that I speak. The Senator from South Carolina has read many books of chivalry, and believes himself a chivalrous knight, with sentiments of honor and courage. Of course he has chosen a mistress to whom he has made his vows, and who, though ugly to others, is always lovely to him; though polluted in the sight of the world, is chaste in his sight—I mean the harlot, Slavery. For her, his tongue is always profuse in words. Let her be impeached in character, or any proposition made to shut her out from the extension of her wantonness, and no extravagance of manner or hardihood of assertion is then too great for this Senator. The frenzy of Don Quixote, in behalf of his wench, Dulcinea del Toboso, is all surpassed. The asserted rights of slavery, which shock equality of all kinds, are cloaked by a fantastic claim of equality. If the slave States cannot enjoy what, in a mockery of the great fathers of this Republic, he misnames equality under the Constitution—in other words, the full power in the National Territories to compel fellow-men to unpaid toil, to separate husband and wife, and to sell little children at the auction block—then, sir, the chivalric Senator will conduct the State of South Carolina out of the Union! Heroic knight! Exalted Senator! A second Moses come for a second exodus!

But not content with this poor menace, . . . the Senator, in the unrestrained chivalry of his nature, has undertaken to apply opprobrious words to those who differ from him on this floor. He calls them "sectional and fanatical;" and opposition to the usurpation in Kansas he denounces as "an uncalculating fanaticism." To be sure, those charges lack all grace of originality, and all sentiment of truth; but the adventurous Senator does not hesitate. He is the uncompromising, the unblushing representative on this floor of a flagrant sectionalism, which now dominates over the Republic, and yet with a ludicrous ignorance of his own position—unable to see himself as others see him—or with an effrontery which even his white head ought not to protect from rebuke, he applies to those here who resist his sectionalism the very epithet which designates himself. The men who strive to bring back the Government to its original policy, when Freedom and not Slavery was national, while Slavery and not Freedom was sectional, he arraigns as sectional. This will not do. It involves too great a perversion of terms. I tell that Senator, that it is to himself, and to the "organization" of which he is the "committed advocate," that his epithet belongs. I now fasten it upon them. For myself, I care little for names; but since the question has been raised here, I affirm that the Republican party of the Union is in no just sense sectional, but, more than any other party, national, and that it now goes forth to dislodge from the high places of the Government the tyrannical sectionalism of which the Senator from South Carolina is one of the maddest zealots.

To the charge of fanaticism I also reply. Sir, fanaticism is found in an enthusiasm or exaggeration of opinions, particularly on religious subjects; but there may be a fanaticism for evil as well as good. Now, I will not deny, that there are persons among us loving Liberty too well for their own personal good, in a selfish generation. Such there may be, and, for the sake of their example, would that there were more! In calling them "fanatics," you cast contumely upon the noble army of martyrs, from the earliest day down to this hour; upon the great tribunes of human rights, by whom life, liberty, and happiness on earth, have been secured; upon the long line of devoted patriots, who, throughout history, have truly loved their country; and, upon all, who, in noble aspirations for the general good and in forgetfulness of self, have stood out before their age, and gathered into their generous bosoms the shafts of tyranny and wrong, in order to make a pathway for Truth. . . .But I tell the Senator, that there are characters badly eminent, of whose fanaticism there can be no question. Such were the ancient Egyptians, who worshipped divinities in brutish forms; the Druids, who darkened the forests of oak, in which they lived, by sacrificing blood; the Mexicans, who surrendered countless victims to the propitiations of their obscene idols. . . . And in this same dreary catalogue faithful history must record all who now, in an enlightened age and in a land of boasted Freedom, stand up, in perversion of the Constitution and in denial of immortal truth, to fasten a new shackle upon their fellow-man. If the Senator wishes to see fanatics, let him look round among his own associates; let him look at himself. . . .

As the Senator from South Carolina is the Don Quixote, the Senator from Illinois [Mr. Douglas] is the squire of Slavery, its very Sancho Panza, ready to do all its humiliating offices. . . . Standing on this floor, the Senator issued his rescript, requiring submission to the Usurped Power of Kansas; and this was accompanied by a manner—all his own—such as befits the tyrannical threat. Very well. Let the Senator try. I tell him now that he cannot enforce any such submission. The Senator, with the Slave Power at his back, is strong, but he is not strong enough for this purpose. He is bold. He shrinks from nothing. . . . The Senator copies the British officer, who, with boastful swagger, said that with the hilt of his sword he would cram the "stamps" down the throat of the American people, and he will meet a similar failure. He may convulse this country with civil feud. Like the ancient madman, he may set fire to this Temple of Constitutional Liberty, grander than the Ephesian dome; but he cannot enforce obedience to that tyrannical Usurpation.

The Senator dreams that he can subdue the North. He disclaims the open threat, but his conduct still implies it. How little that Senator knows himself or the strength of the cause which he persecutes! He is but a mortal man; against him is an immortal principle. With finite power he wrestles with the infinite, and he must fall. Against him are stronger battalions than any marshaled by mortal arm—the inborn, ineradicable, invincible sentiments of the human heart; against him is nature in all her subtle forces; against him is God. Let him try to subdue these. . . .

Preston Brooks Resigns His Seat in the House[*]

At the request of the Senate, the House of Representatives voted to censure Representative Brooks. He responded to that condemnation with the following remarks. Brooks offered an explanation for his attack on Charles Sumner and freely admitted that he had staged the assault. He insisted, however, that the House lacked authority to censure him for actions taken in the Senate chamber. Like many of the events in the United States during the 1850s, this incident, which clearly resulted from the slavery issue, was expanded to include a multitude of constitutional questions and a variety of concerns over liberty and power. Following his resignation, the voters of his district voted overwhelmingly to return Brooks to Congress. Sumner, on the other hand, did not return to

[*]From *Appendix to the Congressional Globe,* 34th Congress, 1st Session, 1856, 831–33.

Harcourt Brace & Company

his Senate seat for more than three years—an absence that convinced his constituents of the brutality of the South.

    Until this moment I have felt that there was a propriety in my remaining silent, and in trusting my defense to friends who are abler and more learned than myself. I have heretofore felt that other and higher interests than any which affect me personally were involved in the proceedings of this case. The interests of my constituents, of the House, and of all, indeed, who are concerned in the Constitution itself, in my view, have been intimately and inseparably complicated. . . .

    I have been content, therefore, to meet personally and in silence all the consequences of these proceedings.

    Some time since a Senator from Massachusetts allowed himself, in an elaborately prepared speech, to offer a great insult to my State and to a venerable friend, who is my State representative, and who was absent at the time.

    Not content with that, he published to the world, and circulated extensively, this uncalled for libel on my State and my blood. Whatever insults my State insults me. Her history and character have commanded my pious veneration; and in her defense I hope I shall always be prepared humbly and modestly, to perform the duty of a son. I should have forfeited my own self-respect, and perhaps the good opinion of my countrymen, if I had failed to resent such an injury by calling the offender in question to a personal account. It was a personal affair, and in taking redress into my own hands I meant no disrespect to the Senate of the United States or to this House. Nor, sir, did I design insult or disrespect to the State of Massachusetts. I was aware of the personal responsibilities I incurred, and was willing to meet them. I know, too, that I was amenable to the laws of the country, which afford the same protection to all, whether they be members of Congress or private citizens. I did not, and do not now, believe that I could be properly punished, not only in a court of law, but here also, at the pleasure and discretion of the House. I did not then, and do not now, believe that the spirit of American freemen would tolerate slander in high places, and permit a member of Congress to publish and circulate a libel on another, and then call upon either House to protect him against the personal responsibilities which he had thus incurred.

    But if I had committed a breach of privilege, it was the privilege of the Senate, and not of this House, which was violated. I was answerable there, and not here. They had no right, as it seems to me, to prosecute me in these Halls, nor have you the right in law or under the Constitution, as I respectfully submit, to take jurisdiction over offenses committed against them. The Constitution does not justify them in making such a request, nor this House in granting it. . . .

    Matters may go smoothly enough when one House asks the other to punish a member who is offensive to a majority of its own body; but how will it be when, upon a pretense of insulted dignity, demands are made of this House to expel a member who happens to run counter to its party predilections, or other demands which may not be so agreeable to grant? It could never have been designed by the Constitution of the United States to expose the two Houses to such temptations to collision, or to extend so far the discretionary power which was given to either House to punish its own members for the violation of its rules and orders. Discretion has been said to be the law of the tyrant, and when exercised under the color of the law, and under the influence of party dictation, it may and will become a terrible and insufferable despotism. . . .

    So far as public interests and constitutional rights are involved, I have now exhausted my means of defense. I may, then, be allowed to take a more personal view of the question at issue. . . .

Sir, I cannot, on my own account, assume the responsibility, in the face of the American people, of commencing a line of conduct which in my heart of hearts I believe would result in subverting the foundations of this Government, and in drenching this Hall in blood. No act of mine, and on my personal account, shall inaugurate revolution; but when you, Mr. Speaker, return to your home, and hear the people of the great North—and they are a great people— speak of me as a bad man, you will do me the justice to say that a blow struck by me at this time would be followed by revolution—and this I know. . . .

At the same time, Mr. Speaker, I am not willing to see the Constitution wounded through me; nor will I submit voluntarily to a wrong if I can avoid it. I will not voluntarily give my name to countenance parliamentary misrule or constitutional aggression. If I am to be tried again for the matter now before us, I will choose my own tribunal. I will appeal from this House to my own constituents. If an expression of public opinion is to be invoked in my case, let my constituents and my fellow-citizens pronounce upon it. From that verdict I will not appeal. The temper of the times is not favorable for a calm and dispassionate judgment of the case; and if, by any act of mine, I can save the majority of this House from the consequences of a rash deci-sion, the time may come when the good men who are pursuing me—and I believe there are such in the Opposition—will admit that I deserve their thanks for the deed. The ax that is uplifted to strike me may fall upon others, and fall upon them after they have parted with the shield of the Constitution to protect them.

For myself I have only to say that, if I cannot preserve my self-respect and constitutional rights, together with a seat in this body, I must renounce the last rather than the former.

I have no desire, sir, to continue an argument which my friends have exhausted. The deter-mination of the majority is fixed, and it is vain to resist it. I will make no appeal to a packed jury, but I protest against its inconsistencies and usurpations. . . . At the first session of the last Congress a member leaped from his seat, and, while the Speaker was in his chair, he passed over several tables toward his antagonist, who drew a weapon in defense, and neither gentleman was subject to the censure of this House. . . .

And yet, sir, the vote which has just been taken transmits me to prosperity as a man unwor-thy, in the judgment of a majority of my peers, of a seat in this Hall. And for what? The mem-ber from New Jersey, [Mr. Pennington]—the prosecuting member . . . says it was for making a "murderous" assault with a "bludgeon;" and he, forsooth, would have the House and the coun-try believe, with an intent to kill. Now, sir, I see that a very respectable and excellent gentleman from Massachusetts has in his hand a cane of the ordinary size for a gentleman of his age, and I beg him to raise it for inspection of the member from New Jersey. . . . Now, sir, I ask that mem-ber to answer as a gentleman—I beg his pardon, that is a word which he cannot compre-hend—but as a man on the witness-stand, is not that cane double the weight and thickness of the one used by me, and which you have impudently and falsely called a "bludgeon?" . . .

If I desired to kill the Senator, why did not I do it? You all admit that I had him in my power. Let me tell the member from New Jersey that it was expressly to avoid taking life that I used an ordinary cane. . . . I went to work very deliberately, as I am charged—and this is admit-ted—and speculated somewhat as to whether I should employ a horsewhip or a cowhide; but knowing that the Senator was my superior in strength, it occurred to me that he might wrest it from my hand, and then—for I never attempt anything I do not perform—I might have been compelled to do that which I would have regretted the balance of my natural life.

The question has been asked in certain newspapers, why did I not invite the Senator to per-sonal combat in the mode usually adopted. Well, sir, as I desire the whole truth to be known about the matter, I will for once notice as newspaper article on the floor of the House, and answer here.

Harcourt Brace & Company

My answer is, that I knew the Senator would not accept a message, and having formed an unalterable determination to punish him, I believed that the offense of "sending a hostile message," superadded to the indictment for assault and battery, would subject me to legal penalties more severe than would be imposed for a simple assault and battery. . . .

For this act, which the Senate, with a solitary exception . . . , have pronounced me guilty of a breach of its privileges—for this act I am complained of by that body to this House. Your committee have declared, and this House has now concurred in the opinion, that my offense is to the Senate, and that no rule or order of this body is violated. . . .

Now, Mr. Speaker, I have nearly finished what I intended to say. If my opponents, who have pursued me with an unparalleled bitterness, are satisfied with the present condition of this affair, I am. I return my thanks to my friends, and especially to those who are from non-slaveowning States, who have magnanimously sustained me, and felt that it was a higher honor to themselves to be just in their judgment of a gentleman than to be a member of Congress for life. In taking my leave, I feel that it is proper that I should say that I believe some of the votes which have been cast against me have been extorted by an outside pressure at home, and that their votes do not express the feelings or opinions of the members who gave them.

To such of these as have given their votes and made their speeches on the constitutional principles involved, and without indulging in personal vilification, I owe my respect. But, sir, they have written me down upon the history of the country as worthy of expulsion, and in no unkindness I must tell them that for all future time my self-respect requires that I shall pass them as strangers.

And now, Mr. Speaker, I announce to you and to this House, that I am no longer a member of the Thirty-Fourth Congress.

President Buchanan Vetoes the Homestead Act, 1860*

Since the earliest years of the republic, the United States had approved a variety of land policies in an effort to encourage western settlement. Land sales, however, provided a major source of income for the nation, so the issue could be quite complex. The Republican party advocated giving much of the land away (they also wanted a high tariff that would compensate for lost revenue) as an effort to develop the West and promote economic growth. Southerners, not surprisingly, viewed any homestead bill as an anti-slavery conspiracy because such a law would create small farms using free labor. Despite southern resistance, Congress approved a Homestead Act in 1860, which President James Buchanan vetoed. In his veto message, Buchanan pointed out specific reservations to the bill, none of which involved slavery. At the same time, he raised broader political concerns about the power and responsibility of the national government.

I return with my objections to the Senate, in which it originated, the bill entitled "An act to secure to actual settlers on the public domain, and for other purposes," presented to me on the 20th instant.

This bill gives to every citizen of the United States "who is head of a family," and to every person of foreign birth residing in the country who has declared his intentions to become a citizen, though he may not be the head of a family, the privilege of appropriating to himself 160 acres of Government land, of settling and residing upon it for five years; and should his resi-

---

*From *A Compilation of the Messages and Papers of the Presidents, 1789–1897*, 10 vols., comp. James D. Richardson (Washington, D.C.: U.S. Government Printing Office, 1896–1899), IV:608–14.

dence continue until the end of this period, he shall then receive a patent on the payment of 25 cents per acre, or one-fifth of the present Government price. During this period the land is protected from all the debts of the settler.

This bill also contains a cession to the States of all the public lands within their respective limits "which have been subject to sale at private entry, and which remain unsold after the lapse of thirty years." This provision embraces a present donation to the States of 12,229,731 acres, and will from time to time transfer to them large bodies of such lands which from peculiar circumstances may not be absorbed by private purchase and settlement.

To the actual settler this bill does not make an absolute donation, but the price is so small that it can scarcely be called a sale. It is nominally 25 cents per acre, but considering that it is not to be paid until the end of five years, it is in fact reduced to about 18 cents per acre, or one-seventh of the present minimum price of the public lands. In regard to the States, it is an absolute and unqualified gift.

1. This state of the facts raises the question whether Congress, under the Constitution, has the power to give away public lands either to States or individuals. On this question I expressed a decided opinion in my message to the House of Representatives . . . returning the agricultural-college bill. This opinion remains unchanged. The argument then used applies as a constitutional objection with greater force to the present bill. There it had the plea of consideration growing out of a specific beneficial purpose; here it is an absolute gratuity to the States, without the pretext of consideration. . . .

I presume the general proposition will be admitted that Congress does not possess the power to make donations of money already in the Treasury, raised by taxes on the people, either to States or individuals.

But it is contended that the public lands are placed upon a different footing from money raised by taxation and that the proceeds arising from their sale are not subject to the limitations of the Constitution, but may be appropriated or given away by Congress, at its own discretion, to States, corporations, or individuals for any purpose they may deem expedient. . . .

It would require clear and strong evidence to induce the belief that the framers of the Constitution, after having limited the powers of Congress to certain precise and specific objects, intended . . . to give that body unlimited power over the vast public domain. It would be a strange anomaly indeed to have created two funds—the one by taxation, confined to the execution of the enumerated powers delegated to Congress, and the other from the public lands, applicable to all subjects, foreign and domestic, which Congress might designate; that this fund should be "disposed of," not to pay the debts of the United States, nor "to raise and support armies," nor "to provide and maintain a navy," nor to accomplish any one of the great objects enumerated in the Constitution, but be diverted from them to pay the debts of the States, to educate their people, and to carry into effect any other measure of their domestic policy. This would be to confer upon Congress a vast and irresponsible authority utterly at war with the well-known jealousy of Federal power which prevailed at the formation of the Constitution. The natural intendment would be that as the Constitution confined Congress to well-defined specific powers, the funds placed at their command, whether in land or money, should be appropriated to the performance of the duties corresponding with those powers. If not, a Government has been created with all its other powers carefully limited, but without any limitation in respect to the public lands. . . .

2. It will prove unequal and unjust in its operation among the actual settlers themselves.

The first settlers of a new country are a meritorious class. They brave the dangers of savage warfare, suffer the privations of a frontier life, and with the hand of toil bring the wilderness into cultivation. The "old settlers," as they are everywhere called, are public benefactors. This class have all paid for their lands the Government price, or $1.25 per acre. They have constructed roads, established schools, and laid the foundations of prosperous commonwealths. Is it just, is it equal, that after they have accomplished all this by their labor new settlers should come in among them and receive their farms at the price of 25 cents or 18 cents per acre? Surely the old settlers, as a class, are entitled to at least equal benefits with the new. If you give the new settlers their land for a comparatively nominal price, upon every principle of equality and justice you will be obliged to refund out of the common Treasury the difference which the old have paid above the new settlers for the land.

3. This bill will do great injustice to the old soldiers who have received land warrants for their services in fighting the battles of their country. It will greatly reduce the market value of these warrants. Already their value has sunk for 160-acre warrants to 67 cents per acre under an apprehension that such a measure as this might become a law. What price would they command when any head of a family may take possession of a quarter section of land and not pay until the end of five years, and then at the rate of only 25 cents per acre? The magnitude of the interest to be affected will appear in the fact that there are outstanding unsatisfied land warrants reaching back to the last war with Great Britain, and even Revolutionary times, amounting in round numbers to seven and a half million acres of land.

4. This bill will prove unequal and unjust in its operation, because from its nature it is confined to one class of our people. It is a boon exclusively conferred upon the cultivators of the soil. Whilst it is cheerfully admitted that these are the most numerous and useful class of our fellow-citizens and eminently deserve all the advantages which our laws have already extended to them, yet there should be no new legislation which would operate to the injury or embarrassment of the large body of respectable artisans and laborers. The mechanic who emigrates to the West and pursues his calling must labor long before he can purchase a quarter section of land, whilst the tiller of the soil who accompanies him obtains a farm at once by the bounty of the Government. The numerous body of mechanics in our large cities can not, even by emigrating to the West, take advantage of the provisions of this bill without entering upon a new occupation for which their habits of life have rendered them unfit.

5. This bill is unjust to the old States of the Union in many respects; and amongst these States, so far as the public lands are concerned, we may enumerate every State east of the Mississippi with the exception of Wisconsin and a portion of Minnesota.

It is a common belief within their limits that the older States of the Confederacy do not derive their proportionate benefit from the public lands. This is not just an opinion. It is doubtful whether they could be rendered more beneficial to these States under any other system than that which at present exists. Their proceeds go into the common Treasury to accomplish the objects of the Government, and in this manner all the States are benefited in just proportion. But to give this common inheritance away would deprive the old States of their just proportion of this revenue without holding out any of the least corresponding advantages. Whilst it is our common glory that the new States have become so prosperous and populous, there is no good reason why the old States should offer premiums to their own citizens to emigrate from them to the West. That land of promise presents in itself sufficient allurements to our young and enterprising citizens without any adventitious aid. The offer of free farms would probably have a powerful effect in encouraging emigration, especially from the States like Illinois, Tennessee, and Kentucky, to the west of the Mississippi, and could not fail to reduce the price of property within their limits. An individual in States thus situated would not pay its fair value for land when by crossing the Mississippi he could go upon the public lands and obtain a farm almost without money and without price.

6. The bill will open one vast field for speculation. Men will not pay $1.25 for lands when they can purchase them for one-fifth of that price. Large numbers of actual settlers will be carried out by capitalists upon agreements to give them half of the land for the improvement of

the other half. This can not be avoided. Secret agreements of this kind will be numerous. In the entry of graduated land the experience of the Land Office justifies this objection.

7. We ought to maintain the most perfect equality between native and naturalized citizens. They are equal, and ought always to remain equal, before the laws. Our laws welcome foreigners to our shores, and their rights will ever be respected. Whilst these are the sentiments on which I have acted through life, it is not, in my opinion, expedient to proclaim to all the nations of the earth that whoever shall arrive in this country from a foreign shore and declare his intention to become a citizen shall receive a farm of 160 acres at a cost of 25 or 20 cents per acre if he will only reside on it and cultivate it. The invitation extends to all, and if this bill becomes a law we may have numerous actual settlers from China and other Eastern nations enjoying its benefits on the great Pacific Slope. The bill makes a distinction in favor of such persons over native and naturalized citizens. When applied to such citizens, it is confined to such as are heads of families, but when applicable to persons of foreign birth recently arrived on our shores there is no such restriction. Such persons need not be the heads of families provided they have filed a declaration of intention to become citizens. Perhaps this distinction was an inadvertence, but it is, nevertheless, a part of the bill.

8. The bill creates an unjust distinction between persons claiming the benefit of the pre-emption laws. Whilst it reduces the price of the land to existing preemptors to 62 1/2 cents per acre and gives them a credit on this sum for two years from the present date, no matter how long they may have hitherto enjoyed the land, future preemptors will be compelled to pay double this price per acre. There is no reason or justice in this discrimination.

9. The effect of this bill on the public revenue must be apparent to all. Should it become a law, the reduction of the price of land to actual settlers to 25 cents per acre, with a credit of five years, and the reduction of its price to existing preemptors to 62 1/2 cents per acre, with a credit of two years, will so diminish the sale of other public lands as to render the expectation of future revenue from that source, beyond the expenses of survey and management, illusory. The Secretary of the Interior estimated the revenue from the public lands for the next fiscal year at $4,000,000, on the presumption that the present land system would remain unchanged. Should this bill become a law, he does not believe that $1,000,000 will be derived from this source.

10. This bill lays the ax at the root of our present and admirable land system. The public land is an inheritance of vast value to us and to our descendants. It is a resource to which we can resort in the hour of difficulty and danger. It has been managed heretofore with the greatest wisdom under existing laws. In this management the rights of actual settlers have been conciliated with the interests of the Government. The price to all has been reduced from $2 per acre to $1.25 for fresh lands, and the claims of actual settlers have been secured by our pre-emption laws. Any man can now acquire a title in fee simple to a homestead of 80 acres, at the minimum price of $1.25 per acre, for $100. Should the present system remain, we shall derive a revenue from public lands of $10,000,000 per annum, when the bounty-land warrants are satisfied, without oppression to any human being. In time of war, when all other sources of revenue are seriously impaired, this will remain intact. It may become the best security for public loans hereafter, in times of difficulty and danger, as it has been heretofore. Why should we impair or destroy the system at the present moment? What necessity exists for it?

The people of the United States have advanced with steady but rapid strides to their present condition of power and prosperity. They have been guided in their progress by the fixed principle of protecting the equal rights of all, whether they be rich or poor. No agrarian sentiment has ever prevailed among them. The honest poor man, by frugality and industry, can in any part of our country acquire a competence for himself and his family, and in doing this he feels that he eats the bread of independence. He desires no charity, either from the Government or from his neighbors. This bill, which proposes to give him land at an almost nominal price out of the property of the Government, will go far to demoralize the people and repress this noble spirit of independence. It may introduce among us those pernicious social theories which have proved so disastrous in other countries.

John Brown's Statement to the Court, 1859*

The North and the South moved further and further apart during the 1850s, and John Brown's raid on Harpers Ferry provided an alarming end to the violent decade. Brown apparently planned to obtain weapons that could be used in an insurrection that would destroy slavery. He failed. Federal troops captured him, authorities put him on trial for treason, and the judge sentenced him to be hanged. In an eloquent statement to the court, presented below, Brown explained his mission. Northerners embraced the remarks as a martyr's final, compassionate words. Southerners viewed Brown differently, and he symbolized the threat that northern power posed to southern liberties. Throughout the 1850s, emotions had been inflamed, blood had been spilled, lives had been lost. Americans would elect a president in 1860 hoping that the crisis could be averted, but fearing that it could not.

I have, may it please the Court, a few words to say. In the first place, I deny everything but what I have all along admitted, of a design on my part to free slaves. I intended certainly to have made a clean thing of that matter, as I did last winter when I went into Missouri, and there took slaves without the snapping of a gun on either side, moving them through the country, and finally leaving them in Canada. I designed to have done the same thing again on a larger scale. That was all I intended to do. I never did intend murder or treason, or the destruction of property, or to excite or incite the slaves to rebellion, or to make insurrection. I have another objection, and that is that it is unjust that I should suffer such a penalty. Had I interfered in the manner which I admit, and which I admit has been fairly proved—for I admire the truthfulness and candor of the greater portion of the witnesses who have testified in this case—had I so interfered in behalf of the rich, the powerful, the intelligent, the so-called great, or in behalf of any of their friends, either father, mother, brother, sister, wife, children, or any of that class, and suffered and sacrificed what I have in this interference, it would have been all right, and every man in this Court would have deemed it an act worthy of reward rather than punishment. This Court acknowledges, too, as I suppose, the validity of the law of God. I see a book kissed, which I suppose to be the Bible, or at least the New Testament, which teaches me that all things whatsoever I would that men should do to me, I should do even so to them. I endeavored to act up to that instruction. I say I am yet too young to understand that God is any respecter of persons. I believe to have interfered as I have done, as I have always freely admitted I have done in behalf of His despised poor, is no wrong, but right. Now, if it is deemed necessary that I should forfeit my life for the furtherance of the ends of justice, and mingle my blood further with the blood of my children, and with the blood of millions in this slave country whose rights are disregarded by wicked, cruel, and unjust enactments, I say let it be done. Let me say one word further. I feel entirely satisfied with the treatment I have received on my trial. Considering all the circumstances, it has been more generous than I expected. But I feel no consciousness of guilt. I have stated from the first what is my intention, and what was not. I never had any design against the liberty of any person, nor any disposition to commit treason or excite slaves to rebel or make any general insurrection. I never encouraged any man to do so, but always discouraged any idea

---

*From *The Life, Trial, and Execution of Captain John Brown* (New York: Robert M. De Witt, 1859), 94–95.

of that kind. Let me say also in regard to the statements by some of those who were connected with me, I fear it has been stated by some of them that I have induced them to join me, but
the contrary is true. I do not say this to injure them, but as regretting their weakness. Not one
but joined me of his own accord, and the greater part at their own expense. A number of them
I never saw, and never had a word of conversation with till the day they came to me, and that
was for the purpose I have stated. Now I am done.

Discussion

1. Why do you think Samuel Morse expressed such fear of the power of the pope, the Jesuits,
    and the St. Leopold Foundation? How and why do you think he saw them as a threat to lib-
    erty and equality? How are his fears similar to or different than the rhetoric of revolutionary
    Americans? How might Republicans have appealed to anti-Catholic nativists to turn their
    anger against southerners?

2. What did Charles Sumner say that made Preston Brooks so angry? How might Brooks have
    justified his attack on Sumner? Do you agree with Brooks's contention that the House of
    Representatives did not have the power to punish him? Why or why not? How might each
    of the two men have argued that the other threatened liberty?

3. How did President James Buchanan express concepts of liberty and equality in his veto of the
    homestead law? What do you think he believed about the power of the national government?
    How might the Republicans have dismissed his comments and insisted that his veto was really
    a pro-slavery statement? Was it a good idea for the government to give away land?

4. How do you think John Brown might have defined liberty and equality? Who do you think
    John Brown believed held power in the United States? Is there anything in his comments to
    suggest that he was not guilty of treason?

5. John Brown insisted that he did not feel any guilt for his raid on Harpers Ferry? Why might
    he have felt that way? What are the implications for power and liberty of such a stance? The
    power of the state executed John Brown, but southerners still feared for their liberties. Why
    do you think they believed that the government could not or would not protect slavery?

Chapter 16
Secession and Civil War, 1860–1862

ABE LINCOLN'S LAST CARD; OR, ROUGE-ET-NOIR.

Most English newspapers and illustrators were either hostile or indifferent to the Northern cause. Here a desperate Abraham Lincoln plays the black ace representing emancipation of the slaves. Jefferson Davis keeps his cards hidden from view.

W *ith the election of 1860, the acrimonious debate over slavery became a bitter war over states' rights and secession. The fundamental question was the nature of the Union under the Constitution. The South claimed that the compact allowed states to secede as an expression of their sovereignty, and, despite the reluctance of many southerners to leave the Union, seven states withdrew by the time Abraham Lincoln became president in March of 1861. Lincoln insisted that no such right of secession existed, and his commitment to the Union led to a crisis at Fort Sumter that brought on war. Once the fighting began, he used the full force of the government to preserve the nation. Southerners, too, fought with all their will. Ironically, each side declared that the other threatened liberty. The South feared that an assertion of federal power would overturn slavery and thereby destroy the one institution that guaranteed equality for white Americans. Lincoln insisted that liberty could only be preserved by a republican government that represented the will of the people. If the southern states left the Union because of discontent with an election, the American experiment in self-government would have failed and liberty would be denied to all.*

A Southerner Speaks Against Secession, 1861*

I n the following speech presented to the Georgia Secession Convention, Alexander H. Stephens urged delegates to move slowly on a decision so monumental as disunion. Like many southerners, however, Stephens swore to support secession wholeheartedly if his state withdrew from the Union. Georgia rejected his counsel and seceded. Stephens honored his promise by becoming the vice president of the Confederacy.

It is well known that my judgment is against secession for existing causes. I have not lost hope of securing our rights in the Union and under the Constitution. My judgment on this point is as unshaken as it was when the Convention was called. I do not now intend to go into my arguments on the subject. No good could be effected by it. That was fully considered in the late canvass, and I doubt not every delegate's mind is made up on the question. I have thought, and still think, that we should not take this extreme step before some positive aggression upon our rights by the General Government, which may never occur; or until we fail, after effort made, to get a faithful performance of their Constitutional obligations, on the part of those Confederate States which now stand so derelict in their plighted faith. I have been, and am still opposed to Secession as a remedy against anticipated aggressions on the part of the Federal Executive, or Congress. I have held, and do now hold, that the point of resistance should be the point of aggression.

Pardon me, Mr. President, for trespassing on your time but for a moment longer. I have ever believed, and do now believe, that it is to the interest of all the States to be and remain united under the Constitution of the United States, with a faithful performance by each of all its con-

*From Alexander H. Stephens, *A Constitutional View of the Late War Between the States . . .*, 2 vols. (Philadelphia: National Publishing Company, 1870), II:305–307.

stitutional obligations. If the Union could be maintained on this basis, and on these principles, I think it would be the best for the security, the liberty, happiness, and common prosperity of all. I do further feel confident, if Georgia would now stand firm, and unite with the Border States, as they are called, in an effort to obtain a redress of these grievances on the part of some of their Northern Confederates, whereof they have such just cause to complain, that complete success would be granted. In this opinion I may be mistaken, but I feel almost as confident of it as I do of my existence. Hence, if upon this test vote, which I trust will be made on the motion pending, to refer both the propositions before us to a committee of twenty-one, a majority shall vote to commit them, then I shall do all I can to perfect the plan of a united Southern co-operation, submitted by the honorable delegate from Jefferson, and put it in such a shape as will, in the opinion of the Convention, best secure its object. That object, as I understand it, does not look to Secession by the 16th of February, or the 4th of March, if redress should not be obtained by that time. In my opinion, it cannot be obtained by the 16th of February, or even the 4th of March. But by the 16th of February we can see whether the Border States and other non-seceding Southern States will respond to our call for the proposed Congress or Convention at Atlanta. If they do, as I trust they may, then that body, so composed of representatives, or delegates, or commissioners as contemplated, from the whole of the slaveholding States, could, and would I doubt not, adopt either our plan or some other, which would fully secure our rights with ample guarantees, and thus preserve and maintain the ultimate peace and Union of the States. Whatever plan of peaceful adjustment might be adopted by such a Congress, I feel confident would be acceded to by the people of every Northern State. This would not be done in a month, or two months, or perhaps short of twelve months, or even longer. Time would necessarily have to be allowed for a consideration of the question submitted to the people of the Northern States, and for their deliberate action on them in view of all their interests, present, and future. How long a time should be allowed, would be a proper question for that Congress to determine. Meanwhile, this Convention could continue its existence, by adjourning over to hear and decide upon the ultimate result of this patriotic effort.

My judgment, as is well known, is against the policy of immediate Secession for any existing causes. It cannot receive the sanction of my vote; but if the judgment of a majority of this Convention, embodying as it does the Sovereignty of Georgia, be against mine; if a majority of the delegates in this Convention shall, by their votes, dissolve the Compact of the Union which has now connected her so long with her Confederate States, and to which I have been so ardently attached, and have made such efforts to continue and perpetuate upon the principles on which it was founded, I shall bow in submission to that decision.

A Southerner Speaks For Secession, 1861*

Opponents to secession, such as Alexander Stephens, could only advise moderation and offer vague promises of a resolution. Many southerners believed that by 1861 they had already shown abundant patience. They understood, as had their forefathers, that power often threatened liberty. They, too, feared the forces that could conspire to destroy their rights, and they saw the Republican electoral victory as such a conspiracy. In a speech to his colleagues, U.S. Senator from Georgia Robert Toombs presented the concerns that he and other secessionists had. Despite the Dred Scott case, President Lincoln and Republican Congressmen had vowed to prohibit the expansion of slavery. To Toombs, the Republican insistence on ignoring the Supreme Court decision was an unconstitutional usurpation of power that justified leaving the Union.

---

*From *The Congressional Globe,* 36th Congress, 2d Session, 1861, 269.

Harcourt Brace & Company

Senators, the Constitution is a compact. It contains all our obligations and duties of the Federal Government. I am content, and have ever been content, to sustain it. While I doubt its perfection; while I do not believe it was a good compact; and while I never saw the day that I would have voted for it as a proposition *de novo*, yet I am bound to it by oath and by that common prudence which would induce men to abide by established forms, rather than to rush into unknown dangers. I have given to it, and intend to give to it, unfaltering support and allegiance; but I choose to put that allegiance on the true ground, not on the false idea that anybody's blood was shed for it. I say that the Constitution is the whole compact. All the obligations, all the chains that fetter the limbs of my people, are nominated in the bond, and they wisely excluded any conclusion against them, by declaring that the powers not granted by the Constitution to the United States, or forbidden by it to the States, belonged to the States respectively or the people. Now I will try it by that standard; I will subject it to that test. The law of nature, the law of justice, would say—and it is so expounded by the publicists—that equal rights in the common property shall be enjoyed. Even in a monarchy the king cannot prevent the subjects from enjoying equality in the disposition of the public property. Even in a despotic Government this principle is recognized. It was the blood and money of the whole people (says the learned Grotius, and say all the publicists) which acquired the public property, and therefore it is not the property of the sovereign. This right of equality being, then, according to justice and natural equity, a right belonging to all States, when did we give it up? You say Congress has a right to pass rules and regulations concerning the Territory and other property of the United States. Very well. Does that exclude those whose blood and money paid for it? Does "dispose of" mean to rob the rightful owners? You must show a better title than that, or a better sword than we have.

But, you say, try the right. I agree to it. But how? By our judgment? No, not until the last resort. What then; by yours? No, not until the same time. How then try it? The South has always said by the Supreme Court. But that is in our favor, and Lincoln says he will not stand that judgment. Then each much judge for himself of the mode and manner of redress. But you deny us that privilege, and finally reduce us to accepting your judgment. We decline it. You say you will enforce it by executing laws; that means your judgment of what the laws ought to be. Perhaps you will have a good time of executing that judgment. The Senator from Kentucky comes to your aid, and says he can find no constitutional right of secession. Perhaps not; but the Constitution is not the place to look for State rights. If that right belongs to the independent States, and they did not cede it to the Federal Government, it is reserved to the States, or to the people. Ask your new commander where he gets your right to judge for us. Is it in the bond?

The northern doctrine was, many years ago, that the Supreme Court was the judge. That was the doctrine in 1800. They denounced Madison for the report of 1799, on the Virginia resolutions; they denounced Jefferson for framing the Kentucky resolutions, because they were presumed to impugn the decisions of the Supreme Court of the United States; and they declared that that court was made, by the Constitution, the ultimate and supreme arbiter. That was the universal judgment—the declaration of every free State in this Union, in answer to the Virginia resolutions of 1798, or of all who did answer, even including the State of Delaware, then under Federal control.

The Supreme Court have decided that, by the Constitution, we have a right to go to the Territories and be protected there with our property. You say, we cannot decide the compact for ourselves. Well, can the Supreme Court decide it for us? Mr. Lincoln says he does not care what the Supreme Court decides, he will turn us out anyway. He says this in the debate with the honorable Senator from Illinois, [Mr. Douglas.] [.] I have it before me. He said he would vote against the decision of the Supreme Court. Then you do not accept the arbiter. You will not take my construction; you will not take the Supreme Court as an arbiter; you will not take the treaties under Jefferson and Madison; you will not take the opinion of Madison upon the very question of prohibition in 1820. You will take nothing but your own judgment; that is, you not only judge for yourselves, not only discard the court, discard our construction, discard the practice of the Government, but you will drive us out, simply because you will it. Come and do it! You have sapped the foundations of society; you have destroyed almost all hope of peace. In a compact where there is no common arbiter, where the parties finally decide for themselves, the sword alone at last becomes the real, if not the constitutional, arbiter. Your party says that you will not take the decision of the Supreme Court. You said so at Chicago; you said so in committee; every man of you in both Houses says so. What are you going to do? You say *we shall submit to your construction.* We shall do it, if you can make us; but not otherwise, or in any other manner. That is settled. You may call it secession, or you may call it revolution; but there is a big fact standing before you—that fact is, freemen with arms in their hands. The cry of the Union will not disperse them; we have passed that point; they demand equal rights; you had better heed the demand. . . .

An Ordinance of Secession, 1861*

The Texas act of secession is typical of other such ordinances in its indictment of the federal government for violating the Constitution and for posing a threat to the property of southerners. Texans, on the other hand, added the charge that national authorities had failed to protect the frontier by ending Indian raids. Unlike the other seceding states, Texas was the only state to present the issue to the voters.

AN ORDINANCE To dissolve the union between the State of Texas and the other States, united under the compact styled "The Constitution of the United States of America."

Whereas, the Federal Government has failed to accomplish the purposes of the compact of union between the States, in giving protection either to the persons of our people upon an exposed frontier, or to the property of our citizens; and, whereas, the action of the Northern States of the Union is violative of the compact between the States and the guarantees of the Constitution; and, whereas, the recent development in Federal affairs, make it evident that the power of the Federal Government is sought to make a weapon with which to strike down the interest and prosperity of the people of Texas and her sister slaveholding States, instead of permitting it to be, as was intended, our shield against outrage and aggression: therefore,

SECTION 1. We, the People of the State of Texas, by delegates in Convention assembled, Do declare and ordain, that the ordinance adopted by our convention of delegates, on the 4th day of July, A. D. 1845, and afterwards ratified by us, under which the Republic of Texas was admitted into union with other States and became a party to the compact styled "The Constitution of the United States of America," be, and is hereby repealed and annulled; that all the powers, which by said compact were delegated by Texas to the Federal Government, are revoked and resumed; that Texas is of right absolved from all restraints and obligations incurred by said compact, and is a separate sovereign State, and that her citizens and people are absolved from all allegiance to the United States, or the Government thereof.

Sec. 2. This ordinance shall be submitted to the people of Texas for their ratification or rejection by the qualified voters thereof, on the 23d day of February, 1861, and, unless rejected by a

---

*From "AN ORDINANCE to dissolve the union between the State of Texas and the other States. . . ," February 1, 1861, in *The Laws of Texas,* 10 vols., ed. H. P. N. Gammel (Austin: Gammel Book Company, 1898), IV:1519–20.

majority of the votes cast, shall take effect and be in force on and after the 2d day of March, A. D. 1861. Provided that in the Representative district of El Paso, said election may be held on the 18th day of February, 1861.

Adopted in Convention, at Austin City, the first day of February, 1861.

The Sumter Crisis, 1861*

Upon his inauguration, Abraham Lincoln faced the difficult task of determining the fate of Fort Sumter. He asked the advice of his cabinet members, and most of them, like Secretary of the Navy Gideon Welles, urged the president not to reinforce or re-supply the post. The majority of the administration proved reluctant to use the power of the government in a way that would turn secession into war. Lincoln, as became typical of his leadership, listened to the various viewpoints and then made his own decision.

In answer to your inquiry of this date, I take it for granted that Fort Sumter cannot be provisioned except by force, and assuming that it is possible to be done by force, is it wise to make the attempt?

The question has two aspects—one military, the other political. The military gentlemen who have been consulted, as well as the officers at the fort, represent that it would be unwise to attempt to succor the garrison under existing circumstance, and I am not disposed to controvert their opinions.

But a plan has been submitted by a gentleman of undoubted courage and intelligence,—not of the army or navy,—to run in supplies by steam tugs, to be chartered in New York. It is admitted to be a hazardous scheme, which, if successful, is likely to be attended with some loss of life and the total destruction of the boats. The force which would constitute the expedition, if undertaken, as well as the officer in command, would not, if I rightly understand the proposition, be of the army or navy. It is proposed to aid and carry out the enterprise by an armed ship at the mouth of the harbor and beyond the range of the shore batteries, which is to drive in the armed boats of the enemy beyond Fort Sumter. But suppose these armed boats of the enemy refuse to go into the inner harbor, as I think they will refuse, and shall station themselves between Sumter and the ship for the express purpose of intercepting your boats, how can you prevent them from taking that station and capturing the tugs? There can be but one way, and that is by opening fire upon them from Sumter, or the ship, or perhaps both. If this is done, will it not be claimed that aggressive war has been commenced by us upon the State and its citizens in their own harbor? It may be possible to provision Fort Sumter by the volunteer expedition, aided by the guns of Sumter and the ship—the military gentlemen admit its possibility, but they question the wisdom of the enterprise in its military aspect, and I would not impeach their conclusion.

In a political view I entertain doubts of the wisdom of the measure, when the condition of the public mind in different sections of the country, and the peculiar exigency of affairs, are considered. Notwithstanding the hostile attitude of South Carolina, and her long and expensive preparations, there is a prevailing belief that there will be no actual collision. An impression has gone abroad that Sumter is to be evacuated, and the shock caused by that announcement has done its work. The public mind is becoming tranquilized under it, and will become fully reconciled to it when the causes which have led to that necessity shall have been made public and

---

*From Gideon Welles to Abraham Lincoln, March 15, 1861, in *Complete Works of Abraham Lincoln,* ed. John G. Nicolay and John Hay, 12 vols. (New York: Lamb Publishing Company, 1905), VI:208–10.

are rightly understood. They are attributable to no act of those who now administer the government.

By sending or attempting to send provisions into Sumter, will not war be precipitated? It may be impossible to escape it under any course of policy that may be pursued, but I am not prepared to advise a course that would provoke hostilities. It does not appear to me that the dignity, strength, or character of the government will be promoted by an attempt to provision Sumter in the manner proposed, even should it succeed, while a failure would be attended with untold disaster.

I do not, therefore, under all the circumstances, think it wise to attempt to provision Fort Sumter.

President Abraham Lincoln Addresses Congress, 1861*

When Congress convened in special session in the summer of 1861, President Abraham Lincoln presented representatives with a summary of the events surrounding the outbreak of war with the Confederacy. In the following selection, he gave an explanation of his decision to re-supply Fort Sumter, the specific act that sparked the fighting. He also defended his suspension of the right to *habeas corpus,* an act that generated widespread criticism. Finally, Lincoln offered his understanding of states' rights, the nature of the Constitution, and the responsibility of the national government. He clearly saw the war as an effort to save the Union and by so doing preserving liberty. The passage underscored Lincoln's commitment to that cause, and it revealed the tremendous intellectual capability that Lincoln brought to the task.

Having been convened on an extraordinary occasion, as authorized by the Constitution, your attention is not called to any ordinary subject of legislation.

At the beginning of the present Presidential term, four months ago, the functions of the Federal Government were found to be generally suspended within the several States of South Carolina, Georgia, Alabama, Mississippi, Louisiana, and Florida, excepting only those of the Post Office Department.

Within these States all the forts, arsenals, dockyards, custom-houses, and the like, including the movable and stationary property in and about them, had been seized and were held in open hostility to this Government, excepting only Forts Pickens, Taylor, and Jefferson, on and near the Florida coast, and Fort Sumter, in Charleston Harbor, South Carolina. The forts thus seized had been in improved condition, new ones had been built, and armed forces had been organized and were organizing, all avowedly with the same hostile purpose.

The forts remaining in the possession of the Federal Government in and near these States were either besieged or menaced by warlike preparations, and especially Fort Sumter was nearly surrounded by well-protected hostile batteries, with guns equal in quality to the best of its own and outnumbering the latter as perhaps ten to one. A disproportionate share of the Federal muskets and rifles had somehow found their way into these States, and had been seized to be used against the Government. Accumulations of the public revenue lying within them had been seized for the same object. The Navy was scattered in distant seas, leaving but a very small part of it within the immediate reach of the Government. Officers of the Federal Army and Navy had resigned in great numbers, and of those resigning a large proportion had taken up arms

---

*From "Special Session Message," July 4, 1861, in *A Compilation of the Messages and Papers of the Presidents, 1789–1897,* 10 vols., comp. James D. Richardson (Washington, D.C.: U.S. Government Printing Office, 1896–1899), VI:20–31.

against the Government. Simultaneously and in connection with all this the purpose to sever the Federal Union was openly avowed. In accordance with this purpose, an ordinance had been adopted in each of these States declaring the States respectively to be separated from the National Union. A formula for instituting a combined government of these States had been promulgated, and this illegal organization, in the character of Confederate States, was already invoking recognition, aid, and intervention from foreign powers.

Finding this condition of things and believing it to be an imperative duty upon the incoming Executive to prevent, if possible, the consummation of such attempt to destroy the Federal Union, a choice of means to that end became indispensable. This choice was made, and was declared in the inaugural address. The policy chosen looked to the exhaustion of all peaceful measures before a resort to any stronger ones. It sought only to hold the public places and property not already wrested from the Government and to collect the revenue, relying for the rest on time, discussion, and the ballot box. It promised a continuance of the mails at Government expense to the very people who were resisting the Government, and it gave repeated pledges against any disturbance to any of the people and any of their rights. Of all that which a President might constitutionally and justifiably do in such a case, everything was forborne without which it was believed possible to keep the Government on foot.

On the 5th of March, the present incumbent's first full day in office, a letter of Major Anderson, commanding at Fort Sumter, . . . expressed the professional opinion of the writer that reinforcements could not be thrown into that fort within the time for his relief rendered necessary by the limited supply of provisions, and with a view of holding possession of the same, with a force of less than 20,000 good and well-disciplined men. . . . Lieutenant-General Scott . . . stated . . . that no such sufficient force was then at the control of the Government or could be raised and brought to the ground in the time when the provisions on the fort would be exhausted. In a purely military point of view this reduced the duty of the Administration in the case to the mere matter of getting the garrison safely out of the fort.

It was believed, however, that to so abandon that position under the circumstances would be utterly ruinous; that the *necessity* under which it was done would not be fully understood; that by many it would be construed as a part of a *voluntary* policy; that at home it would discourage the friends of the Union, embolden its adversaries, and go far to ensure the latter a recognition abroad; that, in fact, it would be our national destruction consummated. This could not be allowed. Starvation was not yet upon the garrison, and ere it would be reached, *Fort Pickens* might be reenforced. This last would be a clear indication of *policy,* and would better enable the country to accept the evacuation of Fort Sumter as a military *necessity.* An order was at once directed to be sent for the landing of the troops from the steamship *Brooklyn* into Fort Pickens. This order could not go by land, but must take the longer and slower route by sea. The first return news from the order was received just one week before the fall of Fort Sumter. The news itself was that the officer commanding the *Sabine,* to which vessel the troops had been transferred from the *Brooklyn*, acting upon some *quasi* armistice of the late Administration (and of the existence of which the present Administration, up to the time the order was dispatched, had only too vague and uncertain rumors to fix attention), had refused to land the troops. To now reenforce Fort Pickens before a crisis would be reached at Fort Sumter was impossible, rendered so by the near exhaustion of provisions in the latter-named fort. In precaution against such a conjecture the Government had a few days before [it] commenced to preparing an expedition, as well adapted as might be, to relieve Fort Sumter, which expedition was intended to be ultimately used or not, according to circumstances. The strongest anticipated case for using it was now presented, and it was resolved to send it forward. As had been intended in this contingency, it was also resolved to notify the governor of South Carolina that he might expect an attempt would be made to provision the fort, and that if the attempt should not be resisted there would be no effort to throw in men, arms, of ammunition without further notice, or in case of an attack upon the fort. This notice was accordingly given, whereupon the fort was attacked and bombarded to its fall, without even awaiting the arrival of the provisioning expedition.

It is thus seen that the assault upon and reduction of Fort Sumter was in no sense a matter of self-defense on the part of the assailants. They well knew that the garrison in the fort could by no possibility commit aggression upon them. They knew—they were expressly notified—that the giving of bread to the few brave and hungry men of the garrison was all which would on that occasion be attempted, unless themselves, by resisting so much, would provoke more. They knew that this Government desired to keep the garrison in the fort, not to assail them, but merely to maintain visible possession, and thus to preserve the Union from actual and immediate dissolution, trusting, as hereinbefore stated, to time, discussion, and the ballot box for a final adjustment; and they assailed and reduced the fort for precisely the reverse object—to drive out the visible authority of the Federal Union, and thus force it to immediate dissolution. That this was their object the Executive well understood; and having said to them in the inaugural address, "You can have no conflict without being yourselves the aggressors," he took pains not only to keep this declaration good, but also to keep the case so free from the power of ingenious sophistry as that the world should not be able to misunderstand it. By the affair at Fort Sumter, with its surrounding circumstance, that point was reached. Then and thereby that assailants of the Government began the conflict of arms, without a gun in sight or in expectancy to return their fire, save only the few in the fort sent to that harbor years before for their own protection, and still ready to give that protection in whatever was lawful. In this act, discarding all else, they have forced upon the country the distinct issue, "Immediate dissolution or blood."

And this issue embraces more than the fate of these United States. It presents to the whole family of man the question whether a constitutional republic, or democracy—a government of the people by the same people—can or can not maintain its territorial integrity against its own domestic foes. It presents the question whether discontented individuals, too few in numbers to control administration according to organic law in any case, can always, upon the pretenses made in this case, or on any other pretenses, or arbitrarily without any pretense, break up their government, and thus practically put an end to free government upon the earth. It forces us to ask, Is there in all republics this inherent and fatal weakness? Must a government of necessity be too *strong* for the liberties of its own people, or too *weak* to maintain its own existence?

So viewing the issue, no choice was left but to call out the war power of the Government and so to resist force employed for its destruction by force for its own preservation. . . .

Soon after the first call for militia it was considered a duty to authorize the Commanding General in proper cases, according to his discretion, to suspend the privilege of the writ of *habeas corpus,* or, in other words, to arrest and detain without resort to the ordinary processes and forms of law such individuals as he might deem dangerous to the public safety. This authority has purposely been executed but very sparingly. Nevertheless, the legality and propriety of what has been done under it are questioned, and the attention of the country has been called to the proposition that one who is sworn to "take care that the laws be faithfully executed," should not himself violate them. Of course some consideration was given to the question of power and propriety before this matter was acted upon. The whole of the laws which were required to be faithfully executed were being resisted and failing of execution in nearly one-third of the States. Must they be allowed to finally fail of execution, even had it been perfectly clear that by the use of the means necessary to their execution some single law, made in such extreme tenderness of the citizen's liberty that practically it relieves more of the guilty than of the innocent, should to a very limited extent be violated? To state the question more directly, Are all the laws *but one* to go unexecuted, and the Government itself go to pieces lest that one be violated? Even in such a case, would not the official oath be broken if the Government should be overthrown when it was believed that disregarding the single law would tend to preserve it? But it was not believed that this question was presented. It was not believed that any law was violated. The provision of the Constitution that "the privilege of the writ of *habeas corpus* shall not be suspended unless when, in cases of rebellion or invasion, the public safety may require it" is equivalent to a provision—is a provision—that such privilege may be suspended when, in cases of rebellion or invasion, the public safety *does* require it. It was decided that we have a case of rebellion and that the public safety does require the qualified suspension of the privilege of the writ which was authorized to be made. Now it is insisted that Congress, and not the Executive, is vested with the power; but the Constitution itself is silent as to which or who is to exercise the power; and as the provision was plainly made for a dangerous emergency, it can not be believed the framers of the instrument intended that in every case the danger should run its course until Congress could be called together, the very assembling of which might be prevented, as was intended in this case, by the rebellion. . . .

It might seem at first thought to be of little difference whether the present movement at the South ought to be called "secession" or "rebellion." The movers, however, will understand the difference. At the beginning they knew they could never raise their treasons to any respectable magnitude by any name which implies *violation* of law. They knew their people possessed as much of moral sense, as much of devotion to law and order, and as much pride in and reverence for the history and Government of their common country as any other civilized and patriotic people. They could make no advancement directly in the teeth of these strong and noble sentiments. Accordingly, they commenced by an insidious debauching of the public mind. They invented an ingenious sophism, which, if conceded, was followed by perfectly logical steps through all the incidents to the complete destruction of the Union. The sophism itself is that any State of the Union may *consistently* with the national Constitution, and therefore *lawfully* and *peacefully*, withdraw from the Union without the consent of the Union or of any other State. The little disguise that the supposed right is to be exercised only for just cause, themselves to be the sole judge of its justice, is too thin to merit any notice.

With rebellion thus sugar coated they have been dragging the public mind of their section for more than thirty years, and until at length they have brought many good men to a willingness to take up arms against the Government the day *after* some assemblage of men have enacted the farcical pretense of taking their State out of the Union who could have been brought to do no such thing the day *before*.

This sophism derives much, perhaps the whole, of its currency from the assumption that there is some omnipotent and sacred supremacy pertaining to a *State*—to each State of our Federal Union. Our States have neither more nor less power than that reserved to them in the Union by the Constitution, no one of them ever having been a State *out* of the Union. The original ones passed into the Union even *before* they cast off their British colonial dependence, and the new ones each came into the Union directly from a condition of dependence, excepting Texas; and even Texas, in its temporary independence, was never designated a State. The new ones each took the designation of States on coming into the Union, while that name was first adopted for the old ones in and by the Declaration of Independence. Therein the "United Colonies" were declared to be free and independent States; but even then the object plainly was not to declare their independence of *one another* or of the *union*, but directly the contrary, as their mutual pledge and their mutual action before, at the time, and afterwards abundantly show. The express plighting of faith by each and all of the original thirteen in the Articles of

Confederation, two years later, that the Union shall be perpetual is most conclusive. Having never been States, either in substance or in name, *outside* of the Union, whence this magical omnipotence of "State rights," asserting a claim of power to lawfully destroy the Union itself? Much is said about the "sovereignty" of the States, but the word even is not in the National Constitution, nor, as is believed, in any of the State constitutions. What is "sovereignty" in the political sense of the term? Would it be far wrong to define it "a political community without political superior"? Tested by this, no one of our States, except Texas, ever was a sovereignty; and even Texas gave up the character on coming into the Union, by which act she acknowledged the Constitution of the United States and the laws and treaties of the United States made in presence of the Constitution to be for her the supreme law of the land. The States have their status in the Union, and they have no other legal status. If they break from this, they can only do so against law and by revolution. . . .

Lest there be some uneasiness in the minds of men as to what is to be the course of the Government toward the Southern States *after* the rebellion shall have been suppressed, the Executive deems it proper to say it will be his purpose then, as ever, to be guided by the Constitution and the laws, and that he probably will have no different understanding of the powers and duties of the Federal Government, relative to the rights of the States and the people under the Constitution than that expressed in the inaugural address.

He desires to preserve the Government, that it may be administered for all as it was administered by the men who made it. Loyal citizens everywhere have the right to claim this of their government, and the government has no right to withhold or neglect it. It is not perceived that in giving it there is any coercion, any conquest, or any subjugation in any just sense of those terms.

The Constitution provides, and all the States have accepted the provision, that "the United States shall guarantee to every State in the Union a republican form of government." But if a State may lawfully go out of the Union, having done so it may also discard the republican form of government; so that to prevent its going out is an indispensable *means* to the *end* of maintaining the guaranty mentioned; and when an end is lawful and obligatory the indispensable means to it are also lawful and obligatory.

It is with the deepest regret that the Executive found the duty of employing the war power in defense of the Government forced upon him. He could but perform this duty or surrender the existence of the Government. No compromise by public servants could in this case be a cure; not that compromises are not often proper, but that no popular government can long survive a marked precedent that those who carry an election can only save the government from immediate destruction by giving up the main point upon which the people gave the election. The people themselves, and not their servants, can safely reverse their own decisions.

As a private citizen the Executive could not have consented that these institutions shall perish; much less could he in betrayal of so vast and so sacred a trust as these free people had confided to him. He felt that he had no moral right to shrink, nor even to count the chances of his own life, in what might follow. In full view of his great responsibility he has so far done what he has deemed his duty. You will now, according to your own judgment, perform yours. He sincerely hopes that your views and your action may so accord with his as to assure all faithful citizens who have been disturbed in their rights of a certain and speedy restoration to them under the Constitution and the laws.

And having thus chosen our course, without guile and with pure purpose, let us renew our trust in God and go forward without fear and with manly hearts.

Harcourt Brace & Company

The Battle of Shiloh, 1862*

While politicians could theorize and debate the nature of republicanism and constitutional government, soldiers fought the war. Well over half a million of them died. When the conflict began, both sides confidently bragged that they could whip the other in just a few months. The Battle of Shiloh in the spring of 1862 was the bloodiest battle in American history up until that time, and it made clear that nothing would be settled within a matter of months. General Ulysses S. Grant filed the following preliminary report on the battle, a Union victory that guaranteed federal control of much of Tennessee and the western theater of operations. The casualty rates of the two days foretold the intensity of the combat that came to characterize the war, and Shiloh offered a portent of the incredible military power that would be required to save the Union. In his initial account of the fighting, however, Grant downplayed the number of casualties he had suffered.

CAPTAIN: It becomes my duty to report another battle fought between two great armies, one contending for the maintenance of the best government ever devised, the other for its destruction. It is pleasant to record the success of the army contending for the former principles.

On Sunday morning our pickets were attacked and driven in by the enemy. Immediately the five divisions stationed at this place were drawn up in line of battle, ready to meet them. The battle soon waxed warm on the left and center, varying at time to all parts of the line. The most continuous firing of musketry and artillery ever heard on this continent was kept up until night-fall, the enemy having forced the entire line to fall back nearly half way from their camps to the Landing.

At a late hour in the afternoon a desperate effort was made by the enemy to turn our left and get possession of the Landing, transports, &c. This point was guarded by the gunboats Tyler and Lexington, Captains Gwin and Shirk, U. S. Navy, commanding, four 20-pounder Parrott guns and a battery of rifled guns. As there is a deep and impassable ravine for artillery or cavalry, and very difficult for infantry, at this point, no troops were stationed here, except the necessary artillerists and a small infantry force for their support. Just at this moment the advance of Major-General Buell's column (a part of the division under General Nelson) arrived, the two generals named both being present. An advance was immediately made upon the point of attack and enemy soon driven back. In this repulse much is due to the presence of the gunboats Tyler and Lexington, and their able commanders, Captains Gwin and Shirk.

During the night the divisions under General Crittenden and McCook arrived. General Lewis Wallace, at Crump's Landing, 6 miles below, was ordered at an early hour in the morning to hold his division in readiness to be moved in any direction to which it might be ordered. At about 11 o'clock the order was delivered to move it up to Pittsburg, but owing to its being led by a circuitous route did not arrive in time to take part in Sunday's action.

During the night all was quiet, and feeling that a great moral advantage would be gained by becoming the attacking party, an advance was ordered as soon as day dawned. The result was a gradual repulse of the enemy at all parts of the line from the morning until probably 5 o'clock in the afternoon, when it became evident the enemy was retreating. Before the close of the action the advance of General T. J. Wood's division arrived in time to take part in the action.

My force was much too fatigued from two days' hard fighting and exposure in the open air to a drenching rain during the intervening night to pursue immediately.

Night closed in cloudy and with heavy rain, making the roads impracticable for artillery by

*From Ulysses S. Grant to N. H. McLean, Adjutant General's Office, Department of the Mississippi, April 9, 1862, *The War of the Rebellion: A Compilation of the Official Records of the Union and Confederate Armies* (Washington, D. C.: Government Printing Office, 1884), vol. X, series I, part I, 108–11.

the next morning. General Sherman, however, followed the enemy, finding that the main part of the army had retreated in good order.

Hospitals of the enemy's wounded were found all along the road as far as a pursuit was made. Dead bodies of the enemy and many graves were also found. . . .

Of the part taken by each separate command I cannot take special notice in this report, but I will do so more fully when reports of division commanders are handed in.

General Buell, coming on the field with a distinct army long under his command, and which did such efficient service, commanded by himself in person on the field, will be much better able to notice those of his command who particularly distinguished themselves than I possibly can.

I feel it a duty, however, to a gallant and able officer, Brig. Gen. W. T. Sherman, to make a special mention. He not only was with his command during the entire two days' action, but displayed great judgment and skill in the management of his men. Although severely wounded in the hand the first day his place was never vacant. He was again wounded, and had three horses killed under him.

In making this mention of a gallant officer no disparagement is intended to other division commanders, Maj. Gens. John A. and Lewis Wallace, and Brig. Gens. S. A. Hurlbut, B. M. Prentiss, and W. H. L. Wallace, all of whom maintained their places with credit to themselves and the cause.

General Prentiss was taken prisoner in the first day's action, and General W. H. L. Wallace severely, probably mortally, wounded. His assistant adjutant general, Captain William McMichael, is missing; probably taken prisoner. . . .

The medical department, under the direction of Surgeon Hewitt, medical director, showed great energy in providing for the wounded and in getting them from the field regardless of the danger.

Colonel Webster was placed in special charge of all the artillery and was constantly upon the field. He displayed, as always heretobefore, both skill and bravery. At least in one instance he was the means of placing an entire regiment in a position of doing most valuable service, and where it would not have been but for his exertions.

Lieutenant-Colonel McPherson, attached to my staff as chief engineer, deserves more than a passing notice for his activity and courage. All the grounds beyond our camps for miles have been reconnoitered by him, and plats carefully prepared under his supervision give accurate information of the nature of the approaches to our lines. During the two days' battle he was constantly in the saddle, leading troops as they arrived to points where their services were required. During the engagement he had one horse shot under him.

The country will have to mourn the loss of many brave men who fell at the battle of Pittsburg, or Shiloh, more properly. The exact loss on killed and wounded will be known in a day or two. At present I can only give it approximately at 1,500 killed and 3,500 wounded.

The loss of artillery was great, many pieces being disabled by the enemy's shots and some losing all their horses and many men. There were probably not less than 200 horses killed.

The loss of the enemy in killed and left upon the field was greater than ours. In wounded the estimate cannot be made, as many of them must have been sent back to Corinth and other points.

The enemy suffered terribly from demoralization and desertion. . . .

Discussion

1. In his speech, Senator Robert Toombs criticized Republicans for ignoring the Dred Scott decision. Was the Republican stance on the decision legitimate or not? What are the implica-

tions for power and liberty of an administration that refuses to accept a court decision. How might the Republicans have justified their position?

2. Senator Robert Toombs insisted that the South wanted to have equal rights. Do you think that statement was sincere? How do you think Toombs, and other southerners, defined equality? Had the North and South ever been equal? Why or why not?

3. Did the southern states have the right to secede? If so, why; if not, why not? Was the Constitution a voluntary compact of the states? Why or why not? Was Texas a special case because it had been an independent republic?

4. Why, if all of his cabinet members rejected the idea of re-supplying Fort Sumter, did Lincoln choose to force the issue in April of 1861? What other options might he have tried? Why couldn't Lincoln just let the Confederate states go in peace?

5. Did President Lincoln exceed his authority during the early weeks of the war? Do you accept his justification for suspending *habeas corpus*? How might that suspension have been justified? What might have been some of the criticisms leveled against Lincoln for revoking the right?

6. Abraham Lincoln described the war as a fundamental question of power. How did he develop that thesis? Who do you think that Lincoln believed held power in the United States? Do you agree with his explanation of the nature of American government? How can a government be strong enough to survive and yet not so powerful as to destroy liberty?

Chapter 17
A New Birth of Freedom, 1862–1865

The unpopular draft triggered resistance in the North and the South. In July, 1863, riots erupted in New York City, aimed at the rich men and war supporters who could buy their way out of military service. Blacks were also blamed for the war, and they were the usual victims of the mobs.

*T*he Civil War marked a true watershed in American history. Although the fighting began in an effort to save the Union, as a military measure President Lincoln emancipated some slaves in 1863 and the Thirteenth Amendment ended slavery altogether two years later. With the liberation of the slaves, the rights of African Americans became a major concern in the United States. Women played important roles in the war efforts of both the North and the South, and they too emerged from the crisis with increased expectations of equal rights. The conflict had additional implications for the nation. Republicans took advantage of their congressional power to pass a number of laws promoting economic growth, which set the stage for the rapid western settlement and industrial expansion that occurred after 1865. The Civil War, then, dramatically altered the nature of liberty, equality, and power in the United States. In a slightly different vein, the war also produced a hero of mythical proportion, and the words of Abraham Lincoln still serve to define the national character of the republic.

The Frémont Incident, 1861*

The two documents that follow touch on several issues important during the early months of the war: the proper approach to the "Border States," civil versus military authority, and emancipation. General John C. Frémont, commander of the Union forces in Missouri, declared martial law in August 1861 to maintain control over that important Border State. In his declaration, Frémont threatened to shoot armed citizens and to free the slaves of Rebel sympathizers. President Lincoln, fearful of Confederate response to the first order and concerned about slave-owning Unionists' reaction to the second, countermanded Frémont. In so doing, Lincoln made clear that the objective of preserving the Union prevailed over freeing the slaves. The President's response also showed his willingness to direct military matters, a dynamic style that came to characterize Lincoln's approach to the war.

Circumstances, in my judgment, of sufficient urgency render it necessary that the commanding general of this department should assume the administrative powers of the State. Its disorganized condition, the helplessness of the civil authority, the total insecurity of life, and the devastation of property by bands of murderers and marauders, who infest nearly every county of the State, and avail themselves of the public misfortunes and the vicinity of a hostile force to gratify private and neighborhood vengeance, and who find an enemy wherever they find plunder, finally demand the severest measures to repress the daily-increasing crimes and outrages which are driving off the inhabitants and ruining the State.

In this condition the public safety and the success of our arms require unity of purpose, without let or hindrance to the prompt administration of affairs. In order, therefore, to suppress disorder, to maintain as far as practicable the public peace, and to give security and protection

---

*From John C. Frémont, "Proclamation," August 30, 1861, and Abraham Lincoln to John C. Frémont, September 2, 1861, both in *The War of the Rebellion: A Compilation of the Official Records of the Union and Confederate Armies,* 129 vols. (Washington, D.C.: U.S. Government Printing Office, 1880–1901), series I, vol. III:466–67, 469–70.

to the persons and property of loyal citizens, I do hereby extend and declare established martial law throughout the State of Missouri.

The lines of the army of occupation in this State are for the present declared to extend from Leavenworth, by way of the posts of Jefferson City, Rolla, and Ironton, to Cape Girardeau, on the Mississippi River.

All persons who shall be taken with arms in their hands within these lines shall be tried by court-martial, and if found guilty will be shot.

The property, real and personal, of all persons in the State of Missouri who shall take up arms against the United States, or who shall be directly proven to have taken an active part with their enemies in the field, is declared to be confiscated to the public use, and their slaves, if any they have, are hereby declared freemen.

All persons who shall be proven to have destroyed, after the publication of this order, railroad tracks, bridges, or telegraphs shall suffer the extreme penalty of the law.

All persons engaged in treasonable correspondence, in giving or procuring aid to the enemies of the United States, in fomenting tumults, in disturbing the public tranquillity by creating and circulating false reports or incendiary documents, are in their own interests warned that they are exposing themselves to sudden and severe punishment.

All persons who have been led away from their allegiance are required to return to their homes forthwith. Any such absence, without sufficient cause, will be held to be presumptive evidence against them.

The object of this declaration is to place in the hands of the military authorities the power to give instantaneous effect to existing laws, and to supply such deficiencies as the conditions of war demand. But this is not intended to suspend the ordinary tribunals of the country, where the law will be administered by the civil officers in the usual manner, and with their customary authority, while the same can be peaceably exercised.

The commanding general will labor vigilantly for the public welfare, and in his efforts for their safety hopes to obtain not only the acquiescence but the active support of the loyal people of the country.

J. C. Frémont

———————

Major-General Frémont:

MY DEAR SIR: Two points in your proclamation of August 30 give me some anxiety:

First, Should you shoot a man, according to the proclamation, the Confederates would very certainly shoot our best men in their hands in retaliation; and so, man for man, indefinitely. It is, therefore, my order that you allow no man to be shot under the proclamation without first having my approbation or consent.

Second, I think there is great danger that the closing paragraph, in relation to the confiscation of property and the liberating slaves of traitorous owners, will alarm our Southern Union friends and turn them against us; perhaps ruin our rather fair prospect for Kentucky. Allow me, therefore, to ask that you will, as of your own motion, modify that paragraph so as to conform to the first and fourth sections of the act of Congress entitled "An act to confiscate property used for insurrectionary purposes," approved August 6, 1861, and a copy of which act I herewith send you.

The letter is written in a spirit of caution and not of censure. I send it by special messenger, in order that it may certainly and speedily reach you. . . .

A. Lincoln

The Emancipation Proclamation, 1863*

Abraham Lincoln personally opposed slavery as a monstrous evil, but early in the war he feared that emancipation would hurt the federal effort to save the Union. By Fall of 1862, however, he decided that freeing the slaves in the rebellious states would significantly improve the North's military situation. With the Union victory at Antietam in September, Lincoln announced that slaves in the Confederacy would be liberated on January 1, 1863. Although the decree could not take effect until the South had been defeated, few Executive Orders have had as significant and as long-lasting implications for the nation. The Emancipation Proclamation marked the birth of a new freedom for thousands of Americans, and it began a tremendous struggle to establish racial equality in the United States.

WHEREAS on the twenty-second day of September of the year of our Lord eighteen hundred and sixty-two, a proclamation was issued by the President of the United States, containing among other things, the following, to wit:

"That on the first day of January, in the year of our Lord eighteen hundred and sixty-three, all persons held as slaves within any state or designated part of a state the people whereof shall then be in rebellion against the United States shall be then, thenceforward, and forever free; and the Executive Government of the United States, including the military and naval authority thereof, will recognize and maintain the freedom of such persons, and will do no act or acts to repress such persons, or any of them, in any efforts they may make for their actual freedom."

"That the Executive will on the first day of January aforesaid, by proclamation, designate the states and parts of states, if any, in which the people thereof, respectively, shall then be in rebellion against the United States; and the fact that any state or the people thereof, shall on that day be in good faith represented in the Congress of the United States by members chosen thereto at elections wherein a majority of the qualified voters of such states shall have participated shall, in the absence of strong countervailing testimony, be deemed conclusive evidence that such state and the people thereof are not then in rebellion against the United States."

Now, therefore, I, ABRAHAM LINCOLN, President of the United States, by virtue of the power in me vested as commander in chief of the army and navy of the United States, in time of actual armed rebellion against the authority and Government of the United States, and as a fit and necessary war measure for suppressing said rebellion, do, on this first day of January, in the year of our Lord eighteen hundred and sixty-three, and in accordance with my purpose so to do, publicly proclaimed for the full period of one hundred days from the first day above mentioned, order and designate as the states and parts of states wherein the people thereof, respectively, are this day in rebellion against the United States the following, to wit:

Arkansas, Texas, Louisiana (except the parishes of St. Bernard, Plaquemines, Jefferson, St. John, St. Charles, St. James, Ascension, Assumption, Terre Bonne, Lafourche, St. Mary, St. Martin, and Orleans, including the city of New Orleans), Mississippi, Alabama, Florida, Georgia, South Carolina, North Carolina, and Virginia (except the forty-eight counties designated as West Virginia, and also the counties of Berkeley, Accomac, Northhampton, Elizabeth City, York, Princess Ann, and Norfolk, including the cities of Norfolk and Portsmouth), and which excepted parts are for the present left precisely as if this proclamation were not issued.

And by virtue of the power and for the purpose aforesaid, I do order and declare that all persons held as slaves within said designated states and parts of states are, and henceforward shall be free; and that the Executive Government of the United States, including the military and naval authorities thereof, will recognize and maintain the freedom of said persons.

---

*From Abraham Lincoln, "A Proclamation," January 1, 1863, *United States Statutes at Large,* XII:1268–69.

And I hereby enjoin upon the so declared to be free to abstain from all violence, unless in necessary self-defense; and I recommend to them that, in all cases when allowed, they labor faithfully for reasonable wages.

And I further declare and make known that such persons of suitable condition, will be received into the armed service of the United States to garrison forts, positions, stations, and other places, and to man vessels of all sorts in said service.

And upon this act, sincerely believed to be an act of justice, warranted by the Constitution upon military necessity, I invoke the considerable judgment of mankind and the gracious favor of Almighty God. . . .

Life in the Civil War South, 1862–1865*

The Civil War, in addition to freeing millions of slaves, changed the lives of thousands of white women. During war, women assume tasks and responsibilities denied them in peace time—a social phenomenon that can serve to erode or alter their traditional roles. Once peace returns, on the other hand, powerful cultural pressures are brought to bear on women to resume their "proper" place. Consequently, the changes in women's status that accompany war may be real and significant, but they are often subtle and limited. The following passage, taken from the memoirs of Victoria Virginia Clayton, wife of a prominent Alabaman, offered a view of the southern home front. The reminiscence may present a rather romantic picture of life in the Civil War South, but it does reveal some of the substantial domestic changes Southerners experienced between 1861 and 1865.

While my husband was at the front during active service, suffering fatigue, privations, and many ills attendant on a soldier's life, I was at home struggling to keep the family comfortable.

We were blockaded on every side, and could get nothing from without, so had to make everything at home; and having been heretofore only an agricultural people, it became necessary for every home to be supplied with spinning wheels and the old-fashioned loom, in order to manufacture clothing for the members of the family. This was no small undertaking. I knew nothing about spinning and weaving cloth. I had to learn myself, and then to teach the negroes. Fortunately for me, most of the negroes knew how to spin thread, the first step toward cloth making. Our work was hard and continuous. To this we did not object, but our hearts sorrowed for our loved ones in the field.

Our home was situated a mile from the town of Clayton. On going to town one day I discovered a small bridge over which we had to pass that needed repairing. It was almost impassable. I went home, called some of our men, and gave them instructions to get up the necessary articles and put the bridge in condition to be passed over safely. I was there giving instructions about the work, when an old gentleman, our Probate Judge, came along. He stopped to see what we were doing. When satisfied, he said to me:

"Madam, I think we will never be conquered, possessing such noble women as we do." . . .

There was no white person on the plantation beside myself and children, the oldest of whom was attending school at Eufaula, as our Clayton schools were closed, and my time was so occupied that it was impossible for me to teach my children. Four small children and myself constituted the white family at home.

---

*From "Home Life of a Southern Lady (1862–1865)," in *American History Told by Contemporaries,* 5 vols., ed. Albert Bushnell Hart (New York: The Macmillan Company, 1914), IV:244–47.

Harcourt Brace & Company

I entrusted the planting and cultivation of the various crops to old Joe. He had been my husband's nurse in infancy, and we always loved and trusted him. I kept a gentle saddle horse, and occasionally, accompanied by Joe, would ride over the entire plantation on a tour of inspection. Each night, when the day's work was done, Joe came in to make a report of everything that had been done on the plantation that day. When Mr. Clayton was where he could receive my letters, I wrote him a letter every night before retiring, and in this way he, being kept informed about the work at home, could write and make suggestions about various things to help me manage successfully.

We made good crops every year, but after the second year we planted provision crops entirely, except enough cotton for home use.

All the coloring matter for cloth had to be gathered from the forest. We would get roots and herbs and experiment with them until we found the color desired, or a near approach to it. We also found out what would dye cotton and what woolen fabrics. We had about one hundred head of sheep; and the wool yielded by these sheep and the cotton grown in the fields furnished us the material for our looms. After much hard work and experience we learned to make very comfortable clothing, some of our cloth being really pretty.

Our ladies would attend services in the church of God, dressed in their home-spun goods, and felt well pleased with their appearances; indeed, better pleased than if they had been dressed in silk of the finest fabric.

We made good warm flannels and other articles of apparel for our soldiers, and every woman learned to knit socks and stockings for her household, and many of the former were sent to the army.

In these dark days the Southern matron, when we sat down at night feeling that the day's work was over, took her knitting in her hands as a pastime, instead of the fancy work which ladies so frequently indulge in now.

I kept one woman at the loom weaving, and several spinning all the time, but found that I could not get sufficient cloth made at home; consequently I gave employment to many a poor woman whose husband was far away. Many a time have I gone ten miles in the country with my buggy filled with thread, to get one of these ladies to weave a piece of cloth for me, and then in return for her labor sent her syrup, sugar, or any of our home produce she wished.

We always planted and raised large crops of wheat, rice, sugar cane, and potatoes. In fact, we grew almost everything that would make food for man or beast. Our land is particularly blessed in this respect. I venture to say there is no land under the sun that will grow a greater variety of products than the land in these Southern states.

Being blockaded, we were obliged to put our ingenuity to work to meet the demands on us as heads of families. Some things we could not raise; for instance, the accustomed necessary luxury of every home—coffee. So we went to work to hunt up a substitute. Various articles were tried, but the best of all was the sweet potato. The potatoes were peeled, sliced, and cut into pieces as large as a coffee bean, dried, and then roasted, just as we prepared coffee. The substitute, mixed with genuine coffee, makes a very palatable drink for breakfast. . . .

Another accustomed luxury of which we were deprived was white sugar. We had, however, a good substitute with which we soon became satisfied; our home-made brown sugar, from the sugar cane. It had the redeeming quality of being pure. . . .

We made many gallons of wine from the scuppernong and other grapes every year. One year I remember particularly. Sheets were spread under the long scuppernong arbors, little negro boys put in top to throw the grapes down, and grown men underneath to gather them in baskets as they fell. When brought to the house they measured thirty-two bushels, and made one hundred and twenty gallons of wine. I did not make so large a quantity from the other varieties of grapes. This wine was kept in the cellar and used for the common benefit. When the negroes would get caught out in the rain, and come to the house wet, they did not hesitate to say, "Mistus, please give me a little wine to keep cold away;" and they always received it. There was never any ill result from the use of domestic wine. We were a temperate family and the use was invariably beneficial.

Closed in as we were on every side, with nearly every white man of proper age and health enlisted in the army, with the country filled with white women, children, and old, infirm men, with thousands of slaves to be controlled, and caused through their systematic labor to feed and clothe the people at home, and to provide for our army, I often wonder, as I contemplate those by-gone days of labor and sorrow, and recall how peacefully we moved on and accomplished what we did.

We were required to give one-tenth of all that was raised, to the government. There being no educated white person on the plantation except myself, it was necessary that I should attend to the gathering and measuring of every crop and the delivery of the tenth to the government authorities. This one-tenth we gave cheerfully and often wished we had more to give.

My duties . . . were numerous and often laborious; the family on the increase continually, and every one added increased labor and responsibility. And this was the case with the typical Southern woman.

The Homestead Act, 1862*

Republicans took advantage of their majority in Congress to pass several important laws in 1862. The Homestead Act provided "free" land to settlers and encouraged the development of the vast public domain. The law did not ensure the survival of yeoman farmers, but it helped stimulate the post–Civil War agricultural production that served as a foundation for incredible economic growth in the United States after 1865.

Be it enacted by . . . Congress . . . , That any person who is the head of a family, or who has arrived at the age of twenty-one years, and is a citizen of the United States, or who shall have filed his declaration of intention to become such, as required by the naturalization laws of the United States, and who has never borne arms against the United States Government or given aid and comfort to its enemies, shall, from and after the first of January, eighteen hundred and sixty-three, be entitled to enter one quarter-section or a less quantity of unappropriated public lands, upon which said person may have filed a preëmption claim, or which may, at the time the application is made, be subject to preëmption at one dollar and twenty-five cents, or less, per acre; or, eighty acres or less of such unappropriated lands at two dollars and fifty cents per acre, to be located in a body, in conformity to the legal subdivisions of the public lands, and after the same shall have been surveyed: *Provided,* That any person owning or residing on land may, under the provisions of this act, enter other land lying contiguous to his or her said land, which shall not, with the land so already owned and occupied, exceed in the aggregate one hundred and sixty acres.

SEC. 2. *And be it further enacted,* That the person applying for the benefit of this act shall upon application to the register of the land office in which he or she is about to make such entry, make affidavit before the said register or receiver that he or she is the head of a family, or is twenty-one or more years of age, or shall have performed service in the army or navy of the United States, and that he has never borne arms against the Government of the United States

---

*From "AN ACT to secure homesteads to actual settlers on the public domain," May 20, 1862, *United States Statutes at Large,* XII:392–39.

or given aid and comfort to its enemies, and that such application is made for his or her exclusive use and benefit, and that said entry is made for the purpose of actual settlement and cultivation, and not, either directly or indirectly, for the use or benefit of any other person or persons whomsoever; and upon filing the said affidavit with the register or receiver, and on payment of ten dollars, he or she shall thereupon be permitted to enter the quantity of land specified: *Provided, however,* That no certificate shall be given or patent issued therefor until the expiration of five years from the date of such entry; and if, at the expiration of such time, or at anytime within two years thereafter, the person making such entry; or, if he be dead, his widow; or in case of her death, his heirs or devisee; or in case of a widow making such an entry, her heirs or devisee, in case of her death; shall prove by two credible witnesses that he, she, or they have resided upon or cultivated the same for the term of five years immediately succeeding the time of filing the affidavit aforesaid, and shall make affidavit that no part of said land has been alienated, and that he has borne true allegiance to the Government of the United States; then, in such case, he, she, or they, if at that time a citizen of the United States, shall be entitled to a patent, as in other cases provided for by law; *And provided, further,* That in case of the death of both father and mother, leaving an infant child or children under twenty-one years of age, the right and fee shall enure to the benefit of said infant child or children; and the executor, administrator, or guardian may, at any time within two years after the death of the surviving parent, and in accordance with the laws of the State in which such children for the time being have their domicile, sell said land for the benefit of the said infants, but for no other purpose; and the purchaser shall acquire the absolute title by the purchase, and be entitled to a patent from the United States, on payment of the office fees and sum of money herein specified.

SEC. 3. *And be it further enacted,* That the register of the land office shall note and such applications on the tract books and plats of his office and keep a register of all such entries. . . .

SEC. 5. *And be it further enacted,* That if, at any time after the filing of the affidavit . . . and before the expiration of the five years aforesaid, it shall be proven, after due notice to the settler, . . . that the person having filed such affidavit shall have actually changed his or her residence, or abandoned the said land for more that six months at any time, then and in that event the land so entered shall revert to the government.

SEC. 6. And be it further enacted, That no individual shall be permitted to acquire title to more than one quarter section under the provisions of this act; and that the Commissioner of the General Land Office is hereby required to prepare and issue such rules and regulations, consistent with this act, as shall be necessary and proper to carry its provisions into effect . . . : *Provided, further,* That no person who has served, or may hereafter serve, for a period of not less than fourteen days in the army or navy of the United States, either regular or volunteer, under the laws thereof, during the existence of an actual war, domestic or foreign, shall be deprived of the benefits of this act on account of not having attained the age of twenty-one years. . . .

The Morrill Act, 1862*

The Morrill Land-Grant College Act gave states the opportunity to support higher public education on an unprecedented scale by giving them federal land to subsidize agricultural and mechanical colleges. With the Republican policy, the wealth of the nation would be used to

---

* "An Act donating Public Lands to the several States and Territories which may provide Colleges for the Benefit of Agriculture and the Mechanic Arts," July 2, 1862, *United States Statutes at Large,* XII:503–505.

provide educational and economic opportunities for thousands of Americans. Approved on July 2, 1862, the bill made possible the creation of many of the major universities in the United States.

Be it enacted by . . . Congress . . . , That there be granted to the several States, for the purpose hereinafter mentioned, an amount of public land, to be appropriated to each State a quantity equal to thirty thousand acres for each senator and representative in Congress to which the States are respectively entitled by the apportionment under the census of eighteen hundred and sixty: Provided, That no mineral lands shall be selected or purchased under the provisions of this act.

SEC. 2. *And be it further enacted,* That the land aforesaid, after being surveyed, shall be apportioned to the several States in sections or subdivisions of sections, not less than one quarter of a section; and whenever there are public lands in a State subject to sale at private entry at one dollar and twenty-five cents per acre, the quantity to which said States shall be entitled shall be selected from such lands within the limits of said States, and the Secretary of the Interior is hereby directed to issue to each of the States in which there is not the quantity of public lands subject to sale at private entry at one dollar and twenty-five cents per acre, to which said State may be entitled under the provisions of this act, land scrip to the amount in acres for the deficiency of its distributive share: said scrip to be sold by said States and the proceeds thereof applied to the uses and purposes in this act, and for no other use or purpose whatsoever: Provided, That in no case shall any State in which land scrip may thus be issued be allowed to locate the same within any other State, or Territory . . . ; *And provided, further,* That not more than one million acres shall be located by . . . assignees in any one of the States: *And provided, further,* That no such location shall be made before one year from the passage of this act.

SEC. 4. *And be it further enacted,* That all moneys derived from the sale of the lands aforesaid by the States to which lands are apportioned, and from the sale of the land scrip hereinbefore provided for, shall be invested in stocks of the United States, or of the States, or some other safe stocks, yielding not less than five percentum upon the par value of said stocks; and that the moneys so invested shall constitute a perpetual fund, the capital of which shall remain forever undiminished, (except so far as may be provided in section fifth of this act,) and the interest of which shall be inviolably appropriated, by each State which may take and claim the benefit of this act, to the endowment, support, and maintenance of at least one college where the leading object shall be, without excluding other scientific and classical studies, and including military tactics, to teach such branches of learning as are related to agriculture and mechanic arts, in such manner as the legislatures of the States may respectively prescribe, in order to promote the liberal and practical education of the industrial classes in the several pursuits and professions of life.

SEC. 5. . . .[Paragraph Six]. No State while in a condition of rebellion or insurrection against the government of the United States shall be entitled to the benefits of this Act. . . .

The Gettysburg Address, 1863*

In 1863, President Lincoln made a few comments at the dedication of a cemetery at Gettysburg. The most famous speech in the history of the United States, the Gettysburg Address offered an eloquent statement of American ideals. Lincoln used the opportunity to define the democratic principles for which the Union fought. The war that had begun to save the Union, and that had brought

---

*From Abraham Lincoln, "The Gettysburg Address," November 19, 1863, in *Select Orations Illustrating American Political History,* ed. Samuel B. Harding (Indianapolis: Hollenbeck Press, 1908), 416.

Harcourt Brace & Company

freedom to African Americans, would, prayed Lincoln, guarantee the survival of government by and for the people.

> Fourscore and seven years ago our fathers brought forth on this continent, a new nation, conceived in liberty, and dedicated to the proposition that all men are created equal. Now we are engaged in a great civil war, testing whether that nation or any nation so conceived and so dedicated, can long endure. We are met on a great battle-field of that war. We have come to dedicate a portion of that field, as a final resting place for those who here gave their lives that that nation might live. It is altogether fitting and proper that we should do this. But, in a larger sense, we can not dedicate, we can not consecrate, we can not hallow, this ground. The brave men, living and dead, who struggled here, have consecrated it, far above our poor power to add or detract. The world will little note, nor long remember what we say here, but it can never forget what they did here. It is for us the living, rather, to be dedicated here to the unfinished work which they who fought here have thus far so nobly advanced. It is rather for us to be here dedicated to the great task remaining before us, that from these honored dead we take increased devotion to that cause for which they gave the last full measure of devotion; that we here highly resolve these dead shall not have died in vain; that this nation, under God, shall have a new birth of freedom, and that government of the people, by the people, and for the people, shall not perish from the earth.

The First South Carolina, U. S. C. T., 1862*

When the federal government established African-American military regiments (designated as United States Colored Troops, or U. S. C. T.), white officers served in command. Blacks could fight, but they could not lead. The discriminatory policy prophesied the overwhelming difficulty former slaves would face in trying to gain equality in the United States. Nevertheless, many of the commanders proved quite sympathetic to the freedmen, as the following selections from one colonel's journal revealed. The excerpts were published in a national magazine, and they provided northerners with one of the earliest descriptions of emancipated slaves. The comments also mirrored many of the attitudes and perceptions that white Americans held about black Americans.

November 24, 1862

> Yesterday afternoon we were steaming over a summer sea, the deck level as a parlor-floor, no land in sight, no sail, until at last appeared one light-house, said to be Cape Romaine, and then a line of trees and two distant vessels and nothing more. The sun set, a great illuminated bubble, emerged in one vast bank of rosy suffusion. . . . Towards morning the boat stopped, and when I came on deck, before six, . . .
>
> Hilton Head lay on one side, the gunboats on the other; all that was raw and bare in the low buildings of the new settlement was softened into picturesqueness by the early light. Stars were still overhead, gulls wheeled and shrieked, and the broad river rippled duskily toward Beaufort.
>
> The shores were low and wooded like any New-England shore; there were a few gunboats, twenty schooners, and some steamers, among them the "Planter," which Robert Small, the slave, presented to the nation. The river-banks were soft and graceful, though low, and as we steamed up to Beaufort, on the flood-tide this morning, it seemed almost as fair as the smooth and lovely canals which Stedman traversed to meet his negro soldiers in Surinam. The air was cool as at

---

*From "Leaves from an Officer's Journal," *The Atlantic Monthly* 14 (July–December 1864), 522–27.

home, yet the foliage seemed green, glimpses of stiff tropical vegetation appeared along the banks, with great clumps of shrubs whose pale seed-vessels looked like tardy blossoms. Then we saw on a picturesque point an old plantation, with stately magnolia avenue, decaying house, and tiny church amid the woods, reminding me of Virginia; behind it stood a neat encampment of white tents, "and there," said my companion, "is your favorite regiment of negro soldiers."

Three miles farther brought us to the pretty town of Beaufort, with its stately houses amid Southern foliage. Reporting to General Saxton, I had the luck to encounter a company of my destined command, marched in to be mustered into the United States service. They were without arms, and all looked as thoroughly black as the most faithful philanthropist could desire; there did not seem to be so much as a mulatto among them. Their coloring suited me, all but the legs, which were clad in a lively scarlet, as intolerable to my eyes as if I had been a turkey. I saw them mustered; General Saxton talked to them a little, in his direct, manly way; they gave close attention, though their faces looked impenetrable. Then I conversed with some of them. The first to whom I spoke had been wounded in a small expedition after lumber, from which a party had just returned, and in which they had been under fire and done very well. I said, pointing to his lame arm,—

"Did you think that was more than you bargained for, my man?"

His answer came promptly and stoutly,—

"I been a-tinking, Mas'r, *dat's jess what I went for.*"

I thought this did well enough for my first interchange of dialogue with my recruits.

―――――――――

December 1, 1862

How absurd is the impression bequeathed by slavery in regard to these Southern blacks, that they are sluggish and inefficient in labor! Last night, after a hard day's work, (our guns and the remainder of our tents being just issued,) an order came from Beaufort that we should be ready in the evening to unload a steamboat's cargo of boards, being some of those captured by them a few weeks since, and now assigned for their use. I wondered if the men would grumble at the nightwork; but the steamboat arrived by seven, and it was bright moonlight when they went at it. Never have I beheld such a jolly scene of labor. Tugging those wet and heavy boards over a bridge of boats ashore, then across the slimy beach at low tide, then up a steep bank, and all in one great uproar of merriment for two hours. Running most of the time, chattering all the time, snatching the boards from each other's back as if they were coveted treasure, getting up eager rivalries between different companies, pouring great choruses of ridicule on the heads of all shirkers, they made the whole scene so enlivening that I gladly stayed out in the moonlight for the whole time to watch it. And all this without any urging or any promised reward, but simply as the most natural way of doing the thing. The steamboat-captain declared that they unloaded the ten thousand feet of boards quicker than any white gang could have done it; and they felt it so little, that, when, later in the night, I reproached one whom I found sitting by a camp-fire, cooking a surreptitious opossum, telling him that he ought to sleep after such a job of work, he answered with the broadest grin,—

"Oh, no, Cunnel, da's no work at all, Cunnel; dat only jess enough *for stretch we.*"

―――――――――

December 2, 1862

I believe I have not yet enumerated the probable drawbacks to the success of this regiment, if any. We are exposed to no direct annoyance from the white regiments, being out of their way;

Harcourt Brace & Company

and we have as yet no discomforts or privations which we do not share with them. I do not as yet see the slightest obstacle, in the nature of the blacks, to making them good soldiers,—but rather the contrary. They take readily to drill, and do not object to discipline; they are not especially dull or inattentive; they seem fully to understand the importance of the contest, and their share of it. They show no jealousy or suspicion towards their officers.

They do show those feelings, however, to the Government itself; and no one can wonder why. Here lies the drawback to rapid recruiting. Were this a wholly new regiment, it would have been full to overflowing, I am satisfied, ere now. The trouble is in the legacy of bitter distrust bequeathed by the abortive regiment of General Hunter,—into which they were driven like cattle, kept for several months in camp, and then turned off without a shilling, by order of the War Department. The formation of that regiment was on the whole a great injury to this one; and the men who came from it, though the best soldiers we have in other respects, are the least sanguine and cheerful; while those who now refuse to enlist have great influence in deterring others. Our soldiers are constantly twitted by their families and friends with the prospect of risking their lives in the service, and being paid nothing; and it is vain that we read them the instructions of the Secretary of War to General Saxton, promising them the full pay of soldiers.[*]

Another drawback is that some of the white soldiers delight in frightening the women on the plantations with doleful tales of plans for putting us in the front rank in all battles, and such silly talk,—the object being, perhaps, to prevent our being employed on active service at all. All these considerations they feel precisely as white men would,—no less, no more; and it is the comparative freedom from such unfavorable influences which makes the Florida men seem more bold and manly, as they undoubtedly do. To-day General Saxton has returned from Fernandina with seventy-six recruits, and the eagerness of the captains to secure them was a sight to me. Yet they cannot deny that some of the very best men in the regiment are South Carolinians.

---

[*]With what utter humiliation were we, their officers, obliged to confess to them, eighteen months afterwards, that it was their distrust which was wise, and our faith in the pledges of the United States Government which was foolishness!

December 3, 1862

What a life is this I lead! It is a dark, mild, drizzling evening, and as the foggy air breeds sand-flies, so it calls out melodies and strange antics from this mysterious race of grown-up children with whom my lot is cast. All over the camp the lights glimmer in the tents, and as I sit at my desk in the open doorway, there come mingled sounds of stir and glee. Boys laugh and shout,—a feeble flute stirs somewhere in some tent, not an officer's,—a drum throbs far away in another,—wild kildeer-plover flit and wail above us, like the haunting souls of dead slave-masters,—and from a neighboring cook-fire comes the monotonous sound of that strange festival, half powwow, half prayer-meeting, which they know only as a "shout." These fires are usually included in a little booth, made neatly of palm-leaves and covered in at top, a regular native African hut, in short, such as is pictured in books, and such as I once got up from dried palm-leaves, for a fair, at home. This hut is now crammed with men, singing at the top of their voices, in one of their quaint, monotonous, endless, negro-Methodist chants, with obscure syllables recurring constantly, and slight variations interwoven, all accompanied with a regular drumming of the feet and clapping of the hands, like castanets. Then the excitement spreads; inside and outside the inclosure men begin to quiver and dance, others join, a circle forms, winding monotonously round some one in the centre; some "heel and toe" tumultuously, others merely trem-

Harcourt Brace & Company

ble and stagger on, others stoop and rise, others whirl, others caper sideways, all keep steadily circling like dervishes; spectators applaud special strokes of skill; my approach only enlivens the scene; the circle enlarges, louder grows the singing, rousing shouts of encouragement come in, half bacchanalian, half devout, "Wak 'em, brudder!" "Stan up to 'em, brudder!"—And still the ceaseless drumming and clapping, in perfect cadence, goes steadily on. Suddenly there comes a sort of *snap*, and the spell breaks, amid general sighing and laughter. And this not rarely and occasionally, but night after night,—while in other parts of the camp the soberest prayers and exhortations are proceeding sedately.

A simple and lovable people, whose graces seem to come by nature, and whose vices by training. Some of the best superintendents confirm the early tales of innocence, and Dr. Zachos told me last night that on his plantation, a sequestered one, "they had absolutely no vices." Nor have these men of mine shown any worth mentioning; since I took command I have heard of no man intoxicated, and there has been but one small quarrel. I suppose that scarcely a white regiment in the army shows so little swearing. Take the "Progressive Friends" and put them in red trousers, and I verily believe they would fill a guard-house sooner than these men. If camp-regulations are violated, it seems to be usually through heedlessness. They love passionately three things, besides their spiritual incantations,—namely, sugar, home, and tobacco. The last affection brings tears to their eyes, almost, when they speak of the urgent need of pay: they speak of their last-remembered quid as if it were some deceased relative, too early lost, and to be mourned forever. As for sugar, no white man can drink coffee after they have sweetened it to their liking.

I see that the pride which military life creates may cause the plantation-trickeries to diminish. For instance, these men make the most admirable sentinels. It is far harder to pass the camp-lines at night than in the camp from which I just came; and I have seen none of that disposition to connive at the offences of members of one's own company which is so troublesome among white soldiers. Nor are they lazy, either about work or drill; in all respects they seem better material for soldiers than I had dared to hope.

There is one company in particular, all Florida men, which I certainly think the finest-looking company I ever saw, white or black; they range admirably in size, have remarkable erectness and ease of carriage, and really march splendidly. Not a visitor but notices them; yet they have been under drill only a fortnight, and part only two days. They have all been slaves, and very few are even mulattoes.

Abraham Lincoln's Second Inaugural Address, 1865*

The war that Americans hoped would last no more than a few weeks dragged on for four years. During that time, it had become for northerners a campaign to make men free—a crusade that cost hundreds of thousands of lives. At his second inauguration, Abraham Lincoln underscored the moral cause the Union now so vigorously pursued. That purpose would be achieved no matter the expense, declared Lincoln, but he also held out hope that the United States would quickly recover from the devastation the conflict had caused.

FELLOW-COUNTRYMEN: At this second appearing to take the oath of the Presidential Office there is less occasion for an extended address than there was at the first. Then a statement

---

*From "Second Inaugural Address," March 4, 1865, in *A Compilation of the Messages and Papers of the Presidents, 1789–1897,* 10 vols., comp. James D. Richardson (Washington, D.C.: U.S. Government Printing Office, 1896–1899), VI:276–77.

somewhat in detail of a course to be pursued seemed fitting and proper. Now, at the expiration of four years, during which public declarations have been constantly called forth on every point and phase of the great contest which still absorbs the attention and engrosses the energies of the nation, little that is new could be presented. The progress of our arms, upon which all else chiefly depends, it is as well known to the public as to myself, and it is, I trust, reasonably satisfactory and encouraging to all. With high hope for the future, no prediction in regard to it is ventured.

On the occasion corresponding to this four years ago all thoughts were anxiously directed to an impending civil war. All dreaded it, all sought to avert it. While the inaugural address was being delivered from this place, devoted altogether to *saving* the Union without war, insurgent agents were in the city seeking to *destroy* it without war—seeking to dissolve the Union and divide effects by negotiation. Both parties deprecated war, but one of them would *make* war rather than let the nation survive, and the other would *accept* war rather than let it perish, and the war came.

One-eighth of the whole population were colored slaves, not distributed generally over the Union, but localized in the southern part of it. These slaves constituted a peculiar and powerful interest. All knew that this interest was somehow the cause of war. To strengthen, perpetuate, and extend this interest was the object for which the insurgents would rend the Union even by war, while the Government claimed no right to do more than to restrict the territorial enlargement of it. Neither party expected for the war the magnitude or the duration which it has already attained. Neither anticipated that the *cause* of the conflict might cease with or even before the conflict itself should cease. Each looked for an easier triumph, and a result less fundamental and astounding. Both read the same Bible and pray to the same God, and each invokes His aid against the other. It may seem strange that any men should dare to ask a just God's assistance in wringing their bread from the sweat of other men's faces, but let us judge not, that we be not judged. The prayers of both could not be answered. That of neither has been answered fully. The Almighty has His own purposes. "Woe unto the world because of offenses; for it must needs be that offenses come, but woe to that man by whom the offense cometh." If we shall suppose that American slavery is one of those offenses which, in the providence of God, must needs come, but which having continued through His appointed time, He now wills to remove, and that He gives to both North and South this terrible war as the woe due to those by whom the offense came, shall we discern therein any departure from those divine attributions which the believers in a living God always ascribe to Him? Fondly do we hope, fervently do we pray, that this mighty scourge of war may speedily pass away. Yet, if God wills that it continue until all the wealth piled by the bondsman's two hundred and fifty years of unrequited toil shall be sunk, and until every drop of blood drawn with the lash shall be paid by another drawn with the sword, as was said three thousand years ago, so still it must be said "the judgments of the lord are true and righteous altogether."

With malice toward none, with charity for all, with firmness in the right as God gives us to see the right, let us strive on to finish the work we are in, to bind up the nation's wounds, to care for him who shall have borne the battle and for his widow and orphan, to do all which may achieve and cherish a just and lasting peace among ourselves and with all nations.

Discussion

1. Based on the four documents by Abraham Lincoln, how do you think Lincoln defined power in the United States? How are the documents in this chapter similar to or different than Lincoln's address to Congress in the previous chapter? How do you think Lincoln viewed liberty and equality?

2. What does the exchange between Lincoln and John C. Frémont imply about civilian versus military power in the United States?

3. Compare the memoirs of Victoria Clayton with the description of Alabama by Harriet Martineau in Chapter 10. Based on those two selections, how was life for southern women similar or different in the 1830s and the 1860s? Clayton expressed no concern that the slaves might revolt, even though so many of the white men were away from home. What power do you believe prevented massive slave insurrections during the Civil War? How do you react to Clayton's description of slavery and the apparent egalitarian treatment her slaves received?

4. How are the Homestead Act and the Morrill Act expressions of Republican faith in liberty and equality? Are the laws expressions of power; why or why not? In what ways do the laws reflect American traditions? In what ways are they innovative and modern? In his farewell address, George Washington encouraged support for "institutions for the general diffusion of knowledge." How do you think Washington might have responded to the Morrill Act? What might he have objected to about the law?

5. What are some of the possible reasons that the U.S. Army placed white officers in charge of black troops? What are the implications of that policy for power and equality? How might their experience as slaves have prepared the troops of the 1st South Carolina, U. S. C. T., for life in the army?

6. The Civil War marked a new birth of freedom and a new emphasis on liberty and equality in the United States. How do the various documents in this chapter support that thesis? Is there anything in the documents that casts doubt on that conclusion?

Chapter 18
Reconstruction, 1863–1877

Staunchly Republican Thomas Nast refined the political cartoon into a modern art form. Post-war Republicans appealed to voters' heated emotions to gather votes. Here Nast equates Republicans with patriotism, as sterotyped Democrats (the Irish, Confederate veterans, and sell-out businessmen) stand over a black Union veteran and the national flag.

*H*aving fought a deadly Civil War, Americans faced the difficult prospect of rebuilding the nation. President Abraham Lincoln began efforts to restore the former Confederate states to the Union while the fighting continued, and after the war Andrew Johnson attempted to enact a policy similar to that of Lincoln. Southern recalcitrance, on the other hand, led to a more extreme approach—the reconstructing of the South. Radical Republicans in Congress eventually gained control of Reconstruction, and they passed several laws to assist the freed slaves and to control the former Rebels. Republicans used federal power to ensure the liberty of slaves and to provide freedpeople some degree of opportunity and political equality. Consequently, southern bitterness over the war and reconstruction, along with northern efforts to enforce the victory they had gained on the battlefield, strained relations between the North and South for more than ten years after Lee's surrender at Appomattox Courthouse. Despite the intense antagonism that Reconstruction caused in the former Confederacy, however, by the 1870s other issues gained importance. After decades of conflict over the slavery question, the United States slowly began to address other concerns.

Abraham Lincoln's "Ten Percent Plan," 1863*

President Lincoln hoped that a broad grant of amnesty would encourage Confederates to abandon the rebellion. Believing that a nucleus of loyal southerners could initiate a quick restoration of the states, Lincoln issued a proclamation offering to recognize governments established by a small percentage of pro-Union voters. Under Lincoln's policy, federal force would put down the insurrection, but he did not want to use the power of the government to punish unduly the majority of southerners. Tragically, Lincoln died before he could fully implement his plan, and his death ended the prospect for a magnanimous reconciliation between the North and South.

Whereas in and by the Constitution of the United States it is provided the President "shall have power to grant reprieves and pardons for offenses against the United States, except in cases of impeachment;" and

Whereas a rebellion now exists whereby the loyal State governments of several States have for a long time been subverted, and many persons have committed and are now guilty of treason against the United States; and

Whereas, with reference to said rebellion and treason, laws have been enacted by Congress declaring forfeitures and confiscation of property and liberation of slaves, all upon terms and conditions therein stated, and also declaring that the President was thereby authorized at any time thereafter, by proclamation, to extend to persons who may have participated in the existing rebellion in any State or part thereof pardon and amnesty, with such exceptions and at such times and on such conditions as he may deem expedient for the public welfare; and

---

*From "Presidential Proclamation," December 8, 1863, *A Compilation of the Messages and Papers of the Presidents, 1789–1897,* 10 vols., comp. James D. Richardson (Washington, D.C.: U.S. Government Printing Office, 1896–1899), VI:213–15..

Whereas the Constitutional declaration for limited and conditional pardon accords with well-established judicial exposition of the pardoning power; and

Whereas, with reference to said rebellion, the President of the United States has issued several proclamations with provisions in regard to the liberation of slaves; and

Whereas it is now desired by some persons heretofore engaged in said rebellion to resume their allegiance to the United States and to reestablish loyal State governments within and for their respective States:

Therefore, I, Abraham Lincoln, President of the United States, do proclaim, declare, and make known to all persons who have, directly or by implication, participated in the existing rebellion, except as hereinafter excepted, that a full pardon is hereby granted to them and each of them, with restoration of all rights of property, except as in slaves and in property cases where rights of third parties shall have intervened, and upon the condition that every such person shall take and subscribe an oath and thenceforward keep and maintain said oath inviolate, and which oath shall be registered for permanent preservation and shall be of the tenor and effect following; to wit:

"I, _____ _____, do solemnly swear, in presence of Almighty God, that I will henceforth faithfully support, protect, and defend the Constitution of the United States and the Union of the States thereunder; and that I will in like manner abide by and faithfully support all acts of Congress passed during the existing rebellion with references to slaves, so long and so far as not repealed, modified, or held void by Congress or by decision of the Supreme Court; and that I will in like manner abide by and faithfully support all proclamations of the President made during the existing rebellion having reference to slaves, so long and so far as not modified or declared void by decision of the Supreme Court. So help me God."

The persons excepted from the benefits of the foregoing provisions are all who are or shall have been civil or diplomatic officers or agents of the so-called Confederate Government; all who have left judicial stations under the United States to aid the rebellion; all who are or who shall have been military or naval officers of the said so-called Confederate Government above the rank of colonel in the army or of lieutenant in the navy; all who left seats in the United States Congress to aid the rebellion; all who resigned commissions in the Army or Navy of the United States and afterwards aided the rebellion; and all who have engaged in any way in treating colored persons, or white persons in charge of such, otherwise than lawfully as prisoners of war, and which persons may have been found in the United States service as soldiers, seamen, or in any other capacity.

And I do further proclaim, declare, and make known that whenever, in any of the States of Arkansas, Texas, Louisiana, Mississippi, Tennessee, Alabama, Georgia, Florida, South Carolina, and North Carolina, a number of persons, not less than one-tenth in number of the votes cast in such State at the Presidential election of the year A.D.1860, each having taken the oath aforesaid, and not having since violated it, and being a qualified voter by the election law of the State existing immediately before the so-called act of secession, and excluding all others, shall reestablish a State government which shall be recognized as the true government of the State, and the State shall receive thereunder the benefits of the constitutional provisions which declares that "the United States shall guarantee to every State in this Union a republican form of government and shall protect each of them against invasion, and, on application of the legislature, or the executive (when the legislature can not be convened), against domestic violence."

And I do further proclaim, declare, and make known that any provision which may be adopted by such State government in relation to the freed people of such State which shall recognize and declare their permanent freedom, provide for their education, and which may yet be consistent as a temporary arrangement with their present condition as a laboring, landless, and homeless class, will not be objected to by the national Executive.

Harcourt Brace & Company

And it is suggested as not improper that in constructing a loyal State government in any State the name of the State, the boundary, the subdivisions, the constitution, and the general code of laws as before the rebellion be maintained, subject only to the modifications made necessary by the conditions hereinbefore stated, and such others, if any, not contravening said conditions and which may be deemed expedient by those framing the new State government.

To avoid misunderstanding, it may be proper to say that this proclamation, so far as it relates to State governments, has no reference to States wherein loyal State governments have all the while been maintained. And for the same reason it may be proper to further say that whether members sent to Congress from any State shall be admitted to seats conditionally rests exclusively with the respective Houses, and not to any extent with the Executive. And, still further, that this proclamation is intended to present the people of the States wherein the national authority has been suspended and loyal State governments have been subverted a mode in and by which the national authority and loyal State governments may be reestablished within said States or in any of them; and while the mode presented is the best the Executive can suggest, with his present impressions, it must not be understood that no other possible mode would be acceptable. . . .

President Andrew Johnson's Amnesty Proclamation*

When Andrew Johnson became president, he used the office much differently than had Lincoln. Johnson had long resented the influence of wealthy southerners, and he viewed Reconstruction as an opportunity to destroy the strength of what he viewed as an arrogant aristocracy. His amnesty proclamation, presented here, made clear his animosity by denying a general pardon to high ranking Confederate officials and to any Confederate worth more than $20,000. At the same time, the decree gave him great discretion in granting special pardons, a practice that later angered many Republicans. That anger eventually became a full-scale power struggle between Congress and Johnson, a conflict with grave ramifications for the president and for the South.

Whereas the President of the United States, on the 8th day of December, A.D. 1863, and on the 26th day of March, A.D. 1864, did, with the object to suppress the existing rebellion, to induce all persons to return to their loyalty, and to restore the authority of the United States, issue proclamations offering amnesty and pardon to certain persons who had, directly or by implication, participated in the said rebellion; and

Whereas many persons who had so engaged in said rebellion have, since the issuance of said proclamations, failed or neglected to take the benefits offered thereby; and

Whereas many persons who have been justly deprived of all claim to amnesty and pardon thereunder by reason of their participation, directly or by implication, in said rebellion and continued hostility to the Government of the United States since the date of said proclamations now desire to apply for and obtain amnesty and pardon.

To the end, therefore, that the authority of the Government of the United States may be restored and that peace, order, and freedom may be established, I, Andrew Johnson, President of the United States, do proclaim and declare that I hereby grant to all persons who have, directly or indirectly, participated in the existing rebellion, except as hereinafter excepted, amnesty and pardon, with restoration of all rights of property, except as to slaves and except in cases

---

*From "Presidential Proclamation," May 29, 1865, *A Compilation of the Messages and Papers of the Presidents, 1789–1897,* 10 vols., comp. James D. Richardson (Washington, D.C.: U.S. Government Printing Office, 1896–1899), VI:310–12.

where legal proceedings under the laws of the Untied States providing for the confiscation of property of persons engaged in rebellion have been instituted; but upon the condition, nevertheless, that every such person shall take and subscribe the following oath (or affirmation) and thence forward keep and maintain said oath inviolate, and which oath shall be registered for permanent preservation and shall be of the tenor and effect following, to wit:

"I _____ _____, do solemnly swear (or affirm) in the presence of Almighty God, that I will henceforth faithfully support, protect, and defend the Constitution of the United States and the Union of the States thereunder, and that I will in like manner abide by and faithfully support all laws and proclamations which have been made during the existing rebellion with references to the emancipation of slaves. So help me God."

The following classes of persons are excepted from the benefits of this proclamation:

First. All who are or shall have been pretended civil or diplomatic officers or otherwise domestic or foreign agents of the pretended Confederate government.

Second. All who left judicial stations under the United States to aid the rebellion.

Third. All who shall have been military or naval officers of said pretended Confederate government above the rank of colonel in the army or lieutenant in the navy.

Fourth. All who left seats in the Congress of the United States to aid the rebellion.

Fifth. All who resigned or tendered resignations of their commissions in the Army or Navy of the United States to evade duty in resisting the rebellion.

Sixth. All who have engaged in any way treating otherwise than lawfully as prisoners of war persons found in the United States service as officers, soldiers, seamen, or in other capacities.

Seventh. All persons who have been or are absentees from the United States for purposes of aiding the rebellion.

Eighth. All military and naval officers in the rebel services who were educated by the Government in the Military Academy at West Point or the United States Naval Academy.

Ninth. All persons who held the pretended offices of governors of States in insurrection against the United States.

Tenth. All persons who left their homes within the jurisdiction and protection of the United States and passed beyond the Federal military lines into the pretended Confederate States for the purpose of aiding the rebellion.

Eleventh. All persons who have been engaged in the destruction of the commerce of the United States upon the high seas and all persons who have made raids into the United States from Canada or been engaged in destroying the commerce of the United States upon the lakes and rivers that separate the British Provinces from the United States.

Twelfth. All persons who, at the time when they seek to obtain the benefits hereof by taking the oath herein prescribed, are in military, naval, or civil confinement or custody, or under bonds of the civil, military, or naval authorities or agents of the United States as prisoners of war, or persons detained for offenses of any kind, either before or after conviction.

Thirteenth. All persons who have voluntarily participated in said rebellion and the estimated value of whose taxable property is over $20,000.

Fourteenth. All persons who have taken the oath of amnesty as prescribed in the President's proclamation of December 8, A.D. 1863, or an oath of allegiance to the Government of the United States since the date of said proclamation and who have not thenceforth kept and maintained the same inviolate.

Provided, That special application may be made to the President for pardon by any person belonging to the excepted classes, and such clemency will be liberally extended as may be consistent with the facts of the cases and the peace and dignity of the United States.

The Secretary of State will establish rules and regulations for administering and recording the said amnesty oath, as to insure its benefit to the people and guard the Government against fraud.

Harcourt Brace & Company

The Freedmen's Bureau, 1865*

Concern for former slaves and other refugees led to the creation of the Bureau of Refugees, Freedmen, and Abandoned Lands just prior to the end of the war. The law creating the bureau provided for some immediate relief measures, but it made the commissioners responsible for most long-term efforts. The Freedmen's Bureau became the primary civilian agency for enforcing Reconstruction policy, and many white southerners despised it as an intrusion of federal power. To the freed slaves, who had their liberty and little else, the bureau offered at least some chance for equitable race relations and fair economic prospects.

> *Be it enacted by . . . Congress . . . ,* That there is hereby established in the War Department, to continue during the present war of rebellion, and for one year thereafter, a bureau of refugees, freedmen, and abandoned lands, to which shall be committed, as hereinafter provided, the supervision and management of all abandoned lands, and the control of all subjects relating to refugees and freedmen from rebel states, or from any district or county within the territory embraced in the operation of the army, under such rules and regulations as may be prescribed by the head of the bureau and approved by the President. The said bureau shall be under the management and control of a commissioner to be appointed by the President, by and with the advice and consent of the Senate, whose compensation shall be three thousand dollars per annum, and such number of clerks as may be assigned to him by the Secretary of War, not exceeding one chief clerk, two of the fourth class, two of the third class, and five of the first class. And the commissioner and all persons appointed under this act, shall, before entering upon their duties, take the oath of office prescribed in an act entitled "An act to prescribe an oath of office, and for other purposes," approved July second, eighteen hundred and sixty-two, and the commissioner and the chief clerk shall, before entering upon their duties, give bonds to the treasurer of the United States, the former in the sum of fifty thousand dollars, and the latter in the sum of ten thousand dollars, conditioned for the faithful discharge of their duties respectively, with securities to be approved as sufficient by the Attorney-General, which bonds shall be filed in the office of the first comptroller of the treasury, to be by him put in suit for the benefit of any injured party upon any breach of the conditions thereof.
>
> SEC. 2. *And be it further enacted,* That the Secretary of War may direct such issues of provisions, clothing, and fuel, as he may deem needful for the immediate and temporary shelter and supply of the destitute and suffering refugees and freedmen and their wives and children, under such rules and regulations as he may direct.
>
> SEC. 3. *And be it further enacted,* That the President may, by and with the advice and consent of the Senate, appoint an assistant commissioner for each of the states declared to be in insurrection, not exceeding ten in number, who shall, under the direction of the commissioner, aid in the execution of the provisions of this act; and he shall give bond to the Treasurer of the United States, in the sum of twenty thousand dollars, in the form and manner prescribed in the first section of this act. Each of said commissioners shall receive an annual salary of two thousand five hundred dollars in full compensation for all services. And any military officer may be detailed and assigned to duty under this act without increase of pay or allowances. The commissioner shall, before the commencement of each regular session of congress, make full report of his proceedings with exhibits of the state of his accounts to the President, who shall communicate the same to congress, and shall also make special reports whenever required to do so

---

*"An Act to Establish a Bureau for the Relief of Freedmen and Refugees," March 3, 1865, *United States Statutes at Large*, XIII:507–509.

by the President or either house of congress; and the assistant commissioner shall make quarterly reports of their proceedings to the commissioner, and also such other reports as from time to time may be required.

SEC. 4. *And be it further enacted,* That the commissioner, under the direction of the President, shall have authority to set apart, for the use of loyal refugees and freedmen, such tracts of land within the insurrectionary states as shall have been abandoned, or to which the United States shall have acquired title by confiscation or sale, or otherwise, and to every male citizen, whether refugee or freedman, as aforesaid, there shall be assigned not more than forty acres of such land, and the person to whom it was so assigned shall be protected in the use and enjoyment of the land for the term of three years at an annual rent not exceeding six per centum upon the value of such land, as it was appraised by the state authorities in the year eighteen hundred and sixty, for the purpose of taxation, and in case no such appraisal can be found, then the rental shall be based upon the estimated value of the land in said year, to be ascertained in such manner as the commissioner may by regulation prescribe. At the end of said term, or at any time during said term, the occupants of any parcels so assigned may purchase the land and receive such title thereto as the United States can convey, upon paying therefore the value of the land, as ascertained and fixed for the purpose of determining the annual rent aforesaid.

Military Reconstruction, 1867*

The following law instituted military Reconstruction in the South, in effect turning most of the former Confederacy into an occupied territory. The great antebellum fear that federal power would end slavery, thereby destroying the liberties and equality of white people, had become an all-too-evident reality. Such a massive extension of government force that appeared designed simply to punish white southerners while helping elevate former slaves to positions of influence created an anger in the South that lasted well into the twentieth century.

WHEREAS no legal State governments or adequate protection for life and property now exists in the rebel States of Virginia, North Carolina, South Carolina, Georgia, Mississippi, Alabama, Louisiana, Florida, Texas, and Arkansas; and whereas it is necessary that peace and good order should be enforced in said States until loyal and republican State governments can be legally established: Therefore,

Be it enacted by . . . Congress . . ., That said rebel States shall be divided into military districts and made subject to the military authority of the United States as hereinafter described, and for that purpose Virginia shall constitute the first district; North and South Carolina the second district; Georgia, Alabama, and Florida the third district; Mississippi and Arkansas the fourth district; and Louisiana and Texas the fifth district.

SEC. 2. *And be it further enacted,* That it shall be the duty of the President to assign to the command of each of said districts an officer of the army, not below the rank of brigadier-general, and to detail a sufficient military force to enable such officer to perform his duties and enforce his authority within the district to which he is assigned.

SEC. 3. *And be it further enacted,* That it shall be the duty of each officer assigned as aforesaid, to protect all persons in their rights of persons and property, to suppress insurrection, disorder, and violence, and to punish, or caused to be punished, all disturbers of the public peace and criminals; and to this end he may allow local civil tribunals to take jurisdiction of and to

---

*"An Act to Provide for the More Efficient Government of the Rebel States," March 2, 1867, *United States Statutes at Large*, XIV:428–30.

Harcourt Brace & Company

try offenders, or, when in his judgment it may be necessary for the trial of offenders, he shall have power to organize military commissions or tribunals for that purpose, and all interference under color of State authority with the exercise of military authority under this act, shall be null and void.

SEC. 4. *And be it further enacted*, That all persons put under military arrest by virtue of this act shall be tried without unnecessary delay, and no cruel or unusual punishment shall be inflicted, and no sentence of any military commission or tribunal hereby authorized, affecting the life or liberty of any person, shall be executed until it is approved by the officer in command of the district, and the laws and regulations for the government of the army shall not be affected by this act, except in so far as they conflict with its provisions; Provided, That no sentence of death under the provisions of this act shall be carried into effect without the approval of the President.

SEC. 5. *And be it further enacted*, That when the people of any one of said rebel States shall have formed a constitution of government in conformity with the Constitution of the United States in all respects, framed by a convention of delegates elected by the male citizens of said State, twenty-one years old and upward, of whatever race, color, or previous condition, who have been resident in said State for one year previous to the day of such election, except such as may be disfranchised for participation in the rebellion or for felony at common law, and when such constitution shall provide that the elective franchise shall be enjoyed by all such persons as have the qualifications herein stated for electors of delegates, and when such constitution shall be ratified by a majority of the persons voting on the question of ratification who are qualified as electors for delegates, and when such constitution shall have been submitted to Congress for examination and approval, and when Congress shall have approved the same, and when said State, by a vote of its legislature elected under said constitution, shall have adopted the amendment to the Constitution of the United States, proposed by the Thirty-ninth Congress, and known as article fourteen, and when said article shall become a part of the Constitution of the United States said State shall be declared entitled to representation on Congress, and senators and representatives shall be admitted therefrom on their taking the oath prescribed by law, and then and thereafter the preceding section of this act shall be inoperative in said State; Provided, That no person excluded from the privilege of holding office by said proposed amendment to the Constitution of the United States shall be eligible to election as a member of the convention to frame a constitution for any of said rebel States, nor shall any such person vote for members of such convention.

SEC. 6. *And be it further enacted*, That, until the people of said rebel States shall be by law admitted to representation in the Congress of the United States, any civil governments which may exist therein shall be deemed provisional only, and in all respects subject to the paramount authority of the United States at any time to abolish, modify, control, or supersede the same; and in all elections to any office under such provisional governments all persons shall be entitled to vote, and no others, who are entitled to vote, under the provisions of the fifth section of this act; and no persons shall be eligible to any office under any such provisional governments who would be disqualified from holding office under the provisions of the third article of said constitutional amendment.

The Election of 1868*

The election of 1868 was a referendum on Reconstruction policy. The Republicans nominated General Ulysses S. Grant, who they believed would guarantee that the northern military victory would not be undone by former Confederates and their sympathizers. Democrats brazenly

---

*Thomas Wentworth Higginson, "Moral Significance of the Republican Triumph," *The Atlantic Monthly* 23 (January–June 1869), 124–28.

Harcourt Brace & Company

campaigned against Radical programs, and their untempered, obviously unreconstructed, rhetoric enraged many northerners. The following essay, by Thomas Wentworth Higginson, editor of *The Atlantic Monthly* magazine, revealed just how much rancor the campaign had generated.

The victory which the Republican party gained in the November election, after the most fiercely contested struggle recorded in our political history, is the crowning victory of the War of the Rebellion, and its real close. A war such as raged in this country between April, 1861 and April, 1865, is ended, not when the defeated party ceases to fight, but when it ceases to hope. The sentiments and principles which led to the Rebellion were overturned, not in 1865, but in 1868. After the exhaustion of physical power, which compelled the Rebels to lay down their arms, came the moral struggle which has resulted in compelling them to surrender their ideas. If these ideas had been on a level with the civilization of the age, or in advance of it; if the "Lost Cause" had been the cause of humanity and freedom, of reason and justice, of good morals and good sense,—such a catastrophe would be viewed by every right-minded man as a great calamity. But the Rebellion was essentially a revolt of tyrants for the privilege to oppress, and of bullies for the right to domineer. Its interpretation of the Constitution was an ingenious reversal of the purposes for which the Constitution was declared to be made, and its doctrine of State Rights was a mere cover for a comprehensive conspiracy against the rights of man. The success of such a "cause" could not have benefited even its defenders, for the worst government for the permanent welfare even of the governing classes is that in which the intelligent systematically prey upon the ignorant, and the strong mercilessly trample on the weak. In a large view, the South is better off to-day for the military defeat which dissipated its wild dream of insolent domination, and for the political defeat which destroyed the last hopes of its reviving passions.

Those who are accustomed to recognize a providence in the direction of human affairs may find in the course and conduct equally of this military and political struggle the strongest confirmation of their faith. The great things that have been done appear to have been done through us, rather than by us. During the war, it seemed as if no mistakes could hinder us from gaining victories, no reverses obstruct our steady advance, no conservative prudence prevent us from being the audacious champion of radical ideas. The march of events swept forward government and people on its own path, converting the distrusted abstraction of yesterday into the "military necessity" of to-day and the constitutional provision of to-morrow. . . .

What was true of the military is true of the political contest. After the armed Rebellion was crushed by arms, and the meaner rebellion of intrigue, bluster, and miscellaneous assassination began, both parties had reason to be surprised at the issue. The Rebels found that their profoundest calculations, their most unscrupulous plottings, their most vigorous action, only led them to a more ruinous defeat. Their opponents had almost equal reason for wonder, for the plan of reconstruction, which they eventually passed and repeatedly sustained by more than two thirds of both Houses of Congress, would not have commanded a majority in either House at the time the problem of reconstruction was first presented. . . .

As it regards the right of the Government of the United States to dictate conditions of reconstruction, it must be remembered that the difference between the President's Plan and the Congressional Plan was not, in this respect, a difference in principle; and that the position held by the Democratic party—that the Rebellion was a rebellion of individuals, and not of States— equally condemns both. This position, however, can only be maintained by the denial of the most obvious facts. The enormous sacrifices of blood and treasure in putting down the Rebellion were made necessary by the circumstances that it was a rebellion of States. . . .

The intellect of the Democratic party is concentrated, to a great degree, in its Copperhead members; and these had become so embittered and vindictive by [Reconstruction policy], that their malignity prevented their ability from having fair play. [In the campaign of 1868, they] assailed the Republicans for not giving peace and prosperity to the nation, and then laid down a programme which proposed to reach peace and prosperity through political and financial anarchy. They selected unpopular candidates, and then placed them on a platform of which revolution and repudiation were the chief planks. Perhaps even with these drawbacks they might have cajoled a sufficient number of voters to succeed in the election, had it not been for the frank brutality of their Southern allies. To carry the North their reliance was on fraud, but the Southern politicians were determined to carry their section by terror and assassination, and no plausible speech could be made by a Northern Democrat the effect of which was not nullified by some Southern burst of eloquence, breathing nothing but proscription and war. The Democratic party was therefore not only defeated, but disgraced. To succeed as it succeeded in New York and New Jersey, in Louisiana and Georgia, did not prevent its fall, but did prevent it from falling with honor. To the infamy of bad ends it added the additional infamy of bad means; and it comes out of an overwhelming general reverse with the mortifying consciousness that its few special victories have been purchased at the expense of its public character. The only way it can recover its *prestige* is by discarding, not only its leaders, but the passions and ideas its leaders represent. . . .

The End of Reconstruction, 1877*

The inauguration of Rutherford B. Hayes marked the end of Reconstruction. A disputed election had raised once again the specter of insurrection, and most Americans celebrated the agreement that had averted yet another crisis. Moreover, the Compromise of 1877 showed that political leaders were anxious to leave sectional differences behind in order to heal the wounds that had festered for so long. In his inaugural address, the new president discussed some of the lingering results of the Civil War, but he also devoted attention to other matters. After 1877, concerns such as governmental reform and international affairs took on increasing importance. The war between the states was over.

FELLOW-CITIZENS: We have assembled to repeat the public ceremonial, begun by Washington, observed by all my predecessors, and now a time-honored custom, which marks the commencement of a new term in Presidential office. Called to the duties of this great trust, I proceed, in compliance with usage, to announce some of the leading principles, on the subjects that now chiefly engage the public attention, by which it is my desire to be guided in the discharge of those duties. I shall not undertake to lay down irrevocably principles or measures of administration, but rather to speak of the motives which should animate us, and to suggest certain important ends to be attained in accordance with our institutions and essential to the welfare of our country.

At the outset of the discussions which preceded the recent Presidential election it seemed to me fitting that I should fully make known my sentiments in regard to several of the important questions which then appeared to demand the consideration of the country. Following the example, and in part adopting the language, of one of my predecessors, I wish now, when every motive for misrepresentation has passed away, to repeat what was said before the election, trusting that my countrymen will candidly weigh and understand it, and that they will feel assured that the sentiments declared in accepting the nomination for the Presidency will be the stan-

*"Inaugural Address," in *A Compilation of the Messages and Papers of the Presidents, 1789–1897,* 10 vols., comp. James D. Richardson (Washington, D.C.: U.S. Government Printing Office, 1896–1899), IX:4394–99.

dard of my conduct in the path before me, charged, as I now am, with the grave and difficult task of carrying them out in the practical administration of the Government so far as depends, under the Constitution and laws, on the Chief Executive of the nation.

The permanent pacification of the country upon such principles and by such measures as will secure the complete protection of all its citizens in the free enjoyment of all their constitutional rights is now the one subject in our public affairs which all thoughtful and patriotic citizens regard as of supreme importance.

Many of the calamitous effects of the tremendous revolution which has passed over the Southern States still remain. The immeasurable benefits which will surely follow, sooner or later, the hearty and generous acceptance of the legitimate results of the revolution have not yet been realized. Difficult and embarrassing questions meet us at the threshold of this subject. The people of those States are still impoverished, and the inestimable blessing of wise, honest, and peaceful local self-government is not fully enjoyed. Whatever difference of opinion may exist as to the cause of this condition of things, the fact is clear that in the progress of events the time has come when such government is the imperative necessity required by all the varied interests, public and private, of those States. But it must not be forgotten that only a local government which recognizes and maintains inviolate the rights of all is a true self-government.

With respect to the two distinct races whose peculiar relations to each other have brought upon us the deplorable complications and perplexities which exist in those States, it must be a government which guards the interests of both races carefully and equally. It must be a government which submits loyally and heartily to the Constitution and the laws—laws of the nation and the laws of the States themselves—accepting and obeying faithfully the whole Constitution as it is. . . .

The sweeping revolution of the entire labor system of a large portion of our country and the advance of 4,000,000 people from a condition of servitude to that of citizenship, upon an equal footing with their former masters, could not occur without presenting problems of the gravest moment, to be dealt with by the emancipated race, by their former masters, and by the General Government, the author of the act of emancipation. That it was a wise, just, and providential act, fraught with good for all concerned, is now generally conceded throughout the country. That a moral obligation rests upon the National Government to employ its constitutional power and influence to establish the rights of the people it has emancipated, and to protect them in the enjoyment of those rights when they are infringed or assailed, is also generally admitted.

The evils which afflict the Southern States can only be removed or remedied by the united and harmonious efforts of both races, actuated by motives of mutual sympathy and regard; and while in duty bound and fully determined to protect the rights of all by every constitutional means at the disposal of my Administration, I am sincerely anxious to use every legitimate influence in favor of honest and efficient local *self*-government as the true resource of those States for the promotion and contentment and prosperity of their citizens. In the effort I shall make to accomplish this purpose I ask the cordial cooperation of all who cherish an interest in the welfare of the country, trusting that party ties and the prejudice of race will be freely surrendered on behalf of the great purpose to be accomplished. In the important work of restoring the South it is not the political situation alone that merits attention. The material development of that section of the country has been arrested by the social and political revolution through which it has passed, and now needs and deserves the considerate care of the national Government within the just limits prescribed by the Constitution and wise public economy.

But at the basis of all prosperity, for that as well as for every other part of the country, lies the improvement of the intellectual and moral condition of the people. Universal suffrage should rest upon universal education. To this end, liberal and permanent provision should be made for the support of free schools by the State Governments, and, if need be, supplemented by legitimate aid from national authority.

Let me assure my countrymen of the Southern States that it is my earnest desire to regard and promote their truest interests—the interests of the white and of the colored people both and equally—and to put forth my best efforts in behalf of a civil policy which will forever wipe out in our political affairs the color line and the distinction between North and South, to the end that we may have not merely a united North or a united South, but a unified country.

I ask the attention of the public to the paramount necessity of reform in our civil service—a reform not merely as to certain abuses and practices of so-called official patronage which have come to have the sanction of usage in the several Departments of our Government, but a change in the system of appointment itself; a reform that shall be thorough, radical, and complete; a return to the principles and practices of the founders of the Government. They neither expected nor desired from the public officers any partisan service. They meant that public officers should owe their whole service to the Government and to the people. They meant that the officer should be secure in his tenure as long as his personal character remained untarnished and the performance of his duties satisfactory. They held that appointments to office were not to be made nor expected merely as rewards for partisan services, nor merely on the nomination of members of Congress, as being entitled in any respect to the control of such appointments. . . .

In furtherance of the reform we seek, and in other important respects a change of great importance, I recommend an amendment to the Constitution prescribing a term of six years for the Presidential office and forbidding a reelection.

With respect to the financial condition of the country, I shall not attempt an extended history of the embarrassment and prostration which we have suffered during the past three years. The depression in all our varied commercial and manufacturing interests throughout the country, which began in September, 1873, still continues. It is very gratifying, however, to be able to say that there are indications all around us of a coming change to prosperous times.

Upon the currency question, intimately connected, as it is, with this topic, I may be permitted to repeat here the statement made in my letter of acceptance, that in my judgment the feeling of uncertainty inseparable from an irredeemable paper currency, with its fluctuation of values, is one of the greatest obstacles to a return to prosperous times. The only safe paper currency is one which rests upon a coin basis and is at all times and promptly converted into coin. . . .

Passing from these remarks upon the condition of our country to consider our relations with other lands, we are reminded by the international complications abroad, threatening the peace of Europe, that our traditional role of noninterference in the affairs of foreign nations has proved of great value in past times and ought to be strictly observed.

The policy inaugurated by my honored predecessor, President Grant, of submitting to arbitration grave questions in dispute between ourselves and foreign powers points to a new, and incomparably the best, instrumentality for the preservation of peace, and will, as I believe, become a beneficent example of the course to be pursued in similar emergencies by other nations.

If, unhappily, questions of difference should at any time during the period of my Administration arise between the United States and any foreign government, it will certainly be my disposition and my hope to aid in their settlement, in the same peaceful and honorable way, thus securing to our country the great blessings of peace and mutual good offices with all the nations of the world.

Fellow-citizens, we have reached the close of a political contest marked by the excitement which usually attends the contests between great political parties whose members espouse and advocate with earnest faith their respective creeds. The circumstances were, perhaps, in no respect extraordinary save in the closeness and the consequent uncertainty of the result.

For the first time in the history of the country it has been deemed best, in view of the peculiar circumstances of the case, that the objections and questions in dispute with reference to the counting of the electoral votes should be referred to the decision of a tribunal appointed for the purpose.

That tribunal—established by law for this sole purpose; its members, all of them, men of long-established reputation for integrity and intelligence, and, with the exception of those who are also members of the supreme judiciary, chosen equally from both political parties; its deliberations enlightened by the research and arguments of able counsel—was entitled to the fullest confidence of the American people. Its decisions have been patiently waited for, and accepted as legally conclusive by the general judgment of the public. For the present, opinion will widely vary as to the wisdom of the several conclusions announced by that tribunal. This is to be anticipated in every instance where matters of dispute are made the subject of arbitration under the forms of law. Human judgment is never unerring, and is rarely regarded as otherwise than wrong by the unsuccessful party in the contest.

The fact that two great political parties have in this way settled a dispute in regard to which good men differ as to the facts and the law no less than as to the proper course to be pursued in solving the question in controversy is an occasion for general rejoicing.

Upon one point there is entire unanimity in public sentiment—that conflicting claims to the Presidency must be amicably and peaceably adjusted, and that when so adjusted the general acquiescence of the nation ought surely to follow.

It has been reserved for a government of the people, where the right of suffrage is universal, to give to the world the first example in history of a great nation, in the midst of the struggle of opposing parties for power, hushing its party tumults to yield the issue of the contest to adjustment according to the forms of law.

Looking for the guidance of that Divine Hand by which the destinies of nations and individuals are shaped, I call upon you, Senators, Representatives, judges, fellow-citizens, here and everywhere, to unite with me in an earnest effort to secure to our country the blessings, not only of material prosperity, but of justice, peace, and union—a union depending not upon the constraint of force, but upon the loving devotion of a free people. . . .

Discussion

1. Compare the three Reconstruction plans presented in this chapter. What similarities or differences exist regarding power? To what degree do any of the documents express concerns for issues of liberty and equality?

2. How might southerners have viewed the law creating the Freedmen's Bureau as an unacceptable assertion of power? How might Radical Republicans have justified the act? To what degree, and how, does the act deal with issues of liberty and with issues of equality?

3. Why might *The Atlantic Monthly* have been so perturbed by the Democrats during the election of 1868? Does the document relate at all to matters of liberty and equality, or were Americans in 1868 primarily concerned with issues of power? How do you think southerners responded to the editorial? How might northern Democrats have reacted to it? What about Republicans?

4. Compare the inaugural address of Rutherford B. Hayes to the magazine editorial from 1868. Are there any differences or similarities in the two documents? How so? What do the two selections suggest about concepts of liberty, equality, and power in 1868 and in 1877?

Harcourt Brace & Company

5. Considering all of the documents from this chapter, how did American concepts of liberty, equality, and power during Reconstruction compare to American attitudes during the Revolutionary era, during the early years of the republic, the 1830s, or the antebellum period?

Photo Credits

Harcourt Brace & Company